Greek

Phrasebook & Dictionary

Acknowledgments
Product Editor Will Allen
Book Designer Wibowo Rusli
Language Writer Thanasis Spilias
Cover Image Researcher Naomi Parker

Published by Lonely Planet Global Limited
CRN 554153

7th Edition – March 2019
ISBN 978 1 78657 378 0
Text © Lonely Planet 2019

Cover Image Oia at night, Santorini, Greece. Maurizio Rellini /
4Corners ©

Printed in China   10 9 8 7 6 5 4 3 2 1

Contact lonelyplanet.com/contact

MIX
Paper from
responsible source
FSC™ C021741

acknowledgments

This 7th edition of Lonely Planet's *Greek phrasebook* is based on the previous edition by the Lonely Planet Language Products team and translator Dr Thanasis Spilias.

Thanasis studied in Greece (University of Thessaloniki) and Australia (University of Melbourne, La Trobe University and University of New England). He has taught Greek language and culture at Deakin and La Trobe Universities and worked as the State Consultant for Greek Language (Victoria, Australia). Thanasis' main research interests are in Greek language and literature, Greek–Australian literature and literary translation. He has published articles in both Greece and Australia, and has co-edited *Reflections: Selected Works from Greek Australian Literature*. With G Betts and S Gauntlett, he has translated Vitsentzos Kornaros' *Erotokritos* into English.

make the most of this phrasebook ...

Anyone can speak another language! It's all about confidence. Don't worry if you can't remember your school language lessons or if you've never learnt a language before. Even if you learn the very basics (on the inside covers of this book), your travel experience will be the better for it. You have nothing to lose and everything to gain when the locals hear you making an effort.

finding things in this book

For easy navigation, this book is in sections. The Basics chapters are the ones you'll thumb through time and again. The Practical section covers basic travel situations like catching transport and finding a bed. The Social section gives you conversational phrases, pick-up lines, the ability to express opinions – so you can get to know people. Food has a section all of its own: gourmets and vegetarians are covered and local dishes feature. Safe Travel equips you with health and police phrases, just in case. Remember the colours of each section and you'll find everything easily; or use the comprehensive Index. Otherwise, check the two-way traveller's Dictionary for the word you need.

being understood

Throughout this book you'll see coloured phrases on each page. They're phonetic guides to help you pronounce the language. You don't even need to look at the language itself, but you'll get used to the way we've represented particular sounds. The pronunciation chapter in Basics will explain more, but you can feel confident that if you read the coloured phrase slowly, you'll be understood.

communication tips

Body language, ways of doing things, sense of humour – all have a role to play in every culture. 'Local talk' boxes show you common ways of saying things, or everyday language to drop into conversation. 'Listen for ...' boxes supply the phrases you may hear. They start with the Greek translation (so a Greek speaker can look up the phrase they want to say to you) and then lead in to the pronunciation guide and the English translation.

social 107

greek

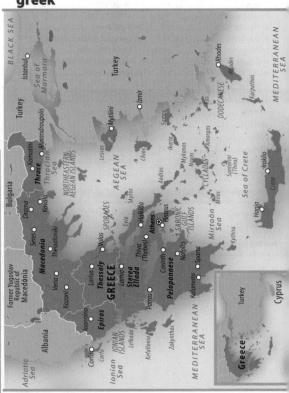

official language

For more details, see the **introduction**.

ristotle, Homer, Plato, Sappho, Herodotus and Alexander the Great can't all be wrong in their choice of language – if you've ver come across arcane concepts such as 'democracy', exotic isciplines like 'trigonometry' or a little-known neurosis termed he Oedipus complex', then you'll have some inkling of the wide-pread influence of Greek language and culture. With just a little Modern Greek under your belt, you'll have a richer understanding f this language's impact on contemporary Western culture.

Greek is the official language of Greece and a co-official lan-uage of Cyprus, in addition to being spoken by emigrant commu-ities in Turkey, Australia, Canada, Germany and the United States. In total, there are over 13 million Greek speakers worldwide.

Modern Greek constitutes a separate branch of the Indo-European language family, with Ancient Greek its only (extinct) relative. The first records of writ-ten Ancient Greek were found in the fragmentary Linear B tablets, dating from the 14th to the 12th centuries BC. By the 9th century BC, the Greeks had adapted the Phoenician alphabet to include vowels – the first alphabet to do so – and the script in use today came to its final form some time in the 5th century BC. The Greek script was the foundation for the Cyrillic script (used in Slavic languages) and the Latin alpha-bet (used in English and other European languages).

Although written Greek may have been remarkably stable

at a glance ...

language name: Greek

name in language:
Ελληνικά e·li·ni·*ka*,
Νέα Ελληνικά ne·a e·li·ni·*ka*
(Greek, Modern Greek)

language family:
Indo-European
(Hellenic branch)

key countries:
Greece, Cyprus

approximate number of speakers:
13 million worldwide

close relatives:
Ancient Greek

donations to English:
anarchy, astronomy,
cosmos, democracy,
drama, logic, politics ...

introduction

9

over the millennia, the spoken language has evolved considerabl In the 5th century, the dialect spoken around Athens (known a 'Attic') became the dominant speech as a result of the city-state cultural and political prestige. Attic gained even greater influenc as the medium of administration for the vast empire of Alexan der the Great, and remained the official language of the Easter Roman Empire and the Orthodox Church after the demise of th Hellenistic world. Once the Ottoman Turks took Constantinop in 1453, the Attic dialect lost its official function. In the meantim the common language – known as *Koine* (Κοινή ki·*ni*) – continue to evolve. It developed a rich history of popular songs (δημοτικ τραγούδια thi·mo·ti·*ka* tra·*ghu*·thia) and absorbed vocabular from Turkish, Italian, Albanian and other Balkan languages.

When an independent Greece returned to the world stage i 1832, it needed to choose a national language. Purists advocate a slightly modernised version of Attic known as *Καθαρεύουσ* ka·tha·*re*·vu·sa (from the Greek word for 'clean'), which no longe resembled the spoken language. *Koine*, or *laiki* as it was also know (λαϊκή la·i·*ki* means 'popular'), had strong support as it was spoke and understood by the majority of Greeks – in the end, this was th language which gained official recognition. By the mid-20th cen tury, *Koine/laiki* was known as 'demotic' and continued in daily us It was banned during Greece's military dictatorship (1967-74) bu then reinstated as the official language of the Hellenic Republic.

This book gives you the practical phrases you need to get by i Greek, as well as all the fun, spontaneous phrases that can lead t a better understanding of Greeks and their culture. Once you'v got the hang of how to pronounce Greek words, the rest is jus a matter of confidence. Local knowledge, new relationships an a sense of satisfaction are on the tip of your tongue. So don't jus stand there, say something!

abbreviations used in this book

a	adjective	n	neuter (after Greek)
acc	accusative	n	noun (after English)
f	feminine	nom	nominative
gen	genitive	pl	plural
inf	informal	pol	polite
lit	literal	sg	singular
m	masculine	v	verb

BASICS > pronunciation
προφορά

The pronunciation of Greek is easy to master, as most of the sounds correspond to those found in English. Use the coloured pronunciation guides to become familiar with them, and then read directly from the Greek when you feel more confident.

vowel sounds

Greek vowels are pronounced separately even when they're written in sequence, eg ζώο zo·o (animal). You'll see though in the table below that some letter combinations correspond to a single sound – ουρά (queue) is pronounced u·ra.

When a word ending in a vowel is followed by another word that starts with the same or a similar vowel sound, one vowel is usually omitted and the two words are pronounced as if they were one – Σε ευχαριστώ se ef·kha·ris·to becomes Σ' ευχαριστώ sef·kha·ris·to (Thank you). Note that the apostrophe (') is used to show that two words have been joined together.

symbol	english equivalent	greek example	transliteration
a	car	αλλά	a·la
e	bet	πλένομαι	ple·no·me
i	lid	πίσω, πόλη, υποφέρω, είδος, οικογένεια, υιός	pi·so, po·li, i·po·fe·ro, i·thos, i·ko·ye·ni·a, i·os
o	lot	πόνος, πίσω	po·nos, pi·so
u	put	ουρά	u·ra
ia	nostalgia	ζητιάνος	zi·tia·nos
io	ratio	πιο	pio

pronunciation

consonant sounds

Most Greek consonant sounds are also found in English – only
the guttural gh and kh might need a bit of practice. Double
consonants are only pronounced once – άλλος *a*·los (other).

symbol	english equivalent	greek example	trans-literation
b	bed	μπαρ	bar
d	dog	ντομάτα	do·*ma*·ta
dz	adds	τζαμί	dza·*mi*
f	fit	φως, αυτή	fos, af·*ti*
g	gap	γκαρσόν	gar·*son*
gh	guttural sound, between goat and loch	γάτα	*gha*·ta
h	heat	χέρι	*he*·ri
k	kit	καλά	ka·*la*
kh	loch (guttural sound)	χαλί	kha·*li*
l	let	λάδι	*la*·thi
m	mat	μαζί	ma·*zi*
n	not	ναός	na·*os*
ng	singer	ελέγχω	e·*leng*·kho
p	pin	πάνω	*pa*·no
ps	lapse	ψάρι	*psa*·ri
r	red (trilled)	ράβω	*ra*·vo
s	sad	στυλό	sti·*lo*
t	top	τι	ti
th	theatre	θέα	*the*·a
ṭh	the	δεν	ṭhen
ts	hats	τσέπη	*tse*·pi
v	vase	βίζα, αύριο	*vi*·za, av·ri·o
y	yes	γέρος	*ye*·ros
z	zoo	ζέστη	*ze*·sti

word stress

Most Greek words have only one stressed syllable, but some have two. Stress can fall on any of the last three syllables. In our pronunciation guides, the stressed syllable is always in italics, but in written Greek, the stressed syllable is always indicated by an accent over the vowel, eg καλά ka·*la*.

If a vowel is represented by two letters, it's written on the second letter, eg ζητιάνος zi·*tia*·nos (beggar). If the accent is marked on the first of these two letters, they should be read separately, like in Μάιος *ma*·i·os (May). Where two vowels occur together but are not stressed, a diaeresis (¨) is used to indicate that they should be pronounced separately, eg λαϊκός la·i·*kos* (popular). When stress falls on a capitalised vowel (like in Έχασα *e*·ha·sa (I lost)), the accent is written to the left of the letter.

intonation

Intonation in mainland Greece is rather flat, except in questions, when the voice is raised at the end of the sentence. Many island dialects have a more 'singing' intonation.

spellbound

You may have noticed that sometimes two Greek letters in combination form one single consonant sound – the combination of the letters μ and π makes the sound b, and the combination of the letters ν and τ makes the sound d. This is particularly the case when each combination appears at the start of a word – in the middle of a word they sound more like the 'mb' in 'amber' and the 'nd' in 'indigo' respectively. In this book, we've used the same symbols regardless of the position of these letters within a word – you'll be understood just fine if you follow our pronunciation guides.

reading & writing

The Greek writing system was simplified in 1982, when the old stress symbols and aspiration marks (ie an accent indicating that a sound is pronounced with a puff of air before it) were abolished, although they may still be found in old books.

The modern Greek alphabet consists of 24 letters. Their pronunciation is shown in the box below for spelling purposes, eg when you need to spell your name to book into a hotel. Many of the letters of the Greek alphabet are also used in the Roman alphabet. Some letters, however, are a little misleading – they look like English letters but are pronounced very differently. For more information, see the consonant table on page 12 and the box on page 34.

Greek punctuation uses the same symbols as in English, except for the question mark – this is written as a semicolon (;).

greek alphabet			
A α *al·*pha	B β *vi·*ta	Γ γ *gha·*ma	Δ δ *thel·*ta
E ε *ep·si·*lon	Z ζ *zi·*ta	H η *i·*ta	Θ θ *thi·*ta
I ι *yio·*ta	K κ *ka·*pa	Λ λ *lam·*tha	M μ mi
N ν ni	Ξ ξ ksi	O o *o·mi·*kron	Π π pi
P ρ ro	Σ σ/ς* *sigh·*ma	T τ taf	Y υ *ip·si·*lon
Φ φ fi	X χ hi	Ψ ψ psi	Ω ω *o·me·*gha

* The letter Σ has two forms for the lower case – σ and ς. The second one is used at the end of words.

BASICS

a–z phrasebuilder
κατασκευή φράσεων

contents

The index below shows the grammatical structures you can use to say what you want. Look under each function – in alphabetical order – for information on how to build your own phrases. For example, to tell the taxi driver where your hotel is, look for **giving instructions** and you'll be directed to information on **negatives**, **prepositions** and **requests**. A glossary of grammatical terms is included at the end of this chapter to help you.

Abbreviations like nom and acc in the literal translations for each example refer the case of the noun or pronoun – this is explained in the glossary and in **case**.

adjectives & adverbs

Adjectives in Greek normally come before the noun, just like in English. They take different endings to agree with the noun they qualify (see **case**, **gender** and **plurals**) – we've given their standard forms below. Adjectives are shown in the nominative form in lists throughout this book and in the **dictionary** – these forms won't always be strictly correct within a sentence, but you'll still be understood. To find out more, see **case**.

	masculine	feminine	neuter
singular	καλός δρόμος ka·*los* thro·mos good road	καλή τύχη ka·*li* ti·hi good fortune	καλό ποτό ka·*lo* po·to good drink
plural	καλοί δρόμοι ka·*li* thro·mi good roads	καλές τύχες ka·*les* ti·hes good fortunes	καλά ποτά ka·*la* po·ta good drinks

Adverbs normally end with the sound a (eg καλά ka·*la* 'well').

He filled in the form quickly.

Συμπλήρωσε το έντυπο   si·*bli*·ro·se to e·di·po
γρήγορα.   *ghri*·gho·ra
(lit: filled-in the-acc form-acc quickly)

articles

The Greek words for 'a' and 'an' change form to agree in gender and case with the noun they refer to.

		masculine	feminine	neuter
indefinite article (a/an)	nom	ένας e·*nas*	μια mia	ένα e·na
	acc	ένα(ν) e·*na(n)*	μια mia	ένα e·na
	gen	ενός e·*nos*	μιας *mi*·as	ενός e·*nos*

a–z phrasebuilder

The Greek equivalents of 'the' also change form according to the noun – see also **case**, **gender** and **plurals**.

			masculine		feminine		neuter	
definite article (the)	nom	sg	o	o	η	i	το	to
		pl	οι	i	οι	i	τα	ta
	acc	sg	το(ν)	to(n)	τη(ν)	ti(n)	το	to
		pl	τους	tus	τις	tis	τα	ta
	gen	sg	του	tu	της	tis	του	tu
		pl	των	ton	των	ton	των	ton

Articles alway come before the noun:

a road	**ένας** δρόμος	*e·*nas *thro·*mos
the road	**ο** δρόμος	o *thro·*mos

be

making statements

The verb είμαι *i·*me (be) changes depending on who or what is the subject (doer) of the sentence. These are the forms for the present and past tenses.

present			past		
I am	είμαι	*i·*me	I was	ήμουν	*i·*mun
you are sg inf	είσαι	*i·*se	you were sg inf	ήσουν	*i·*sun
you are sg pol	είστε	*i·*ste	you were sg pol	ήσαστε	*i·*sa·ste
he/she/it is	είναι	*i·*ne	he/she/it was	ήταν	*i·*tan
we are	είμαστε	*i·*ma·ste	we were	ήμαστε	*i·*ma·ste
you are pl	είστε	*i·*ste	you were pl	ήσαστε	*i·*sa·ste
they are	είναι	*i·*ne	they were	ήταν	*i·*tan

BASICS

18

The future tense is formed by placing the word θα tha (will) in front of the present tense forms.

I'll be there tomorrow.
Θα είμαι εκεί αύριο.   tha *i*·me e·*ki* av·ri·o
(lit: will be there tomorrow)

case

**doing things • indicating location •
naming people/things • possessing**

Greek uses four different cases, usually shown by word endings, to indicate a noun's role and its relationship to other words in the sentence. Adjectives, articles, demonstratives and pronouns also change their form to agree with the noun they go with.

nominative **nom** – shows the subject of a sentence

The car won't start.
Το αυτοκίνητο δεν αρχίζει.   to af·to·*ki*·ni·to then ar·*hi*·zi
(lit: the-**nom** car-**nom** not starts)

accusative **acc** – shows the direct object of a sentence

Please bring the menu.
Παρακαλώ φέρε το μενού.   pa·ra·ka·*lo* fe·re to me·*nu*
(lit: please bring the-**acc** menu-**acc**)

genitive **gen** – shows possession or the indirect object of a sentence

What's the address of the hotel?
Ποια είναι η διεύθυνση του   pia *i*·ne i *thi*·ef·thin·si tu
ξενοδοχείου;   kse·no·tho·*hi*·u
(lit: which is the-**nom** address-**nom** the-**gen** hotel-**gen**)

vocative **voc** – to address someone directly

Officer, I think there's been a mistake.
Κύριε, νομίζω ότι έχει γίνει   *ki*·ri·e no·*mi*·zo o·ti e·xi *yi*·ni
κάποιο λάθος   *ka*·pio *la*·thos
(lit: sir-**voc** I-think that has been some-**nom** mistake-**nom**)

Greek nouns in the **dictionaries**, the **menu decoder** and word lists in this book are given in the nominative case. You can use this form as a default and, although this won't always be grammatically correct within sentences, you'll still be understood.

demonstratives

indicating location • naming people/things • pointing things out

The words for 'this' and 'that' in Greek change their endings depending on the form of the noun they determine (see **case**, **gender** and **plurals**). We've only given the nominative forms here – in most cases you'll be understood just fine.

		masculine		feminine		neuter	
this	sg	αυτός	af·*tos*	αυτή	af·*ti*	αυτό	af·*to*
	pl	αυτοί	af·*ti*	αυτές	af·*tes*	αυτά	af·*ta*
that	sg	εκείνος	e·*ki*·nos	εκείνη	e·*ki*·ni	εκείνο	e·*ki*·no
	pl	εκείνοι	e·*ki*·ni	εκείνες	e·*ki*·nes	εκείνα	e·*ki*·na

Does this train go to Lamia?
Πηγαίνει αυτό το τρένο   pi·*ye*·ni af·*to* to *tre*·no
στη Λαμία;   sti la·*mi*·a
(lit: goes this-**nom** the-**nom** train-**nom** to Lamia-**acc**)

That bag is mine.
Εκείνη η τσάντα είναι   e·*ki*·ni i *tsa*·da *i*·ne
δική μου.   thi·*ki* mu
(lit: that-**nom** the-**nom** bag-**nom** is mine)

This is my bag.
Αυτή η σάκα είναι δική μου.   af·*ti* i *sa*·ka *i*·ne thi·*ki* mu
(lit: this-**nom** the-**nom** bag-**nom** is mine)

BASICS

gender

Greek nouns have gender – masculine **m**, feminine **f** or neuter **n**. You need to learn the grammatical gender for each noun as you go, but you can often identify it by the noun's ending as shown in the table below. Adjectives, articles and pronouns take the same gender to agree with the noun they qualify.

common noun endings				
masculine	sg	**-ας** πατέρας pa·*te*·ras father	**-ης** ναύτης *naf*·tis sailor	**-ος** δρόμος *thro*·mos road
	pl	**-ες** πατέρες pa·*te*·res fathers	**-ες** ναύτες *naf*·tes sailors	**-οι** δρόμοι *thro*·mi roads
feminine	sg	**-α** πόρτα *por*·ta door	**-η** τύχη *ti*·hi fortune	
	pl	**-ες** πόρτες *por*·tes doors	**-ες** τύχες *ti*·hes fortunes	
neuter	sg	**-μα** όνομα o·*no*·ma name	**-ι** αγόρι a·*gho*·ri boy	**-ο** ποτό po·*to* drink
	pl	**-τα** ονόματα o·*no*·ma·ta names	**-α** αγόρια a·*gho*·ria boys	**-α** ποτά po·*ta* drinks

have

The verb έχω *e*·kho (have) only changes form according to who or what is the subject (doer) of the sentence. To form the future tense (as in the example on page 22), just place the word θα tha (will) in front of the present tense forms.

present			past		
I have	έχω	e·kho	I had	είχα	i·kha
you have sg inf	έχεις	e·his	you had sg inf	είχες	i·hes
you have sg pol	έχετε	e·he·te	you had sg pol	είχατε	i·kha·te
he/she/it has	έχει	e·hi	he/she/it had	είχε	i·he
we have	έχουμε	e·khu·me	we had	είχαμε	i·kha·me
you have pl	έχετε	e·he·te	you had pl	είχατε	i·kha·te
they have	έχουν	e·khun	they had	είχαν	i·khan

I'll have no money by the end of my trip!

Δεν θα έχω χρήματα με
το τέλος του ταξιδιού!
(lit: not will I-have money-acc with
the-acc end-acc the-gen trip-gen)

ţhen tha e·kho khri·ma·ta me
to te·los tu tak·si·ţhiu

negatives

giving instructions · negating

To make a statement negative, add the word δεν ţhen (not)
before the verb:

I speak Greek.

Μιλώ Ελληνικά.
(lit: speak Greek)

mi·lo e·li·ni·ka

I don't speak Greek.

Δεν μιλώ Ελληνικά.
(lit: not speak Greek)

ţhen mi·lo e·li·ni·ka

In commands, use the word μην min (not) instead:

Don't swim here.

Μην κολυμπάς εδώ.
(lit: not swim here)

min ko·li·bas e·ţho

Note that, unlike English, Greek has double negatives:

I don't want anything.
Δεν θέλω τίποτε.　　　　　　　ţhen *the·*lo *ti·*po·te
(lit: not want nothing)

personal pronouns

doing things • making statements

In Greek, there are two words for 'you' – an informal one, εσύ
e·*si* (used with friends, younger people or family members),
and a formal one, εσείς e·*sis* (used when addressing strangers,
authority figures or older people). In this phrasebook we've
used the form of 'you' (and the verb form) appropriate for each
situation.

	subject nom	
I	εγώ	e·*gho*
you sg inf	εσύ	e·*si*
you sg pol	εσείς	e·*sis*
he/she/it	αυτός/αυτή/αυτό	af·*tos*/af·*ti*/af·*to*
we	εμείς	e·*mis*
you pl	εσείς	e·*sis*
they m/f/n	αυτοί/αυτές/αυτά	af·*ti*/af·*tes*/af·*ta*

	direct object acc		**indirect object** gen	
me	με	me	μου	mu
you sg inf	σε	se	σου	su
you sg pol	σας	sas	σας	sas
him/her/it	τον/την/το	ton/tin/to	του/της/του	tu/tis/tu
us	μας	mas	μας	mas
you pl	σας	sas	σας	sas
them m/f/n	τους/τις/τα	tus/tis/ta	τους	tus

Greek pronouns vary according to case – the subject or doer of an action is in the nominative case while the object is in the accusative or genitive case.

Both direct and indirect object pronouns are placed before the verb. If you have both in a sentence, the indirect pronoun comes first. In commands, they come after the verb.

I gave my passport to him.

Του έδωσα το
διαβατήριό μου.
tu e·tho·sa to
thia·va·ti·ri·o mu

(lit: him-gen I-gave the-acc passport-acc my)

I gave it to him.

Του το έδωσα.
tu to e·tho·sa

(lit: him-gen it-acc I-gave)

It's not necessary to use a subject pronoun in Greek, as verb endings show who the subject is. A subject pronoun can be used for emphasis or when there's no verb in the sentence.

I go to school everyday.

Πηγαίνω στο σχολείο
κάθε μέρα.
pi·ye·no sto skho·li·o
ka·the me·ra

(lit: go-I to school-acc every day)

I did it.

Εγώ το έκανα.
e·gho to e·ka·na

(lit: I-nom it-acc did)

plurals

Plural nouns take different endings depending on gender – see the table under **gender** for the most common ones. Adjectives, articles, demonstratives and pronouns also have plural forms to agree with the plural noun.

possessives

Possession can be expressed not only with the verb 'have' but with possessive pronouns and adjectives as well.

The possessive adjectives (my, your, his etc) are placed after the noun, with the definite article before the noun (also see **articles**). They don't change for case, gender or number.

possessive adjectives		
my	μου	mu
your sg inf	σου	su
your sg pol	σας	sas
his/her/its	του/της/του	tu/tis/tu
our	μας	mas
your pl	σας	sas
their	τους	tus

I've lost my car keys.

Έχασα τα κλειδιά   e·kha·sa ta kli·*thia*
του αυτοκινήτου μου.   tu af·to·ki·*ni*·tu mu
(lit: lost the-**acc** keys-**acc** the-**gen** car-**gen** my)

Possessive pronouns (mine, yours etc) are formed by adding the word δικός/δική/δικό thi·*kos*/thi·*ki*/thi·*ko* m/f/n in front of the possessive adjective. This word agrees in gender and case with the noun it refers to – endings are the same as those the adjectives take (see **adjectives & adverbs**). To keep things simple we've only given the nominative case in the next table.

possessive pronouns			
	masculine	**feminine**	**neuter**
mine	δικός μου ᶁhi·*kos* mu	δική μου ᶁhi·*ki* mu	δικό μου ᶁhi·*ko* mu
yours sg inf	δικός σου ᶁhi·*kos* su	δική σου ᶁhi·*ki* su	δικό σου ᶁhi·*ko* su
yours sg pol	δικός σας ᶁhi·*kos* sas	δική σας ᶁhi·*ki* sas	δικό σας ᶁhi·*ko* sas
his/hers/its	δικός του/της/του ᶁhi·*kos* tu/tis/tu	δική του/της/του ᶁhi·*ki* tu/tis/tu	δικό του/της/του ᶁhi·*ko* tu/tis/tu
ours	δικός μας ᶁhi·*kos* mas	δική μας ᶁhi·*ki* mas	δικό μας ᶁhi·*ko* mas
yours pl	δικός σας ᶁhi·*kos* sas	δική σας ᶁhi·*ki* sas	δικό σας ᶁhi·*ko* sas
theirs	δικός τους ᶁhi·*kos* tus	δική τους ᶁhi·*ki* tus	δικό τους ᶁhi·*ko* tus

Those bags are ours.

Εκείνες οι τσάντες είναι   e·*ki*·nes i *tsa*·des *i*·ne
δικές μας.   ᶁhi·*kes* mas
(lit: those-**nom** the-**nom** bags-**nom** are ours)

prepositions

giving instructions • indicating location •
pointing things out

Many prepositions require the noun used after them to be in
a particular case (see **case**) – σε se (to/at/in), από a·*po* (from),
με me (with), για yia (for), προς pros (towards), κάτω από ka·to
a·*po* (under), πάνω σε *pa*·no se (on) are all followed by the accusative. The genitive is used after μεταξύ me·tak·*si* (between).

I'd like to book a seat to Athens.

Θα ήθελα να κρατήσω   tha *i*·the·la na kra·*ti*·so
μια θέση για την Αθήνα.   mia *the*·si yia tin a·*thi*·na
(lit: I-would like to book
a seat-acc for the-acc Athens-acc)

What's the difference between 1st and 2nd class?

Ποια είναι η διαφορά μεταξύ   pia *i*·ne i thia·fo·*ra* me·tak·*si*
πρώτης και δεύτερης θέσης;   *pro*·tis ke *thef*·te·ris *the*·sis
(lit: which is the-nom difference-nom between
first-gen and second-gen class-gen)

questions

asking questions

To ask a yes/no question, just raise the intonation at the end
of a sentence. Note that Greek uses a semicolon (;) instead of
a question mark.

The bus stop is over there.

Η στάση του λεωφορείου   i *sta*·si tu le·o·fo·*ri*·u
είναι εκεί πέρα.   *i*·ne e·*ki* pe·ra
(lit: the-nom stop-nom the-gen bus-gen is there over)

Is the bus stop over there?

Η στάση του λεωφορείου   i *sta*·si tu le·o·fo·*ri*·u
είναι εκεί πέρα;   *i*·ne e·*ki* pe·ra
(lit: the-nom stop-nom the-gen bus-gen is there over)

The subject and the verb are often reversed in questions (see
word order). You can also start a question with a question
word – the verb comes in the second place, just like in English.
The table on the next page lists the main question words.

question words		
How?	Πώς;	pos
How many?	Πόσοι/Πόσες/Πόσα; m/f/n pl	po·si/po·ses/po·sa
How much?	Πόσος/Πόση/Πόσο; m/f/n	po·sos/po·si/po·so
What?	Τι;	ti
When?	Πότε;	po·te
Where?	Πού;	pu
Who?	Ποιος/Ποια/Ποιο; m/f/n sg Ποιοι/Ποιες/Ποια; m/f/n pl	pios/pia/pio pii/pies/pia
Which?	Ποιος/Ποια/Ποιο; m/f/n sg Ποιοι/Ποιες/Ποια; m/f/n pl	pios/pia/pio pii/pies/pia
Why?	Γιατί;	yi·a·ti

How do you pronounce this?
Πώς προφέρεις αυτό;   pos pro·fe·ris af·to
(lit: how you-pronounce this-acc)

How much is it?
Πόσο κάνει;   po·so ka·ni
(lit: how-much makes)

When's the first bus?
Πότε είναι το πρώτο   po·te i·ne to pro·to
λεωφορείο;   le·o·fo·ri·o
(lit: when is the-nom first-nom bus-nom)

Who is that?
Ποιος είναι εκείνος;   pios i·ne e·ki·nos
(lit: who-nom is that-nom)

Why can't I board this train?
Γιατί δεν μπορώ να ανεβώ   yia·ti then bo·ro na a·ne·vo
σ'αυτό το τρένο;   saf·to to tre·no
(lit: why not can to board to-this-acc the-acc train-acc)

BASICS

requests

giving instructions

A simple and polite way to make a request is to use the verb as found in the table on page 30, in its second-person present form, followed by παρακαλώ pa·ra·ka·*lo* ('please'). Use the informal (singular) form with people you know well, and the polite (plural) form with others.

Would you please open the window?

ανοίγεις το παράθυρο,   a·*ni*·yis to pa·*ra*·thi·ro
παρακαλώ; sg inf   pa·ra·ka·*lo*
(lit: open the window please)

Would you please open the window?

ανοίγετε το παράθυρο,   a·*ni*·ye·te to pa·*ra*·thi·ro
παρακαλώ; pl pol   pa·ra·ka·*lo*
(lit: open the window please)

For the negative form, see **negatives**.

verbs

doing things

The dictionary form of all Greek verbs ends in -ω ·o or -ομαι o·me, which is the present tense form of the first person singular (like in 'I eat'). The ending -ω represents 'active' verbs (which show someone actively doing something – πηγαίνω pi·*ye*·no 'go'), while -ομαι is for 'stative' verbs (which show a state or condition, and don't require movement – κάθομαι *ka*·tho·me 'sit'). These endings change according to the subject of the sentence. Sometimes changes in the verb stem (the form of the verb before the ending) occur, but if you use the endings shown on the next page, you'll be understood just fine.

present

Active and stative verbs have different sets of endings.

	active verb eg 'write'		stative verb eg 'think'	
dictionary form	γράφω	*ghra*·fo	σκέφτομαι	*skef*·to·me
I	γράφ**ω**	*ghra*·fo	σκέφτ**ομαι**	*skef*·to·me
you sg inf	γράφ**εις**	*ghra*·fis	σκέφτ**εσαι**	*skef*·te·se
you sg pol	γράφ**ετε**	*ghra*·fe·te	σκέφτ**εστε**	*skef*·tes·te
he/she/it	γράφ**ει**	*ghra*·fi	σκέφτ**εται**	*skef*·te·te
we	γράφ**ουμε**	*ghra*·fu·me	σκεφτ**όμαστε**	*skef*·to·ma·ste
you pl	γράφ**ετε**	*ghra*·fe·te	σκέφτ**εστε**	*skef*·tes·te
they	γράφ**ουν**	*ghra*·fun	σκέφτ**ονται**	*skef*·ton·de

past

The past tense endings for all verbs are provided below. There are some irregularities, however – as the stress in the verb moves back to the third syllable from the end, the prefix ε e· (augment) is added to the verb when there are less than three syllables. Also, the final letter before the ending sometimes changes.

	all verbs eg 'write'	
I	έγραψα	*e*·ghra·psa
you sg inf	έγραψες	*e*·ghra·pses
you sg pol	γράψατε	*ghra*·psa·te
he/she/it	έγραψε	*e*·ghra·pse
we	γράψαμε	*ghra*·psa·me
you pl	γράψατε	*ghra*·psa·te
they	έγραψαν	*e*·ghra·psan

future

The easiest way to express an action in the future is by using the present tense forms and adding the word θα tha (will) in front of them.

I'll send you a postcard everyday.
> Θα σου στέλνω μία   tha su *stel*·no mia
> κάρτα κάθε μέρα.   *kar*·ta *ka*·the *me*·ra
> (lit: will you-**gen** send a-**acc** postcard-**acc** every day)

word order

asking questions • making statements • negating

While the sentence order of subject–verb–object is most common in Greek, all other combinations are correct too – the word order is relatively free as Greek uses case (meaning that different word endings express the role of a word in the sentence). You might notice, however, that emphasised words are usually at the beginning of the sentence (see also **negatives** and **questions**).

The cashier didn't give me the correct change.
> Ο ταμίας δεν μου έδωσε   o ta·*mi*·as then mu *e*·tho·se
> τα σωστά ρέστα.   ta so·*sta re*·sta
> (lit: the-**nom** cashier-**nom** not me-**gen** gave
> the-**acc** correct-**acc** change-**acc**)

The cashier didn't give me the correct change.
> Δεν μου έδωσε τα σωστά   then mu *e*·tho·se ta so·*sta*
> ρέστα ο ταμίας.   *re*·sta o ta·*mi*·as
> (lit: not me-**gen** gave the-**acc** correct-**acc**
> change-**acc** the-**nom** cashier-**nom**)

Note that the indirect object comes before the direct object.

glossary

active verb	a verb that involves someone actively doing something – 'he **travelled** for many moons'
adjective	a word that describes something – '**ancient** hero'
adverb	a word that explains how an action was done – 'he **heroically** set out to find his father'
article	the words 'a', 'an' and 'the'
case (marking)	word ending that shows the role of the thing or person in the sentence
demonstrative	a word that means 'this' or 'that'
gender	Greek nouns can be masculine, feminine or neuter
imperative	a command – '**prove** to me that you are Odysseus'
noun	a thing, person or idea – 'an odyssey'
number	whether a word is singular or plural – 'journey' or 'journeys'
object (direct)	the thing or person that's directly affected by the action – 'Penelope offered **dinner** to her suitors'
object (indirect)	the person in the sentence that benefits from an action – 'Penelope offered **them** dinner'
personal pronoun	a word that means 'I', 'you', etc
possessive pronoun	a word that means 'mine', 'yours', etc
preposition	a word like 'for' or 'before' in English
stative verb	a verb that doesn't require movement – 'Penelope **missed** her husband very much'
subject	the thing or person that does the action – '**the suitors** took advantage of her hospitality'
tense	marking on the verb that tells you whether the action is in the present, past or future – 'travel**led**'
verb	the word that tells you what action happened – 'Odysseus **disguises** himself as a beggar'
verb stem	the part of a verb which does not change – like 'charm' in 'charmed' and 'charming'

language difficulties

Do you speak (English)?
Μιλάς (Αγγλικά);
mi·*las* (ang·gli·*ka*)

Does anyone speak (English)?
Μιλάει κανείς (Αγγλικά);
mi·*la*·i ka·*nis* (ang·gli·*ka*)

Do you understand?
Καταλαβαίνεις;
ka·ta·la·*ve*·nis

Yes, I understand.
Ναι, καταλαβαίνω.
ne ka·ta·la·*ve*·no

No, I don't understand.
Όχι, δεν καταλαβαίνω.
o·hi ţhen ka·ta·la·*ve*·no

I (don't) understand.
(Δεν) καταλαβαίνω.
(ţhen) ka·ta·la·*ve*·no

Pardon?
Συγνώμη;
sigh·*no*·mi

I speak (English).
Μιλώ (Αγγλικά).
mi·*lo* (ang·gli·*ka*)

I don't speak Greek.
Δεν μιλώ Ελληνικά.
ţhen mi·*lo* e·li·ni·*ka*

I speak a little.
Μιλώ λίγο.
mi·*lo* li·gho

Let's speak Greek.
Ας μιλήσουμε Ελληνικά.
as mi·*li*·su·me e·li·ni·*ka*

---

tongue-tied

If you're after a challenge, try this tongue twister for size.

Ο παπάς ο παχύς έφαγε παχιά φακή.
Γιατί, παπά παχύ, έφαγες παχιά φακή;
o pa·*pas* o pa·*his* e·fa·ye pa·*hia* fa·*ki*
yia·*ti* pa·*pa* pa·*hi* e·fa·yes pa·*hia* fa·*ki*
(The fat priest ate thick lentil soup.
Why, fat priest, did you eat thick lentil soup?)

I would like to practise Greek.

Θα ήθελα να εξασκήσω
τα Ελληνικά μου.

tha *i*·the·la na ek·sa·*ski*·so
ta e·li·ni·*ka* mu

What does (μώλος) mean?

Τι σημαίνει (μώλος);

ti si·*me*·ni (*mo*·los)

How do you ...?
  pronounce this
  write 'Madhuri'

Πώς ...;
  προφέρεις αυτό
  γράψεις
  'Μαδουρή'

pos ...
  pro·*fe*·ris af·*to*
  ghrap·sis
  ma·thu·*ri*

**Could you
please ...?**
  repeat that
  **speak more
  slowly**
  write it down

Θα μπορούσες
παρακαλώ να ...;
  το επαναλάβεις
  μιλάς πιο αργά

  το γράψεις

tha bo·*ru*·ses
pa·ra·ka·*lo* na ...
  to e·pa·na·*la*·vis
  mi·*las* pio ar·*gha*

  to *ghrap*·sis

---

alphabet soup

Some Greek letters might look like English ones, but they're
pronounced quite differently.

upper case	lower case	pronunciation
Β	β	v
Η	η	i
Ρ	ρ	r
Υ	υ	i
Χ	χ	h
Ν	ν	n
Ξ	ξ	ks
Σ	σ/ς	s
Ω	ω	o

See the box on page 14 for the full Greek alphabet.

numbers & amounts

cardinal numbers

απόλυτοι αριθμοί

In Greek, some numbers (one, three, four, and numbers linked to them like 21 and 13) change according to gender – that is, they have different forms when the noun they're associated with is masculine m, feminine f or neuter n. When simply counting, you use the neuter form.

1	ένας/μία/ένα m/f/n	e·nas/mi·a/e·na
2	δύο	thi·o
3	τρεις/τρία m&f/n	tris/tri·a
4	τέσσερις m&f	te·se·ris
	τέσσερα n	te·se·ra
5	πέντε	pe·de
6	έξι	ek·si
7	εφτά	ef·ta
8	οχτώ	okh·to
9	εννέα	e·ne·a
10	δέκα	the·ka
11	έντεκα	e·de·ka
12	δώδεκα	tho·the·ka
13	δεκατρείς m&f	the·ka·tris
	δεκατρία n	the·ka·tri·a
14	δεκατέσσερις m&f	the·ka·te·se·ris
	δεκατέσσερα n	the·ka·te·se·ra
15	δεκαπέντε	the·ka·pe·de
16	δεκαέξι	the·ka·ek·si
17	δεκαεφτά	the·ka·ef·ta
18	δεκαοχτώ	the·ka·okh·to
19	δεκαεννέα	the·ka·e·ne·a
20	είκοσι	i·ko·si
21	είκοσι ένας/μία m/f	i·ko·si e·nas/mi·a
	είκοσι ένα n	i·ko·si e·na

22	είκοσι δύο	i·ko·si thi·o
30	τριάντα	tri·a·da
40	σαράντα	sa·ra·da
50	πενήντα	pe·ni·da
60	εξήντα	ek·si·da
70	εβδομήντα	ev·tho·mi·da
80	ογδόντα	ogh·tho·da
90	ενενήντα	e·ne·ni·da
100	εκατό	e·ka·to
200	διακόσια	thia·ko·sia
1000	χίλια	hi·lia
1,000,000	ένα εκατομμύριο	e·na e·ka·to·mi·rio

ordinal numbers

Ordinals agree in gender with the noun they're associated with.

1st	πρώτος/πρώτη m/f	pro·tos/pro·ti
	πρώτο n	pro·to
2nd	δεύτερος/δεύτερη m/f	thef·te·ros/thef·te·ri
	δεύτερο n	thef·te·ro
3rd	τρίτος/τρίτη/τρίτο m/f/n	tri·tos/tri·ti/tri·to
4th	τέταρτος/τέταρτη m/f	te·tar·tos/te·tar·ti
	τέταρτο n	te·tar·to
5th	πέμπτος/πέμπτη m/f	pem·tos/pem·ti
	πέμπτο n	pem·to
6th	έκτος/έκτη/έκτο m/f/n	ek·tos/ek·ti/ek·to
7th	έβδομος/έβδομη m/f	ev·tho·mos/ev·tho·mi
	έβδομο n	ev·tho·mo
8th	όγδοος/όγδοη m/f	ogh·tho·os/ogh·tho·i
	όγδοο n	ogh·tho·o
9th	ένατος/ένατη/ένατο m/f/n	e·na·tos/e·na·ti/e·na·to
10th	δέκατος/δέκατη m/f	the·ka·tos/the·ka·ti
	δέκατο n	the·ka·to

fractions

κλάσματα

a quarter	ένα τέταρτο n	*e*·na *te*·tar·to
a third	ένα τρίτο n	*e*·na *tri*·to
a half	μισό n	mi·*so*
three-quarters	τρία τέταρτα n pl	*tri*·a *te*·tar·ta
all	όλα n pl	*o*·la
none	τίποτε	*ti*·po·te

useful amounts

χρήσιμα ποσά

The words for 'How much?' and 'How many?' take different forms for the gender of the noun they refer to, as shown below.

How much?	Πόσος/Πόση m/f	po·sos/*po*·si
	Πόσο; n	*po*·so
How many?	Πόσοι/Πόσες m/f	*po*·si/*po*·ses
	Πόσα; n	*po*·sa
How much water?	Πόσο νερό; n	*po*·so ne·*ro*
How much sugar?	Πόση ζάχαρη; f	*po*·si *za*·kha·ri
How many men?	Πόσοι άντρες; m	*po*·si *a*·dres
How many women?	Πόσες γυναίκες; f	*po*·ses yi·*ne*·kes

I'd like (a) ...	Θα ήθελα ...	tha i·the·la ...
Please give me (a) ...	Παρακαλώ δώσε μου ...	pa·ra·ka·lo tho·se mu ...
(100) grams	(εκατό) γραμμάρια	(e·ka·to) ghra·ma·ria
half a dozen	μισή ντουζίνα	mi·si du·zi·na
dozen	μια ντουζίνα	mia du·zi·na
half a kilo	μισό κιλό	mi·so ki·lo
kilo	ένα κιλό	e·na ki·lo
bottle	ένα μπουκάλι	e·na bu·ka·li
jar	ένα βάζο	e·na va·zo
tin	ένα κουτί	e·na ku·ti
packet	ένα πακέτο	e·na pa·ke·to
slice	μια φέτα	mia fe·ta
few	λίγα	li·gha
less	λιγότερο	li·gho·te·ro
(just) a little	(μόνο) λιγάκι	(mo·no) li·gha·ki
lot	πολύ	po·li
many	πολλά	po·la
more	πιο πολύ	pio po·li
some ...	μερικά ...	me·ri·ka ...

To find out how to put these amounts to use, see **self-catering**, page 171.

---

what's in a name?

Although Greeks have moved around their own country and emigrated worldwide, you can sometimes tell from their surnames where they originally come from. People whose name ends in -ακης -a·kis are from Crete, -ατος -a·tos from Cephallonia, -ιδης -i·this from Macedonia, and -πουλος -pu·los from the Peloponnese.

telling the time

λέγοντας την ώρα

Telling the time in Greek is straightforward. For 'It's ... o'clock' simply say είναι *i*·ne (lit: it-is) followed by the number, then η ώρα i *o*·ra (lit: the hour). Note that η ώρα is optional. To give times after the hour say the number of hours, then και ke (lit: and) and the number of minutes. For times before the hour say the number of hours, then παρά pa·*ra* (lit: minus) and the minutes. Instead of 30 or 15 minutes, say μισή mi·*si* (half) for the half hour and τέταρτο *te*·tar·to (quarter).

What time is it?
Τι ώρα είναι;   ti *o*·ra *i*·ne

It's (ten) o'clock.
Είναι (δέκα) η ώρα.   *i*·ne (*the*·ka) i *o*·ra

Five past (ten).
(Δέκα) και πέντε.   (*the*·ka) ke *pe*·de

Quarter past (ten).
(Δέκα) και τέταρτο.   (*the*·ka) ke *te*·tar·to

Half past (ten).
(Δέκα) και μισή.   (*the*·ka) ke mi·*si*

Quarter to (ten).
(Δέκα) παρά τέταρτο.   (*the*·ka) pa·*ra te*·tar·to

Twenty to (ten).
(Δέκα) παρά είκοσι.   (*the*·ka) pa·*ra i*·ko·si

At what time ...?
Τι ώρα ...;   ti *o*·ra ...

At (ten).
Στις (δέκα).   stis (*the*·ka)

At (7.57pm).
Στις (7.57μ.μ.).   stis (ef·*ta* ke pe·*ni*·da ef·*ta*
                                me·*ta* to me·si·*me*·ri)

The times 'am' and 'pm' are written 'π.μ.' and 'μ.μ.', but you always say the full name – πριν το μεσημέρι prin to me·si·*me*·ri (am) and μετά το μεσημέρι me·*ta* to me·si·*me*·ri (pm).

the calendar

το ημερολόγιο

days

Monday	Δευτέρα	ţhef·*te*·ra
Tuesday	Τρίτη	*tri*·ti
Wednesday	Τετάρτη	te·*tar*·ti
Thursday	Πέμπτη	*pem*·ti
Friday	Παρασκευή	pa·ra·ske·*vi*
Saturday	Σάββατο	*sa*·va·to
Sunday	Κυριακή	ki·ria·*ki*

months

January	Ιανουάριος	i·a·nu·*a*·ri·os
February	Φεβρουάριος	fev·ru·*a*·ri·os
March	Μάρτιος	*mar*·ti·os
April	Απρίλιος	a·*pri*·li·os
May	Μάιος	*ma*·i·os
June	Ιούνιος	i·*u*·ni·os
July	Ιούλιος	i·*u*·li·os
August	Αύγουστος	*av*·ghu·stos
September	Σεπτέμβριος	sep·*tem*·vri·os
October	Οκτώβριος	ok·*tov*·ri·os
November	Νοέμβριος	no·*em*·vri·os
December	Δεκέμβριος	ţhe·*kem*·vri·os

dates

What date is it today?

Τι ημερομηνία είναι σήμερα;   ti i·me·ro·mi·*ni*·a *i*·ne *si*·me·ra

It's (18 October).

Είναι (18 Οκτωβρίου).   *i*·ne (ţhe·ka·okh·*to* ok·tov·*ri*·u)

seasons

spring	άνοιξη f	*a*·nik·si
summer	καλοκαίρι n	ka·lo·*ke*·ri
autumn	φθινόπωρο n	fthi·*no*·po·ro
winter	χειμώνας m	hi·*mo*·nas

present

παρόν

now	τώρα	*to*·ra
today	σήμερα	*si*·me·ra
tonight	το βράδι	to *vra*·thi
this week	αυτή την εβδομάδα	af·*ti* tin ev·tho·*ma*·tha
this ...	αυτό το ...	af·*to* to ...
morning	πρωί	pro·*i*
afternoon	απόγευμα	a·*po*·yev·ma
month	μήνα	*mi*·na
year	χρόνο	*khro*·no

past

παρελθόν

(three days) ago	(τρεις μέρες) πριν	(tris *me*·res) prin
day before yesterday	προχτές	prokh·*tes*
since (May)	από (το Μάιο)	a·*po* (to *ma*·i·o)
yesterday ...	χτες το ...	khtes to ...
morning	πρωί	pro·*i*
afternoon	απόγευμα	a·*po*·yev·ma
evening	βράδι	*vra*·thi

last night/week

την περασμένη νύχτα/εβδομάδα	tin pe·raz·*me*·ni *nikh*·ta/ev·tho·*ma*·tha

last month/year

τον περασμένο μήνα/χρόνο	ton pe·raz·*me*·no *mi*·na/*khro*·no

future

μέλλον

tomorrow ...	αύριο το ...	*av*·ri·o to ...
morning	πρωί	pro·*i*
afternoon	απόγευμα	a·*po*·yev·ma
evening	βράδι	*vra*·thi
tomorrow	αύριο	*av*·ri·o
day after tomorrow	μεθαύριο	me·*thav*·ri·o
next week	την επόμενη εβδομάδα	tin e·*po*·me·ni ev·tho·*ma*·tha
next month	τον επόμενο μήνα	ton e·*po*·me·no *mi*·na
next year	τον επόμενο χρόνο	ton e·*po*·me·no *khro*·no
in (six days)	σε (έξι μέρες)	se (*ek*·si *me*·res)
until (June)	μέχρι (τον Ιούνιο)	*meh*·ri (ton i·*u*·ni·o)

during the day

κατά τη διάρκεια της ημέρας

afternoon	απόγευμα n	a·*po*·yev·ma
dawn	αυγή f	av·*yi*
day	ημέρα f	i·*me*·ra
evening	βράδι n	*vra*·thi
midday	μεσημέρι n	me·si·*me*·ri
midnight	μεσάνυχτα n pl	me·*sa*·nikh·ta
morning	πρωί n	pro·*i*
night	νύχτα f	*nikh*·ta
sunrise	ανατολή του ήλιου f	a·na·to·*li* tu *i*·liu
sunset	δύση του ήλιου f	*thi*·si tu *i*·liu

but the most important time of day ...

... is probably the μεσημεριανή ανάπαυση me·si·*me*·ria·*ni* a·*na*·paf·si (siesta). Don't miss out!

How much is it?
Πόσο κάνει;   *po·so ka·ni*

It's (12) euros.
Κάνει (δώδεκα) ευρώ.   *ka·ni (tho·the·ka) ev·ro*

It's free.
Είναι δωρεάν.   *i·ne tho·re·an*

Can you write down the price?
Μπορείς να γράψεις την τιμή;   bo·*ris* na *ghrap*·sis tin ti·*mi*

Do you accept …?	Δέχεσαι …;	*the*·he·se …
credit cards	πιστωτικές	pi·sto·ti·*kes*
	κάρτες	*kar*·tes
debit cards	χρεωτικές	khre·o·ti·*kes*
	κάρτες	*kar*·tes
travellers	ταξιδιωτικές	tak·si·thio·ti·*kes*
cheques	επιταγές	e·pi·ta·*yes*
Where's a/an …?	Πού είναι …;	pu *i*·ne …
automated	μια αυτόματη	mia af·*to*·ma·ti
teller machine	μηχανή	mi·kha·*ni*
	ανάληψης	a·*na*·lip·sis
	χρημάτων	khri·*ma*·ton
foreign exchange	ένα γραφείο	e·na ghra·*fi*·o
office	αλλαγής	a·la·*yis*
	χρημάτων	khri·*ma*·ton

The official currency in Greece is the ευρώ ev·ro (euro), which is made up of 100 λεπτά lep·ta (euro cents). Some vendors are also happy to take foreign currencies.

What's the ...?	Πόσο είναι ...;	po·so i·ne ...
charge	το κόστος	to kos·tos
exchange rate	η τιμή	i ti·mi
	συναλλάγματος	si·na·lagh·ma·tos
I'd like to ...	Θα ήθελα να ...	tha i·the·la na ...
cash a cheque	εξαργυρώσω	ek·sar·yi·ro·so
	μια επιταγή	mia e·pi·ta·yi
change money	αλλάξω χρήματα	a·lak·so khri·ma·ta
change a	αλλάξω μια	a·lak·so mia
travellers	ταξιδιωτική	tak·si·thio·ti·ki
cheque	επιταγή	e·pi·ta·yi
get a cash	κάμω μια	ka·mo mia
advance	ανάληψη	a·na·lip·si
	σε μετρητά	se me·tri·ta
withdraw	αποσύρω	a·po·si·ro
money	χρήματα	khri·ma·ta
I'd like ...,	Θα ήθελα ...,	tha i·the·la ...
please.	παρακαλώ.	pa·ra·ka·lo
my change	τα ρέστα μου	ta re·sta mu
a refund	μια επιστροφή	mia e·pi·stro·fi
	χρημάτων	khri·ma·ton
to return this	να επιστρέψω αυτό	na e·pi·strep·so af·to

There's a mistake in the bill.

Υπάρχει κάποιο λάθος
στο λογαριασμό.

i·par·hi ka·pio la·thos
sto lo·gha·riaz·mo

Do I need to pay upfront?

Χρειάζεται να πληρώσω
από πριν;

khri·a·ze·te na pli·ro·so
a·po prin

I don't have that much money.

Δεν έχω τόσα πολλά
χρήματα.

then e·kho to·sa po·la
khri·ma·ta

getting around

κυκλοφορώντας

Which ... goes to (Athens)?	Ποιο ... πηγαίνει στην (Αθήνα);	pio ... pi·ye·ni stin (a·thi·na)
Is this the ... to (Athens)?	Είναι αυτό το ... για την (Αθήνα);	i·ne af·to to ... yia tin (a·thi·na)
boat	πλοίο	pli·o
bus	λεωφορείο	le·o·fo·ri·o
ferry	φέρυ	fe·ri
plane	αεροπλάνο	a·e·ro·pla·no
train	τρένο	tre·no
When's the ... (bus)?	Πότε είναι το ... (λεωφορείο);	po·te i·ne to ... (le·o·fo·ri·o)
first	πρώτο	pro·to
last	τελευταίο	te·lef·te·o
next	επόμενο	e·po·me·no

What time does it leave?
Τι ώρα φεύγει;   ti o·ra fev·yi

What time does it get to (Thessaloniki)?
Τι ώρα φτάνει στη (Θεσσαλονίκη);   ti o·ra fta·ni sti (the·sa·lo·ni·ki)

How long will it be delayed?
Πόση ώρα θα καθυστερήσει;   po·si o·ra tha ka·thi·ste·ri·si

Is this seat free?
Είναι αυτή η θέση ελεύθερη;   i·ne af·ti i the·si e·lef·the·ri

That's my seat.
Αυτή η θέση είναι δική μου.   af·ti i the·si i·ne thi·ki mu

transport

45

Please tell me when we get to (Thessaloniki).

Παρακαλώ πέστε μου
όταν φτάσουμε στη
(Θεσσαλονίκη).

pa·ra·ka·*lo* pe·ste mu
o·tan *fta*·su·me sti
(the·sa·lo·*ni*·ki)

How long do we stop here?

Πόση ώρα θα
σταματήσουμε εδώ;

po·si *o*·ra tha
sta·ma·*ti*·su·me e·*tho*

Are you waiting for more people?

Περιμένεις για
περισσότερο κόσμο;

pe·ri·*me*·nis yia
pe·ri·*so*·te·ro *koz*·mo

Can you take us around the city, please?

Μπορείς να μας πάρεις
γύρω στην πόλη,
παρακαλώ;

bo·*ris* na mas *pa*·ris
yi·ro stin *po*·li,
pa·ra·ka·*lo*

How many people can ride on this?

Πόσοι άνθρωποι μπορούν
να ανεβούν σ'αυτό;

po·si *an*·thro·pi bo·*run*
na a·ne·*vun* saf·*to*

Can you take me as well?

Μπορείς να πάρεις
και εμένα;

bo·*ris* na *pa*·ris
ke e·*me*·na

tickets

Where do I buy a ticket?

Πού αγοράζω εισιτήριο;

pu a·gho·*ra*·zo i·si·*ti*·ri·o

Do I need to book?

Χρειάζεται να κλείσω θέση;

khri·*a*·ze·te na *kli*·so *the*·si

A bunch of (10) tickets, please.

Μια δέσμη από (δέκα)
εισιτήρια, παρακαλώ.

mia *thez*·mi a·*po* (*the*·ka)
i·si·*ti*·ri·a pa·ra·ka·*lo*

Do you have a timetable (in English)?

Έχεις ένα πρόγραμμα
(στα αγγλικά);

e·his e·na *pro*·ghra·ma
(sta ang·gli·*ka*)

Can I get a tourist rail pass?

Μπορώ να έχω ένα		bo·ro na e·kho e·na
τουριστικό πάσο		tu·ri·sti·ko pa·so
για το τρένο;		yia to tre·no

A ... ticket	Ένα εισιτήριο ...	e·na i·si·ti·ri·o ...
to (Patras).	για την (Πάτρα).	yia tin (pa·tra)
1st-class	πρώτη θέση	pro·ti the·si
2nd-class	δεύτερη θέση	thef·te·ri the·si
child's	παιδικό	pe·thi·ko
deck class (boat)	κατάστρωμα	ka·ta·stro·ma
one-way	απλό	a·plo
return	με επιστροφή	me e·pi·stro·fi
student's	μαθητικό	ma·thi·ti·ko
tourist class	τουριστική θέση	tu·ri·sti·ki the·si

I'd like a/an ...	Θα ήθελα μια	tha i·the·la mia
seat.	θέση ...	the·si ...
aisle	στο διάδρομο	sto thia·thro·mo
(non)smoking	στους (μη)	stus (mi)
	καπνίζοντες	kap·ni·zo·des
window	στο παράθυρο	sto pa·ra·thi·ro

---

listen for ...

Ακυρώστε το εισιτήριο.	a·ki·ro·ste to i·si·ti·rio	**Punch the ticket.**
ακυρώθηκε	a·ki·ro·thi·ke	**cancelled**
απεργία f	a·per·yi·a	**strike**
αυτό	af·to	**this one**
εκείνο	e·ki·no	**that one**
γεμάτο	ye·ma·to	**full**
καθυστέρησε	ka·thi·ste·ri·se	**delayed**
θυρίδα αγοράς εισιτιρίων f	thi·ri·tha a·gho·ras i·si·ti·ri·on	**ticket window**
πλατφόρμα f	plat·for·ma	**platform**
πρόγραμμα n	pro·ghra·ma	**timetable**
ταξιδιωτικός πράκτορας m	tak·si·thio·ti·kos prak·to·ras	**travel agent**

transport

Is there (a) …?	Υπάρχει …;	i·par·hi …
air conditioning	έρκοντίσιον	e·kon·di·si·on
blanket	κουβέρτα	ku·ver·ta
sick bag	σακούλα εμετού	sa·ku·la e·me·tu
toilet	τουαλέτα	tu·a·le·ta

Can I get a sleeping berth?
Μπορώ να έχω μια θέση
με κρεβάτι;
bo·ro na e·kho mia the·si
me kre·va·ti

How much is it?
Πόσο κάνει;
po·so ka·ni

How long does the trip take?
Πόσο διαρκεί το ταξίδι;
po·so thi·ar·ki to tak·si·thi

Is it a direct route?
Πηγαίνει κατ'ευθείαν;
pi·ye·ni ka·tef·thi·an

Can I get a stand-by ticket?
Μπορώ να μπω στον
κατάλογο αναμονής
για εισιτήριο;
bo·ro na bo ston
ka·ta·lo·gho a·na·mo·nis
yia i·si·ti·ri·o

What time should I check in?
Τι ώρα να έρθω στον
έλεγχο;
ti o·ra na er·tho ston
e·leng·kho

I'd like to … my ticket, please.	Θα ήθελα να … το εισιτήριό μου παρακαλώ.	tha i·the·la na … to i·si·ti·ri·o mu pa·ra·ka·lo
cancel	ακυρώσω	a·ki·ro·so
change	αλλάξω	a·lak·so
confirm	επικυρώσω	e·pi·ki·ro·so

luggage

Where can I find a/the …?	Πού μπορώ να βρω …;	pu bo·*ro* na vro …
baggage claim	το χώρο αποσκευών	to *kho*·ro a·pos·ke·*von*
left-luggage office	φύλαξη αποσκευών	*fi*·lak·si a·pos·ke·*von*
luggage locker	τη φύλαξη αντικειμένων	ti *fi*·lak·si a·di·ki·*me*·non
trolley	ένα καροτσάκι	e·na ka·rot·*sa*·ki

My luggage has been …	Οι αποσκευές μου έχουν …	i a·pos·ke·*ves* mu e·khun …
damaged	πάθει ζημιά	*pa*·thi zi·*mia*
lost	χαθεί	kha·*thi*
stolen	κλαπεί	kla·*pi*

That's (not) mine.
Αυτό (δεν) είναι δικό μου.   af·*to* (then) *i*·ne thi·*ko* mu

Can I have some coins/tokens?
Μπορώ να έχω μερικά   bo·*ro* na *e*·kho me·ri·*ka*
κέρματα/κουπόνια;   *ker*·ma·ta/ku·*po*·nia

transport

plane

αεροπλάνο

Where does flight (10) arrive/depart?
Πού προσγειώνεται/   pu pros·yi·*o*·ne·te/
απογειώνεται η πτήση (δέκα);   a·po·yi·*o*·ne·te i *pti*·si (*the*·ka)

Where's (the) ...?
	Πού είναι ...;	pu *i*·ne ...
airport shuttle	το λεωφορείο	to le·o·fo·*ri*·o
	του αεροδρομίου	tu a·e·ro·thro·*mi*·u
arrivals hall	η αίθουσα των	i *e*·thu·sa ton
	αφίξεων	a·*fik*·se·on
departures hall	η αίθουσα των	i *e*·thu·sa ton
	ανα χωρήσεων	*a*·na kho·*ri*·se·on
duty-free shops	τα αφορολόγητα	ta a·fo·ro·*lo*·yi·ta
gate (9)	η θύρα (εννέα)	i *thi*·ra (e·*ne*·a)

bus, trolley bus & coach

λεωφορεία, τρόλεϊ και πούλμαν

How often do buses come?
Κάθε πότε έρχονται τα   *ka*·the *po*·te *er*·kho·de ta
λεωφορεία;   le·o·fo·*ri*·a

Does it stop at (Iraklio)?
Σταματάει στο (Ηράκλειο);   sta·ma·*ta*·i sto (i·*ra*·kli·o)

What's the next stop?
Ποια είναι η επόμενη στάση;   pia *i*·ne i e·*po*·me·ni *sta*·si

I'd like to get off (at Iraklio).
Θα ήθελα να κατεβώ   tha *i*·the·la na ka·te·*vo*
(στο Ηράκλειο).   (sto i·*ra*·kli·o)

Where's the trolley bus stop?
Πού είναι η στάση του τρόλεϊ;   pu *i*·ne i *sta*·si tu *tro*·le·i

city a	αστικό	a·sti·*ko*
intercity a	υπεραστικό	i·pe·ra·sti·*ko*
local a	τοπικό	to·pi·*ko*

train & metro

Where's the nearest metro station?
Πού είναι ο πιο κοντινός   pu i·ne o pio ko·di·nos
σταθμός του μετρό;   stath·mos tu me·tro

Which line goes to (the port)?
Ποια γραμμή πηγαίνει   pia ghra·mi pi·ye·ni
(στο λιμάνι);   (sto li·ma·ni)

What station is this?
Ποιος σταθμός είναι αυτός;   pios stath·mos i·ne af·tos

What's the next station?
Ποιος είναι ο επόμενος   pios i·ne o e·po·me·nos
σταθμός;   stath·mos

Does it stop at (Kalamata)?
Σταματάει στην (Καλαμάτα);   sta·ma·ta·i stin (ka·la·ma·ta)

Do I need to change?
Χειάζεται να αλλάξω;   khri·a·ze·te na a·lak·so

Is it direct/express?
Είναι κατ'ευθείαν/εξπρές;   i·ne ka·tef·thi·an/eks·pres

Which carriage is ...?	Ποια άμαξα είναι (για) ...;	pia a·mak·sa i·ne (yia) ...
1st class	πρώτη θέση	pro·ti the·si
for dining	φαγητό	fa·yi·to
for (Kalamata)	την (Καλαμάτα)	tin (ka·la·ma·ta)

north & south

On Greek maps and road signs, 'N' stands for Νότια no·ti·a
(south) and 'B' stands for βόρια vo·ri·a (north).

transport

51

boat

βάρκα

Where's the port/port police?

Πού είναι το λιμάνι/
λιμεναρχείο;

pu *i*·ne to li·*ma*·ni/
li·me·nar·*hi*·o

Can I have the ferry timetable?

Μπορώ να έχω το
πρόγραμμα του φέρι;

bo·*ro* na *e*·kho to
pro·ghra·ma tu *fe*·ri

Where does the boat to (Chios) leave from?

Από πού φεύγει το πλοίο
για τη (Χίο);

a·*po* pu *fev*·yi to *pli*·o
yia ti (*hi*·o)

When is the next boat for (Naxos)?

Πότε είναι το επόμενο
πλοίο για τη (Νάξο);

po·te *i*·ne to e·*po*·me·no
pli·o yia ti (*nak*·so)

Does this ferry go to (Rhodos)?

Πηγαίνει αυτό το φέρι
στη (Ρόδο);

pi·*ye*·ni af·*to* to *fe*·ri
sti (*ro*·tho)

TICAL

How many hours is it to (Milos)?

Πόσες ώρες είναι για   *po·*ses *o·*res *i·*ne yia
τη (Μήλο);   ti (*mi·*lo)

How many stops does the boat make?

Πόσες στάσεις κάνει   *po·*ses *sta·*sis *ka·*ni
το πλοίο;   to *pli·*o

Where can I get a taxi boat?

Πού μπορώ να νοικιάσω   pu bo·*ro* na ni·*kia·*so
μια βάρκα με βαρκάρη;   mia *var·*ka me var·*ka·*ri

Where can we hire an uncrewed boat?

Πού μπορώ να νοικιάσω   pu bo·*ro* na ni·*kia·*so
μόνο μια βάρκα;   *mo·*no mia *var·*ka

I'd like a/an …	Θα ήθελα …	tha *i·*the·la …
cabin for	μια καμπίνα για	mia ka·*bi·*na yia
one/two	ένα/δύο	*e·*na/*thi·*o
inside/outside	μια εσωτερική/	mia e·so·te·ri·*ki*/
cabin	εξωτερική καμπίνα	ek·so·te·ri·*ki* ka·*bi·*na

What's the sea like today?

Πώς είναι η θάλασσα   pos *i·*ne i *tha·*la·sa
σήμερα;   *si·*me·ra

Are there life jackets?

Υπάρχουν σωσίβια;   i·*par·*khun so·*si·*vi·a

What island is this?

Ποιο νησί είναι αυτό;   pio ni·*si i·*ne af·*to*

What beach is this?

Ποια παραλία είναι αυτή;   pia pa·ra·*li·*a *i·*ne af·*ti*

I feel seasick.

Αισθάνομαι ναυτία.   es·*tha·*no·me naf·*ti·*a

cabin	καμπίνα f	ka·*bi*·na
caïque (large fishing boat)	καΐκι n	ka·*i*·ki
captain	καπετάνιος m	ka·pe·*ta*·nios
car deck	χώρος για αυτοκίνητο στο κατάστρωμα m	*kho*·ros yia af·to·*ki*·ni·to sto ka·*ta*·stro·ma
catamaran	σχεδία καταμαράν f	she·*thi*·a ka·ta·ma·*ran*
cruise	κρουαζέρα f	kru·a·*ze*·ra
deck	κατάστρωμα n	ka·*ta*·stro·ma
excursion boat	εκδρομική βάρκα f	ek·thro·mi·*ki* *var*·ka
ferry	φέρι n	*fe*·ri
hammock	αιώρα f	e·*o*·ra
hydrofoil	ιπτάμενο δελφίνι n	ip·*ta*·me·no thel·*fi*·ni
inter-island boat	πλοίο συγκοινωνίας μεταξύ νησιών n	*pli*·o si·gi·no·*ni*·as me·tak·*si* ni·*sion*
jolly roger	βάρκα πλοίου f	*var*·ka *pli*·u
lifeboat	ναυαγοσωστική λέμβος f	na·va·gho·so·sti·*ki* *lem*·vos
life jacket	σωσίβιο n	so·*si*·vi·o
muster station	χώρος συγκέντρωσης m	*kho*·ros si·*ge*·dro·sis
purser's office	γραφείο λογιστή n	ghra·*fi*·o lo·yi·*sti*
sailing boat	ιστιοφόρο n	i·sti·o·*fo*·ro
small fishing boat	μικρή βάρκα για ψάρεμα f	mi·*kri* *var*·ka yia *psa*·re·ma
yacht	γιωτ n	yiot

taxi

ταξί

I'd like a taxi …	Θα ήθελα ένα ταξί …	tha *i*·the·la *e*·na tak·*si* …
at (9am)	στις (εννέα π.μ.)	stis (e·*ne*·a prin to me·si·*me*·ri)
now	τώρα	*to*·ra
tomorrow	αύριο	*av*·ri·o

Where's the taxi rank?
Πού είναι η στάση για ταξί;   pu *i*·ne i *sta*·si yia tak·*si*

Is this taxi available?
Είναι αυτό το ταξί ελεύθερο;   *i*·ne af·*to* to tak·*si* e·*lef*·the·ro

Please put the meter on.
Παρακαλώ βάλε το   pa·ra·ka·*lo va*·le to
ταξίμετρο.   tak·*si*·me·tro

How much is it (to Petroupoli)?
Πόσο κάνει (για Πετρούπολη);   *po*·so *ka*·ni (yia pe·*tru*·po·li)

Please take me to (this address).
Παρακαλώ πάρε με σε   pa·ra·ka·*lo pa*·re me se
(αυτή τη διεύθυνση).   (af·*ti* ti thi·*ef*·thin·si)

How much do you charge for the luggage?
Πόσο χρεώνεις για   *po*·so khre·*o*·nis yia
τις αποσκευές;   tis a·pos·ke·*ves*

Please ...	Παρακλώ ...	pa·ra·ka·*lo* ...
slow down	πήγαινε πιο σιγά	*pi*·ye·ne pio si·*gha*
stop here	σταμάτα εδώ	sta·*ma*·ta e·*tho*
wait here	περίμενε εδώ	pe·*ri*·me·ne e·*tho*

car & motorbike

αυτοκίνητο και μοτοσακό

car & motorbike hire

I'd like to hire a/an ...	Θα ήθελα να ενοικιάσω ένα ...	tha *i*·the·la na e·ni·ki·*a*·so e·na ...
4WD	4W ντράιβ	for·ghu·*il* dra·iv
automatic	αυτόματο	af·*to*·ma·to
car	αυτοκίνητο	af·to·*ki*·ni·to
manual	με ταχύτητες	me ta·*hi*·ti·tes
motorbike	μοτοσακό	mo·to·sa·*ko*

with ...	με ...	me ...
air conditioning	έρκοντίσιον	e·kon·*di*·si·on
a driver	οδηγό	o·thi·*gho*

How much for daily/weekly hire?

Πόσο νοικάζεται την
ημέρα/εβδομάδα;

*po·so ni·kia·ze·te tin
i·me·ra/ev·tho·ma·tha*

Does that include insurance/mileage?

Αυτό συμπεριλαμβάνει
ασφάλεια/χιλιόμετρα;

*af·to si·be·ri·lam·va·ni
as·fa·li·a/hi·lio·me·tra*

Can I take the car on a ferry?

Μπορώ να πάρω το
αυτοκίνητο στο φέρι;

*bo·ro na pa·ro to
af·to·ki·ni·to sto fe·ri*

Do you have a guide to the road rules in English?

Έχετε οδικό κώδικα
κυκλοφορίας στα Αγγλικά;

*e·he·te o·thi·ko ko·thi·ka
ki·klo·fo·ri·as sta ang·gli·ka*

Do you have a road map?

Έχετε οδικό χάρτη;

e·he·te o·thi·ko khar·ti

on the road

What's the speed limit?

Ποιο είναι το όριο ταχύτητας;   *pio i·ne to o·ri·o ta·hi·ti·tas*

Is this the road to (Lamia)?

Είναι αυτός ο δρόμος για
(τη Λαμία);

*i·ne af·tos o thro·mos yia
(ti la·mi·a)*

Where's a petrol station?

Πού είναι ένα πρατήριο
βενζίνας;

*pu i·ne e·na pra·ti·ri·o
ven·zi·nas*

Fill it up, please.

Γεμίστε το, παρακαλώ.   *ye·mis·te to pa·ra·ka·lo*

signs		
Απαγορεύεται η είσοδος	a·pa·gho·re·ve·te i i·so·thos	No Entry
Διόδια	thi·o·thi·a	Toll
Είσοδος	i·so·thos	Entrance (Freeway)
Έξοδος Εθνικής Οδού	ek·so·thos e·th·ni·kis o·thu	Exit Freeway
Προσοχή	pro·so·hi	Drive With Care
Μονόδρομος	mo·no·thro·mos	One-Way

άδεια οδήγησης f	a·thi·a o·thi·yi·sis	**drivers licence**
βενζίνα f	ven·zi·na	**petrol (gas)**
δωρεάν	tho·re·an	**free** a
επί τόπου	e·pi to·pu	**on-the-spot**
ασφάλεια f	as·fa·li·a	**insurance**
παρκόμετρο n	par·ko·me·tro	**parking meter**
Πράσινη κάρτα f	pra·si·ni kar·ta	**Green Card (international third-party insurance)**
χιλιόμετρα n pl	hi·lio·me·tra	**kilometres**

diesel	ντίζελ n	di·zel
leaded	μολυβδούχος f	mo·liv·thu·khos
LPG	υγραέριο n	igh·ra·e·ri·o
premium unleaded	σούπερ αμόλυβδος f	su·per a·mo·liv·thos
regular unleaded	απλή f αμόλυβδος f	ap·li a·mo·liv·thos

Can you check the ...?	Μπορείς να κοιτάξεις ...;	bo·ris na ki·tak·sis ...
oil	το λάδι	to la·thi
tyre pressure	την πίεση των τροχών	tin pi·e·si ton tro·khon
water	το νερό	to ne·ro

(How long) Can I park here?
(Πόση ώρα) Μπορώ να παρκάρω εδώ;   (po·si o·ra) bo·ro na par·ka·ro e·tho

Do I have to pay?
Πρέπει να πληρώσω;   pre·pi na pli·ro·so

problems

I need a mechanic.
Χρειάζομαι μηχανικό.   khri·a·zo·me mi·kha·ni·ko

I've had an accident.
Είχα ένα ατύχημα.   i·kha e·na a·ti·hi·ma

The car/motorbike has broken down (at Corinth).
Το αυτοκίνητο/μοτοσακό   to af·to·ki·ni·to/mo·to·sa·ko
χάλασε (στην Κόρινθο).   ha·la·se (stin ko·rin·tho)

The car/motorbike won't start.
Το αυτοκίνητο/μοτοσακό   to af·to·ki·ni·to/mo·to·sa·ko
δεν αρχίζει.   then ar·hi·zi

I have a flat tyre.
Μ'έπιασε λάστιχο.   me·pia·se la·sti·kho

I've lost my car keys.
Έχασα τα κλειδιά του   e·ha·sa ta kli·thia tu
αυτοκινήτου μου.   af·to·ki·ni·tu mu

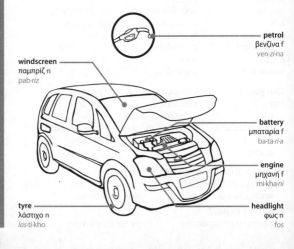

petrol
βενζίνα f
ven·zi·na

windscreen
παμπρίζ n
pab·riz

battery
μπαταρία f
ba·ta·ri·a

engine
μηχανή f
mi·kha·ni

tyre
λάστιχο n
las·ti·kho

headlight
φως n
fos

I've locked the keys inside.
Κλείδωσα τα κλειδιά μου
στο αυτοκίνητου.
*kli·tho·sa ta kli·thia mu
sto af·to·ki·ni·to*

I've run out of petrol.
Μου τελείωσε η βενζίνα.
mu te·li·o·se i ven·zi·na

Can you fix it (today)?
Μπορείς να το
επισκευάσεις (σήμερα);
*bo·ris na to
e·pis·ke·va·sis (si·me·ra)*

How long will it take?
Πόση ώρα θα κάμει;
po·si o·ra tha ka·mi

bicycle

ποδήλατο

I'd like ...	Θα ήθελα ...	*tha i·the·la ...*
my bicycle repaired	να επισκευάσω το ποδήλατό μου	*na e·pis·ke·va·so to po·thi·la·to mu*
to buy a bicycle	να αγοράσω ένα ποδήλατο	*na a·gho·ra·so e·na po·thi·la·to*
to hire a bicycle	να νοικιάσω ένα ποδήλατο	*na ni·kia·so e·na po·thi·la·to*

I'd like a ... bike.	Θα ήθελα ένα ...	*tha i·the·la e·na ...*
mountain	ποδήλατο για βουνό	*po·thi·la·to yia vu·no*
racing	ποδήλατο κούρσας	*po·thi·la·to kur·sas*
second-hand	μεταχειρισμένο ποδήλατο	*me·ta·hi·riz·me·no po·thi·la·to*

How much is it per day?
Πόσο κοστίζει την ημέρα;
po·so ko·sti·zi tin i·me·ra

How much is it per hour?
Πόσο κοστίζει την ώρα;
po·so ko·sti·zi tin o·ra

Do I need a helmet?
Χρειάζομαι κράνος;   khri·*a*·zo·me *kra*·nos

Is there a bicycle-path map?
Υπάρχει χάρτης για δρόμο   i·*par*·hi *khar*·tis yia *thro*·mo
ποδηλάτου;   po·*thi*·*la*·tu

Is this road OK for bicycles?
Είναι αυτός ο δρόμος   *i*·ne af·*tos* o *thro*·mos
κατάλληλος για ποδήλατα;   ka·*ta*·li·los yia po·*thi*·la·ta

I have a puncture.
Τρύπησε η ρόδα μου.   *tri*·pi·se i *ro*·tha mu

gut feelings

Greeks tend to get pretty physical when they talk about
their emotions:

I'm not impressed.
Δεν μου γεμίζει το μάτι.   then mu ye·*mi*·zi to *ma*·ti
(lit: It doesn't fill my eye.)

I can't stand him/her.
Δεν τον/την χωνεύω.   then ton/tin tso·ne·*vo*
(lit: I can't digest him/her.)

I've had enough of you.
Μ'έπρηξες.   me·prik·ses
(lit: You've made me swollen.)

I regretted it.
Μου βγήκε από τη μύτη.   mu *vyi*·ke a·*po* ti *mi*·ti
(lit: It came out of my nose.)

He/She put me under pressure.
Μου βαλε τα δυο πόδια   mu·va·le ta thio po·*thia*
σ' ένα παπούτσι.   se·na pa·*put*·si
(lit: He/She put both my feet in one shoe.)

border crossing

περνώντας τα σύνορα

I'm ...	Είμαι ...	*i*·me ...
in transit	τράνζιτ	*tran*·zit
on business	για δουλειά	yia thu·*lia*
on holiday	σε διακοπές	se thia·ko·*pes*

I'm here for	Είμαι εδώ για	*i*·me e·*tho* yia
(three) ...	(τρεις) ...	(tris) ...
days	μέρες	*me*·res
weeks	εβδομάδες	ev·tho·*ma*·thes
months	μήνες	*mi*·nes

I'm going to (Limassol).
Πηγαίνω στη (Λεμεσό).　　　pi·*ye*·no sti (le·me·*so*)

I'm staying at (the Xenia).
Μένω στο (Ξενία).　　　　*me*·no sto (kse·*ni*·a)

The children are on this passport.
Τα παιδιά είναι σ'αυτό　　　ta pe·*thia i*·ne saf·*to*
το βιαβατήριο.　　　　　to thia·va·*ti*·ri·o

listen for ...

άδεια f	*a*·thi·a	**export permit**
εξαγωγής	ek·sa·gho·*yis*	
βίζα f	*vi*·za	**visa**
διαβατήριο n	thia·va·*ti*·ri·o	**passport**
μόνος m	*mo*·nos	**alone**
οικογένεια f	i·ko·ye·*ni*·a	**family**
ομάδα f	o·*ma*·tha	**group**
ταυτότητα f	taf·*to*·ti·ta	**ID card**

Can you stamp a separate paper instead of the passport?

Μπορείτε να σφραγίσετε ena χωριστό χαρτί αντί για το διαβατήριο;

bo·ri·te na sfra·yi·se·te e·na kho·ri·sto khar·ti a·di yia to thia·va·ti·ri·o

Where can I get a travel permit for (Mt Athos)?

Πού μπορώ να πάρω μια άδεια ταξιδιού για (το Άγιο Όρος);

pu bo·ro na pa·ro mia a·thi·a tak·si·thiu yia (to a·yi·o o·ros)

at customs

I have nothing to declare.

Δεν έχω τίποτε να δηλώσω.

then e·kho ti·po·te na thi·lo·so

I have something to declare.

Έχω κάτι να δηλώσω.

e·kho ka·ti na thi·lo·so

Do I have to declare this?

Πρέπει να το δηλώσω αυτό;

pre·pi na to thi·lo·so af·to

That's (not) mine.

Αυτό (δεν) είναι δικό μου.

af·to (then) i·ne thi·ko mu

I didn't know I had to declare it.

Δεν ήξερα πως έπρεπε να το δηλώσω.

then ik·se·ra pos e·pre·pe na to thi·lo·so

I have a doctor's certificate for this medication.

Έχω πιστοποιητικό γιατρού για αυτό το φάρμακο.

e·kho pis·to·pi·i·ti·ko yia·tru yia af·to to far·ma·ko

signs

Αφορολόγητα	a·fo·ro·lo·yi·ta	**Duty-Free**
Έλεγχος	e·len·ghos	**Passport Control**
Διαβατηρίων	thia·va·ti·ri·on	
Καραντίνα	ka·ran·di·na	**Quarantine**
Τελωνείο	te·lo·ni·o	**Customs**
Μετανάστευση	me·ta·na·stef·si	**Immigration**

Where's (the tourist office)?
Πού είναι (το τουριστικό
γραφείο);
pu i·ne (to tu·ri·sti·ko
ghra·fi·o)

What's the address?
Ποια είναι η διεύθυνση;
pia i·ne i thi·ef·thin·si

How far is it?
Πόσο μακριά είναι;
po·so ma·kri·a i·ne

How do I get there?
Πώς πηγαίνω εκεί;
pos pi·ye·no e·ki

What street is this?
Ποιος δρόμος είναι αυτός;
pios thro·mos i·ne af·tos

What village is this?
Ποιο χωριό είναι αυτό;
pio kho·rio i·ne af·to

Can you show me (on the map)?
Μπορείς να μου δείξεις
(στο χάρτη);
bo·ris na mu thik·sis
(sto khar·ti)

It's …	Είναι …	i·ne …
close	κοντά	ko·da
behind …	πίσω …	pi·so …
here	εδώ	e·tho
in front of …	μπροστά από …	bros·ta a·po …
near …	κοντά …	ko·da …
next to …	δίπλα από …	thip·la a·po …
on the corner	στη γωνία	sti gho·ni·a
opposite …	απέναντι …	a·pe·na·di …
straight ahead	κατ'ευθείαν	ka·tef·thi·an
there	εκεί	e·ki

north	βόρια	vo·ri·a
south	νότια	no·ti·a
east	ανατολικά	a·na·to·li·ka
west	δυτικά	thi·ti·ka

directions

63

χιλιόμετρα	hi·*lio*·me·tra	**kilometres**
λεπτά	lep·*ta*	**minutes**
μέτρα	*me*·tra	**metres**

avenue	λεωφόρος f	le·o·*fo*·ros
lane	πάροδος f	pa·ro·ţhos
street	οδός f	o·ţhos
by bus/taxi	με λεωφορείο/ταξί	me le·o·fo·*ri*·o/tak·*si*
on foot	με πόδια	me po·ţhia
Turn ...	Στρίψε ...	*strip*·se ...
at the corner	στη γωνία	sti gho·*ni*·a
at the traffic lights	στα φανάρια	sta fa·*na*·ria
left	αριστερά	a·ris·te·*ra*
right	δεξιά	ţhek·si·*a*

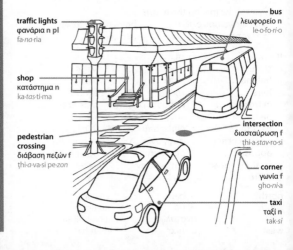

traffic lights φανάρια n pl fa·*na*·ria

shop κατάστημα n ka·*tas*·ti·ma

pedestrian crossing διάβαση πεζών f ţhi·*a*·va·si pe·*zon*

bus λεωφορείο n le·o·fo·*ri*·o

intersection διασταύρωση f ţhi·a·*stav*·ro·si

corner γωνία f gho·*ni*·a

taxi ταξί n tak·*si*

finding accommodation

βρίσκοντας κατάλυμα

Where's (a) ...?	Πού είναι ...;	pu *i*·ne ...
bed and breakfast	κατάλυμα με πρόγευμα	ka·*ta*·li·ma me *pro*·ghev·ma
camping ground	χώρος για κάμπινγκ	*kho*·ros yia *kam*·ping
guesthouse	ξενώνας	kse·*no*·nas
(3-star) hotel	ξενοδοχείο (τριών αστέρων)	kse·no·*tho*·hi·o (tri·*on* a·*ste*·ron)
mountain refuge	ορεινό καταφύγιο	o·ri·*no* ka·ta·*fi*·yi·o
pension	πανσιόν	pan·*sion*
room for rent	δωμάτιο για νοίκιασμα	tho·*ma*·ti·o yia *ni*·kiaz·ma
self-contained apartment	ξεχωριστό διαμέρισμα	kse·kho·ri·*sto* thi·a·*me*·riz·ma
some traditional accommodation	παραδοσιακό κατάλυμα	pa·ra·*tho*·si·a·*ko* ka·*ta*·li·ma
youth hostel	γιουθ χόστελ	yiuth *kho*·stel

Can you	Μπορείτε να	bo·*ri*·te na
recommend	συστήσετε	si·*sti*·se·te
somewhere ...?	κάπου ...;	*ka*·pu ...
cheap	φτηνό	fti·*no*
good	καλό	ka·*lo*
nearby	κοντινό	ko·di·*no*
romantic	ρομαντικό	ro·ma·di·*ko*

What's the address?

Ποια είναι η διεύθυνση; pia *i*·ne i thi·*ef*·thin·si

For responses, see **directions**, page 63.

booking ahead & checking in

κλείσιμο θέσης από πριν και εγκατάσταση

I'd like to book a room, please.

Θα ήθελα να κλείσω ένα tha *i*·the·la na *kli*·so *e*·na
δωμάτιο, παρακαλώ. tho·*ma*·ti·o pa·ra·ka·*lo*

I have a reservation.

Έχω κάμει κάποια κράτηση. *e*·kho *ka*·mi *ka*·pia *kra*·ti·si

My name's ...

Με λένε ... me *le*·ne ...

For (three) nights/weeks.

Για (τρεις) νύχτες/ yia (tris) *nikh*·tes/
εβδομάδες. ev·tho·*ma*·thes

From (2 July) to (6 July).

Από (τις δύο Ιουλίου) a·*po* (tis *thi*·o i·u·*li*·u)
μέχρι (τις έξι Ιουλίου). *me*·khri (tis *ek*·si i·u·*li*·u)

Ελεύθερα δωμάτια	e·*lef*·the·ra tho·*ma*·ti·a	**Vacancy**
Μπάνιο	*ba*·nio	**Bathroom**
Πλήρες	*pli*·res	**No Vacancy**

Do you have a ... room?	Έχετε ένα ... δωμάτιο	e·he·te *e*·na ... tho·*ma*·ti·o
single	μονό	mo·*no*
double	διπλό	thi·*plo*
twin	δίκλινο	*thi*·kli·no

How much is it per ...?	Πόσο είναι για κάθε ...;	po·so *i*·ne yia *ka*·the ...
night	νύχτα	*nikh*·ta
person	άτομο	*a*·to·mo
week	εβδομάδα	ev·tho·*ma*·tha

Can I see it?
Μπορώ να το δω;   bo·*ro* na to tho

I'll take it.
Θα το πάρω.   tha to *pa*·ro

Do I need to pay upfront?
Χρειάζεται να πληρώσω   khri·*a*·ze·te na pli·*ro*·so
από πριν;   a·*po* prin

Can I pay by ...?	Μπορώ να πληρώσω με ...;	bo·*ro* na pli·*ro*·so me ...
credit card	πιστωτική κάρτα	pi·sto·ti·*ki kar*·ta
travellers cheque	ταξιδιωτική επιταγή	tak·si·*thio*·ti·*ki* e·pi·ta·*yi*

For other methods of payment, see **shopping**, page 77.

accommodation

requests & queries

When/Where is breakfast served?

Πότε/Πού σερβίρεται το
πρόγευμα;

po·te/pu ser·*vi*·re·te to
pro·yev·ma

Please wake me at (seven).

Παρακαλώ ξύπνησέ με
στις (εφτά).

pa·ra·ka·*lo* ksip·ni·*se* me
stis (ef·*ta*)

Do you ... here?	... εδώ;	... e·*tho*
arrange tours	Κανονίζετε	ka·no·*ni*·ze·te
	ξεναγήσεις	kse·na·*yi*·sis
change money	Αλλάζετε	a·*la*·ze·te
	χρήματα	*khri*·ma·ta

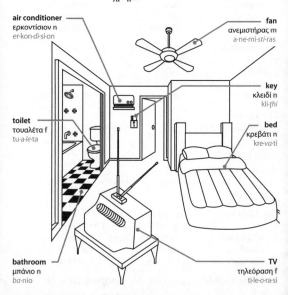

air conditioner
ερκοντίσιον n
er·kon·*di*·si·on

toilet
τουαλέτα f
tu·a·*le*·ta

bathroom
μπάνιο n
ba·nio

fan
ανεμιστήρας m
a·ne·mi·*sti*·ras

key
κλειδί n
kli·*thi*

bed
κρεβάτι n
kre·*va*·ti

TV
τηλεόραση f
ti·le·o·ra·si

Can I use the ...?	Μπορώ να χρησιμοποιήσω ...;	bo·ro na khri·si·mo·pi·i·so ...
kitchen	την κουζίνα	tin ku·zi·na
laundry	το πλυντήριο	to pli·di·ri·o
telephone	το τηλέφωνο	to ti·le·fo·no

Do you have a/an ...?	Έχετε ...;	e·he·te ...
elevator	ασανσέρ	a·san·ser
laundry service	υπηρεσία πλυντηρίου	i·pi·re·si·a pli·di·ri·u
message board	πίνακα μηνυμάτων	pi·na·ka mi·ni·ma·ton
safe	χρηματοκιβώτιο	khri·ma·to·ki·vo·ti·o
swimming pool	πισίνα	pi·si·na

Could I have (a/an) ..., please?	Μπορώ να έχω ... παρακαλώ;	bo·ro na e·kho ... pa·ra·ka·lo
extra blanket	μια κουβέρτα ακόμη	mia ku·ver·ta a·ko·mi
my key	το κλειδί μου	to kli·thi mu
mosquito net	μια κουνουπιέρα	mia ku·nu·pie·ra
receipt	μια απόδειξη	mia a·po·thik·si

Is there hot water all day?
Υπάρχει ζεστό νερό όλη την ημέρα;
i·par·hi ze·sto ne·ro o·li tin i·me·ra

Is there a message for me?
Υπάρχει μήνυμα για μένα;
i·par·hi mi·ni·ma yia me·na

Can I leave a message for someone?
Μπορώ να αφήσω ένα μήνυμα για κάποιον;
bo·ro na a·fi·so e·na mi·ni·ma yia ka·pion

I'm locked out of my room.
Κλειδώθηκα έξω από το δωμάτιό μου.
kli·tho·thi·ka ek·so a·po to tho·ma·ti·o mu

complaints

It's too ...	Είναι πάρα πολύ ...	*i*·ne *pa*·ra po·*li* ...
bright	φωτεινό	fo·ti·*no*
cold	κρύο	*kri*·o
dark	σκοτεινό	sko·ti·*no*
expensive	ακριβό	a·kri·*vo*
noisy	θορυβώδες	tho·ri·*vo*·thes
small	μικρό	mi·*kro*

The ... doesn't work.	... δεν δουλεύει.	... then thu·*le*·vi
air conditioner	Το ερκοντίσιον	to er·kon·*di*·si·on
fan	Ο ανεμιστήρας	o a·ne·mi·*sti*·ras
toilet	Η τουαλέτα	i tu·a·*le*·ta

Can I get another (blanket)?
Μπορώ να πάρω μια άλλη   bo·*ro* na *pa*·ro mia *a*·li
(κουβέρτα);   (ku·*ver*·ta)

This (pillow) isn't clean.
Αυτό (το μαξιλάρι) δεν   af·*to* (to mak·si·*la*·ri) then
είναι καθαρό.   *i*·ne ka·tha·*ro*

---

a knock at the door ...

Who is it?
Ποιος είναι;   pios *i*·ne
Just a moment.
Μια στιγμή.   mia stigh·*mi*
Come in.
Περάστε.   pe·*ra*·ste
Come back later, please.
Έλα αργότερα, παρακαλώ.   *e*·la ar·*gho*·te·ra pa·ra·ka·*lo*

checking out

What time is checkout?
Τι ώρα είναι η αναχώρηση;   ti o·ra i·ne i a·na·kho·ri·si

Can I have a late checkout?
Μπορώ να φύγω αργά;   bo·ro na fi·gho ar·gha

Can you call a taxi for me (for 11 o'clock)?
Μπορείτε να καλέσετε ένα   bo·ri·te na ka·le·se·te e·na
ταξί (για τις έντεκα);   tak·si (yia tis e·de·ka)

I'm leaving now.
Φεύγω τώρα.   fev·gho to·ra

Can I leave my bags here?
Μπορώ να αφήσω τις   bo·ro na a·fi·so tis
βαλίτσες μου εδώ;   va·lit·ses mu e·tho

There's a mistake in the bill.
Υπάρχει κάποιο λάθος   i·par·hi ka·pio la·thos
στο λογαριασμό.   sto lo·gha·riaz·mo

Could I have my ..., please?	Μπορώ να έχω ... παρακλώ;	bo·ro na e·kho ... pa·ra·ka·lo
deposit	την προκαταβολή μου	tin pro·ka·ta·vo·li mu
passport	το διαβατήριό μου	to thia·va·ti·rio mu
valuables	τα κοσμήματά μου	ta koz·mi·ma·ta mu

I'll be back ...	Θα επιστρέψω ...	tha e·pi·strep·so ...
in (three) days	σε (τρεις) μέρες	se (tris) me·res
on (Tuesday)	την (Τρίτη)	tin tri·ti

I had a great stay, thank you.
Είχα υπέροχη διαμονή,   i·kha i·pe·ro·hi thia·mo·ni
ευχαριστώ.   ef·kha·ri·sto

I'll recommend it to my friends.
Θα το συστήσω στους   tha to si·sti·so stus
φίλους μου.   fi·lus mu

camping

Do you have (a) …?	Έχετε …	e·he·te …
electricity	ηλεκτρισμό	i·lek·triz·mo
laundry	πλυντήριο	pli·di·ri·o
site	χώρο	kho·ro
shower facilities	εγκαταστάσεις για ντουζ	e·ga·ta·sta·sis yia duz
tents for hire	τέντες για νοίκιασμα	te·des yia ni·kiaz·ma

How much is it per …?	Πόσο κοστίζει για κάθε …;	po·so ko·sti·zi yia ka·the …
caravan	τροχόσπιτο	tro·kho·spi·to
person	άτομο	a·to·mo
tent	τέντα	te·da
vehicle	αυτοκίνητο	af·to·ki·ni·to

Can I camp here?
Μπορώ να κατασκηνώσω εδώ;
bo·ro na ka·ta·ski·no·so e·tho

Can I park next to my tent?
Μπορώ να παρκάρω δίπλα στην τέντα μου;
bo·ro na par·ka·ro thi·pla stin te·da mu

Who do I ask to stay here?
Ποιον ρωτάω για να μείνω εδώ;
pion ro·ta·o yia na mi·no e·tho

Could I borrow …?
Μπορώ να δανειστώ …;
bo·ro na tha·ni·sto …

Is it coin-operated?
Λειτουργεί με κέρματα;
li·tur·yi me ker·ma·ta

Is the water drinkable?
Είναι το νερό πόσιμο;
i·ne to ne·ro po·si·mo

When you're making a request, make it sound more polite by starting your question with μήπως *mi*·pos, the equivalent of the English 'Do you, by any chance, …?'.

Do you, by any chance, have a room with a view?

Μήπως έχετε ένα	*mi*·pos *e*·hete *e*·na
δωμάτιο με θέα;	tho·*ma*·tio me *the*·a

See the **phrasebuilder** for more on requests.

renting

νοικιάζοντας

I'm here about	Είμαι εδώ για το …	*i*·me e·*tho* yia to …
the … for rent.	που νοικιάζεται.	pu ni·*kia*·ze·te
Do you have	Έχεις ένα … για	*e*·his *e*·na … yia
a/an … for rent?	νοίκιασμα;	*ni*·kiaz·ma
apartment	διαμέρισμα	thi·a·*me*·riz·ma
house	σπίτι	*spi*·ti
room	δωμάτιο	tho·*ma*·ti·o
I'm here about	Είμαι εδώ για την	*i*·me e·*tho* yia tin
the … for rent.	… που νοικιάζεται.	… pu ni·*kia*·ze·te
Do you have	Έχεις μια … για	*e*·his mia … yia
a … for rent?	νοίκιασμα;	*ni*·kiaz·ma
cabin	καμπίνα	ka·*bi*·na
villa	έπαυλη	*e*·pav·li
furnished	με έπιπλα	me *e*·pi·pla
partly furnished	με λίγα έπιπλα	me *li*·gha *e*·pi·pla
unfurnished	χωρίς έπιπλα	kho·*ris* *e*·pi·pla

διαμονή με τους ντόπιους

Can I stay at your place?

Μπορώ να μείνω στο
σπίτι σου;

bo·ro na *mi*·no sto
spi·ti su

Is there anything I can do to help?

Μπορώ να κάνω κάτι για
να βοηθήσω;

bo·ro na *ka*·no *ka*·ti yia
na vo·i·*thi*·so

I have my own ...   Έχω το δικό μου ...   e·kho to thi·*ko* mu ...
    mattress   στρώμα   *stro*·ma
    sleeping bag   σλίπινγκ μπαγκ   *sli*·ping bag

Can I ...?   Μπορώ να ...;   bo·*ro* na ...
    bring anything   φέρω κάτι   *fe*·ro *ka*·ti
    for the meal   για το φαγητό   yia to fa·yi·*to*
    do the dishes   πλύνω τα πιάτα   *pli*·no ta *pia*·ta
    set/clear the   στρώσω/μαζέψω   *stro*·so/ma·*zep*·so
    table   το τραπέζι   to tra·*pe*·zi
    take out the   βγάλω έξω τα   *vgha*·lo *ek*·so ta
    rubbish   σκουπίδια   sku·*pi*·thia

Thanks for your hospitality.

Ευχαριστώ για τη
φιλοξενία σας.

ef·kha·ri·*sto* yia ti
fi·lok·se·*ni*·a sas

If you're dining with your hosts, see **eating out**, page 157, for additional phrases.

foreign visitors

Punctuality for social engagements is not taken as seriously as you might be used to. An invitation for 9pm means that most people won't show up before 9.30pm. An evening coffee can sometimes extend to dinner, and not end until after midnight. Such a long visit is known in Greek as an αρμένικη βίζιτα ar·*me*·ni·ki *vi*·si·ta (Armenian visit).

looking for ...

ψάχνοντας για ...

Where's ...?	Πού είναι ...;	pu *i*·ne ...
a department store	ένα κατάστημα	*e*·na ka·*ta*·sti·ma
the flea market	το παζάρι	to pa·*za*·ri
the food market	η αγορά τροφίμων	i a·gho·*ra* tro·*fi*·mon
a kiosk	ένα περίπτερο	*e*·na pe·*rip*·te·ro
the street market	η λαϊκή αγορά	i la·i·*ki* a·gho·*ra*
a supermarket	ένα σούπερ-μάρκετ	*e*·na *su*·per *mar*·ket
a souvenir shop	ένα κατάστημα με σουβενίρ	*e*·na ka·*ta*·sti·ma me su·ve·*nir*

On which day is the street market held?

Ποια μέρα έχει λαϊκή;   pia *me*·ra *e*·hi la·i·*ki*

Where can I buy (a padlock)?

Πού μπορώ να αγοράσω (μια κλειδαριά);   pu bo·*ro* na a·gho·*ra*·so (mia kli·ṱha·*ria*)

For phrases on directions, see **directions**, page 63.

listen for ...	
Μπορώ να σας βοηθήσω; bo·*ro* na sas vo·i·*thi*·so	Can I help you?
Τίποτε άλλο; *ti*·po·te *a*·lo	Anything else?
Όχι, δεν έχουμε. *o*·hi ṱhen *e*·khu·me	No, we don't have any.
Να το τυλίξω; na to ti·*lik*·so	Shall I wrap it?

making a purchase

I'm just looking.
Απλά κοιτάζω.
a·*pla* ki·*ta*·zo

I'd like to buy (an adaptor plug).
Θα ήθελα να αγοράσω
(ένα μετασχηματιστή).
tha *i*·the·la na a·gho·*ra*·so
(e·na me·ta·shi·ma·ti·*sti*)

Can I look at it?
Μπορώ να το κοιτάξω;
bo·*ro* na to ki·*tak*·so

Do you have any others?
Έχετε άλλα;
e·he·te *a*·la

How much is it?
Πόσο κάνει;
po·so *ka*·ni

Can you write down the price?
Μπορείς να γράψεις την τιμή;
bo·*ris* na *ghrap*·sis tin ti·*mi*

Does it have a guarantee?
Έχει εγγύηση;
e·hi e·*gi*·i·si

Could I have it wrapped?
Μπορείς να μου το τυλίξεις;
bo·*ris* na mu to ti·*lik*·sis

Could I have a bag/receipt, please?
Μπορώ να έχω μια τσάντα/
απόδειξη, παρακαλώ;
bo·*ro* na e·kho mia *tsa*·da/
a·*po*·thik·si pa·ra·ka·*lo*

Can I have it sent overseas?
Μπορείς να το στείλεις
στο εξωτερικό;
bo·*ris* na to *sti*·lis
sto ek·so·te·ri·*ko*

Can you order it for me?
Μπορείς να το παραγγείλεις
για μένα;
bo·*ris* na to pa·ra·*gi*·lis
yia *me*·na

Can I pick it up later?
Μπορώ να το πραλάβω
αργότερα;
bo·*ro* na to pa·ra·*la*·vo
ar·*gho*·te·ra

It's faulty.
Είναι ελαττωματικό.
i·ne e·la·to·ma·ti·*ko*

bargain	ευκαιρία f	ef·ke·*ri*·a
rip-off	γδάρσιμο n	*ghthar*·si·mo
sale	έκπτωση f	ek·pto·si
specials	προσφορές f pl	pros·fo·*res*

Do you accept ...?	Δέχεστε ...;	*the*·he·ste ...
credit cards	πιστωτικές κάρτες	pi·sto·ti·*kes kar*·tes
debit cards	χρεωτικές κάρτες	khre·o·ti·*kes kar*·tes
travellers cheques	ταξιδιωτικές επιταγές	tak·si·thio·ti·*kes* e·pi·ta·*yes*
I'd like ..., please.	Θα ήθελα ..., παρακαλώ.	tha *i*·the·la ... pa·ra·ka·*lo*
a refund	επιστροφή χρημάτων	e·pi·stro·*fi* khri·*ma*·ton
my change	τα ρέστα μου	ta *re*·sta mu
to return this	να επιστρέψω αυτό	na e·pi·*strep*·so af·*to*

bargaining

παζάρεμα

That's too expensive.
Είναι πάρα πολύ ακριβό.   *i*·ne *pa*·ra po·*li* a·kri·*vo*

I don't have that much money.
Δεν έχω τόσα πολλά χρήματα.   then e·kho *to*·sa po·*la* khri·*ma*·ta

Do you have something cheaper?
Έχεις κάτι πιο φτηνό;   e·his *ka*·ti pio fti·*no*

Can you lower the price?
    Μπορείς να κατεβάσεις   bo·*ris* na ka·te·*va*·sis
    την τιμή;   tin ti·*mi*

How much for (two)?
    Πόσο κάνει για (δύο);   *po*·so *ka*·ni yia (*thi*·o)

I'll give you (five euros).
    Θα σου δώσω (πέντε ευρώ).   tha su *tho*·so (*pe*·de ev·*ro*)

books & reading

βιβλία και διάβασμα

Is there an English-language bookshop/section?
    Υπάρχει ένα βιβλιοπωλείο/   i·*par*·hi *e*·na viv·li·o·po·*li*·o/
    τμήμα Αγγλικής γλώσσας;   *tmi*·ma ang·gli·*kis* ghlo·sas

Can you recommend a book for me?
    Μπορείς να μου συστήσεις   bo·*ris* na mu si·*sti*·sis
    ένα βιβλίο;   *e*·na viv·*li*·o

Do you have Lonely Planet guidebooks?
    Έχετε βιβλία-οδηγούς του   *e*·he·te viv·*li*·a·o·thi·*ghus* tu
    Λόνλι Πλάνετ;   *lon*·li *pla*·net

Do you have ...?	Έχεις ένα ...;	*e*·his *e*·na ...
a book by (Nikos	βιβλίο (του Νίκου	viv·*li*·o (tu *ni*·ku
Kazantzakis)	Καζαντζάκη)	ka·za·*dza*·ki)
an entertainment	οδηγό	o·*thi*·*gho*
guide	διασκεδάσεων	thias·ke·*tha*·se·on

I'd like a ...	Θα ήθελα ...	tha *i*·the·la ...
dictionary	ένα λεξικό	*e*·na lek·si·*ko*
newspaper	μια εφημερίδα	mia e·fi·me·*ri*·tha
(in English)	(στα Αγγλικά)	(sta ang·gli·*ka*)
notepad	ένα μπλοκ για	*e*·na blok yia
	σημειώσεις	si·mi·*o*·sis

clothes

My size is ...	Το νούμερό μου είναι ...	to *nu*·me·*ro* mu *i*·ne ...
(40)	(σαράντα)	(sa·*ra*·da)
small	μικρό	mi·*kro*
medium	μεσαίο	me·*se*·o
large	μεγάλο	me·*gha*·lo

Can I try it on?
Μπορώ να το προβάρω;   bo·*ro* na to pro·*va*·ro

It doesn't fit.
Δε μου κάνει.   ţhe mu *ka*·ni

electronic goods

Where can I buy duty-free electronic goods?
Πού μπορώ να αγοράσω   pu bo·*ro* na a·gho·*ra*·so
αφορολόγητα ηλεκτρονικά   a·fo·ro·*lo*·yi·ta i·lek·tro·ni·*ka*
είδη;   *i*·ţhi

Is this the latest model?
Είναι αυτό το τελευταίο   *i*·ne af·*to* to te·lef·*te*·o
μοντέλο;   mo·*de*·lo

Is this (240) volts?
Είναι αυτό   *i*·ne af·*to*
(240) βολτ;   (ţhia·*ko*·sia sa·*ra*·da) volt

I need an adaptor plug.
Χρειάζομαι ένα   khri·*a*·zo·me *e*·na
μετασχηματιστή.   me·ta·shi·ma·ti·*sti*

boy-words & girl-words

Some phrases in this book are marked with m/f – they refer
as a rule to the speaker. Follow the m (masculine) form if
you're a 'he' and the f (feminine) form if you're a 'she'.

hairdressing

I'd like (a) ...	Θα ήθελα ένα ...	tha *i*·the·la e·na ...
blow wave	στέγνωμα	*stegh*·no·ma
	με πιστολάκι	me pis·to·*la*·ki
colour	βάψιμο	*vap*·si·mo
haircut	κούρεμα	*ku*·re·ma
my beard	ψαλίδισμα	psa·*li*·thiz·ma
trimmed	στο μούσι μου	sto *mu*·si mu
shave	ξύρισμα	*ksi*·riz·ma

Don't cut it too short.

Μην τα κόψεις πολύ κοντά.   min ta *kop*·sis po·*li* ko·*da*

Please use a new blade.

Παρακαλώ χρησιμοποίησε   pa·ra·ka·*lo* khri·si·mo·*pi*·i·se
καινούργιο ξυράφι.   ke·*nur*·yio ksi·*ra*·fi

Shave it all off!

Ξύρισέ τα όλα.   *ksi*·ri·*se* ta o·la

I should never have let you near me!

Δεν θα έπρεπε ποτέ να σε   then tha e·pre·pe po·*te* na se
αφήσω κοντά μου!   a·*fi*·so ko·*da* mu

barber	κουρέας m	ku·*re*·as
beauty salon	ινστιτούτο	in·sti·*tu*·to
	αισθητικής n	es·thi·ti·*kis*
for both sexes	και για τα δύο φύλα	ke yia ta *thi*·o *fi*·la
men's	κομμωτής	ko·mo·*tis*
hairdresser	για άντρες m	yia *a*·dres
women's	κομμωτής	ko·mo·*tis*
hairdresser	για γυναίκες m	yia yi·*ne*·kes

music & DVD

I'd like a CD/DVD.
Θα ήθελα ένα CD/DVD.　　　tha *i*·the·la *e*·na si·*di*/di·vi·*di*

I'm looking for something by (Anna Vissi).
Ψάχνω για κάτι　　　　　*psakh*·no yia *ka*·ti
(της Άννας Βίσση).　　　(tis *a*·na *vi*·si)

What's his/her best recording?
Ποια είναι η καλύτερη　　　pia *i*·ne i ka·*li*·te·ri
ηχογράφησή του/της;　　　i·kho·*ghra*·fi·si tu/tis

Does this work on all DVD players?
Παίζει σε όλα τα DVD;　　　*pe*·zi se *o*·la ta di·vi·*di*

Is this for a (PAL/NTSC) system?
Είναι κατάλληλο για　　　*i*·ne ka·*ta*·li·lo yia
σύστημα (PAL/NTSC);　　　*si*·sti·ma (pal/en·ti·es·*si*)

video & photography

Can you ...?	Μπορείς να ...;	bo·*ris* na ...
develop	εμφανίσεις	em·fa·*ni*·sis
digital	ψηφιακές	psi·fi·a·*kes*
photos	φωτογραφίες	fo·to·ghra·*fi*·es
develop this	εμφανίσεις	em·fa·*ni*·sis
film	αυτό το φιλμ	af·*to* to film
load my film	βάλεις το φιλμ	*va*·lis to film
	στη μηχανή μου	sti mi·kha·*ni* mu
recharge the	φορτίσεις την	for·*ti*·sis tin
battery for	μπαταρία για την	ba·ta·*ri*·a yia tin
my digital	ψηφιακή μου	psi·fi·a·*ki* mu
camera	μηχανή	mi·kha·*ni*
transfer	μεταφέρεις	me·ta·*fe*·ris
photos from	φωτογραφίες από	fo·to·ghra·*fi*·es a·*po*
my camera	την φωτογραφική	ti fo·to·ghra·fi·*ki*
to CD	μου μηχανή στο CD	mu mi·kha·*ni* sto si·*di*

I need ... film for this camera.	Χρειάζομαι φιλμ ... για αυτή τη μηχανή.	khri·a·zo·me film ... yia af·ti ti mi·kha·ni
APS	APS	e·i·pi·es
B&W	μαυρόασπρο	mav·ro·a·spro
colour	έγχρωμο	eng·khro·mo
slide	σλάιντ	sla·id
(200) speed	ταχύτητα (200)	ta·hi·ti·ta (thia·ko·si·on)

Do you have ... for this camera?	Έχεις ... για αυτή τη φωτογραφική μηχανή;	e·his ... yia af·ti ti fo·to·ghra·fi·ki mi·kha·ni
batteries	μπαταρίες	ba·ta·ri·es
memory cards	κάρτες μνήμης	kar·tes mni·mis

I need a cable to connect my camera to a computer.

Χρειάζομαι ένα καλώδιο
για να συνδέσω τη μηχανή
μου στο κομπιούτερ.

khri·a·zo·me e·na ka·lo·thi·o
yia na sin·the·so ti mi·kha·ni
mu sto kom·piu·ter

I need a cable to recharge this battery.

Χρειάζομαι ένα καλώδιο
για να φορτίσω αυτή
τη μπαταρία.

khri·a·zo·me e·na ka·lo·thi·o
yia na for·ti·so af·ti
ti ba·ta·ri·a

I need a video cassette for this camera.

Χρειάζομαι μια
βιντεοκασέτα για
αυτή τη μηχανή.

khri·a·zo·me mia
vi·de·o·ka·se·ta yia
af·ti ti mi·kha·ni

Do you have disposable (underwater) cameras?

Έχεις (υποβρύχιες)
φωτογραφικές μηχανές
μιας χρήσης;

e·his (i·pov·ri·hi·es)
fo·to·ghra·fi·kes mi·kha·nes
mias khri·sis

When will it be ready?

Πότε θα είναι έτοιμο;

po·te tha i·ne e·ti·mo

How much is it?

Πόσο κάνει;

po·so ka·ni

I need a passport photo taken.

Θέλω να βγάλω φωτογραφία
για διαβατήριο.

the·lo na vga·lo fo·to·ghra·fi·a
yia thia·va·ti·ri·o

I'm not happy with these photos.

Δεν είμαι ικανοποιημένος/
ικανοποιημένη με αυτές
τις φωτογραφίες. **m/f**

then *i*·me i·ka·no·pi·i·*me*·nos/
i·ka·no·pi·i·*me*·ni me af·*tes*
tis fo·to·ghra·*fi*·es

I don't want to pay the full price.

Δεν θέλω να πληρώσω
ολόκληρη την τιμή.

then *the*·lo na pli·*ro*·so
o·*lo*·kli·ri tin ti·*mi*

repairs

επισκευές

Can I have my … repaired here?	Μπορώ να επισκευάσω εδώ …;	bo·*ro* na e·pi·ske·*va*·so e·*tho* …
backpack	το σάκο μου	to *sa*·ko mu
camera	τη φωτογραφική μηχανή μου	ti fo·to·ghra·fi·*ki* mi·kha·*ni* mu
shoes	τα παπούτσια μου	ta pa·*pu*·tsia mu
sunglasses	τα γιαλιά μου του ήλιου	ta yia·*lia* mu tu *i*·liu

When will my … be ready?	Πότε θα είναι έτοιμα τα …;	*po*·te tha *i*·ne e·ti·ma ta …
glasses	γιαλιά μου	yia·*lia* mu
shoes	παπούτσια μου	pa·*put*·sia mu
sunglasses	γιαλιά μου του ήλιου	yia·*lia* mu tu *i*·liu

When will my camera be ready?

Πότε θα είναι έτοιμη η
φωτογραφική μηχανή μου;

po·te tha *i*·ne e·ti·mi i
fo·to·ghra·fi·*ki* mi·kha·*ni* mu

When will my backpack be ready?

Πότε θα είναι έτοιμος
ο σάκος μου;

po·te tha *i*·ne e·ti·mos
o *sa*·kos mu

shopping

83

backgammon board	τάβλι n	*tav·li*
baskets	καλάθια n pl	ka·*la*·thia
bouzouki	μπουζούκι n	bu·*zu*·ki
bronzeware	μπρούτζινα n pl	*bru*·dzi·na
carpets	χαλιά n pl	kha·*lia*
ceramics	κεραμικά n pl	ke·ra·mi·*ka*
copperware	χάλκινα n pl	*khal*·ki·na
cushion covers	μαξιλαροθήκες f pl	mak·si·la·ro·*thi*·kes
evil eye (blue eye warding off evil spirits)	φυλαχτό n	fi·lakh·*to*
icons	εικόνες f pl	i·*ko*·nes
lace	δαντέλλα f	than·*te*·la
leather work	δερμάτινα n pl	ther·*ma*·ti·na
pottery	είδη αγγειοπλαστικής n pl	*i*·thi a·gi·o·pla·sti·*kis*
rugs	τάπητες m pl	*ta*·pi·tes
sculptures	γλυπτά n pl	ghlip·*ta*
worry beads	κομπολόγια n pl	ko·bo·*lo*·yia
woven shoulder bag	υφαντή τσάντα ώμου f	i·fa·*di* tsa·da *o*·mu
... jewellery	... κοσμήματα n pl	... koz·*mi*·ma·ta
filigree	φιλιγκράν	fi·li·*gran*
gold	χρυσά	khri·*sa*
silver	ασημένια	a·si·*me*·nia

post office

ταχυδρομείο

I want to send a ...	Θέλω να στείλω ...	*the*·lo na *sti*·lo ...
fax	ένα φαξ	*e*·na faks
letter	ένα γράμμα	*e*·na *ghra*·ma
parcel	ένα δέμα	*e*·na *the*·ma
postcard	μια κάρτα	mia *kar*·ta
telegram	ένα τηλεγράφημα	*e*·na ti·le·*ghra*·fi·ma
I want to buy a/an ...	Θέλω να αγοράσω ένα ...	*the*·lo na a·gho·*ra*·so *e*·na ...
aerogram	αερόγραμμα	a·e·*ro*·ghra·ma
envelope	φάκελο	*fa*·ke·lo
stamp	γραμματόσημο	ghra·ma·*to*·si·mo
customs declaration	δήλωση τελωνείου f	*thi*·lo·si te·lo·*ni*·u
domestic a	εσωτερικό	e·so·te·ri·*ko*
fragile a	εύθραυστο	*ef*·thraf·sto
international a	διεθνές	thi·eth·*nes*
mail	αλληλογραφία f	a·li·lo·ghra·*fi*·a
mailbox	ταχυδρομικό κουτί n	ta·hi·thro·mi·*ko* ku·*ti*
postcode	ταχυδρομικός τομέας m	ta·hi·thro·mi·*kos* to·*me*·as

snail mail

airmail	αεροπορικώς	a·e·ro·po·ri·*kos*
express mail	εξπρές	eks·*pres*
registered mail	συστημένο	si·sti·*me*·no
sea mail	ατμοπλοϊκώς	at·mo·plo·i·*kos*
surface mail	δια ξηράς	thi·*a* ksi·*ras*

Please send it by airmail to (Australia).

Παρακαλώ στείλτε το
αεροπορικώς στην
(Αυστραλία).

pa·ra·ka·*lo* stil·te to
a·e·ro·po·ri·*kos* stin
(af·stra·*li*·a)

Please send it by surface mail to (New Zealand).

Παρακαλώ στείλτε το δια
ξηράς στην (Νέα Ζηλανδία).

pa·ra·ka·*lo* stil·te to thi·*a*
ksi·*ras* stin (*ne*·a zi·nan·*thi*·a)

It contains (souvenirs).

Περιέχει (σουβενίρ).

pe·ri·e·hi (su·ve·*nir*)

Where's the poste restante section?

Πού είναι το ποστ ρεστάντ;

pu *i*·ne to post re·*stant*

Is there any mail for me?

Υπάρχουν γράμματα
για μένα;

i·*par*·khun *ghra*·ma·ta
yia *me*·na

I'd like to collect a parcel.

Θα ήθελα να παραλάβω
ένα δέμα.

tha *i*·the·la na pa·ra·*la*·vo
e·na *the*·ma

Where can I find a fax and telegram service?

Πού μπορώ να βρω
υπηρεσία για φαξ και
για τηλεγράφημα;

pu bo·*ro* na vro
i·pi·re·*si*·a yia faks ke
yia ti·le·*ghra*·fi·ma

How much is a fax per page?

Πόσο κοστίζει το φαξ
η σελίδα;

po·so ko·*sti*·zi to faks
i se·*li*·tha

Do you have Internet services?

Έχετε υπηρεσία
Διαδικτύου;

e·he·te i·pi·re·*si*·a
thi·a·thik·*ti*·u

---

medusa

Medusa, famous for turning mortals to stone, had hair
much like the tentacles of a jellyfish. In fact the jellyfish
is named after her in Greek (μέδουσα me·thu·sa), French
(*méduse* me·*dooz*) and Spanish (*medusa* me·*doo*·sa), to
name just a few languages.

phone

τηλέφωνο

What's your phone number?
Τι αριθμό τηλεφώνου έχεις;   ti a·rith·mo ti·le·fo·nu e·his

Where's the nearest public phone?
Πού είναι το πιο κοντινό   pu i·ne to pio ko·di·no
δημόσιο τηλέφωνο;   thi·mo·si·o ti·le·fo·no

Where's the nearest telephone office?
Πού είναι το πιο κοντινό   pu i·ne to pio ko·di·no
τηλεφωνικό κέντρο;   ti·le·fo·ni·ko ke·dro

Do you have a metered phone?
Έχεις τηλέφωνο με μετρητή;   e·his ti·le·fo·no me me·tri·ti

Can I look at a phone book?
Μπορώ να κοιτάξω τον   bo·ro na ki·tak·so ton
τηλεφωνικό κατάλογο;   ti·le·fo·ni·ko ka·ta·lo·gho

I want to …	Θέλω να …	*the*·lo na …
buy a (2000 unit) phonecard	αγοράσω μια τηλεφωνική κάρτα (2000 μονάδων)	a·gho·ra·so mia ti·le·fo·ni·ki kar·ta (thi·o hi·lia·thon mo·na·thon)
buy a discount card	αγοράσω μια κάρτα με έκπτωση	a·gho·ra·so mia kar·ta me ek·pto·si
call (Singapore)	τηλεφωνήσω (στη Σιγγαπούρη)	ti·le·fo·ni·so (sti sing·ga·pu·ri)
make a (local) call	κάμω ένα (τοπικό) τηλέφωνο	ka·mo e·na (to·pi·ko) ti·le·fo·no
reverse the charges	αντιστρέψω τα έξοδα	a·di·strep·so ta ek·so·tha
speak for (three) minutes	μιλήσω για (τρία) λεπτά	mi·li·so yia (tri·a) lep·ta

Ποιος μιλάει; pios mi·*la*·i	**Who's calling?**
Σε ποιον θέλετε να μιλήσετε; se pion *the*·le·te na mi·*li*·se·te	**Who do you want to speak to?**
Μια στιγμή. mia stigh·*mi*	**One moment.**
Δεν είναι εδώ. then *i*·ne e·*tho*	**He's/She's not here.**
Λάθος αριθμός. *la*·thos a·rith·*mos*	**Wrong number.**

How much does ... cost?	Πόσο κοστίζει ...;	*po*·so ko·*sti*·zi ...
a (three)- minute call	ένα τηλεφώνημα (τριών) λεπτών	*e*·na ti·le·*fo*·ni·ma (tri·*on*) lep·*ton*
each extra minute	κάθε έξτρα λεπτό	*ka*·the *eks*·tra lep·*to*

The number is ...
Ο αριθμός είναι ...   o a·rith·*mos i*·ne ...

What's the code for (New Zealand)?
Ποιος είναι ο κωδικός   pios *i*·ne o ko·thi·*kos*
αριθμός για   a·rith·*mos* yia
(τη Νέα Ζηλανδία);   (ti *ne*·a zi·lan·*thi*·a)

It's engaged.
Είναι κατειλημμένη.   *i*·ne ka·ti·li·*me*·ni

I've been cut off.
Με διέκοψαν.   me thi·e·*kop*·san

The connection's bad.
Η σύνδεση είναι κακή.   i *sin*·the·si *i*·ne ka·*ki*

Hello.
Εμπρός.   e·*bros*

It's ...
Είμαι ...   *i*·me ...

Is ... there?
Είναι ... εκεί;   *i*·ne ... e·*ki*

Can I speak to ...?
Μπορώ να μιλήσω με ...;   bo·*ro* na mi·*li*·so me ...

Can I leave a message?
Μπορώ να αφήσω ένα μήνυμα;   bo·*ro* na a·*fi*·so e·na *mi*·ni·ma

Please tell him/her I called.
Παρακαλώ πες του/της
ότι τηλεφώνησα.   pa·ra·ka·*lo* pes tu/tis
o·ti ti·le·*fo*·ni·sa

My number is ...
Ο αριθμός μου είναι ...   o a·rith·*mos* mu *i*·ne ...

I don't have a contact number.
Δεν έχω αριθμό για
επικοινωνία.   then *e*·kho a·rith·*mo* yia
e·pi·ki·no·*ni*·a

I'll call back later.
Θα τηλεφωνήσω αργότερα.   tha ti·le·fo·*ni*·so ar·*gho*·te·ra

mobile/cell phone

κινητό τηλέφωνο

I'd like a ...	Θα ήθελα ...	tha *i*·the·la ...
charger for	ένα φορτιστή για	e·na for·ti·*sti* yia
my phone	το τηλέφωνό μου	to ti·*le*·fo·no mu
mobile/cell	να νοικιάσω ένα	na ni·*kia*·so e·na
phone for hire	κινητό τηλέφωνο	ki·ni·*to* ti·*le*·fo·no
prepaid mobile/	ένα	e·na
cell phone	προπληρωμένο	pro·pli·ro·*me*·no
	κινητό τηλέφωνο	ki·ni·*to* ti·*le*·fo·no
SIM card for	μια κάρτα SIM	mia *kar*·ta sim
your network	για το δίκτυό σας	yia to *thik*·tio sas

What are the rates?
Ποιες είναι οι τιμές;   pies *i*·ne i ti·*mes*

(40c) per (30) seconds.
(40λ) για (30)
δευτερόλεπτα.   (sa·*ra*·da lep·*ta*) yia (tri·*a*·da)
thef·te·ro·lep·ta

communications

89

the internet

Where's the local Internet cafe?
Πού είναι το τοπικό   pu *i*·ne to to·pi·*ko*
καφενείο με διαδίκτυο;   ka·fe·*ni*·o me thi·a·*thik*·ti·o

I'd like to ...	Θα ήθελα να ...	tha *i*·the·la na ...
check my	ελέγξω την	e·*leng*·so tin
email	ηλεκτρονική	i·lek·tro·ni·*ki*
	αλληλογραφία μου	a·li·lo·ghra·*fi*·a mu
get Internet	έχω πρόσβαση	e·kho *pros*·va·si
access	στο Διαδίκτυο	sto thi·a·*thik*·ti·o
use a printer	χρησιμοποιήσω	khri·si·mo·pi·*i*·so
	έναν εκτυπωτή	e·nan ek·ti·po·*ti*
use a scanner	χρησιμοποιήσω	khri·si·mo·pi·*i*·so
	ένα σκάνερ	e·na *ska*·ner

Do you have ...?	Έχετε ...;	e·he·te ...
Macs	Κομπιούτερ Mac	kom·*piu*·ter mak
PCs	Κομπιούτερ PC	kom·*piu*·ter pi si
a Zip drive	Zip drive	zip *dra*·iv

How much	Πόσο κοστίζει	po·so ko·*sti*·zi
per ...?	κάθε ...;	*ka*·the ...
hour	ώρα	o·ra
page	σελίδα	se·*li*·tha

How do I log on?
Πώς μπαίνω μέσα;   pos *be*·no *me*·sa

Please change it to the (English)-language setting.
Παρακαλώ άλλαξέ το στην   pa·ra·ka·*lo* a·lak·se to stin
(αγγλική) γλώσσα.   (ang·gli·*ki*) *glo*·sa

Do you have (English) keyboards?
έχεις (Αγγλικό) πληκτρολόγιο;   e·his (ang·gli·*ko*) plik·tro·*lo*·yi·o

It's crashed.
κατέρρευσε.   ka·*te*·ref·se

I've finished.
Τελείωσα.   te·*li*·o·sa

What time does the bank open?

Τι ώρα ανοίγει η τράπεζα;   ti o·ra a·ni·yi i tra·pe·za

Where's a/an ...?   Πού είναι ...;   pu i·ne ...
  automated   μια αυτόματη   mia af·to·ma·ti
  teller machine   μηχανή   mi·kha·ni
     χρημάτων   khri·ma·ton
  foreign exchange   ένα γραφείο   e·na ghra·fi·o
  office   αλλαγής   a·la·yis
     χρημάτων   khri·ma·ton

Where can I ...?   Πού μπορώ να ...;   pu bo·ro na ...
I'd like to ...   Θα ήθελα να ...   tha i·the·la na ...
  cash a cheque   εξαργυρώσω   ek·sar·yi·ro·so
     μια επιταγή   mia e·pi·ta·yi
  change money   αλλάξω χρήματα   a·lak·so khri·ma·ta
  change a   αλλάξω μια   a·lak·so mia
  travellers   ταξιδιωτική   tak·si·thio·ti·ki
  cheque   επιταγή   e·pi·ta·yi
  get a cash   κάμω μια   ka·mo mia
  advance   ανάληψη   a·na·lip·si
     σε μετρητά   se me·tri·ta
  withdraw   αποσύρω   a·po·si·ro
  money   χρήματα   khri·ma·ta

What's the ...?   Ποια είναι ... ;   pia i·ne ...
  exchange rate   η τιμή   i ti·mi
     συναλλάγματος   si·na·lagh·ma·tos
  charge for that   η χρέωση   i khre·o·si
     για αυτό   yia af·to

Has my money arrived yet?

Έχουν φτάσει τα
χρήματά μου;

e·khun *fta*·si ta
khri·ma·*ta* mu

How long will it take to arrive?

Σε πόσο καιρό θα φτάσουν;

se *po*·so ke·*ro* tha *fta*·sun

The automated teller machine took my card.

Η αυτόματη μηχανή
χρημάτων κράτησε
την κάρτα μου.

i af·*to*·ma·ti mi·kha·*ni*
khri·*ma*·ton *kra*·ti·se
tin *kar*·ta mu

I've forgotten my PIN.

Ξέχασα τον κωδικό
αριθμό μου.

kse·ha·sa ton ko·*thi*·*ko*
a·rith·*mo* mu

Can I use my credit card to withdraw money?

Μπορώ να χρησιμοποιήσω
την πιστωτική μου κάρτα
για να αποσύρω χρήματα;

bo·*ro* na khri·si·mo·pi·*i*·so
tin pi·sto·ti·*ki* mu *kar*·ta
yia na a·po·*si*·ro *khri*·ma·ta

---

listen for ...

διαβατήριο n	*thia*·va·*ti*·ri·o	**passport**
ταυτότητα f	taf·*to*·ti·ta	**identification**

Δεν μπορούμε να το κάνουμε αυτό.
then bo·*ru*·me na
to *ka*·nu·me af·*to*
We can't do that.

Τελείωσαν τα χρήματά σας.
te·*li*·o·san ta *khri*·ma·*ta* sas
You have no funds left.

Υπάρχει ένα πρόβλημα.
i·*par*·hi e·na *prov*·li·ma
There's a problem.

Υπογράψτε εδώ.
i·po·*ghrap*·ste e·*tho*
Sign here.

I'd like a/an ...	Θα ήθελα ...	tha i·the·la ...
audio set	ακουστικά	a·ku·sti·ka
catalogue	ένα κατάλογο	e·na ka·ta·lo·gho
guide	έναν οδηγό	e·nan o·thi·gho
guidebook in	έναν οδηγό στα	e·nan o·thi·gho sta
(English)	(Αγγλικά)	(ang·gli·ka)
(local) map	ένα (τοπικό)	e·na (to·pi·ko)
	χάρτη	khar·ti

Do you have	Έχετε	e·he·te
information	πληροφορίες για	pli·ro·fo·ri·es yia
on ... sights?	... χώρους;	... kho·rus
ancient	αρχαίους	ar·he·us
archaic	αρχαϊκούς	ar·kha·i·kus
archeological	αρχαιολογικούς	ar·he·o·lo·yi·kus
architectural	αρχιτεκτονικούς	ar·hi·tek·to·ni·kus
Byzantine	Βυζαντινούς	vi·za·di·nus
classical	κλασσικούς	kla·si·kus
cultural	πολιτιστικούς	po·li·ti·sti·kus
Hellenistic	Ελληνιστικούς	e·li·ni·sti·kus
historical	ιστορικούς	i·sto·ri·kus
neoclassical	νεοκλασσικούς	ne·o·kla·si·kus
Orthodox	Ορθόδοξους	or·tho·dok·sus
Ottoman	Οθωμανικούς	o·tho·ma·ni·kus
religious	θρησκευτικούς	thris·kef·ti·kus
Roman	Ρωμαϊκούς	ro·ma·i·kus

signs

Ανδρών	an·thron	**Men**
Είσοδος	i·so·thos	**Entrance**
Έξοδος	ek·so·thos	**Exit**
Τουαλέτες	tu·a·le·tes	**Toilets**
Γυναικών	yi·ne·kon	**Women**

I'd like to see (the) …	Θα ήθελα να δω …	tha *i*·the·la na tho …
Acropolis	την Ακτόπολη	tin ak·*ro*·po·li
amphitheatre	το αμφιθέατρο	to am·fi·*the*·a·tro
Archeological Museum	το Αρχαιολογικό Μουσείο	to ar·he·o·lo·yi·*ko* mu·*si*·o
Byzantine frescoes	Βυζαντινά φρέσκο	vi·za·di·*na* *fres*·ko
labyrinth	τον λαβύρινθο	ton la·*vi*·rin·tho
mosaics	τα μωσαϊκά	ta mo·sa·i·*ka*
Mt Athos monasteries	τα μοναστήρια του Αγίου Όρους	ta mo·na·*sti*·ria tu a·*yi*·u *o*·rus
Mycaenian tombs	Μυκηναϊκούς τάφους	mi·ki·na·i·*kus* *ta*·fus
oracle of Delphi	το μαντείο των Δελφών	to ma·*di*·o ton thel·*fon*
palace	το παλάτι	to pa·*la*·ti
ruins	τα ερείπια	ta e·*ri*·pi·a
sculptures	τα γλυπτά	ta ghlip·*ta*
statues	τα αγάλματα	ta a·*ghal*·ma·ta
temple	το ναό	to na·*o*

What's that?
Τι είναι εκείνο; ti *i*·ne e·*ki*·no

Who made it?
Ποιος το έκαμε; pios to *e*·ka·me

How old is it?
Πόσο χρονώ είναι; *po*·so khro·*no i*·ne

When was this discovered?
Πότε ανακαλύφτηκε αυτό; *po*·te a·na·ka·*lif*·ti·ke af·*to*

When were the excavations done?
Πότε έγιναν οι ανασκαφές; *po*·te *e*·yi·nan i a·nas·ka·*fes*

Could you take a photograph of me?
Μπορείς να μου πάρεις μια φωτογραφία; bo·*ris* na mu *pa*·ris mia fo·to·ghra·*fi*·a

Can I take a photo (of you)?
Μπορώ να (σου) πάρω μια φωτογραφία; bo·*ro* na (su) *pa*·ro mia fo·to·ghra·*fi*·a

getting in

What time does it open?
Τι ώρα ανοίγει;   ti *o*·ra a·*ni*·yi

What time does it close?
Τι ώρα κλείνει;   ti *o*ra *kli*·ni

Is it open every day?
Είναι ανοιχτό κάθε μέρα;   *i*·ne a·nikh·*to ka*·the *me*·ra

What's the admission charge?
Πόσο κοστίζει η είσοδος;   *po*·so ko·*sti*·zi i *i*·so·ṭhos

Can I go in wearing these clothes?
Μπορώ να μπω με αυτά   bo·*ro* na bo me af·*ta*
τα ρούχα;   ta *ru*·kha

sightseeing

95

Is there a discount for ...?	Υπάρχει έκπτωση για ...;	i·par·hi ek·pto·si yia ...
children	παιδιά	pe·thia
families	οικογένειες	i·ko·ye·ni·es
groups	γκρουπ	grup
older people	υπερήλικους	i·pe·ri·li·kus
pensioners	συνταξιούχους	si·dak·si·u·khus
students	σπουδαστές	spu·tha·stes

tours

περιηγήσεις

Can you recommend a tour?
Μπορείς να συστήσεις
κάποια περιήγηση;
bo·ris na si·sti·sis
ka·pia pe·ri·i·yi·si

When's the next tour?
Πότε είναι η επόμενη
περιήγηση;
po·te i·ne i e·po·me·ni
pe·ri·i·yi·si

How long is the tour?
Πόσην ώρα διαρκεί η
περιήγηση;
po·sin o·ra thi·ar·ki i
pe·ri·i·yi·si

The guide will pay.
Ο/Η οδηγός θα πληρώσει. m/f
o/i o·thi·ghos tha pli·ro·si

The guide has paid.
Ο/Η οδηγός έχει πληρώσει. m/f
o/i o·thi·ghos e·hi pli·ro·si

What time should we be back?
Τι ώρα πρέπει να
επιστρέψουμε;
ti o·ra pre·pi na
e·pi·strep·su·me

I'm with them.
Είμαι με αυτούς.
i·me me af·tus

I've lost my group.
Έχασα την ομάδα μου.
e·kha·sa tin o·ma·tha mu

doing business

επιχειρησήσεις

I'm attending a ...	Παρακολουθώ ...	pa·ra·ko·lu·tho ...
conference	ένα συνέδριο	e·na sin·e·thri·o
course	μια σειρά μαθημάτων	mia si·ra ma·thi·ma·ton
meeting	μια συνεδρίαση	mia sin·e·thri·a·si
trade fair	μια εμπορική έκθεση	mia e·bo·ri·ki ek·the·si
I'm with ...	Είμαι με ...	i·me me ...
(Olympiaki)	(την Ολυμπιακή)	(tin o·li·bi·a·ki)
my colleague	τον συνάδελφό μου m	ton sin·a·thel·fo mu
	την συναδέλφισσά μου f	tin sin·a·thel·fi·sa mu
my colleagues	τους συναδέλφους μου	tus sin·a·thel·fus mu

I'm alone.
Είμαι μόνος/μόνη. m/f   i·me mo·nos/mo·ni

I have an appointment with ...
Έχω ένα ραντεβού με ...   e·kho e·na ra·de·vu me ...

I'm staying at (the Xenia), room (10).
Μένω στο (Ξενία),   me·no sto (kse·ni·a)
δωμάτιο (10).   tho·ma·ti·o (the·ka)

I'm here for (two) days/weeks.
Είμαι εδώ για (δύο)   i·me e·tho yia (thi·o)
μέρες/εβδομάδες.   me·res/ev·tho·ma·thes

Here's my business card.
Ορίστε η κάρτα μου.   o·ri·ste i kar·ta mu

Can I have your business card?
Μπορώ να έχω την κάρτα σου;   bo·ro na e·kho tin kar·ta su

Here's my ...	Ορίστε ... μου.	o·ri·ste ... mu
What's your ...?	Ποια είναι η δική	pia i·ne i thi·ki
	σου η ...;	su i ...
address	διεύθυνση	thi·ef·thin·si
email address	ηλεκτρονική	i·lek·tro·ni·ki
	διεύθυνση	thi·ef·thin·si

Here's my ...	Εδώ είναι	e·tho i·ne
number.	ο αριθμός ... μου.	o a·rith·mos ... mu
What's your	Ποιος είναι ο	pios i·ne o
... number?	δικός σου ο	thi·kos su o
	αριθμός ...;	a·rith·mos ...
fax	του φαξ	tu faks
mobile	του κινητού	tu ki·ni·tu
pager	του	tu
	τηλεειδοποιητή	ti·le·i·tho·pi·i·ti
work	της δουλειάς	tis thu·lias

Where's the ...?	Πού είναι ...;	pu i·ne ...
business	ο χώρος	o kho·ros
centre	εργασίας	er·gha·si·as
conference	το συνέδριο	to sin·e·thri·o
meeting	η συνεδρίαση	i sin·e·thri·a·si

I need (a/an) ...	Χρειάζομαι ...	khri·a·zo·me ...
computer	ένα κομπιούτερ	e·na kom·piu·ter
Internet	σύνδεση στο	sin·the·si sto
connection	διαδύκτιο	thi·a·thik·ti·o
interpreter	διερμηνέα	thi·er·mi·ne·a
more business	περισσότερες	pe·ri·so·te·res
cards	κάρτες	kar·tes
some space to	χώρο να τοποθε-	kho·ro na to·po·the·
set up	τήσω τα πράγματα	ti·so ta ragh·ma·ta
to send a fax	να στείλω ένα φαξ	na sti·lo e·na faks

Thank you for your time.
Ευχαριστώ για το χρόνο σου.   ef·kha·ri·sto yia to khro·no su

That went very well.
Πήγε πολύ καλά.   pi·ye po·li ka·la

Shall we go for a drink/meal?
Πάμε για ποτό/φαγητό;   pa·me yia po·to/fa·yi·to

looking for a job

Where are jobs advertised?

| Πού διαφημίζονται | pu thi·a·fi·mi·zo·de |
| οι δουλειές; | i thu·lies |

I'm enquiring about the position advertised.

| ζητώ πληροφορίες για τη | zi·to pli·ro·fo·ri·es yia ti |
| θέση που διαφημίστηκε. | the·si pu thi·a·fi·mi·sti·ke |

I've had experience.

| Έχω πείρα. | e·kho pi·ra |

What's the wage?

| Τι μισθό έχει; | ti mi·stho e·hi |

I'm looking	Ψάχνω για	psakh·no yia
for ... work.	δουλειά ...	thu·lia ...
bar	σε μπαρ	se bar
casual	προσωρινή	pro·so·ri·ni
English-	να διδάσκω	na thi·tha·sko
teaching	αγγλικά	ang·gli·ka
fruit-picking	να μαζεύω	na ma·ze·vo
	φρούτα	fru·ta
full-time	με πλήρη	me pli·ri
	απασχόληση	a·pa·skho·li·si
labouring	χειρωνακτική	hi·ro·nak·ti·ki
office	γραφείου	ghra·fi·u
part-time	μερικής	me·ri·kis
	απασχόλησης	a·pa·skho·li·sis
waitering	γκαρσόν	gar·son

Do I need	Χειάζομαι ...;	khri·a·zo·me ...
(a/an)...?		
contract	συμβόλαιο	sim·vo·le·o
experience	πείρα	pi·ra
insurance	ασφάλεια	as·fa·li·a
my own	δικό μου	thi·ko mu
transport	μεταφορικό μέσο	me·ta·fo·ri·ko me·so
paperwork	ντοκουμέντα	do·ku·men·ta
uniform	στολή	sto·li
work permit	άδεια εργασίας	a·thi·a er·gha·si·as

Here is/are my ...	Ορίστε ...	o·ri·ste ...
bank account	ο τραπεζικός μου	o tra·pe·zi·kos mu
details	λογαριασμός	lo·gha·riaz·mos
CV/résumé	το βιογραφικό	to vi·o·ghra·fi·ko
	μου σημείωμα	mu si·mi·o·ma
residency	η άδεια	i a·thi·a
permit	παραμονής μου	pa·ra·mo·nis mu
visa	η βίζα μου	i vi·za mu
work permit	η άδεια	i a·thi·a
	εργασίας μου	er·gha·si·as mu
What time do I ...?	Τι ώρα ...;	ti o·ra ...
finish	τελειώνω	te·li·o·no
have a break	έχω διάλειμμα	e·kho thia·li·ma
start	αρχίζω	ar·hi·zo

🏛🏛🏛🏛🏛🏛 🏛🏛🏛🏛🏛

I can start ...	Μπορώ να	bo·ro na
	αρχίσω ...	ar·hi·so ...
Can you start ...?	Μπορείς να	bo·ris na
	αρχίσεις ...;	ar·hi·sis ...
at (eight)	στις (οχτώ)	stis (okh·to)
o'clock		
next week	την επόμενη	tin e·po·me·ni
	εβδομάδα	ev·tho·ma·tha
today	σήμερα	si·me·ra
tomorrow	αύριο	av·ri·o
advertisement	διαφήμιση f	thi·a·fi·mi·si
contract	συμβόλαιο n	sim·vo·le·o
employee	υπάλληλος m&f	i·pa·li·los
employer	εργοδότης m	er·gho·tho·tis
	εργοδότρια f	er·gho·tho·tri·a
job	δουλειά f	thu·lia
work experience	πείρα στη δουλειά f	pi·ra sti thu·lia

PRACTICAL

100

senior & disabled travellers
υπερήλικοι και ανάπηροι ταξιδιώτες

I have a disability.
Έχω μια αναπηρία.   *e*·kho mia a·na·pi·*ri*·a

I need assistance.
Χρειάζομαι βοήθεια.   khri·*a*·zo·me vo·*i*·thi·a

What services do you have for people with a disability?
Τι υπηρεσίες έχετε για   ti i·pi·re·*si*·es *e*·he·te yia
άτομα με ειδικές ανάγκες;   *a*·to·ma me i·thi·*kes* a·*na*·ges

Are there disabled toilets?
Υπάρχουν τουαλέτες για   i·*par*·khun tu·a·*le*·tes yia
άτομα με ειδικές ανάγκες;   *a*·to·ma me i·thi·*kes* a·*na*·ges

Are there disabled parking spaces?
Υπάρχει πάρκινγκ για   i·*par*·hi *par*·king yia
άτομα με ειδικές ανάγκες;   *a*·to·ma me i·thi·*kes* a·*na*·ges

Is there wheelchair access?
Υπάρχει δρόμος για   i·*par*·hi *thro*·mos yia
αναπηρικές καρέκλες;   a·na·pi·ri·*kes* ka·*re*·kles

How wide is the entrance?
Πόσο πλατιά είναι η είσοδος;   po·so pla·*tia i*·ne i *i*·so·thos

Is there somewhere I can sit down?
Υπάρχει κάπου να καθίσω;   i·*par*·hi *ka*·pu na ka·*thi*·so

I'm deaf.
Είμαι κουφός.   *i*·me ku·*fos*

I have a hearing aid.
Έχω ακουστικά.   *e*·kho a·ku·sti·*ka*

Are guide dogs permitted?
Επιτρέπεται στα σκυλιά   e·pi·*tre*·pe·te sta ski·*lia*
για τυφλούς;   yia ti·*flus*

How many steps are there?
Πόσα σκαλοπάτια υπάρχουν;   po·sa ska·lo·*pa*·tia i·*par*·khun

Is there a lift?
Υπάρχει ασανσέρ;   i·*par*·khi a·san·*ser*

Are there rails in the bathroom?

Υπάρχουν στηρίγματα   i·*par*·khun sti·*righ*·ma·ta
στο μπάνιο;   sto *ba*·nio

Could you call me a disabled taxi?

Μπορείς να καλέσεις   bo·*ris* na ka·*le*·sis
ένα ταξί για άτομα με   *e*·na tak·*si* yia a·*to*·ma me
ειδικές ανάγκες;   i·thi·*kes* a·*na*·ges

Could you help me cross the street safely?

Μπορείς να με βοηθήσεις   bo·*ris* na me vo·i·*thi*·sis
να περάσω το δρόμο   na pe·*ra*·so to *thro*·mo
με ασφάλεια;   me as·*fa*·li·a

guide dog	σκυλί για τυφλούς n	ski·*li* yia ti·*flus*
older person	υπερήλικος m	i·pe·*ri*·li·kos
	υπερήλικη f	i·pe·*ri*·li·ki
person with a disability	άτομο με ειδικές	*a*·to·mo me i·thi·*kes*
	ανάγκες n	a·*na*·ges
ramp	ράμπα f	*ram*·pa
walking frame	περπατούσα f	per·pa·*tu*·sa
walking stick	μπαστούνι n	ba·*stu*·ni
wheelchair	αναπηρική	a·na·pi·ri·*ki*
	καρέκλα f	ka·*re*·kla

---

gobbledy gook

So you're having one of those days when you can't make heads or tails of the Greek signs around you, and you're dying to say 'It's all Greek to me!'. In your shoes, a Greek speaker would say:

This is Chinese to me.

Αυτά για μένα είναι Κινέζικα.   af·*ta* yia *me*·na *i*·ne ki·*ne*·zi·ka

travelling with children

ταξιδεύοντας με παιδιά

Is there a ...?	Υπάρχει ...;	i·*par*·hi ...
baby change room	δωμάτιο για άλλαγμα μωρών	tho·*ma*·ti·o yia *a*·lagh·ma mo·*ron*
child-minding service	υπηρεσία διαφύλαξης παιδιών	i·pi·re·*si*·a thi·a·*fi*·lak·sis pe·*thion*
children's menu	παιδικό μενού	pe·thi·*ko* me·*nu*
child's portion	παιδική μερίδα	pe·thi·*ki* me·*ri*·tha
crèche	βρεφοκομείο	vre·fo·ko·*mi*·o
discount for children	έκπτωση για παιδιά	*ek*·pto·si yia pe·*thia*
family ticket	οικογενειακό εισιτήριο	i·ko·ye·ni·a·*ko* i·si·*ti*·ri·o

I need a/an ...	Χρειάζομαι ...	khri·*a*·zo·me ...
baby seat (English-speaking) babysitter	κάθισμα μωρού (αγγλομαθή) μπέημπι σίτερ	*ka*·thiz·ma mo·*ru* (ang·glo·ma·*thi*) be·*i*·bi *si*·ter
booster seat	ανυψωμένο κάθισμα	a·nip·so·*me*·no *ka*·thiz·ma
cot	παιδικό κρεβάτι	pe·thi·*ko* kre·*va*·ti
highchair	παιδική καρέκλα	pe·thi·*ki* ka·*re*·kla
plastic sheet	πλαστικό σεντόνι	pla·sti·*ko* se·*do*·ni
plastic bag	πλαστική σακούλα	pla·sti·*ki* sa·*ku*·la
potty	γιογιό	yio·*yio*
pram	παιδικό καροτσάκι	pe·thi·*ko* ka·rot·*sa*·ki
sick bag	σακούλα εμετού	sa·*ku*·la e·me·*tu*
stroller	καροτσάκι	ka·rot·*sa*·ki

Where's the nearest …?	Πού είναι το πιο κοντινό …;	pu *i*·ne to pio ko·di·*no* …
park	πάρκο	*par*·ko
playground	γήπεδο	*yi*·pe·do
toy shop	κατάστημα παιγνιδιών	ka·*ta*·sti·ma pegh·ni·*thion*

Where's the nearest …?	Πού είναι η πιο κοντινή …;	pu *i*·ne i pio ko·di·*ni* …
drinking fountain	βρύση με πόσιμο νερό	*vri*·si me *po*·si·mo ne·*ro*
swimming pool	πισίνα	pi·*si*·na
tap	βρύση	*vri*·si
theme park	παιδική χαρά	pe·*thi·ki* kha·*ra*

Do you sell …?	Πουλάτε …;	pu·*la*·te …
baby wipes	πετσέτες για σκούπισμα μωρών	pet·*se*·tes yia *sku*·piz·ma mo·*ron*
painkillers for infants	παυσίπονα για μωρά	paf·*si*·po·na yia mo·*ra*
disposable nappies/diapers	πάνες μιας χρήσης	*pa*·nes mias *khri*·sis
tissues	χαρτομάντηλα	khar·to·*ma*·di·la

Do you hire out …?	Νοικιάζετε …;	ni·*kia*·ze·te …
prams	παιδικά καροτσάκια	pe·thi·*ka* ka·rot·*sa*·kia
strollers	καροτσάκια	ka·rot·*sa*·kia

Are there any good places to take children around here?

Υπάρχουν καλά μέρη εδώ κοντά για τα παιδιά;	i·*par*·khun ka·*la* me·ri e·*tho* ko·*da* yia ta pe·*thia*

Is there space for a pram?

Υπάρχει χώρος για το παιδικό καροτσάκι;	i·*par*·hi *kho*·ros yia to pe·thi·*ko* ka·rot·*sa*·ki

Are children allowed?

Επιτρέπεται στα παιδιά;	e·pi·*tre*·pe·te sta pe·*thia*

Where can I change a nappy?

Πού μπορώ να αλλάξω την πάνα;	pu bo·*ro* na a·*lak*·so tin *pa*·na

Do you mind if I breast-feed here?
Σε πειράζει αν θηλάσω   se pi·*ra*·zi an thi·*la*·so
εδώ το μωρό;   e·*tho* to mo·*ro*

Could I have some paper and pencils, please?
Μπορώ να έχω λίγο χαρτί   bo·*ro* na *e*·kho *li*·gho khar·*ti*
και μολύβια, παρακαλώ.   ke mo·*li*·via pa·ra·ka·*lo*

Is this suitable for (five)-year-old children?
Είναι αυτό κατάλληλο για   *i*·ne af·*to* ka·*ta*·li·lo yia
παιδιά (πέντε) χρονών;   pe·*thia* (*pe*·de) khro·*no*

Do you know a dentist/doctor who is good with children?
Ξέρεις ένα οδοντίατρο/   *kse*·ris *e*·na o·tho·*di*·a·tro/
γιατρό που είναι καλός   yia·*tro* pu *i*·ne ka·*los*
με τα παιδιά;   me ta pe·*thia*

If your child is sick, see **health**, page 195.

talking with children

μιλώντας με τα παιδιά

What's your name?
Πώς σε λένε;   pos se *le*·ne

How old are you?
Πόσο χρονώ είσαι;   *po*·so khro·*no i*·se

When's your birthday?
Πότε είναι τα   *po*·te *i*·ne ta
γενέθλιά σου;   ye·*neth*·li·a su

Do you go to school/kindergarten?
Πηγαίνεις στο σχολείο/   pi·*ye*·nis sto skho·*li*·o/
νηπιαγωγείο;   ni·pi·a·gho·*yi*·o

What grade are you in?
Σε ποια τάξη είσαι;   se pia *tak*·si *i*·se

Do you like ...?	Σου αρέσει ...;	su a·*re*·si ...
music	η μουσική	i mu·si·*ki*
school	το σχολείο	to skho·*li*·o
your teacher	ο δάσκαλός σου m	o *tha*·ska·los su
	η δασκάλα σου f	i tha·*ska*·la su

children

105

Do you like sport?
Σου αρέσουν τα σπορ;   su a·re·sun ta spor

What do you do after school?
Τι κάνεις μετά το σχολείο;   ti ka·nis me·ta to skho·li·o

Do you learn English?
Μαθαίνεις αγγλικά;   ma·the·nis ang·gli·ka

talking about children

When's the baby due?
Πότε είναι να γεννηθεί   po·te i·ne na ye·ni·thi
το μωρό;   to mo·ro

What are you going to call the baby?
Πώς θα το ονομάσεις   pos tha to·o·no·ma·sis
το μωρό;   to mo·ro

Is this your first child?
Είναι το πρώτο σου παιδί;   i·ne to pro·to su pe·thi

How many children do you have?
Πόσα παιδιά έχεις;   po·sa pe·thia e·his

What a beautiful child!
Τι όμορφο παιδί!   ti o·mor·fo pe·thi

Is it a boy or a girl?
Είναι αγόρι ή κορίτσι;   i·ne a·gho·ri i ko·rit·si

How old is he/she?
Πόσο χρονώ είναι;   po·so khro·no i·ne

Does he/she go to school?
Πηγαίνει στο σχολείο;   pi·ye·ni sto skho·li·o

What's his/her name?
Πώς τον/την λένε;   pos ton/tin le·ne

Is he/she well-behaved?
Είναι καλό παιδί;   i·ne ka·lo pe·thi

He/She has your eyes.
Έχει τα μάτια σου.   e·hi ta ma·tia su

He/She looks like you.
Σου μοιάζει.   su mia·zi

basics

βασικά

Yes.	Ναι.	ne
No.	Όχι.	o-hi
Please.	Παρακαλώ.	pa-ra-ka-lo
Thank you (very much).	Ευχαριστώ (πολύ).	ef-kha-ri-sto (po-li)
You're welcome.	Παρακαλώ.	pa-ra-ka-lo
Sorry.	Συγνώμη.	si-ghno-mi
Excuse me.	Με συγχωρείτε.	me sing-kho-ri-te
I beg your pardon?	Ορίστε;/Συγνώμη;	o-ri-ste/si-ghno-mi
Here you are.	Ορίστε.	o-ri-ste

greetings & goodbyes

χαιρετισμοί και αποχαιρετισμοί

Greeks shakes hands when greeting each other and saying goodbye. When greeting friends, male or female, they kiss each other on both cheeks.

Hello/Hi.	Γεια σου.	yia su
Good afternoon.	Χαίρετε.	he-re-te
Good morning.	Καλή μέρα.	ka-li me-ra
Good evening.	Καλή σπέρα.	ka-li spe-ra

when in greece ...

Be sure not to turn up empty-handed when you visit a Greek friend's house. It's customary to bring ένα κουτί γλυκά e-na ku-ti ghli-ka (a box of sweets) or μια ανθοδέσμη mia an-tho-thes-mi (a bunch of flowers).

meeting people

How are you?
Τι κάνεις; ti *ka*·nis

So-so.
Έτσι και έτσι. *et*·si ke *et*·si

Fine. And you?
Καλά. Εσύ; ka·*la* e·*si*

What's your name?
Πώς σε λένε; pos se *le*·ne

My name is …
Με λένε … me *le*·ne …

I'm pleased to meet you.
Χαίρω πολύ. *he*·ro po·*li*

I'd like to introduce you to … (a man).
Θα ήθελα να σε tha *i*·the·la na se
συστήσω στο … si·*sti*·so sto …

I'd like to introduce you to … (a woman).
Θα ήθελα να σε tha *i*·the·la na se
συστήσω στη … si·*sti*·so sti …

This is my …	Από εδώ …	a·*po* e·*tho* …
child	το παιδί μου	to pe·*thi* mu
colleague	ο συνάδελφός μου m	o sin·*a*·thel·*fos* mu
	η συναδέλφισσά μου f	i sin·a·*thel*·fi·sa mu
friend	ο φίλος μου m	o *fi*·los mu
	η φίλη μου f	i *fi*·li mu
husband	ο σύζυγός μου	o *si*·zi·ghos mu
partner	ο σύντροφός μου m	o *si*·dro·fos mu
(intimate)	η σύντροφός μου f	i *si*·dro·*fos* mu
wife	η σύζυγός μου	i *si*·zi·*ghos* mu

For other family members, see **family**, page 114.

See you later/Goodbye/Bye.
Αντίο. a·*di*·o

Good night.
Καλή νύχτα. ka·*li* nikh·ta

Bon voyage!
Καλό ταξίδι! ka·*lo* tak·si·*thi*

addressing people

The Greek language has two forms of the word 'you'. Use the polite form εσείς e·sis with adult strangers, elders, or those in a position of authority. In all other cases, you can use the informal form εσύ e·si. The polite form is simply the plural form of 'you', and you use it even when addressing one person. In this book we've chosen the appropriate form for the situation that the phrase is used in – it's normally the polite form unless we've marked it otherwise. For phrases where either form might be suitable, we've given both.

Also note that when speaking to older people you know well, their first name comes after Κύριε ki·ri·e (Sir), or Κυρία ki·ri·a (Madam).

Mr/Sir	Κύριε	ki·ri·e
Ms/Mrs	Κα	ki·ri·a
Miss	Δις	thes·pi·nis
Madam	Κυρία	ki·ri·a

on friendly terms

People will indicate when you can use the informal form of the word 'you' (εσύ e·si). If you want to initiate a more informal conversation with a Greek acquaintance, say:

Please speak to me in the singular.
Μίλα μου στον ενικό.   mi·la mu ston e·ni·ko

And here are a few casual terms to address your Greek pals:

friend	φίλε/φίλη m/f	fi·le/fi·li
dude	ρε μάγκα	re ma·ga
mate (Cyprus only)	κουμπάρε	ku·ba·re

meeting people

making conversation

How are you going?
Πώς πάμε;   pos *pa*·me

What's happening?
Τι γίνεται;   ti *yi*·ne·te

What's new?
Τι νέα;   ti *ne*·a

What a beautiful day!
Τι όμορφη μέρα!   ti o·mor·fi *me*·ra

Nice/Awful weather, isn't it?
Καλός/απαίσιος καιρός,   ka·*los*/a·*pe*·si·os ke·*ros*
έτσι δεν είναι;   *et*·si then i·*ne*

Where are you going?
Πού πηγαίνεις;   pu pi·*ye*·nis

What are you doing?
Τι κάνεις;   ti *ka*·nis

What's this called?
Πώς το λένε αυτό;   pos to *le*·ne af·*to*

That's (beautiful), isn't it!
Είναι (όμορφο),   *i*·ne (o·mor·fo)
έτσι δεν είναι!   *et*·si then *i*·ne

---

don't mention the war

Sometimes, discretion is the better part of conversation –
these topics are best avoided:

• anything linked to Το Μακεδονικό to ma·ke·tho·ni·*ko*
(the Macedonian issue). A northern region of Greece is
called Macedonia, and many Greek patriots object to the
Former Yugoslav Republic of Macedonia usurping 'their'
name.

• any mention of Το Κυπριακό to kip·ri·a·*ko* (the Cyprus
problem). Displaced Greek Cypriots object to the Turkish
occupation of Northern Cyprus.

Can I take a photo (of you)?
Μπορώ να (σου) πάρω
μια φωτογραφία;
bo·ro na (su) *pa*·ro
mia fo·to·ghra·*fi*·a

Do you live here?
Μένεις εδώ;
me·nis e·*tho*

Are you here on holiday?
Είσαι εδώ για διακοπές;
i·se e·*tho* yia thia·ko·*pes*

I'm here ...
Είμαι εδώ για ...
i·me e·*tho* yia ...
  for a holiday   διακοπές   thia·ko·*pes*
  on business   δουλειά   thu·*lia*
  to study   σπουδές   spu·*thes*

How long are you here for?
Πόσον καιρό θα είσαι εδώ;
po·son ke·ro tha *i*·se e·*tho*

I'm here for (four) weeks/days.
Θα είμαι εδώ για (τέσσερις)
εβδομάδες/μέρες.
tha *i*·me e·*tho* yia (*te*·se·ris)
ev·tho·*ma*·thes/*me*·res

Do you like it here?
Σου αρέσει εδώ;
su a·*re*·si e·*tho*

I love it here.
Μου αρέσει εδώ.
mu a·*re*·si e·*tho*

nationalities

Where are you from?
Από πού είσαι;
a·po pu *i*·se

I'm from ...
Είμαι από ...
i·me a·*po* ...
  Australia   την Αυστραλία   tin af·stra·*li*·a
  Canada   τον Καναδά   ton ka·na·*tha*
  Singapore   τη Σιγγαπούρη   ti si·ga·*pu*·ri

age

How old ...?	Πόσο χρονώ ...;	*po*·so khro·*no* ...
are you	είσαι	*i*·se
is your son	είναι ο γιος σου	*i*·ne o yios su
is your daughter	είναι η κόρη σου	*i*·ne i *ko*·ri su

I'm ... years old.
Είμαι ... χρονώ.   *i*·me ... khro·*no*

He/She is ... years old.
Αυτός/αυτή είναι ... χρονών.   af·*tos*/af·*ti i*·ne ... khro·*no*

I'm younger than I look.
Είμαι νεώτερος/νεώτερη   *i*·me ne·*o*·te·ros/ne·*o*·te·ri
από ό,τι φαίνομαι. m/f   a·*po o*·ti *fe*·no·me

For your age, see **numbers & amounts**, page 35.

---

local talk

Absolutely!	Απολύτως!	a·po·*li*·tos
Don't stress!	Μην κάνεις έτσι!	min *ka*·nis *et*·si
Enough!	Αρκετά!	ar·ke·*ta*
Exactly!	Ακριβώς!	a·kri·*vos*
Great!	Απίθανο!	a·*pi*·tha·no
Hey!	Εε!	*e*·e
I don't care.	Δεν με νιάζει.	then me *nia*·zi
I don't give a stuff.	Δεν δίνω δεκάρα.	then *thi*·no the·*ka*·ra
It's OK.	Είναι εντάξει.	*i*·ne e·*dak*·si
Just a minute.	Μισό λεπτό.	mi·*so* lep·*to*
Just joking.	Αστειεύομαι.	a·sti·*e*·vo·me
Maybe.	Ίσως.	*i*·sos
No problem.	Δεν υπάρχει	then i·*par*·hi
	πρόβλημα.	*prov*·li·ma
No way!	Αποκλείεται!	a·po·*kli*·e·te
Rubbish!	Σαχλαμάρες!	sakh·la·*ma*·res
Sure.	Σίγουρα.	*si*·ghu·ra
Well now ...	Λοιπόν ...	li·*pon* ...
You're wrong.	Κάνεις λάθος.	*ka*·nis *la*·thos

Dogs in Greece don't 'woof' – instead, they say ghav. Greek cows, on the other hand, seem to speak English. Here are some animal noises as they sound to Greek ears:

bird	τσίου-τσίου	*tsi*·u *tsi*·u
cat	νιάου	*nia*·ou
chick	κο-κο-κο	ko·ko·*ko*
cow	μου	mu
crow	κρα	kra
dog	γαβ	ghav
hen	κα-κα-κα	ka·ka·*ka*
rooster	κι-κιρίκου	ki·ki·*ri*·ku

occupations & studies

επαγγέλματα και σπουδές

What's your occupation?

Τι δουλειά κάνεις;   ti thu·*lia* ka·nis

I'm a …	Είμαι …	*i*·me …
businessperson	επιχειρηματίας m&f	e·pi·hi·ri·ma·*ti*·as
journalist	δημοσιογράφος m&f	thi·mo·si·o·*ghra*·fos
salesperson	πωλητής m	po·li·*tis*
	πωλήτρια f	po·*li*·tri·a
student	σπουδαστής m	spu·tha·*stis*
	σπουδάστρια f	spu·*tha*·stri·a
teacher	δάσκαλος m	*tha*·ska·los
	δασκάλα f	*tha*·ska·la
waiter	γκαρσόν m	gar·*son*
waitress	γκαρσόνα	gar·*so*·na

I work in …	Δουλεύω …	thu·*le*·vo …
administration	στη διοίκηση	sti thi·*i*·ki·si
health	στην υγεία	stin i·*yi*·a
sales &	στις πωλήσεις	stis po·*li*·sis
marketing	και μάρκετινγκ	ke *mar*·ke·ting

I'm ...	Είμαι ...	i·me ...
retired	συνταξιούχος m/f	si·dak·si·u·khos
self-	ιδιωτικός/ιδιωτική	i·thi·o·ti·kos/i·thi·o·ti·ki
employed	υπάλληλος m/f	i·pa·li·los
unemployed	άνεργος/άνεργη m/f	an·er·ghos/an·er·yi

What are you studying?	Τι σπουδάζεις;	ti spu·tha·zis

I'm studying ...	Σπουδάζω ...	spu·tha·zo ...
Greek	Ελληνικά	e·li·ni·ka
languages	γλώσσες	ghlo·ses
science	θετικές επιστήμες	the·ti·kes e·pi·sti·mes

family

οικογένεια

Are you married? (to a man)
Είσαι παντρεμένος;   i·se pa·dre·me·nos

Are you married? (to a woman)
Είσαι παντρεμένη;   i·se pa·dre·me·ni

I live with someone. (with a woman)
Ζω με κάποια.   zo me ka·pia

I live with someone. (with a man)
Ζω με κάποιον.   zo me ka·pion

I'm ...	Είμαι ...	i·me ...
married	παντρεμένος m	pa·dre·me·nos
	παντρεμένη f	pa·dre·me·ni
separated	χωρισμένος m	kho·riz·me·nos
	χωρισμένη f	kho·riz·me·ni
single	ανύπαντρος m	a·ni·pa·dros
	ανύπαντρη f	a·ni·pa·dri

Do you have a/an ...?
Έχεις ...;   e·his ...

I (don't) have a/an ...
(Δεν) έχω ...   (then) e·kho ...

aunt	θεία f	*thi*·a
brother	αδερφό m	a·ther·*fo*
brother-in-law	γαμπρό m	gha·*bro*
cousin	ξάδερφο m	ksa·ther·fo
	ξαδέρφη f	ksa·*ther*·fi
daughter	κόρη f	*ko*·ri
daughter-in-law	νύφη f	*ni*·fi
family	οικογένεια f	i·ko·ye·ni·a
father	πατέρα m	pa·*te*·ra
father-in-law	πεθερό m	pe·the·*ro*
granddaughter	εγγονή f	e·go·*ni*
grandfather	παπού m	pa·*pu*
grandmother	γιαγιά f	yia·*yia*
grandson	εγγονο m	e·go·*no*
husband	σύζυγο m	*si*·zi·gho
mother	μητέρα f	mi·*te*·ra
mother-in-law	πεθερά f	pe·the·*ra*
nephew	ανιψιό m	a·nip·*sio*
niece	ανιψιά f	a·nip·*sia*
partner (intimate)	σύντροφο m&f	*si*·dro·fo
sister	αδερφή f	a·ther·*fi*
sister-in-law	νύφη f	*ni*·fi
son	γιο m	yio
son-in-law	γαμπρό m	gha·*bro*
uncle	θείο m	*thi*·o
wife	σύζυγο f	*si*·zi·gho

farewells

Tomorrow is my last day here.

Αύριο είναι η τελευταία
μέρα μου εδώ.

av·ri·o *i*·ne i te·lef·*te*·a
me·ra mu e·*tho*

It's been great meeting you.

Είναι υπέροχο που σε
συνάντησα.

i·ne i·*pe*·ro·kho pu se
si·*na*·di·sa

If you come to (Scotland) you can stay with me.
Αν έρθεις (στη Σκωτία)   an er·this (sti sko·ti·a)
μπορείς να μείνεις μαζί μου.   bo·ris na mi·nis ma·zi mu

Here's my address.
Εδώ είναι η διεύθυνσή μου.   e·tho i·ne i thi·ef·thin·si mu

What's your address?
Ποια είναι η δική σου   pia i·ne i thi·ki su
διεύθυνση;   thi·ef·thin·si

What's your …?   Ποιο είναι το … σου;   pio i·ne to … su
Here's my …   Εδώ είναι το … μου.   e·tho i·ne to … mu
  phone number   τηλέφωνό   ti·le·fo·no
  email address   ημέιλ   i·me·il

Keep in touch!
Μη χαθούμε!   mi kha·thu·me

We'll talk again soon.
Θα τα πούμε.   tha ta pu·me

Farewell.
Γεια χαρά.   yia ha·ra

Adieu.
Αντίο.   a·di·o

---

well-wishing

Bless you!	Ο Θεός να σε φυλάει!	o the·os na se fi·la·i
Bon voyage!	Καλό ταξίδι!	ka·lo tak·si·thi
Congratulations!	Συγχαρητήρια!	sing·kha·ri·ti·ri·a
Good luck!	Καλή τύχη!	ka·li ti·hi
Happy Birthday!	Χαρούμενα γενέθλια!	kha·ru·me·na ye·ne·thli·a
Have a nice/ good time!	Καλά/Ωραία να περάσεις!	ka·la/or·e·a na pe·ra·sis
Merry Christmas!	Καλά Χριστούγεννα!	ka·la khri·stu·ye·na

If you're lost for words on a special occasion, just wish people Χρόνια πολλά! khro·nia po·la (Many years!) – this works for just about any festive occasion.

SOCIAL

common interests

κοινά ενδιαφέροντα

What do you do in your spare time?

Τι κάνεις τον ελεύθερο		ti *ka*·nis ton e·*lef*·the·ro
χρόνο σου;		*khro*·no su

Do you like ...?	Σου αρέσει ...;	su a·*re*·si ...
I (don't) like ...	(Δεν) μου αρέσει ...	(then) mu a·*re*·si ...
billiards	το μπιλιάρδο	to bi·*liar*·tho
chess	το σκάκι	to *ska*·ki
cooking	η μαγειρική	i ma·yi·ri·*ki*
dancing	ο χορός	o kho·*ros*
dominoes	το ντόμινο	to *do*·mi·no
drawing	το σχέδιο	to *she*·thi·o
gardening	η κηπουρική	i ki·pu·ri·*ki*
music	η μουσική	i mu·si·*ki*
painting	η ζωγραφική	i zo·ghra·fi·*ki*
reading	το διάβασμα	to *thia*·vaz·ma

Do you like ...?	Σου αρέσουν ...;	su a·*re*·sun ...
I (don't) like ...	(Δεν) μου αρέσουν	(then) mu a·*re*·sun
	τα ...	ta ...
films	φιλμ	film
sport	σπορ	spor

Do you like ...?	Σου αρέσει να ...;	su a·*re*·si na ...
shopping	ψωνίζεις	pso·*ni*·zis
travelling	ταξιδεύεις	tak·si·*the*·vis

I (don't) like ...	(Δεν) μου αρέσει	(then) mu a·*re*·si
	να ...	na ...
shopping	ψωνίζω	pso·*ni*·zo
travelling	ταξιδεύω	tak·si·*the*·vo

For sporting activities, see **sport**, page 141.

astrology	αστρολογία f	a·stro·lo·yi·a
backgammon	τάβλι n	tav·li
bouzouki	μπουζούκι n	bu·zu·ki
(instrument)		
current affairs	επίκαιρα θέματα n pl	e·pi·ke·ra the·ma·ta
playing cards	χαρτιά n pl	khar·tia
politics	πολιτική f	po·li·ti·ki
sirtaki	συρτάκι n	sir·ta·ki
(Greek dancing)		

music

μουσική

What music do you like?

Τι μουσική σου αρέσει; ti mu·si·ki su a·re·si

Which bands/singers do you like?

Τι μπάντες/τραγουδιστές ti ba·des/tra·ghu·thi·stes
σου αρέσουν; su a·re·sun

traditional greek dances

Many traditional dances are specific to certain regions of Greece, while others are popular throughout the country. The most common ones are the Ζεμπέκικο ze·be·ki·ko (Zembekiko), the Τσάμικο tsa·mi·ko (Tsamiko), Καλαματιανό ka·la·ma·tia·no (Kalamatiano) – also called the Συρτό sir·to (Sirto) – and the Χασαποσέρβικο ha·sa·po·ser·vi·ko (Zorba Dance).

In most of these dances, the participants hold hands to form a semicircle and, moving in repetitive steps, they follow the lead dancer in an anticlockwise direction. The one exception is the Zembekiko, which is danced by individuals – although sometimes called the 'drunken sailor's dance' for its seeming clumsiness, it actually takes great skill to perform.

Other popular dances are the Κότσαρι kot·sa·ri (Kotsari), the Κρητικός kri·ti·kos (Kritikos) and the Ποντιακός po·di·a·kos (Pontiakos).

Do you …?

dance	Χορεύεις;	kho·re·vis
go to concerts	Πηγαίνεις σε κονσέρτα;	pi·ye·nis se kon·ser·ta
listen to music	Ακούς μουσική;	a·kus mu·si·ki
play an instrument	Παίζεις κανένα όργανο;	pe·zis ka·ne·na or·gha·no
sing	Τραγουδάς;	tra·ghu·thas

blues	μπλουζ n	bluz
classical music	κλασσική μουσική f	kla·si·ki mu·si·ki
electronic music	ηλεκτρονική μουσική f	i·lek·tro·ni·ki mu·si·ki
Greek folk music	Ελληνική παραδοσιακή μουσική f	e·li·ni·ki pa·ra·tho·si·a·ki mu·si·ki
jazz	τζαζ f	tzaz
pop music	ποπ f	pop
rembetika	ρεμπέτικα n pl	re·be·ti·ka
rock music	μουσική ροκ f	mu·si·ki rok
traditional music	παραδοσιακή μουσική f	pa·ra·tho·si·a·ki mu·si·ki

Planning to go to a concert? See **tickets**, page 46, and **going out**, page 127.

cinema & theatre

I feel like going to a …	Θέλω να πάω σε …	the·lo na pa·o se …
ballet	μπαλέτο	ba·le·to
film	φιλμ	film
play	έργο	er·gho

What's showing at the cinema/theatre tonight?

Τι παίζει στο σινεμά/   ti *pe*·zi sto si·ne·*ma*/
θέατρο απόψε;   the·a·tro a·*pop*·se

Is it in English/Greek?

Είναι στα Αγγλικά/Ελληνικά;   *i*·ne sta ang·gli·*ka*/e·li·ni·*ka*

Does it have (English) subtitles?

Έχει (Αγγλικούς) υπότιτλους;   e·hi (ang·gli·*kus*) i·*po*·tit·lus

Is this seat taken?

Είναι αυτή η θέση πιασμένη;   *i*·ne af·*ti* i *the*·si piaz·*me*·ni

Have you seen …?

Έχεις δει …;   e·his thi …

Who's in it?

Ποιος παίζει σ' αυτό;   pios *pe*·zi saf·*to*

Did you like the (film)?

Σου άρεσε το (φιλμ);   su *a*·re·se to (film)

I thought it was …	Νομίζω πως ήταν …	no·*ni*·zo pos *i*·tan …
excellent	εξαιρετικό	ek·se·re·ti·*ko*
long	μεγάλο	me·*gha*·lo
OK	εντάξει	e·*dak*·si

I (don't) like …	(Δεν) μου αρέσουν …	(then) mu a·*re*·sun …
action movies	οι ταινίες δράσης	i te·*ni*·es *thra*·sis
animated films	τα φιλμ κινουμένων σχεδίων	ta film ki·nu·*me*·non she·*thi*·on
comedies	οι κωμωδίες	i ko·mo·*thi*·es
documentaries	τα ντοκυμαντέρ	ta do·ki·man·*ter*
drama	τα δραματικά έργα	ta thra·ma·ti·*ka* er·gha
Greek cinema	τα ελληνικά έργα	ta e·li·ni·*ka* er·gha
horror movies	τα έργα τρόμου	ta *er*·gha tro·mu
sci-fi	τα έργα επιστημονικής φαντασίας	ta *er*·gha e·pi·sti·mo·ni·*kis* fa·da·*si*·as
short films	τα φιλμ μικρής διάρκειας	ta film mi·*kris* thi·*ar*·ki·as
thrillers	τα θρίλερ	ta *thri*·ler
war movies	τα πολεμικά έργα	ta po·le·mi·*ka* er·gha

feelings

αισθήματα

Are you ...?	Είσαι ...;	*i*·se ...
I'm (not) ...	(Δεν) Είμαι ...	(then) *i*·me ...
annoyed	ενοχλημένος m	e·no·khli·*me*·nos
	ενοχλημένη f	e·no·khli·*me*·ni
disappointed	απογοητευμένος m	a·po·gho·i·tev·*me*·nos
	απογοητευμένη f	a·po·gho·i·tev·*me*·ni
embarrassed	αμήχανος m	a·*mi*·kha·nos
	αμήχανη f	a·*mi*·kha·ni
happy	ευτυχισμένος m	ef·ti·hiz·*me*·nos
	ευτυχισμένη f	ef·ti·hiz·*me*·ni
hot	ζεστός m	ze·*stos*
	ζεστή f	ze·*sti*
hungry	πεινασμένος m	pi·naz·*me*·nos
	πεινασμένη f	pi·naz·*me*·ni
in a hurry	βιαστικός m	via·sti·*kos*
	βιαστική f	via·sti·*ki*
sad	στενοχωρημένος m	ste·no·kho·ri·*me*·nos
	στενοχωρημένη f	ste·no·kho·ri·*me*·ni
surprised	έκπληκτος m	*ek*·plik·tos
	έκπληκτη f	*ek*·plik·ti
thirsty	διψασμένος m	thip·saz·*me*·nos
	διψασμένη f	thip·saz·*me*·ni
tired	κουρασμένος m	ku·raz·*me*·nos
	κουρασμένη f	ku·raz·*me*·ni
worried	ανύσυχος m	a·*ni*·si·khos
	ανύσυχη f	a·*ni*·si·hi
I'm (not) cold.	(Δεν) Κρυώνω.	(then) kri·o·no

If you're not feeling well, see **health**, page 195.

mixed feelings		
a little	λίγο	*li*·gho
I'm a little sad.	Είμαι λίγο στενοχωρημένος/ στενοχωρημένη. m/f	*i*·me *li*·gho ste·no·kho·ri·*me*·nos ste·no·kho·ri·*me*·ni
very	πολύ	po·*li*
I feel very lucky.	Αισθάνομαι πολύ τυχερός/τυχερή. m/f	es·*tha*·no·me po·*li* ti·he·*ros*/ti·he·*ri*
extremely	πάρα πολύ	*pa*·ra po·*li*
I'm extremely sorry.	Λυπάμαι πάρα πολύ.	li·*pa*·me *pa*·ra po·*li*

opinions

γνώμες

Did you like it?
Σου άρεσε;   su *a*·re·se

What do you think of it?
Τι νομίζεις για αυτό;   ti no·*mi*·zis yia af·*to*

I thought it was …	Νομίζω ήταν …	no·*mi*·zo *i*·tan …
It's …	Είναι …	*i*·ne …
awful	απαίσιο	a·*pe*·si·o
beautiful	όμορφο	o·mor·fo
boring	πληκτικό	plik·ti·*ko*
great	καταπληκτικό	ka·ta·plik·ti·*ko*
interesting	ενδιαφέρον	en·thia·*fe*·ron
OK	εντάξει	e·*dak*·si
strange	παράξενο	pa·*rak*·se·no
too expensive	πάρα πολύ ακριβό	*pa*·ra po·*li* a·kri·*vo*

politics & social issues

πολιτική και κοινωνικά θέματα

Who do you vote for?	Ποιον ψηφίζεις;	pion psi·fi·zis
I support the ... party.	Εγώ υποστηρίζω το κόμμα ...	e·gho i·po·sti·ri·zo to ko·ma ...
I'm a member of the ... party.	Είμαι μέλος του κόμματος ...	i·me me·los tu ko·ma·tos ...
coalition	συνασπισμός	si·nas·piz·mos
communist	κομμουνιστικό	ko·mu·ni·sti·ko
conservative	συντηρητικό	si·di·ri·ti·ko
democratic	δημοκρατικό	thi·mo·kra·ti·ko
green	οικολογικό	i·ko·lo·yi·ko
liberal	φιλελεύθεροι	fil·e·lef·the·ri
republican	ρεπουμπλικανικό	re·pu·bli·ka·ni·ko
social	κοινωνικό	ki·no·ni·ko
democratic	δημοκρατικό	thi·mo·kra·ti·ko
socialist	σοσιαλιστικό	so·si·a·li·sti·ko

Did you hear about ...?		
Άκουσες για ...;		a·ku·ses yia ...

Do you agree with it?
Συμφωνείς με αυτό ...;   sim·fo·nis me af·to ...

I (don't) agree with ...
(Δεν) Συμφωνώ με ...   (then) sim·fo·no me ...

How do people feel about ...?
Πώς αισθάνονται οι   pos es·tha·no·de i
άνθρωποι για ...;   an·thro·pi yia ...

How can we support ...?
Πώς μπορούμε να   pos bo·ru·me na
υποστηρίξουμε ...;   i·po·sti·rik·su·me ...

How can we protest against ...?
Πώς μπορούμε να   pos bo·ru·me na
διαμαρτυρηθούμε για ...;   thi·a·mar·ti·ri·thu·me yia ...

Although it may sound like 'no', remember that ναι ne really means 'yes'.

abortion	εκτρώσεις f	ek·*tro*·sis
animal rights	δικαιώματα	thi·ke·o·ma·ta
	των ζώων n	ton *zo*·on
civil servants	δημοσίους	tus thi·mo·*si*·us
	υπαλλήλους m	i·pa·*li*·lus
crime	έγκλημα n	*eng*·li·ma
democracy	δημοκρατία f	thi·mo·kra·*ti*·a
diaspora	διασπορά f	thi·a·spo·*ra*
discrimination	διακρίσεις f	thi·a·*kri*·sis
drugs	ναρκωτικά n	nar·ko·ti·*ka*
the economy	οικονομία f	i·ko·no·*mi*·a
education	εκπαίδευση f	ek·*pe*·thef·si
the environment	περιβάλλον n	pe·ri·*va*·lon
equal opportunity	ίσες ευκαιρίες f	*i*·ses ef·ke·*ri*·es
euthanasia	ευθανασία f	ef·tha·na·*si*·a
the European	Ευρωπαϊκή	ev·ro·pa·i·*ki*
Union	Ένωση f	*e*·no·si
gay rights	δικαιώματα	thi·ke·o·ma·ta
	των γκέι n	ton *ge*·i
globalisation	παγκοσμιοποίηση f	pa·goz·mi·o·*pi*·i·si
human rights	ανθρώπινα	an·*thro*·pi·na
	δικαιώματα n	thi·ke·o·ma·ta
immigration	μετανάστευση f	me·ta·*na*·stef·si
inequality	ανισότητα f	a·ni·*so*·ti·ta
inflation	πληθωρισμό m	pli·tho·riz·*mo*
the military junta	στρατιωτική	stra·ti·o·ti·*ki*
	χούντα f	*khu*·da
the Macedonian	Μακεδονικό	ma·ke·tho·ni·*ko*
question	ζήτημα n	*zi*·ti·ma
the monarchy	μοναρχία f	mo·nar·*hi*·a
NATO	ΝΑΤΟ n	*na*·to
parliament	κοινοβούλιο n	ki·no·*vu*·li·o

the partition of Cyprus	διχοτόμηση της Κύπρου f	thi·kho·*to*·mi·si tis *ki*·pru
party politics	πολιτική του κόμματος f	po·li·ti·*ki* tu *ko*·ma·tos
privatisation	ιδιοτικοποίηση f	i·thi·o·ti·ko·*pi*·i·si
poverty	φτώχεια f	*fto*·hia
racism	ρατσισμό n	rat·siz·*mo*
refugees	πρόσφυγες m	*pros*·fi·yes
relations with Turkey	σχέσεις με την Τουρκία f	*she*·sis me tin tur·*ki*·a
sexism	σεξισμό m	sek·siz·*mo*
social welfare	κοινωνική πρόνοια f	ki·no·ni·*ki pro*·ni·a
strikes	απεργίες f	ap·er·*yi*·es
terrorism	τρομοκρατία f	tro·mo·kra·*ti*·a
traffic restrictions	περιορισμό της κυκλοφορίας m	pe·ri·o·riz·*mo* tis ki·klo·fo·*ri*·as
unemployment	ανεργία f	an·er·*yi*·a
US military bases	στρατιωτικές βάσεις των ΗΠΑ f	stra·ti·o·ti·*kes va*·sis ton *i*·pa
the war in (the Balkans)	πολέμους (στα Βαλκάνια) m	po·*le*·mus (sta val·*ka*·ni·a)

the environment

το περιβάλλον

Is there a … problem here?
Υπάρχει κλάποιο πρόβλημα εδώ με …;
i·*par*·hi ka·pio *pro*·vli·ma e·*tho* me …

What should be done about …?
Τι θα πρέπει να γίνει με …;
ti tha *pre*·pi na *yi*·ni me …

beach cleaning	καθαρισμό	ka·tha·riz·mo
	των ακτών m	ton ak·ton
conservation	προστασία	pro·sta·si·a
	του περιβάλλοντος f	tu pe·ri·va·lo·dos
deforestation	αποδάσωση f	a·po·tha·so·si
drought	ανομβρία f	a·nom·vri·a
earthquakes	σεισμούς m	siz·mus
ecosystem	οικοσύστημα n	i·ko·si·sti·ma
endangered	είδη υπό	i·thi i·po
species	εξαφάνιση n	ek·sa·fa·ni·si
erosion	διάβρωση f	thi·av·ro·si
forest fires	φωτιές στα δάση f	fo·tyes sta tha·si
genetically	γενετικά	ye·ne·ti·ka
modified food	μεταλλαγμένο	me·ta·lagh·me·no
	φαγητό n	fa·yi·to
hunting	κυνήγι n	ki·ni·yi
hydroelectricity	υδροηλεκτρισμό m	i·thro·i·lek·triz·mo
irrigation	άρδευση f	ar·thef·si
marine	θαλάσσια	tha·la·si·a
reserves	διαφύλαξη f	thi·a·fi·lak·si
national parks	εθνικά πάρκα n	eth·ni·ka par·ka
nuclear energy	πυρηνική ενέργεια f	pi·ri·ni·ki e·ner·yi·a
nuclear testing	πυρηνικές δοκιμές f	pi·ri·ni·kes tho·ki·mes
ozone layer	στρώμα του όζοντος n	stro·ma tu o·zo·dos
pesticides	φυτοφάρμακα n	fi·to·far·ma·ka
pollution	μόλυνση f	mo·lin·si
recycling	πρόγραμμα	pro·ghra·ma
program	ανκύκλωσης n	a·na·ki·klo·sis
smog	νέφος n	ne·fos
toxic waste	τοξικά απόβλητα n	tok·si·ka a·pov·li·ta
urban	αστική	a·sti·ki
encroachment	εξάπλωση f	ek·sa·plo·si
water supply	παροχή ύδατος f	pa·ro·hi i·tha·tos
Is this a	Είναι αυτό	i·ne af·to
protected ...?	προστατευόμενο ...;	pro·sta·te·vo·me·no
forest	δάσος	tha·sos
park	πάρκο	par·ko
species	είδος	i·thos

SOCIAL

where to go

πού να πάμε

What's there to do in the evenings?

	Τι μπορούμε να κάνουμε το βράδι;	ti bo·*ru*·me na *ka*·nu·me to *vra*·thi

What's on …?	Τι γίνεται …;	ti *yi*·ne·te …
locally	εδώ γύρω	e·*tho yi*·ro
this weekend	αυτό το Σαββατοκύριακο	af·*to* to sa·va·to·*ki*·ria·ko
today	σήμερα	*si*·me·ra
tonight	απόψε	a·*pop*·se
Where can I find …?	Πού μπορώ να βρω …;	pu bo·*ro* na vro …
a *bouzouki* place (venue with live Greek music)	ταβέρνα με μπουζούκια	ta·*ver*·na me bu·*zu*·kia
clubs	κλαμπ	klab
gay venues	Χώρους συνάντησης για γκέη	*kho*·rus si·*na*·di·sis yia *ge*·i
an open-air cinema	θερινό κινηματογράφο	the·ri·*no* ki·ni·ma·to·*ghra*·fo
places to eat	εστιατόρια	e·sti·a·*to*·ri·a
pubs	μπυραρίες	bi·ra·*ri*·es
Is there a local … guide?	Υπάρχει τοπικός οδηγός για …;	i·*par*·hi to·pi·*kos* o·thi·*ghos* yia …
entertainment	διασκεδάσεις	thias·ke·*tha*·sis
film	φιλμ	film
gay	γκέη	*ge*·i
music	μουσική	mu·si·*ki*

I feel like going to a ...	Έχω όρεξη να πάω σε ...	e·kho o·rek·si na pa·o se ...
ballet	μπαλέτο	ba·*le*·to
bar	μπαρ	bar
café	καφενείο	ka·fe·*ni*·o
concert	κονσέρτο	kon·*ser*·to
film	φιλμ	film
karaoke bar	καραόκι μπαρ	ka·ra·o·ki bar
nightclub	νυχτερινό κέντρο	nikh·te·ri·*no ke*·dro
party	πάρτυ	*par*·ti
performance	θέαμα	the·*a*·ma
play	έργο	*er*·gho
pub	μπυραρία	bi·ra·*ri*·a
rebetika club	κέντρο με ρεμπέτικα	*ke*·dro me re·*be*·ti·ka
restaurant	εστιατόριο	e·sti·a·*to*·ri·o
sports match	αθλητικό παιγνίδι	ath·li·ti·*ko* pegh·*ni*·thi

For more on bars and drinks, see **romance**, page 131, and **eating out**, pages 166–170.

invitations

προσκλήσεις

What are you doing ...?	Τι κάνεις ...;	ti *ka*·nis ...
now	τώρα	*to*·ra
this weekend	το Σαββατοκύριακο	to sa·va·to·*ki*·ria·ko
tonight	απόψε	a·*pop*·se

Do you know a good restaurant?
Ξέρεις κανένα καλό εστιατόριο;   *kse*·ris ka·*ne*·na ka·*lo* e·sti·a·*to*·ri·o

My round.
Η σειρά μου.   i si·*ra* mu

We're having a party.
Έχουμε πάρτι.   e·*khu*·me *par*·ti

Would you like to go (for a) …?	Θα ήθελες να πας …;	tha *i*·the·les na pas …
coffee	για καφέ	yia ka·*fe*
dancing	για χορό	yia kho·*ro*
drink	για ποτό	yia po·*to*
meal	για φαγητό	yia fa·yi·*to*
out somewhere	κάπου έξω	*ka*·pu *ek*·so
walk	βόλτα	*vol*·ta

responding to invitations

Sure!
Μάλιστα! — *ma*·li·sta

Yes, I'd love to.
Ναι, θα ήθελα πολύ. — ne tha *i*·the·la po·*li*

That's very kind of you.
Πολύ ευγενικό εκ μέρους σου. — po·*li* ev·ye·ni·*ko* ek *me*·rus su

No, I'm afraid I can't.
Όχι, φοβάμαι πως δεν . μπορώ — *o*·hi fo·*va*·me pos then bo·*ro*

What about tomorrow?
Τι θα έλεγες για αύριο; — ti tha e·le·yes yia *av*·ri·o

Where shall we go?
Πού θα πάμε; — pu tha *pa*·me

arranging to meet

What time will we meet?
Τι ώρα θα συναντηθούμε; — ti *o*·ra tha si·na·di·*thu*·me

Where will we meet?
Πού θα συναντηθούμε; — pu tha si·na·di·*thu*·me

Let's meet at ...	Ας	as
	συναντηθούμε ...	si·na·di·*thu*·me ...
(eight) o'clock	στις (οχτώ)	stis (okh·*to*)
the entrance	στην είσοδο	stin *i*·so·tho

I'll pick you up.
Θα σε πάρω εγώ. tha se *pa*·ro e·*gho*

Are you ready?
Είσαι έτοιμος/έτοιμη; m/f *i*·se e·ti·mos/e·ti·mi

I'm ready.
Είμαι έτοιμος/έτοιμη. m/f *i*·me e·ti·mos/e·ti·mi

Where will you be?
Πού θα είσαι; pu tha *i*·se

If I'm not there by (nine), don't wait for me.
Αν δεν είμαι εκεί μέχρι an then *i*·me e·*ki* me·khri
(τις εννέα), μή με περιμένεις. (tis e·*ne*·a) mi me pe·ri·*me*·mis

I'm looking forward to it.
Το περιμένω πώς και πώς. to pe·ri·*me*·no pos ke pos

OK!	Εντάξει!	e·*dak*·si
I'll see you then.	Θα σε δω τότε.	tha se tho *to*·te
Sorry I'm late.	Συγνώμη που	sigh·*no*·mi pu
	άργησα.	*ar*·yi·sa

drugs

ναρκωτικά

Do you have a light?
Έχεις φωτιά; *e*·his fo·*tia*

Do you want to have a smoke?
Θέλεις να καπνίσεις; *the*·lis na kap·*ni*·sis

I don't take drugs.
Δεν παίρνω ναρκωτικά. then *per*·no nar·ko·ti·*ka*

I take ... occasionally.
Παίρνω ... καμιά φορά. *per*·no ... ka·*mia* fo·*ra*

asking someone out

ζητώντας να βγείτε έξω

Where would you like to go (tonight)?
Πού θα ήθελες να πάμε (απόψε); — pu tha *the*·lis na *pa*·me (a·*pop*·se)

Would you like to do something (tomorrow)?
Θα ήθελες να κάνουμε κάτι (αύριο); — tha i·the·les na *ka*·nu·me *ka*·ti (av·ri·o)

Yes, I'd love to.
Ναι, θα το ήθελα πολύ. — ne tha to i·the·la po·*li*

Sorry, I can't.
Συγνώμη, δεν μπορώ. — sigh·*no*·mi then bo·*ro*

pick-up lines

χώροι γνωριμίας

Would you like a drink?
Θα ήθελες ένα ποτό; — tha i·the·les *e*·na po·*to*

You look like someone I know. (to a man)
Μοιάζεις με κάποιον που ξέρω. — *mia*·zis me *ka*·pion pu *kse*·ro

You look like someone I know. (to a woman)
Μοιάζεις με κάποια που ξέρω. — *mia*·zis me *ka*·pia pu *kse*·ro

You're a fantastic dancer. (to a man)
Είσαι απίθανος χορευτής. — i·se a·*pi*·tha·nos kho·*ref*·tis

You're a fantastic dancer. (to a woman)
Είσαι απίθανη χορεύτρια. — i·se a·*pi*·tha·ni kho·*ref*·tria

Can I ...?	Μπορώ να ...;	bo·ro na ...
dance with you	χορέψω μαζί σου	kho·rep·so ma·zi su
sit here	καθίσω εδώ	ka·thi·so e·tho
take you home	σε πάρω στο σπίτι	se pa·ro sto spi·ti

rejections

No, thank you.
Όχι, ευχαριστώ.   o·hi ef·kha·ri·sto

I'd rather not.
Νομίζω όχι.   no·mi·zo o·hi

I'm here with my boyfriend.
Είμαι εδώ με τον φίλο μου.   i·me e·tho me ton fi·lo mu

I'm here with my girlfriend.
Είμαι εδώ με την φίλη μου.   i·me e·tho me tin fi·li mu

Excuse me, I have to go now.
Συγνώμη, πρέπει να   sigh·no·mi pre·pi na
πηγαίνω τώρα.   pi·ye·no to·ra

Leave me alone! (a man)
Άσε με ήσυχο!   a·se me i·si·kho

Leave me alone! (a woman)
Άσε με ήσυχη!   a·se me i·si·khi

Piss off!
Άντε από δω, ρε!   a·de a·po tho re

He's a babe.
Είναι κούκλος.   *i*·ne *ku*·klos

She's a babe.
Είναι κούκλα.   *i*·ne *ku*·kla

He's hot.
Είναι θερμός.   *i*·ne ther·*mos*

She's hot.
Είναι θερμή.   *i*·ne ther·*mi*

getting closer

πλησιάζοντας πιο κοντά

I like you very much.
Μου αρέσεις πολύ.   mu a·*re*·sis po·*li*

You're great.
Είσαι θαύμα.   *i*·se *thav*·ma

Can I kiss you?
Μπορώ να σε φιλήσω;   bo·*ro* na se fi·*li*·so

Do you want to come inside for a while?
Θέλεις να έρθεις μέσα,   *the*·lis na er·this *me*·sa
για λίγο;   yia *li*·gho

Do you want a massage?
Θέλεις ένα μασάζ;   *the*·lis e·na ma·*saz*

Can I stay over?
Μπορώ να μείνω τη νύχτα;   bo·*ro* na *mi*·no ti *nikh*·ta

romance

Kiss me.	Φίλα με.	*fi*·la me
I want you.	Σε θέλω.	se *the*·lo
Touch me here.	Πιάσε με εδώ.	*pia*·se me e·*tho*
Let's go to bed.	Πάμε στο κρεβάτι.	*pa*·me sto kre·*va*·ti

Do you like this?
Σου αρέσει αυτό;   su a·*re*·si af·*to*

I (don't) like that.
(Δεν) Μου αρέσει αυτό.   (ṭhen) mu a·*re*·si af·*to*

I think we should stop now.
Νομίζω πως πρέπει να   no·*mi*·zo pos *pre*·pi na
σταματήσουμε τώρα.   sta·ma·*ti*·su·me *to*·ra

Do you have a condom?
Έχεις προφυλακτικό;   *e*·his pro·fi·lak·ti·*ko*

Let's use a condom.
Ας χρησιμοποιήσουμε   as khri·si·mo·pi·*i*·su·me
προφυλακτικό.   pro·fi·lak·ti·*ko*

I won't do it without protection.
Δεν το κάνω χωρίς   ṭhen to *ka*·no kho·*ris*
προφύλαξη.   pro·*fi*·lak·si

It's my first time.
Είναι η πρώτη μου φορά.   *i*·ne i *pro*·ti mu fo·*ra*

It helps to have a sense of humour.
Βοηθάει να έχεις την   vo·i·*tha*·i na *e*·his tin
αίσθηση του χιούμορ.   *es*·thi·si tu *hiu*·mor

Oh my god!
Ω, θεέ μου!   o the·*e* mu

That's great.
Είναι απίθανο.   *i*·ne a·*pi*·tha·no

Easy tiger! (to a man)
σιγά ρε γόη!   si·*gha* re *gho*·i

Easy tiger! (to a woman)
σιγά ρε γόισσα!   si·*gha* re *gho*·i·sa

That was …	Ήταν …	*i*·tan …
amazing	καταπληκτικό	ka·ta·plik·ti·*ko*
romantic	ρομαντικό	ro·ma·di·*ko*
wild	άγριο	*a*·ghri·o

love

αγάπη

I think we're good together.
Νομίζω ταιριάζουμε.   no·*mi*·zo te·*ria*·zu·me

I love you.
Σ'αγαπώ.   sa·gha·*po*

Will you …?	Θα …;	tha …
go out with me	έρθεις έξω	er·this ek·so
	μαζί μου	ma·*zi* mu
marry me	με παντρευτείς	me pa·dref·*tis*
meet my	συναντήσεις τους	si·na·*di*·sis tus
parents	γονείς μου	gho·*nis* mu

sweet talk

my baby	μωρό μου	mo·*ro* mu
my darling	μάνα μου	*ma*·na mu
my doll	κουκλί μου	ku·*kli* mu
my hunk	τζουτζούκο μου	tzu·*tzu*·ko mu
my soul	ψυχούλα μου	psi·*hu*·la mu
my treasure	χρυσό μου	khri·*so* mu
sweetheart	καρδούλα μου	kar·*thu*·la mu

problems

Are you seeing someone else? (to a woman)
βλέπεις κάποιον άλλο;   e·his ka·pion a·lon

Are you seeing someone else? (to a man)
βλέπεις κάποια άλλη;   e·his ka·pia a·li

He/She is just a friend.
Είναι απλά φίλος/φίλη.   i·ne a·pla fi·los/fi·li

You're just using me for sex.
Με θέλεις μόνο για το σεξ.   me the·lis mo·no yia to seks

I never want to see you again.
Δεν θέλω να σε ξαναδώ.   then the·lo na se ksa·na·tho

I don't think it's working out.
Δεν νομίζω ότι δουλεύει.   then no·mi·zo o·ti thu·le·vi

We'll work it out.
Θα τα βρούμε.   tha ta vru·me

leaving

I have to leave (tomorrow).
Πρέπει να φύγω (αύριο).   pre·pi na fi·gho (av·ri·o)

I'll ...	Θα ...	tha ...
keep in touch	βρίσκομαι σε επαφή	vris·ko·me se e·pa·fi
miss you	μου λείψεις	mu lip·sis
visit you	σε επισκεφτώ	se e·pis·kef·to

it's a tragedy

The poet Thespis (Θέσπις thes·pis) was one of the founders of the theatrical tragedy genre during the 6th century BC. His name survives in the English word 'Thespian', meaning 'dramatic' or 'relating to drama or theatre'.

SOCIAL

religion

θρησκεία

What's your religion?
Ποια είναι η θρησκεία σου;   pia *i*·ne i thris·*ki*·a su

I'm not religious.
Δεν είμαι θρήσκος.   then *i*·me *thris*·kos

I'm ...	Είμαι ...	*i*·me ...
agnostic	αγνωστικιστής m	agh·no·sti·ki·*stis*
	αγνωστικίστρια f	agh·no·sti·*ki*·stri·a
Buddhist	Βουδιστής m	vu·țhi·*stis*
	Βουδίστρια f	vu·*țhi*·stri·a
Catholic	Καθολικός m	ka·tho·li·*kos*
	Καθολική f	ka·tho·li·*ki*
Christian	Χριστιανός m	khri·stia·*nos*
	Χριστιανή f	khri·stia·*ni*
Hindu	Ινδουιστής m	in·țhu·i·*stis*
	Ινδουίστρια f	in·țhu·i·*stri*·a
Jewish	Ιουδαίος m	i·u·*the*·os
	Ιουδαία f	i·u·*the*·a
Muslim	Μουσουλμάνος m	mu·sul·*ma*·nos
	Μουσουλμάνα f	mu·sul·*ma*·na
Orthodox	Ορθόδοξος m	or·*tho*·thok·sos
	Ορθόδοξη f	or·*tho*·thok·si

I (don't) believe in ...	(Δεν) Πιστευω ...	(țhen) pi·*ste*·vo ...
astrology	στην αστρολογία	stin a·stro·lo·*yi*·a
fate	στη μοίρα	sti *mi*·ra
God	στο Θεό	sto the·*o*

Can I ... here?	Μπορώ να ... εδώ;	bo·ro na ... e·tho
Where can I ...?	Πού μπορώ να ...;	pu bo·ro na ...
attend mass	παρακολουθήσω	pa·ra·ko·lu·thi·so
	τη λειτουργία	ti li·tur·yi·a
attend a	παρακολουθήσω	pa·ra·ko·lu·thi·so
service	την ακολουθία	tin a·ko·lu·thi·a
pray	προσευχηθώ	pro·sef·hi·tho
worship	προσκυνήσω	pros·ki·ni·so

cultural differences

πολιτιστικές διαφορές

Is this a local or national custom?
Είναι αυτό τοπικό ή
εθνικό έθιμο;
i·ne af·*to* to·pi·*ko* i
eth·ni·*ko* e·thi·mo

I'm not used to this.
Δεν είμαι συνηθισμένος
σ'αυτό.
then *i*·me si·ni·thiz·*me*·nos
saf·*to*

I'd rather not join in.
Θα προτιμούσα να μη
λάβω μέρος.
tha pro·ti·*mu*·sa na mi
la·vo me·ros

I'll try it.
Θα το δοκιμάσω.
tha to tho·ki·*ma*·so

I didn't mean to do anything wrong.
Δεν ήθελα να κάμω κάτι
που δεν έπρεπε.
then *i*·the·la na *ka*·mo *ka*·ti
pu then e·pre·pe

I didn't mean to say anything wrong.
Δεν ήθελα πω κάτι
που δεν έπρεπε.
then *i*·the·la po *ka*·ti
pu then e·pre·pe

I don't want to offend you.
Δεν θέλω να σε προσβάλω.
then *the*·lo na se proz·*va*·lo

I'm sorry, it's against my ...
Συγνώμη, είναι
αντίθετο με ... μου.
sigh·*no*·mi *i*·ne
a·*di*·the·to me ... mu
beliefs την πίστη tin *pi*·sti
religion τη θρησκεία ti thris·*ki*·a

When's the museum open?

Πότε είναι ανοιχτό το μουσείο; · · · · · · · · po·te i·ne a·nikh·to to mu·si·o

When's the gallery open?

Πότε είναι ανοιχτή · · · · · · · · · · · · · · · · · po·te i·ne a·nikh·ti
η πινακοθήκη; · i pi·na·ko·thi·ki

What kind of art are you interested in?

Τι είδους τέχνη σε ενδιαφέρει; · · · · · · · · · ti i·thus tekh·ni se en·thia·fe·ri

I'm interested in ...

Με ενδιαφέρει ... · · · · · · · · · · · · · · · · · · me en·thia·fe·ri ...

What's in the collection?

Τι υπάρχει στη συλλογή; · · · · · · · · · · · · · ti i·par·hi sti si·lo·yi

It's an exhibition of ...

Είναι μια έκθεση ... · · · · · · · · · · · · · · · · i·ne mia ek·the·si ...

Where are the exhibits from (Knossos)?

Πού είναι τα εκθέματα · · · · · · · · · · · · · · pu i·ne ta ek·the·ma·ta
από την (Κνωσσό); · · · · · · · · · · · · · · · · · a·po tin (kno·so)

What style is this?

Τι στυλ είναι αυτό; · · · · · · · · · · · · · · · · ti stil i·ne af·to

Is it an original or a copy?

Είναι αυθεντικό ή αντίγραφο; · · · · · · · · · i·ne af·the·di·ko i a·di·ghra·fo

What do you think of ...?

Πώς σου φαίνεται ...; · · · · · · · · · · · · · · · pos su fe·ne·te ...

I like the works of ...

Μου αρέσουν τα έργα ... · · · · · · · · · · · · mu a·re·sun ta er·gha

It reminds me of ...

Μου θυμίζει ... · mu thi·mi·zi ...

Byzantine	Βυζαντινός	vi·za·di·nos
classical	κλασσικός	kla·si·kos
Hellenistic	Ελληνιστικός	e·li·ni·sti·kos
modern	μοντέρνος	mo·der·nos
Roman	Ρωμαϊκός	ro·ma·i·kos

... civilisation	... πολιτισμός m	... po·li·tiz·*mos*
Cycladic	Κυκλαδικός	ki·kla·thi·*kos*
Minoan	Μινωικός	mi·no·i·*kos*
Mycenean	Μυκηναϊκός	mi·ki·ma·i·*kos*
... style	... ρυθμός m	... rith·*mos*
Corinthian	Κορινθιακός	ko·rin·thi·a·*kos*
Doric	Δωρικός	tho·ri·*kos*
Ionic	Ιωνικός	i·o·ni·*kos*
architecture	αρχιτεκτονική f	ar·hi·tek·to·ni·*ki*
artwork	καλλιτέχνημα n	ka·li·*tekh*·ni·ma
column	κολόνα f	ko·*lo*·na
curator	έφορος μουσείου m	e·fo·ros mu·*si*·u
decorative arts	διακοσμητικές τέχνες f pl	thi·a·koz·mi·ti·*kes* *tekh*·nes
etching	χαλκογραφία f	khal·ko·ghra·*fi*·a
exhibit	έκθεση f	*ek*·the·si
exhibition hall	αίθουσα έκθεσης f	e·thu·sa *ek*·the·sis
fresco	φρέσκο n	*fres*·ko
metalwork	μεταλλικά αντικείμενα n pl	me·ta·li·*ka* a·di·*ki*·me·na
mosaic	μωσαϊκό n	mo·sa·i·*ko*
painter	ζωγράφος m	zo·*ghra*·fos
painting (artwork)	πίνακας m	*pi*·na·kas
painting (the art)	ζωγραφική f	zo·ghra·fi·*ki*
period	περίοδος f	pe·*ri*·o·thos
permanent collection	μόνιμη συλλογή f	*mo*·ni·mi si·lo·*yi*
print	αντίγραφο n	a·*di*·ghra·fo
sculptor	γλύπτης m	*ghlip*·tis
sculpture	γλυπτική f	ghlip·ti·*ki*
shield	ασπίδα f	a·*spi*·tha
spear	δόρυ n	*tho*·ri
sword	σπαθί n	spa·*thi*
statue	άγαλμα n	*a*·ghal·ma
terracotta pot	αγγείο τερακότα n	a·*gi*·o te·ra·*ko*·ta
tunic	χιτώνας m	hi·*to*·nas
vessel	αγγείο n	a·*gi*·o

sporting interests

αθλητικά ενδιφέροντα

What sport do you follow/play?
Τι σπορ ακολουθείς/παίζεις; ti spor a·ko·lu·*this/pe*·zis

I follow (basketball).
Παρακολουθώ (μπάσκετ). pa·ra·ko·lu·*tho (ba*·sket)

I play (football).
Παίζω (ποδόσφαιρο). *pe*·zo (po·*thos*·fe·ro)

I do ...	Κάνω ...	*ka*·no ...
athletics	αθλήματα	ath·*li*·ma·ta
hiking	πεζοπορία	pe·zo·po·*ri*·a
sailing	ιστιοπλοΐα	i·sti·o·plo·*i*·a
scuba diving	υπόγειες	i·*po*·yi·es
	καταδύσεις	ka·ta·*thi*·sis
sailboarding	γουιντσέρφινγκ	ghu·id·*ser*·fing
water-skiing	θαλάσσιο σκι	tha·*la*·si·o ski

For more sports, see the **dictionary**.

---

top sport

soccer	ποδόσφαιρο n	po·*thos*·fe·ro
	ευρωπαϊκό	ev·ro·pa·i·ko
basketball	μπάσκετ n	*bas*·ket
volleyball	βόλεϊ n	*vo*·le·i
gymnastics	κλασσικός	kla·si·*kos*
	αθλητισμός m	ath·li·tiz·*mos*
swimming	κολύμπι n	ko·*lim*·bi

To exercise you brain, try Greece's favourite nonphysical pastime:

backgammon	τάβλι n	*tav*·li

I ...	Εγώ ...	e·gho ...
cycle	κάνω ποδήλατο	ka·no po·thi·la·to
run	τρέχω	tre·kho
walk	βαδίζω	va·thi·zo

Do you like (football)?
Σου αρέσει (το ποδόσφαιρο);   su a·re·si (to po·thos·fe·ro)

Yes, very much.
Ναι, πάρα πολύ.   ne pa·ra po·li

Not really.
Όχι.   o·hi

I like watching it.
Μου αρέσει να το κοιτάζω.   mu a·re·si na to ki·ta·zo

What's your favourite team?
Ποια ομάδα υποστηρίζεις;   pia o·ma·tha i·po·sti·ri·zis

Who's your favourite sportsperson?
Ποιος αθλητής σου αρέσει;   pios ath·li·tis su a·re·si

going to a game

πηγαίνοντας σε ένα παιγνίδι

Would you like to go to a game?
Θα ήθελες να πας σε   tha i·the·les na pas se
ένα παιγνίδι;   e·na pegh·ni·thi

Who are you supporting?
Ποιον υποστηρίζεις;   pion i·po·sti·ri·zis

Who's playing/winning?
Ποιος παίζει/κερδίζει;   pios pe·zi/ker·thi·zi

scoring

What's the score?	Ποιο είναι το σκορ;	pio i·ne to skor
draw/even	ισοπαλία	i·so·pa·li·a
love/zero/nil	μηδέν	mi·then
match-point	πόντος για	po·dos yia
	παιγνίδι	pegh·ni·thi

What a ...!	Τι ...!	ti ...
goal	γκολ	gol
hit	χτύπημα	*khti*·pi·ma
kick	κλωτσιά	klot·*sia*
pass	πάσα	*pa*·sa
performance	απόδοση	a·*po*·tho·si

That was a ... game!	Ήταν ... παιγνίδι!	*i*·tan ... pegh·*ni*·thi
bad	άσχημο	*a*·shi·mo
boring	πληκτικό	plik·ti·*ko*
great	υπέροχο	i·*pe*·ro·kho

playing sport

παίζοντας σπορ

Do you want to play?
Θέλεις να παίξεις; — *the*·lis na *pek*·sis

Can I join in?
Να παίξω και εγώ; — na *pek*·so ke e·*gho*

That would be great.
Αυτό θα ήταν υπέροχο. — af·*to* tha *i*·tan i·*pe*·ro·kho

I can't.
Δεν μπορώ. — then bo·*ro*

I have an injury.
Έχω ένα τραύμα. — *e*·kho *e*·na *trav*·ma

Your/My point.
Δικός σου/μου πόντος. — thi·*kos* su/mu *po*·dos

Kick it to me!
κλώτσα την σε μένα! *klot·*sa tin se *me·*na

Pass it to me!
ρίξ'την σε μένα! *riks·*tin se *me·*na

You're a good player.
Είσαι καλός παίχτης. *i·*se ka·*los pekh·*tis

Thanks for the game.
Ευχαριστώ για το παιγνίδι. ef·kha·ri·*sto* yia to pegh·*ni·*thi

Where's a good place to …?	Πού είναι ένα καλό μέρος για να … κανείς;	pu *i·*ne *e·*na ka·*lo me·*ros yia na … ka·*nis*
fish	ψαρέψει	psa·*rep·*si
go horse riding	κάμει ιππασία	*ka·*mi i·pa·*si·*a
run	τρέξει	*trek·*si
snorkel	κάμει κατάδυση	*ka·*mi ka·*ta·*thi·si
surf	σερφάρει	ser·*fa·*ri

Where's the nearest ...?	Πού είναι το πιο κοντινό ...;	pu *i*·ne to pio ko·*di*·no ...
golf course	γήπεδο του γκολφ	*yi*·pe·ţho tu golf
gym	γυμναστήριο	yim·na·*sti*·ri·o
tennis court	γήπεδο του τένις	*yi*·pe·ţho tu *te*·nis

Where's the nearest swimming pool?

Πού είναι η πιο κοντινή πισίνα; — pu *i*·ne i pio ko·di·*ni* pi·*si*·na

Do I have to be a member to attend?

Πρέπει να είμαι μέλος — *pre*·pi na *i*·me *me*·los
για να πάω; — yia na *pa*·o

Is there a women-only session?

Υπάρχει ορισμένη ώρα — i·*par*·hi o·riz·*me*·ni *o*·ra
μόνο για γυναίκες; — *mo*·no yia yi·*ne*·kes

Can I book a lesson?

Μπορώ να κλείσω ένα — bo·*ro* na *kli*·so *e*·na
μάθημα; — *ma*·thi·ma

Where are the changing rooms?

Πού είναι τα αποδυτήρια; — pu *i*·ne ta a·po·ţhi·*ti*·ri·a

What's the charge per ...?	Πόσο κοστίζει ...;	*po*·so ko·*sti*·zi ...
day	την ημέρα	tin i·*me*·ra
game	το παιγνίδι	to pegh·*ni*·ţhi
hour	την ώρα	tin *o*·ra
visit	την επίσκεψη	tin e·*pis*·kep·si

Can I hire a ...?	Μπορώ να νοικιάσω ...;	bo·*ro* na ni·*kia*·so ...
ball	μια μπάλα	mia *ba*·la
bicycle	ένα ποδήλατο	*e*·na po·*ţhi*·la·to
court	το γήπεδο	to *yi*·pe·ţho
racquet	μια ρακέτα	mia ra·*ke*·ta

fishing

Where are the good spots?
Πού είναι τα καλά μέρη; pu *i*·ne ta ka·*la* me·ri

Do I need a fishing permit?
Χρειάζομαι άδεια για khri·*a*·zo·me *a*·ṭhi·a yia
ψάρεμα; *psa*·re·ma

Do you do fishing tours?
Κάνετε εκδρομές για *ka*·ne·te ek·ṭhro·*mes* yia
ψάρεμε; *psa*·re·ma

What's the best bait?
Ποιο είναι το καλύτερο pio *i*·ne to ka·*li*·te·ro
δόλωμα; ṭho·lo·ma

Are they biting?
Τσιμπάει; tsi·*ba*·i

What kind of fish are you landing?
Τι ψάρι βγάζεις; ti *psa*·ri *vgha*·zis

How much does it weigh?
Πόσο ζυγίζει; *po*·so zi·*yi*·zi

bait	δόλωμα n	ṭho·lo·ma
fishing line	πετονιά f	pe·to·*nia*
flare	φανάρι n	fa·*na*·ri
float	φελλός f	fe·*los*
hooks	αγκίστρια n pl	a·*gi*·stri·a
lifejacket	σωσίβιο n	so·*si*·vi·o
lure	δόλωμα n	ṭho·lo·ma
rod	καλάμι n	ka·*la*·mi
sinkers	βαρύδια n pl	va·*ri*·ṭhia

not biting?

Fishing with dynamite used to be a popular pastime in Greece, but this 'sport' has been outlawed because of its environmental impact. Look out for signs warning Απαγορεύεται η χρήση δυναμίτη (No Dynamite).

horse riding

How much is a (one-)hour ride?
Πόσο κοστίζει η ιππασία
(την) ώρα;
po·so kos·*ti*·zi i i·pa·*si*·a
(tin) *o*·ra

How long is the ride?
πόση ώρα διαρκεί η
διαδρομή με το άλογο;
po·si o·ra thi·ar·*ki* i
thi·a·thro·*mi* me to *a*·lo·gho

I'm (not) an experienced rider.
(Δεν) Είμαι πεπειραμένος
αναβάτης.
(then) *i*·me pe·pi·ra·me·*nos*
a·na·*va*·tis

Can I rent a hat and boots?
Μπορώ να νοικάσω ένα
καπέλο και μπότες;
bo·*ro* na ni·*kia*·so *e*·na
ka·*pe*·lo ke *bo*·tes

bit	στομίδα f	sto·*mi*·tha
bridle	χαλινάρι n	kha·li·*na*·ri
canter	τριποδισμός m	tri·po·thiz·*mos*
crop	μαστίγιο ιππασίας n	mas·*ti*·yi·o i·pa·*si*·as
gallop	καλπασμός m	kal·paz·*mos*
groom	ιπποκόμος m	i·po·*ko*·mos
horse	άλογο n	*a*·lo·gho
pony	πουλάρι n	pu·*la*·ri
race	κούρσα f	*kur*·sa
reins	γκέμια n pl	*ge*·mia
saddle	σέλλα f	*se*·la
stable	στάβλος m	*stav*·los
stirrup	σκάλα f	*ska*·la
trot	τροχασμός m	tro·khaz·*mos*
walk	βάδισμα n	*va*·thiz·ma

soccer/football

Who plays for (Iraklis)?
Ποιος παίζει στον (Ηρακλή);   pios *pe*·zi ston (i·ra·*kli*)

He's a great (player).
Είναι μεγάλος (παίχτης).   *i*·ne me·*gha*·los (*pekh*·tis)

He played brilliantly in the match against (Italy).
Έπαιξε υπέροχα στο ματς   *e*·pek·se i·*pe*·ro·kha sto mats
εναντίον (της Ιταλίας).   e·na·*di*·on (tis i·ta·*li*·as)

Which team is at the top of the league?
Ποια ομάδα είναι στην   pia o·*ma*·tha *i*·ne stin
κορυφή της πρώτης εθνικής;   ko·ri·*fi* tis *pro*·tis eth·ni·*kis*

What a great/terrible team!
Τι μεγάλη/κουρέλα ομάδα!   ti me·*gha*·li/ku·*re*·la o·*ma*·tha

ball	μπάλα f	*ba*·la
coach	προπονητής m	pro·po·ni·*tis*
corner (kick)	κόρνερ n	*kor*·ner
expulsion	αποβολή n	a·po·vo·*li*
fan	οπαδός m	o·pa·*thos*
foul	φάουλ n	*fa*·ul
free kick	φρίκικ n	*fri*·kik
goal (structure)	γκολπόστ n	gol·*post*
goalkeeper	γκολκήπερ m	gol·*ki*·per
manager	μάνατζερ m	*ma*·na·dzer
offside	οφσάιτ n	of·*sa*·it
penalty	πέναλτι n	*pe*·nal·ti
player	παίχτης m	*pekh*·tis
red card	κόκκινη κάρτα f	*ko*·ki·ni *kar*·ta
referee	διαιτητής m	thi·e·ti·*tis*
throw in	αναπληρωματικός m	a·na·pli·ro·ma·ti·*kos*
yellow card	κίτρινη κάρτα n	*ki*·tri·ni *kar*·ta

tennis & table tennis

I'd like to …	Θα ήθελα να …	tha i·the·la na …
book a time	κλείσω ώρα να	kli·so o·ra na
to play	παίξω	pek·so
play table tennis	παίξω πινγκ πονγκ	pek·so ping pong
play tennis	παίξω τένις	pek·so te·nis

Can we play at night?
Μπορούμε να παίξουμε
τη νύχτα;
bo·ru·me na pek·su·me
ti nikh·ta

I need my racquet restrung.
Η ρακέτα μου χρειάζεται
επισκευή.
i ra·ke·ta mu khri·a·ze·te
e·pis·ke·vi

ace	άσος m	a·sos
advantage	πλεονέκτημα n	ple·o·nek·ti·ma
bat	ρακέτα f	ra·ke·ta
clay	πήλινη σφαίρα f	pi·li·ni sfe·ra
fault	φάουλ n	fa·ul
game, set, match	παιγνίδι, σετ, ματς n	pegh·ni·thi set mats
grass	γρασίδι n	ghra·si·thi
hard court	σκληρό γήπεδο n	skli·ro yi·pe·tho
net	δίχτυ n	thikh·ti
ping-pong ball	μπαλάκι του	ba·la·ki tu
	πινγκ πονγκ n	ping pong
play doubles v	παίζουμε ζευγάρια	pe·zu·me zev·gha·ria
racket	ρακέτα f	ra·ke·ta
serve v	σερβ	serv
tennis ball	μπαλάκι του τένις n	ba·la·ki tu te·nis
table-tennis	τραπέζι του	tra·pe·zi tu
table	πινγκ πονγκ n	ping pong

sport

149

water sports

Can I hire (a) …?	Μπορώ να νοικιάσω …;	bo·ro na ni·kia·so …
boat	μια βάρκα	mia var·ka
canoe	ένα κανό	e·na ka·no
kayak	ένα καγιάκ	e·na ka·yiak
life jacket	ένα σωσίβιο	e·na so·si·vi·o
snorkelling	μια στολή	mia sto·li
gear	κατάδυσης	ka·ta·thi·sis
water-skis	θαλάσσια σκι	tha·la·si·a ski
wetsuit	αδιάβροχη στολή	a·thiav·ro·hi sto·li

Are there any …?	Υπάρχουν …;	i·par·khun …
reefs	ξέρες	kse·res
rips	δύνες	thi·nes
water	θαλάσσιοι	tha·la·si·i
hazards	κίνδυνοι	kin·thi·ni

guide	οδηγός m&f	o·thi·ghos
motorboat	βάρκα με μηχανή f	var·ka me mi·kha·ni
oars	κουπιά n pl	ku·pia
sailboarding	γουιντσέρφινγκ n	ghu·id·ser·fing
sailing boat	βάρκα με ιστία f	var·ka me i·sti·a
surfboard	σέρφμπορντ n	serf·bord
surfing	σέρφινγκ n	ser·fing
wave	κύμα n	ki·ma

---

diving in

During the summer months, ask around for diving classes:

Is there a diving school here?

Υπάρχει σχολή καταδύσεων εδώ;	i·par·hi skho·li ka·ta·thi·se·on e·tho

Do you offer diving lessons (in English)?

Προσφέρετε μαθήματα καταδύσεων (στα αγγλικά);	pros·fe·re·te ma·thi·ma·ta ka·ta·thi·se·on (sta ang·gli·ka)

hiking

πεζοπορία

Where can I ...?	Πού μπορώ να ...;	pu bo·ro na ...
buy supplies	αγοράσω προμήθειες	a·gho·ra·so pro·mi·thi·es
find someone who knows this area	βρω κάποιον που ξέρει αυτή την περιοχή	vro ka·pion pu kse·ri af·ti tin pe·ri·o·hi
get a map	πάρω ένα χάρτη	pa·ro e·na khar·ti
hire hiking gear	νοικιάσω εξοπλισμό για πεζοπορία	ni·kia·so ek·so·pliz·mo yia pe·zo·po·ri·a
How ...?	Πόσο ...;	po·so ...
high is the climb	ψηλό είναι το ανέβασμα	psi·lo i·ne to a·ne·vaz·ma
long is the trail	μακρύ είναι το μονοπάτι	ma·kri i·ne to mo·no·pa·ti
Do we need to take ...?	Χρειάζεται να πάρουμε ...;	khri·a·ze·te na pa·ru·me ...
bedding	σκεπάσματα	ske·paz·ma·ta
food	φαγητό	fa·yi·to
water	νερό	ne·ro

Do we need a guide?
Χρειαζόμαστε οδηγό;   khri·a·zo·ma·ste o·thi·gho

Are there guided treks?
Υπάρχουν μονοπάτια με σήματα;   i·par·khun mo·no·pa·tia me si·ma·ta

Is there a path to (Profitis Ilias)?
Υπάρχει μονοπάτι για (τον Προφήτη Ηλία);   i·par·hi mo·no·pa·ti yia (ton pro·fi·ti i·li·a)

151

Is it safe?
Είναι ασφαλές;   i·ne as·fa·*les*

Is it steep?
Είναι απόκρημνο;   i·ne a·*po*·krim·no

Are there any rockfalls?
Πέφτουν πουθενά πέτρες;   *pef*·tun pu·the·*na* pet·res

Is there a hut?
Υπάρχει κανένα καλύβι;   i·*par*·hi ka·ne·na ka·*li*·vi

When does it get dark?
Πότε σκοτεινιάζει;   *po*·te sko·ti·*nia*·zi

Is the track ...?	Είναι ο δρόμος ...;	i·ne o *thro*·mos ...
(well-)	σημαδεμένος	si·ma·the·*me*·nos
marked	(καλά)	(ka·*la*)
open	ανοιχτός	a·nikh·*tos*
scenic	γραφικός	ghra·fi·*kos*

Which is the ...	Ποια είναι η πιο	pia *i*·ne i pio
route?	... διαδρομή;	... thi·a·*thro·mi*
easiest	εύκολη	*ef*·ko·li
most interesting	ενδιαφέρουσα	en·thia·*fe*·ru·sa
shortest	κοντινή	ko·di·*ni*

Where can I	Πού μπορώ	pu bo·*ro*
find the ...?	να βρω το ...	na vro to ...
camping	χώρο του	*kho*·ro tu
ground	κάμπινγκ	*kam*·ping
nearest village	πιο κοντινό	pio ko·di·*no*
	χωριό	kho·*rio*
showers	ντουζ	duz
toilets	την τουαλέτα	tin tu·a·*le*·ta

Where have you come from?
Από πού ήρθες;   a·*po* pu *ir*·thes

How long did it take?
Πόση ώρα σου πήρε;   *po*·si *o*·ra su *pi*·re

Does this path go to ...?
Πηγαίνει αυτό το   pi·*ye*·ni af·*to* to
μονοπάτι στο ...;   mo·no·*pa*·ti sto ...

Can I go through here?
Μπορώ να πάω μέσα
από εδώ;

bo·*ro* na *pa*·o *me*·sa
a·*po* e·*tho*

Is the water OK to drink?
Είναι εντάξει το νερό
για να πιω;

i·ne e·*dak*·si to ne·*ro*
yia na pio

I'm lost.
Χάθηκα.

kha·thi·ka

beach

παραλία

Where's the ...	Πού είναι η ...	pu *i*·ne i ...
beach?	παραλία;	pa·ra·*li*·a
best	καλύτερη	ka·*li*·te·ri
nearest	κοντινότερη	ko·di·*no*·te·ri
public	δημόσια	thi·*mo*·si·a

Where's the nudist beach?
Πού είναι η πλαζ γυμνιστών;

pu *i*·ne i plaz yim·ni·*ston*

Do we have to pay?
Πρέπει να πληρώσουμε;

pre·pi na pli·*ro*·su·me

What time is high/low tide?
Τι ώρα είναι η παλίρροια/
άμπωτις;

ti *o*·ra *i*·ne i pa·*li*·ri·a/
a·bo·tis

Is it safe to dive/swim here?
Είναι ασφαλές να κάμω
βουτιές/κολυμπήσω εδώ;

i·ne as·fa·*les* na *ka*·mo
vu·*ties*/ko·li·*bi*·so e·*tho*

---

listen for ...

Είναι επικίνδυνο!
i·ne e·pi·*kin*·thi·no — **It's dangerous!**

Πρόσεχε το υπόγειο ρεύμα!
pro·*se*·he to i·*po*·yi·o *rev*·ma — **Be careful of the undertow!**

outdoors

153

Απαγορεύεται το κολύμπι	a·pa·gho·*re*·ve·te to ko·*li*·bi	**No Swimming**
Απαγορεύονται οι βουτιές	a·pa·gho·*re*·vo·de i vu·*ties*	**No Diving**

Are there any …?	Υπάρχουν …;	i·*par*·khun …
currents	ρεύματα	*rev*·ma·ta
jelly fish	μέδουσες	*me*·thu·ses
rocks	βράχια	*vra*·hia
sea urchins	αχινοί	a·hi·*ni*

How much for a/an …?	Πόσο για μια …;	*po*·so yia mia …
chair	καρέκλα	ka·*re*·kla
hut	καλύβα	ka·*li*·va
umbrella	ομπρέλα	o·*bre*·la

weather

καιρός

What's the weather like?

Πώς είναι ο καιρός;   pos *i*·ne o ke·*ros*

What will the weather be like tomorrow?

Πώς θα είναι ο καιρός αύριο;   pos tha *i*·ne o ke·*ros* av·ri·o

It's …	Είναι …	*i*·ne …
cloudy	συννεφιά	si·ne·*fia*
dry	ξηρασία	ksi·ra·*si*·a
fine	καλός καιρός	ka·*los* ke·*ros*
freezing	παγωνιά	pa·gho·*nia*
humid	υγρασία	i·ghra·*si*·a
mild	μαλακός καιρός	ma·la·*kos* ke·*ros*
sunny	λιακάδα	lia·*ka*·tha

It's …		
raining	Βρέχει.	*vre*·hi
snowing	Χιονίζει.	hio·*ni*·zi
windy	Φυσάει.	fi·*sa*·i
drizzling	Ψιχαλίζει.	psi·kha·*li*·zi

It's …	Κάνει …	*ka*·ni …
cold	κρύο	*kri*·o
hot	πολλή ζέστη	po·*li ze*·sti
warm	ζέστη	*ze*·sti

Where can I buy a/an …?	Πού μπορώ να αγοράσω …;	pu bo·*ro* na a·gho·*ra*·so …
rain jacket	ένα αδιάβροχο	*e*·na a·*thiav*·ro·kho
umbrella	μια ομπρέλα	mia o·*bre*·la

weathering the local storms

heatwave	καύσωνας m	*kaf*·so·nas
strong northerly wind	μελτέμι n	mel·*te*·mi
strong cold wind	βαρδάρης m	var·*tha*·ris
thunderstorm	καταιγίδα f	ka·te·*yi*·tha

flora & fauna

χλωρίδα και πανίδα

What … is that?	Τι … είναι εκείνο;	ti … *i*·ne e·*ki*·no
animal	ζώο	*zo*·o
flower	λουλούδι	lu·*lu*·thi
plant	φυτό	fi·*to*
tree	δέντρο	*the*·dro

What's it used for?

Σε τι χρησιμοποιείται;   se ti khri·si·mo·pi·*i*·te

Can you eat the fruit?

Μπορείς να φας τον καρπό;   bo·*ris* na fas ton kar·*po*

outdoors

Is it ...?	Είναι ...;	i·ne ...
common	κοινό	ki·no
dangerous	επικίνδυνο	e·pi·kin·thi·no
endangered	υπό εξαφάνιση	i·po ek·sa·fa·ni·si
poisonous	δηλητηριώδες	thi·li·ti·ri·o·thes
protected	προστατευόμενο	pro·sta·te·vo·me·no

local plants & animals

basil	βασιλικός m	va·si·li·kos
carnation	γαρύφαλο n	gha·ri·fa·lo
carob	χαρούπι n	kha·ru·pi
Dalmatian pelican	Δαλματικός πελεκάνος m	thal·ma·ti·kos pe·le·ka·nos
dolphin	δελφίνι n	thel·fi·ni
falcon	γεράκι n	ye·ra·ki
fig	σύκο n	si·ko
iris	κρίνος m	kri·nos
lizard	σαύρα f	sav·ra
monk seal	φώκια f	fo·kia
olive	ελιά f	e·lia
orchid	ορχιδέα f	or·hi·the·a
pine	πεύκο n	pef·ko
rose	τριαντάφυλλο n	tri·a·da·fi·lo
sea gull	γλάρος m	gla·ros
sea turtle	θαλάσσια χελώνα f	tha·la·si·a khe·lo·na
snake	φίδι n	fi·thi
swallow	χελιδόνι n	he·li·tho·ni
wildflowers	αγριολούλουδα n pl	a·ghri·o·lu·lu·tha

basics

βασικά

breakfast	πρόγευμα n	pro·yev·ma
lunch	γεύμα n	yev·ma
dinner	δείπνο n	thip·no
snack	μεζεδάκι n	me·ze·tha·ki
eat v	τρώγω	tro·gho
drink v	πίνω	pi·no
I'd like …	Θα ήθελα …	tha i·the·la …
Please.	Παρακαλώ.	pa·ra·ka·lo
Thank you.	Ευχαριστώ.	ef·kha·ri·sto
I'm starving!	Πεινώ τρομερά!	pi·no tro·me·ra
Enjoy your meal.	Καλή όρεξη.	ka·li o·rek·si

food glorious food

For breakfast, Greeks usually have a hot cup of milk, tea or coffee with φρυγανιά fri·gha·nia (dry sweet toast). If eating out, a typical order is a τυρόπιτα ti·ro·pi·ta (cheese pie) or σπανακόπιτα spa·na·ko·pi·ta (spinach pie).

Lunch, the day's main meal, is an early afternoon affair, usually followed by a απογευματινός ύπνος a·po·yev·ma·ti·nos ip·nos (siesta). A typical lunch will be a meat dish with rice, pasta or potatoes, or fish with a side salad. Legume dishes such as φακές fa·kes (lentil broth) and φασολάδα fa·so·la·tha (bean broth) are especially popular in winter.

Dinner is a light meal eaten between eight and nine o'clock.

Dessert is rarely served. Instead, seasonal fresh fruit finishes off a meal.

eating out

157

finding a place to eat

Can you recommend a ...?	Μπορείς να συστήσεις ένα ...;	bo·ris na si·sti·sis e·na ...
bar	μπαρ	bar
café	καφεστιατόριο	ka·fe·sti·a·to·ri·o
restaurant	ρεστωράν	re·sto·ran

Where would you go for (a) ...?	Πού θα πήγαινες για ...;	pu tha pi·ye·nes yia ...
celebration	μια γιορτή	mia yior·ti
cheap meal	ένα φτηνό γεύμα	e·na fti·no yev·ma
local specialities	τοπικές λιχουδιές	to·pi·kes li·khu·thies

I'd like to reserve a table for ...	Θα ήθελα να κρατήσω ένα τραπέζι για ...	tha i·the·la na kra·ti·so e·na tra·pe·zi yia ...
(two) people	(δύο) άτομα	(thi·o) a·to·ma
(eight) o'clock	τις (οχτώ)	stis (okh·to)

listen for ...

Δεν υπάρχει άδειο τραπέζι. then i·par·hi a·thio tra·pe·zi	We're full.
Κλείσαμε. kli·sa·me	We're closed.
Μια στιγμή. mia stigh·mi	One moment.
Πού θα θέλατε να καθίσετε; pu tha the·la·te na ka·thi·se·te	Where would you like to sit?
Τι μπορώ να σας φέρω; ti bo·ro na sas fe·ro	What can I get for you?
Ορίστε! o·ri·ste	Here you go!

I'd like (a/the) …, please.	Θα ήθελα …, παρακαλώ.	tha *i*·thela … pa·ra·ka·*lo*
children's menu	ένα μενού για παιδιά	*e*·na me·*nu* yia pe·*thia*
drink list	τον κατάλογο με τα ποτά	ton ka·*ta*·lo·gho me ta po·*ta*
half portion	μισή μερίδα	mi·*si* me·*ri*·tha
menu (in English)	ένα μενού (στα αγγλικά)	*e*·na me·*nu* (sta ang·gli·*ka*)
mixed plate	μια ποικιλία	mia pi·ki·*li*·a
nonsmoking	στους μη καπνίζοντες	stus mi kap·*ni*·zo·des
smoking	στους καπνίζοντες	stus kap·*ni*·zo·des
table for (five)	ένα τραπέζι για (πέντε)	*e*·na tra·*pe*·zi yia (*pe*·de)
table outside	ένα τραπέζι έξω	*e*·na tra·*pe*·zi ek·so

Are you still serving food?

Σερβίρετε ακόμη φαγητό;   ser·*vi*·re·te a·*ko*·mi fa·ghi·*to*

How long is the wait?

Πόση ώρα θα περιμένουμε;   *po*·si *o*·ra tha pe·ri·*me*·nu·me

eateries

Act like a local and order some μερικά παξιμάδια me·ri·*ka* pak·si·*ma*·thia (dried bread) for dunking in your coffee or other hot drinks the next time you're at one of these eateries:

καφετηρία f	ka·fe·ti·*ri*·a	cafeteria
καφενείο n	ka·fe·*ni*·o	coffee shop
γλακτοπωλείο n	gha·lak·to·po·*li*·o	dairy shop
φαστφουντάδικο n	fast·fun·*da*·thi·ko	fast-food eatery
ουζερί n	u·ze·*ri*	ouzeria
οινοπωλείο n	i·no·po·*li*·o	liquor shop
ταβέρνα f	ta·*ver*·na	taverna

at the restaurant

What would you recommend?
Τι θα συνιστούσες; — ti tha si·ni·*stu*·ses

What are you serving today?
Τι έχετε σήμερα; — ti *e*·he·te *si*·me·ra

What's that called?
Πώς το λένε αυτό; — pos to *le*·ne af·*to*

What's in that dish?
Τι περιέχει αυτό το φαγητό; — ti pe·ri·e·hi af·*to* to fa·ghi·*to*

I'll have that.
Θα πάρω αυτό. — tha *pa*·ro af·*to*

Πώς θα το θέλατε ψημένο;
pos tha to *the*·la·te
psi·*me*·no
How would you like that cooked?

Σας αρέσει ...;
sas a·*re*·si ...
Do you like ...?

Συνιστώ ...
si·ni·*sto* ...
I suggest the ...

Is it savoury or sweet?
Είναι πικάντικο ή γλυκό;
i·ne pi·*ka*·di·ko i ghli·*ko*

I'd like it hot, please.
Θα το ήθελα ζεστό,
παρακαλώ.
tha to *i*·the·la ze·*sto*
pa·ra·ka·*lo*

Does it take long to prepare?
Θα αργήσει να ετοιμαστεί;
tha ar·*ghi*·si na e·ti·ma·*sti*

Is it self-serve?
Είναι σελφ σέρβις;
i·ne self *ser*·vis

Is there a cover charge?
Υπάρχει προσαύξηση τιμής;
i·*par*·hi pro·*saf*·ksi·si ti·*mis*

Is service included in the bill?
Συμπεριλαμβάνεται
και η εξυπηρέτηση στο
λογαριασμό;
si·be·ri·lam·*va*·ne·te
ke i ek·si·pi·*re*·ti·si sto
lo·gha·riaz·*mo*

Are these complimentary?
Είναι αυτά δωρεάν;
i·ne af·*ta* tho·re·*an*

How much is that?
Πόσο κάνει αυτό;
po·so *ka*·ni af·*to*

I'd like (a/the) ...	Θα ήθελα ...	tha *i*·the·la ...
chicken	το κοτόπουλο	to ko·*to*·pu·lo
local speciality	μια τοπική	mia to·pi·*ki*
	λιχουδιά	li·khu·*thia*
meal fit for	ένα λουκούλλειο	*e*·na lu·*ku*·li·o
a king	γεύμα	*yev*·ma
menu	το μενού	to me·*nu*
sandwich	ένα σάντουιτς	*e*·na *sa*·du·its
that dish	εκείνο το φαγητό	e·*ki*·no to fa·yi·*to*

look for ...

Ορεκτικά	o·rek·ti·*ka*	Appetisers
Σούπες	*su*·pes	Soups
Προδόρπια	pro·*thor*·pi·a	Entrees
Σαλάτες	sa·*la*·tes	Salads
Κύρια φαγητά	*ki*·ri·a fa·yi·*ta*	Main Courses
Ψητά της ώρας	psi·*ta* tis *o*·ras	Freshly Grilled Dishes
Μαγειρεμένα φαγητά	ma·yi·re·*me*·na fa·yi·*ta*	Precooked Dishes
Σαλάτες	sa·*la*·tes	Side Dishes
Μακαρόνια	ma·ka·*ro*·nia	Pasta
Ψάρια	*psa*·ria	Fish
Θαλασσινά	tha·la·si·*na*	Seafood
Επιδόρπια	e·pi·*thor*·pi·a	Desserts
Ποτά	po·*ta*	Drinks
Απεριτίφ	a·pe·ri·*tif*	Apéritifs
Αναψυκτικά	a·nap·sik·ti·*ka*	Soft Drinks
Οινοπνευματώδη ποτά	i·nop·nev·ma·*to*·thi po·*ta*	Spirits
Μπύρες	*bi*·res	Beers
Σαμπάνια	sam·*pa*·nia	Sparkling Wines
Άσπρο κρασί	*as*·pro kra·*si*	White Wines
Κόκκινο κρασί	*ko*·ki·no kra·*si*	Red Wines
Επιδόρπια κρασιά	e·pi·*thor*·pi·a kra·*sia*	Dessert Wines
Ρετσίνα	ret·*si*·na	Retsina
Χωνευτικά	kho·nef·ti·*ka*	Digestifs

If you've got the munchies, try one of these snacks:

κουλούρι n	ku·*lu*·ri	crisp sesame-coated bread rings
γύρος m	*yi*·ros	spit-roast lamb
πασατέμπο n	pa·sa·*tem*·po	pumpkin seeds
σουβλάκι n	suv·*la*·ki	skewered marinated meat
σπανακόπιτα f	spa·na·*ko*·pi·ta	spinach & cheese pie
τυρόπιτα f	ti·*ro*·pi·ta	cheese pie
ψημένα κάστανα n pl	psi·*me*·na *ka*·sta·ma	roasted chestnuts
ψημένο καλαμπόκι n	psi·*me*·no ka·la·*bo*·ki	roasted corn

I'd like it with/ without ...	Θα το ήθελα με/ χωρίς ...	tha to *i*·the·la me/ kho·ris ...
cheese	τυρί	ti·*ri*
chilli	πιπεριά	pi·pe·*ria*
chilli sauce	σάλτσα πιπεριάς	*salt*·sa pi·pe·*rias*
garlic	σκόρδο	*skor*·tho
ketchup	σάλτσα	*salt*·sa
nuts	καρύδια	ka·*ri*·thia
oil	λάδι	*la*·thi
pepper	πιπέρι	pi·*pe*·ri
salt	αλάτι	a·*la*·ti
tomato sauce	σάλτσα ντομάτας	*salt*·sa do·*ma*·tas
vinegar	ξύδι	ksi·thi

For additional items, see the **menu decoder**, page 175.
For other specific meal requests, see **vegetarian & special meals**, page 173.

eating out

163

at the table

Please bring (a/the) ...	Παρακαλώ φέρε ...	pa·ra·ka·*lo* fe·re ...
bill	το λογαριασμό	to lo·gha·riaz·*mo*
cloth	ένα τραπεζομάντηλο	e·na tra·pe·zo·*ma*·di·lo
glass	ένα ποτήρι	e·na po·*ti*·ri
serviette	μια πετσέτα	mia pet·*se*·ta
wineglass	ένα ποτήρι κρασιού	e·na po·*ti*·ri kra·*siu*

This is ...	Αυτό είναι ...	af·*to* i·ne ...
(too) cold	(πολύ) κρύο	(po·*li*) kri·o
spicy	πιπεράτο	pi·pe·*ra*·to
superb	καταπληκτικό	ka·ta·plik·ti·*ko*

There's a mistake in the bill.
Υπάρχει κάποιο λάθος   i·*par*·hi ka·pio la·thos
στο λογαριασμό.   sto lo·gha·riaz·*mo*

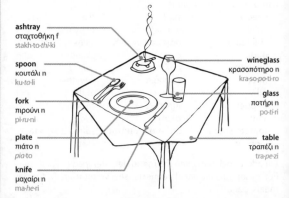

ashtray
σταχτοθήκη f
stakh·to·*thi*·ki

spoon
κουτάλι n
ku·*ta*·li

fork
πιρούνι n
pi·*ru*·ni

plate
πιάτο n
pia·to

knife
μαχαίρι n
ma·*he*·ri

wineglass
κρασοπότηρο n
kra·so·po·ti·ro

glass
ποτήρι n
po·*ti*·ri

table
τραπέζι n
tra·*pe*·zi

talking food

I love this dish.
Μου αρέσει πολύ αυτό
το φαγητό.
mu a·*re*·si po·*li* af·to
to fa·yi·to

I love the local cuisine.
Μου αρέσει η τοπική κουζίνα.
mu a·*re*·si i to·pi·*ki* ku·*zi*·na

That was delicious!
Ήταν νοστιμότατο!
i·tan no·sti·*mo*·ta·to

My compliments to the chef.
Τα συγχαρητήριά μου στο σεφ.
ta sing·kha·ri·*ti*·ri·a mu sto sef

methods of preparation

I'd like it …	Θα το ήθελα …	tha to *i*·the·la …
I don't want it …	Δεν το θέλω …	then to *the*·lo …
boiled	βρασμένο	vraz·*me*·no
broiled	ψημένο στη σχάρα	psi·*me*·no sti *skha*·ra
deep-fried	τηγανισμένο σε καυτό λίπος	ti·gha·niz·*me*·no se kaf·*to li*·pos
fried	τηγανητό	ti·gha·ni·*to*
grilled	στα κάρβουνα	sta *kar*·vu·na
mashed	πουρέ	pu·*re*
reheated	ξαναζεσταμένο	ksa·na·ze·sta·*me*·no
steamed	βρασμένο στον ατμό	vraz·*me*·no ston at·*mo*

how would you like that?		
medium	ψημένο κανονικά	psi·*me*·no ka·no·ni·*ka*
rare	μισοψημένο	mi·sop·si·*me*·no
well-done	καλοψημένο	ka·lop·si·*me*·no

nonalcoholic drinks

μη οινοπνευματώδη ποτά

... mineral water	... μεταλλικό νερό n	... me·ta·li·ko ne·ro
sparkling	γαζόζα	gha·zo·za
still	χωρίς ανθρακικό	kho·ris an·thra·ki·ko
(hot) water	(ζεστό) νερό n	(ze·sto) ne·ro
bottled water	εμφιαλωμένο νερό n	em·fi·a·lo·me·no ne·ro
tap water	νερό βρύσης n	ne·ro vri·sis
apple juice	χυμός μήλου m	hi·mos mi·lu
hot chocolate	ζεστό κακάο n	ze·sto ka·ka·o
herbal tea	τσάι από βότανα n	tsa·i a·po vo·ta·na
morello cherry juice	βισινάδα f	vi·si·na·tha
orange juice	χυμός πορτοκάλι m	hi·mos por·to·ka·li
soft drink	αναψυκτικό n	a·nap·sik·ti·ko
(cup of) tea	(ένα φλυτζάνι) τσάι n	(e·na fli·dza·ni) tsa·i
(cup of) coffee	(ένα φλυτζάνι) καφέ m	(e·na fli·dza·ni) ka·fe
with milk	με γάλα	me gha·la
with lemon	με λεμόνι	me le·mo·ni
sweetened	με ζάχαρη	me za·kha·ri
unsweetened	χωρίς ζάχαρη	kho·ris za·kha·ri

coffee time

black	χωρίς γάλα	kho·ris gha·la
decaffeinated	χωρίς καφεΐνη	kho·ris ka·fe·i·ni
Greek	ελληνικός	e·li·ni·kos
iced	φραπέ	fra·pe
instant	στιγμιαίος	stigh·mi·e·os
medium	μέτριος	me·tri·os
plain (no sugar)	σκέτος	ske·tos
strong	δυνατός	thi·na·tos
sweet	γλυκός	ghli·kos
weak	ελαφρύς	e·la·fris
white	με γάλα	me gha·la

κουμανταρία f	ku·ma·da·*ri*·a	traditional Cypriot wine
ζιβανία f	zi·va·*ni*·a	a clear Cypriot apéritif made from grapes
ούζο n	*u*·zo	spirit distilled from grapes with a strong aniseed flavour
ρετσίνα f	ret·*si*·na	pine-resinated wine, served chilled
τσίπουρο n	*tsi*·pu·ro	spirit made from grapes, high in alcohol
τσικουδιά f	tsi·ku·*thia*	Crete's version of τσίπουρο

alcoholic drinks

οινοπνευματώδη ποτά

To get drinks at a bar in Greece, you don't have to memorise numerous standard measurements – standard serves are ordered using 'one'. For example: μία μπύρα *mi*·a *bi*·ra (one beer) or ένα ούζο *e*·na *u*·zo (one ouzo). See also **numbers & amounts**, page 35.

beer	μπύρα f	*bi*·ra
brandy	μπράντι n	*bran*·di
champagne	σαμπάνια f	sam·*pa*·nia
cocktail	κοκτέηλ n	kok·*te*·il
a shot of ...	ένα ... m	*e*·na ...
gin	τζιν	dzin
rum	ρούμι	*ru*·mi
whisky	ουίσκι	u·*i*·ski

a shot of ...	μία ... f	mia ...
tequila	τεκίλα	te·*ki*·la
vodka	βότκα	*vot*·ka

a bottle/glass of ... wine	ένα μπουκάλι/ ποτήρι ... κρασί n	e·na bu·*ka*·li/ po·*ti*·ri ... kra·*si*
dessert	επιδόρπιο	e·pi·*thor*·pi·o
dry	ξηρό	ksi·*ro*
red	κόκκινο	*ko*·ki·no
rosé	ροζέ	ro·*ze*
sparkling	σαμπάνια	sam·*pa*·nia
sweet	γλυκό	ghli·*ko*
white	άσπρο	*a*·spro

a ... of beer	ένα ... μπύρα n	e·na ... *bi*·ra
glass	ποτήρι	po·*ti*·ri
pint	μεγάλο ποτήρι	me·*gha*·lo po·*ti*·ri
small bottle	μικρό μπουκάλι	mi·*kro* bu·*ka*·li
large bottle	μεγάλο μπουκάλι	me·*gha*·lo bu·*ka*·li

a ... of beer	μια ... μπύρα f	mia ... *bi*·ra
carafe	καράφα	ka·*ra*·fa
jug	κανάτα	ka·*na*·ta

give it a go

Try more traditional Greek delicacies from these eateries:

αρτοποιείο n	ar·to·pi·*i*·o	bakery
ζαχαροπλαστείο n	za·kha·ro·pla·*sti*·o	patisserie or sweet shop
φαστφουντάδικο n	fast·fu·*da*·thi·ko	fast-food eatery
καντίνα f	kan·*ti*·na	canteen or food van
πιτσαρία f	pit·sa·*ri*·a	barbecue-style eatery
σουβλατζίδικο n	suv·lat·*zi*·thi·ko	kebab and souvlaki shop
τυροπωλείο n	ti·ro·po·*li*·o	cheese shop
ψαροταβέρνα f	psa·ro·ta·*ver*·na	taverna serving fish
ψησταριά f	psi·sta·*ria*	eatery serving spit-roasted meats

FOOD

in the bar

Excuse me!
Συγνώμη!   sigh·*no*·mi

I'm next.
Είναι η δική μου σειρά.   *i*·ne i ţhi·*ki* mu si·*ra*

I'll have …
Θα πάρω …   tha *pa*·ro …

Same again, please.
Από τα ίδια, παρακαλώ.   a·*po* ta *i*·ţhia pa·ra·ka·*lo*

No ice, thanks.
Όχι πάγο, ευχαριστώ.   *o*·hi *pa*·gho ef·kha·ri·*sto*

I'll buy you a drink.
Θα σε κεράσω εγώ.   tha se ke·*ra*·so e·*gho*

What would you like?
Τι θα ήθελες;   ti tha *i*·the·les

I don't drink alcohol.
Δεν πίνω αλκοόλ.   ţhen *pi*·no al·ko·*ol*

It's my round.
Είναι η σειρά μου.   *i*·ne i si·*ra* mu

How much is that?
Πόσο κάνει αυτό;   *po*·so *ka*·ni af·*to*

Do you serve meals here?
Σερβίρετε φαγητό εδώ;   ser·*vi*·re·te fa·yi·*to* e·*ţho*

listen for …

Τι θα πάρεις;
ti tha *pa*·ris   **What are you having?**

Νομίζω ήπιες αρκετά.
no·*mi*·zo *i*·pies ar·ke·*ta*   **I think you've had enough.**

Τελευταίες παραγγελίες.
te·lef·*te*·es pa·ra·ghe·*li*·es   **Last orders.**

Τα ποτά τα κερνάει το κατάστημα.
ta po·*ta* ta ker·*na*·i
to ka·*ta*·sti·ma   **Drinks are on the house.**

eating out

drinking up

Cheers!
Εις υγείαν! · is i·*yi*·an

I feel fantastic!
Είμαι στα κέφια μου! · *i*·me sta *ke*·fia mu

I think I've had one too many.
Νομίζω ήπια παραπάνω. · no·*mi*·zo *i*·pia pa·ra·*pa*·no

I'm feeling drunk.
Μέθυσα. · *me*·thi·sa

I feel ill.
Δεν αισθάνομαι καλά. · ţhen es·*tha*·no·me ka·*la*

Where's the toilet?
Πού είναι η τουαλέτα; · pu *i*·ne i tu·a·*le*·ta

I'm tired, I'd better go home.
Είμαι κουρασμένος/ · *i*·me ku·raz·*me*·nos/
κουρασμένη, καλύτερα · ku·raz·*me*·ni ka·*li*·te·ra
να πάω σπίτι. m/f · na *pa*·o *spi*·ti

Can you call a taxi for me?
Μπορείς να μου καλέσεις · bo·*ris* na mu ka·*le*·sis
ένα ταξί; · *e*·na tak·*si*

I don't think you should drive.
Νομίζω ότι δεν πρέπει να · no·*mi*·zo *o*·ti ţhen *pre*·pi na
οδηγήσεις. · o·ţhi·*yi*·sis

---

pot plant

When you're in Greece, make sure that you don't eat the
decoration – βασιλικός va·si·li·*kos* (basil) is favoured as an
ornamental plant and is rarely used in cooking.

What's the local speciality?
Ποιες είναι οι τοπικές
λιχουδιές;
pies *i*·ne i to·pi·*kes*
li·khu·*thies*

What's that?
Τι είναι εκείνο;
ti *i*·ne e·*ki*·no

Can I taste it?
Μπορώ να το δοκιμάσω;
bo·*ro* na to tho·ki·*ma*·so

Can I have a bag, please?
Μπορώ να έχω μια
σακούλα, παρακαλώ;
bo·*ro* na *e*·kho mia
sa·*ku*·la pa·ra·ka·*lo*

How much is (a kilo of cheese)?
Πόσο κάνει (ένα κιλό τυρί);
po·so ka·ni (*e*·na ki·*lo* ti·*ri*)

I'd like ...	Θα ήθελα ...	tha *i*·the·la ...
(three) pieces	(τρία) κομμάτια	(*tri*·a) ko·*ma*·tia
(six) slices	(έξι) φέτες	(*ek*·si) *fe*·tes
that one	εκείνο	e·*ki*·no
this one	αυτό	af·*to*

Less.	Πιο λίγο.	pio *li*·gho
A bit more.	Λιγάκι πιο πολύ.	li·*gha*·ki pio po·*li*
Enough.	Αρκετά.	ar·ke·*ta*

For more on quantities, see **numbers & amounts**, page 35.

For more on quantities, see **numbers & amounts**, page 35.

---

listen for ...

Δεν υπάρχει άλλο. then i·*par*·hi *a*·lo	**There isn't any.**
Μπορώ να σας βοηθήσω; bo·*ro* na sas vo·i·*thi*·so	**Can I help you?**
Τι θα θέλατε; ti tha *the*·la·te	**What would you like?**
Τίποτε άλλο; *ti*·po·te *a*·lo	**Anything else?**

self-catering

171

food stuff

cooked	μαγειρεμένο	ma·yi·re·*me*·no
cured	παστό	pa·*sto*
dried	ξηρό	ksi·*ro*
fresh	φρέσκο	*fre*·sko
frozen	κατεψυγμένο	ka·tep·sigh·*me*·no
grilled	στα κάρβουνα	sta *kar*·vu·na
raw	ωμό	o·*mo*
roasted	ψητό	psi·*to*
savoury	πικάντικο	pi·*ka*·di·ko
smoked	καπνιστό	kap·ni·*sto*
sweet	γλυκό	ghli·*ko*

Do you have ...?	Έχετε κάτι ...;	*e*·he·te *ka*·ti ...
anything cheaper	πιο φτηνό	pio fti·*no*
other kinds	διαφορετικό	thia·fo·re·ti·*ko*

Where can I find the ... section?	Πού μπορώ να βρω το μέρος με ...;	pu bo·*ro* na vro to *me*·ros me ...
bread	το ψωμί	to pso·*mi*
dairy	τα γαλακτικά	ta gha·lak·ti·*ka*
fish	τα ψάρια	ta *psa*·ria
frozen goods	τα κατεψυγμένα	ta ka·tep·sigh·*me*·na
fruit and vegetable	τα φρούτα και τα λαχανικά	ta *fru*·ta ke ta la·kha·ni·*ka*
meat	το κρέας	to *kre*·as
poultry	τα πουλερικά	ta pu·le·ri·*ka*
seafood	τα θαλασσινά	ta tha·la·si·*na*

Could I please borrow a ...?	Μπορώ παρακαλώ να δανειστώ ...;	bo·*ro* pa·ra·ka·*lo* na tha·ni·*sto* ...
I need a ...	Χρειάζομαι ...	khri·*a*·zo·me ...
chopping board	μια σανίδα κοπής	mia sa·*ni*·tha ko·*pis*
frying pan	ένα τηγάνι	*e*·na ti·*gha*·ni
knife	ένα μαχαίρι	*e*·na ma·*he*·ri
saucepan	μια κατσαρόλα	mia kat·sa·*ro*·la

For more cooking implements, see the **dictionary** (p207).

ordering food

παραγγέλλοντας φαγητό

Do you have ... food?	Έχετε φαγητό ...;	*e*·he·te fa·*yi*·*to* ...
halal	χαλάλ	kha·*lal*
kosher	κόσια	*ko*·si·a
Lent	Σαρακοστιανό	sa·ra·ko·stia·*no*
pulse-based	με όσπρια	me *os*·pri·a
vegetarian	για χορτοφάγους	yia khor·to·*fa*·ghus

Is there a ... restaurant near here?
Υπάρχει ένα εστιατόριο ...   i·*par*·hi e·na e·sti·a·*to*·ri·o ...
εδώ κοντά;   e·*tho* ko·*da*

Is it cooked in/with ...?
Είναι μαγειρεμένο   *i*·ne ma·yi·re·*me*·no
σε/με ...;   se/me ...

Could you prepare a meal without ...?
Μπορείτε να κάνετε   bo·*ri*·te na *ka*·ne·te
φαγητό χωρίς ...;   fa·*yi*·to kho·*ris* ...

I don't eat ...	Δεν τρώγω ...	ţhen *tro*·gho ...
butter	βούτυρο	*vu*·ti·ro
eggs	αβγά	av·*gha*
fish	ψάρι	*psa*·ri
fish stock	ζουμί από ψάρι	zu·*mi* a·po *psa*·ri
lamb	αρνί	ar·*ni*
(red) meat	(κόκκινο) κρέας	(*ko*·ki·no) *kre*·as
meat stock	ζουμί από κρέας	zu·*mi* a·po *kre*·as
oil	λάδι	*la*·ţhi
olives	ελιές	e·*lies*
pork	χοιρινό	hi·ri·*no*
poultry	πουλερικά	pu·le·ri·*ka*

Is this ...?	Είναι αυτό ...;	i·ne af·to ...
decaffeinated	χωρίς καφεΐνη	kho·ris ka·fe·i·ni
gluten-free	χωρίς γλουτένη	kho·ris ghlu·te·ni
low in fat	χαμηλό σε λίπος	kha·mi·lo se li·pos
low in sugar	χαμηλό σε ζάχαρη	kha·mi·lo se za·kha·ri
organic	οργανικό	or·gha·ni·ko
salt-free	χωρίς αλάτι	kho·ris a·la·ti

special diets & allergies

ειδική δίαιτα και αλλεργίες

I'm on a special diet.

Κάνω ειδική δίαιτα.   ka·no i·thi·ki thi·e·ta

I'm allergic to ...	Είμαι αλλεργικός/ αλλεργική ... m/f	i·me a·ler·yi·kos a·ler·yi·ki ...
dairy produce	στα γαλακτικά	sta gha·lak·ti·ka
eggs	στα αβγά	sta av·gha
gluten	στη γλουτένη	sti ghlu·te·ni
honey	στο μέλι	sto me·li
MSG	στο MSG	sto em si dzi
nuts	στους ξηρούς καρπούς	stus ksi·rus kar·pus
seafood	στα θαλασσινά	sta tha·la·si·na
shellfish	στα οστρακοειδή	sta os·tra·ko·i·thi

I'm (a) ...	Είμαι ...	i·me ...
Buddhist	Βουδιστής m	vu·thi·stis
	Βουδίστρια f	vu·thi·stri·a
Hindu	Ινδουιστής m	in·thu·i·stis
	Ινδουίστρια f	in·thu·i·stri·a
Jewish	Ιουδαίος m	i·u·the·os
	Ιουδαία f	i·u·the·a
Muslim	Μουσουλμάνος m	mu·sul·ma·nos
	Μουσουλμάνα f	mu·sul·ma·na
vegan	βέγκαν m&f	ve·gan
vegetarian	χορτοφάγος m&f	khor·to·fa·ghos

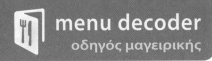

menu decoder
οδηγός μαγειρικής

This miniguide lists dishes and ingredients used in Greek cuisine. It's designed to help you get the most out of your gastronomic experience by providing you with food terms that you may see on menus. For certain dishes we've marked the region or city where they're most popular.

The **menu decoder** has been ordered according to the Greek alphabet:

Αα Ββ Γγ Δδ Εε Ζζ Ηη Θθ Ιι Κκ Λλ Μμ
Νν Ξξ Οο Ππ Ρρ Σσ/ς Ττ Υυ Φφ Χχ Ψψ Ωω

Α α

αβγολέμονο ⑩ av-gho-*le*-mo-no *egg and lemon sauce added to meat, chicken or fish soup and other dishes*

αβγοτάραχο ⑩ av-gho-*ta*-ra-kho *dried & salted grey mullet roe, coated in beeswax*

αγγινάρες ① pl a-gi-*na*-res *globe artichokes*
— **αλαπολίτα** a-la-po-*li*-ta *'Constantinople-style artichokes' – artichokes, carrots & potatoes in dill-spiked chicken stock*
— **καλογρές** ka-lo-*ghres* *'nuns' – artichoke hearts braised in creamy onion broth (Crete)*

αγγουροντομάτα σαλάτα ①
ang-gu-ro-do-*ma*-ta sa-*la*-ta *cucumber slices, tomato wedges & parsley with oil, lemon juice, salt & pepper*

αγγουροσαλάτα ① ang-gu-ro-sa-*la*-ta *sliced cucumbers sprinkled with salt & served with oil & vinegar*

άγρια χόρτα pl *a*-ghri-a *khor*-ta *seasonal wild greens*

άγρια σπαράγγια ⑩ pl *a*-ghri-a spa-*rang*-gi-a *wild asparagus*

άγριες αγγινάρες ① pl *a*-ghri-es ang-gi-*na*-res *small prickly artichokes, eaten raw with salt & lemon juice*

αμπελοπούλια ⑩ pl am-be-lo-*pu*-lia *tiny birds preserved in vinegar & wine, eaten whole (Cyprus)*

αμελέτητα ⑩ pl a-me-*le*-ti-ta *lamb testicles*

αμπελοφάσουλα ⑩ pl am-be-lo-*fa*-su-la *green beans*

αμπερόριζα ① am-be-ro-ri-za *rose geranium (leaves are used as a flavouring for cakes, pastries & preserved fruits)*

αμύγδαλα ⑩ pl *migh*-tha-la *almonds*

αμυγδαλωτά ⑩ pl a-migh-tha-lo-*ta* *almond shortbread sprinkled with icing sugar & chopped almonds*

αμυγδαλωτό γλύκισμα ⑩
a-migh-tha-lo-*to* ghli-kiz-ma *nougat*

αναρή ① a-na-*ri* *soft ricotta-like cheese from goat's or sheep's milk (Cyprus)*

αρακάς ⑩ a-ra-*kas* *fresh peas*
— **λαδερός** la-*the*-ros *peas stewed with carrots, garlic bulbs & herbs in oil & paprika (Corfu)*

αρνάκι ⑩ ar-*na*-ki *milk-lamb (very young lamb)*
— **γεμιστό** ye-mi-*sto* *Easter dish of stuffed roast lamb (Dodecanese Islands)*

αρνί ⑩ ar-*ni* *lamb*
— **βραστό** vra-*sto* *slow-boiled mutton served with mutton-stock soup (Crete)*
— **γιαχνί** yiakh-*ni* *lamb stewed with tomatoes, onions, carrots & celery*
— **γιουβέτσι με κριθαράκι** yiu-*vet*-si me kri-tha-*ra*-ki *lamb baked with tomatoes & barley-shaped pasta in an earthenware pot*
— **εξοχικό** ek-so-hi-*ko* *'country-style lamb' – baked filo parcels of lamb, potato, feta & **κεφαλοτύρι***

menu decoder

— **φρικασέ με μαρούλι**
fri·ka·*se* me ma·*rou*·li *poached lamb with shredded lettuce, egg & lemon sauce*
— **κεφαλάκι ριγανάτο**
ke·fa·*la*·ki ri·gha·*na*·to *lamb's head (generally roasted) complete with tongue, cheek, brains & eyes*
— **κοκκινιστό** ko·ki·ni·*sto* *lamb braised in white wine with onions & bay leaves*
— **οφτό** of·*to* *roast lamb on the spit*
— **στη σούβλα** sti *souv*·la *spit-roast lamb basted with olive oil, lemon juice & garlic – a traditional Easter dish*
— **στο φούρνο** sto *fur*·no *roasted leg or shoulder of lamb*

αρνίσια παϊδάκια ⓝ pl ar·*ni*·sia pa·i·*tha*·kia *marinated & chargrilled lamb cutlets*

αστακός a·sta·*kos* ⓜ *lobster, usually boiled or chargrilled*

αφέλια ⓝ pl a·*fe*·lia *meat braised with potato & mushrooms in red wine*

αχηβάδα ⓕ a·hi·*va*·tha *clam*

αχινοί ⓜ pl a·hi·*ni* *sea urchins*
— **σαλάτα** sa·*la*·ta *sea urchin salad*
— **γεμιστοί** ye·mi·*sti* *sea urchin stuffed with rice, onions & tomatoes*

B β

βασιλόπιτα ⓕ va·si·*lo*·pi·ta *New Year loaf decorated with almonds – whoever finds the coin in the bread gets good luck*

βατόμουρο ⓝ va·*to*·mu·ro *blackberry • raspberry*

βατραχοπόδαρα τηγανητά ⓝ pl va·tra·kho·*po*·tha·ra ti·gha·ni·*ta* *fried frog's legs (Western Greece)*

βυσσινάδα ⓕ vi·si·*na*·tha *syrup of morello cherries – mixed with cold water for summer-time cordials*

βύσσινο ⓝ *vi*·si·no *morello cherry • sour black cherry*
— **γλυκό** ghli·*ko* *morello cherry preserve*

βλίτο ⓝ *vli*·to *amaranth – its sweet nutty flavour & soft texture make it popular for warm salads*

βοδινό ⓝ vo·thi·*no* *beef*
— **καπαμά** ka·pa·*ma* *beef stewed with tomatoes, red wine, cinnamon & cloves*

— **με λαχανικά** me la·kha·ni·*ka* *beef braised with carrots, potatoes & celery*

βολβοί ⓜ pl vol·*vi* *grape hyacinth bulbs*
— **βραστοί** vra·*sti* *bulbs boiled, dressed with dill vinaigrette & accompanied by* **σκορδαλιά**

βρούβα ⓕ *vru*·va *charlock • field green with sharp peppery taste*

Γ γ

γαϊδουρελιά ⓕ gha·i·*thu*·re·*lia* *'donkey olive' – named so because of its large size*

γαλακτομπούρεκο ⓝ gha·lak·to·*bu*·re·ko *baked custard-cream filo pie sprinkled with a lemony syrup*

γαλοπούλα ⓕ gha·lo·*pu*·la *turkey*
— **γεμιστή** ye·mi·*sti* *stuffed roast turkey*

γαλύπες ⓕ pl gha·*li*·pes *a sea anemone*
— **τηγανητές** ti·gha·ni·*tes* *lightly battered & fried sea anemone*

γαλυποκεφτέδες ⓜ pl gha·li·po·kef·*te*·thes *sea anemone rissoles*

γαρδούμια ⓝ pl ghar·*thu*·mia *small offal rolls made from strips of lamb's stomach, bound with intestines then roasted*

γαρίδες ⓕ pl gha·*ri*·thes *prawns • shrimps*
— **σαγανάκι** sa·gha·*na*·ki *prawns fried with tomatoes & red wine, topped with feta & baked*
— **τηγανητές** ti·gha·ni·*tes* *fried prawns*
— **βραστές** vra·*stes* *boiled prawns accompanied by* **λαδολέμονο**
— **γιουβετσάκι** yiu·vet·*sa*·ki *prawns with tomatoes, parsley, oregano & feta chunks baked in earthenware pots*

γαριδοσαλάτα ⓕ gha·ri·tho·sa·*la*·ta *prawn salad*

γαύρος ⓜ *ghav*·ros *fresh anchovy*

γεμιστά ⓝ pl ye·mi·*sta* *stuffed vegetables*

γεμιστός ye·mi·*stos* *method of stuffing meat, fish or vegetables prior to cooking*

γιαούρτι ⓝ yia·*ur*·ti *thick, heavy yogurt with a tangy bite, made from sheep's, goat's or cow's milk*
— **αγελάδος** a·ye·*la*·thos *cow's milk yogurt*
— **φρούτων** *fru*·ton *fruit yogurt*
— **με μέλι** me *me*·li *yogurt with honey*
— **πρόβειο** *pro*·vio *sheep's milk yoghurt*

γιαουρτογλού ① yia·ur·to·*ghlu*
pie cooked with finely sliced grilled meat, topped with a yogurt sauce

γιαουρτόπιτα ① yia·ur·to·*pi*·ta
light moist cake made with yogurt, sugar, lemon rind & lots of eggs

γίδα βραστή ① *yi*·tha vra·*sti*
aromatic dish of boiled goat

γύρος *yi*·ros 'to spin' – seasoned lamb packed onto a spit & rotisseried upright, carved into meat platters or served in **πίτα** with tomatoes, onions & **τζατζίκι**

γιορτή ① yior·*ti* small pieces of pork & goat boiled with corn, topped with melted butter, cinnamon & pepper (Samos)

γιουβαρλάκια ⑩ pl yiu·var·*la*·kia egg-shaped rissoles of minced beef or lamb simmered in a light stock

γιουβέτσι ⑩ yiu·*vet*·si casserole of meat & seafood with tomatoes & barley pasta
— **με θαλασσινά** me tha·la·si·*na* casserole of seafood, barley pasta, tomatoes & chicken stock (Ionian Islands)

γιουσλεμέδες ⑩ pl yiuz·le·*me*·thes golden pies filled with eggs & **κεφαλοτύρι**, deep-fried then served with grated cheese (Lesvos)

γλιστρίδα ① ghli·*stri*·tha purslane – small-leafed plant with lemony flavour & crisp texture used mainly in salads
— **με καππαρόφυλλα σαλάτα** me ka·pa·ro·*fi*·la sa·*la*·ta purslane leaves, sliced tomatoes, black olives & caper leaves with oil & lemon dressing
— **με γιαούρτι** me yia·*ur*·ti chopped purslane beaten with strained yogurt, garlic, salt & oil (Crete)

γλυκά κουταλιού ⑩ pl ghli·*ka* ku·ta·*liu* 'spoon sweets' – preserved fruits

γλυκάνισο ⑩ ghli·*ka*·ni·so aniseed

γλυκά ταψιού ⑩ pl ghli·*ka* tap·*siu* sweets made with filo pastry

γλύκισμα ⑩ pl *ghli*·kiz·ma sweet pastry • cake

γλυκοκολοκύθα ① ghli·ko·ko·lo·*ki*·tha marrow • pumpkin • squash

γλώσσα ① *ghlo*·sa tongue (fish) • generic name for any flat fish

— **μοσχαρίσια κρασάτη** mo·sha·*ri*·sia kra·*sa*·ti tongue (fish) fried in butter, then poached in white wine

γουρουνάκι (του γάλακτος) ⑩ ghu·ru·*na*·ki (tu *gha*·lak·tos)
piglet • suckling pig
— **στη σούβλα** sti *suv*·la a whole suckling pig spit-roasted until tender
— **γεμιστό με φέτα** ye·mi·*sto* me *fe*·ta suckling pig stuffed with feta & roasted

γυαλιστερές ① pl yia·li·ste·*res* shellfish eaten alive with a squeeze of lemon juice (Dodecanese Islands)

Δ δ

δάχτυλα ⑩ pl *thakh*·ti·la 'fingers' – deep-fried, nut-filled pastries (Cyprus)

δίπλες ① pl *thi*·ples sweet pastry, deep-fried & drizzled with honey & sesame seeds
— **Δράμας** *thra*·mas yogurt pie with vine leaves

δρύλοι αλευρολέμονο ⑩ pl *thri*·li a·lev·ro·*le*·mo·no wild greens in lemon

Ε ε

ελαιόλαδο ⑩ e·le·o·la·*tho* olive oil

ελαιόπιτες ① pl e·le·o·*pi*·tes small olive & leek pies (Cyprus)

ελαιώτη ① e·le·o·*ti* bread with a layer of chopped black olives & onions (Cyprus)

ελαιόψωμο ⑩ e·le·*op*·so·mo olive bread

ελιές ① pl e·*lies* olives
— **Αμφίσσης** am·*fi*·sis large blue-black olives with nutty flavour
— **Αταλάντης** a·ta·*lan*·dis big fruity greenish-purple or purple olives
— **χαμούρες** ha·*mu*·res dried newly fallen olives
— **Ιονίων πράσινες** i·o·*ni*·on *pra*·si·nes mild green olives (Ionian Islands)
— **Καλαμάτας** ka·la·*ma*·tas large black olives with pungent flavour
— **μαύρες** *mav*·res black olives
— **Ναυπλίου** naf·*pli*·u nutty flavoured green olives (Nafplio)
— **παστές** pa·*stes* dried salted olives
— **πελτέ** pel·*te* olive paste
— **πράσινες** *pra*·si·nes green olives

— **τσακιστές** tsa·ki·*stes* cracked green olives marinated in oil, lemon & herbs

— **τουρσί** tur·*si* pickled olives

ελίτσες ① pl e·*lit*·ses tiny sweet black olives

εντόσθια ⑩ pl en·*do*·sthi·a offal • innards (usually lamb)

— **κοκκινιστά** ko·ki·ni·*sta* chicken giblets in a rich gravy

— **πουλιών** pu·*lion* giblets

Ζ ζ

ζαχαροπούλια ⑩ pl za·kha·ro·*pu*·lia marzipan sweets (Lesvos)

ζαχαρωτό με αμύγδαλο ⑩ za·kha·ro·*to* me a·*migh*·tha·lo marzipan

ζαμπόν ⑩ zam·*bon* ham

ζαργάνα ① zar·*gha*·na garfish

ζύμη ① *zi*·mi pastry

— **με γιαούρτι** me yia·*ur*·ti baked pasta dish consisting of homemade macaroni, strained yogurt & onions (Kos)

Θ θ

θαλασσινά ⑩ pl tha·la·si·*na* seafood

— **του Αιγαίου** tu e·*ye*·u paella-style rice dish cooked with seafood (Hydra)

θρούμπες ① pl *thru*·mbes ripe black olives

θυμάρι ⑩ thi·*ma*·ri thyme

Ι ι

ιμάμ-μπαϊλντί ⑩ i·mam·ba·il·*di* Turkish-inspired dish of eggplant stuffed with eggplant pulp, tomato, garlic, onion, parsley, then baked

Κ κ

καβούρι ⑩ ka·*vu*·ri crab

— **βραστό** vra·*sto* crab boiled & dressed with λαδολέμονο

καϊμάκι ⑩ ka·i·*ma*·ki froth that forms on top of Greek coffee while it brews

— **πηγμένο** pigh·*me*·no clotted cream

κακαβιά ① ka·ka·*via* saltwater fish soup

καλαμαράκια ⑩ pl ka·la·ma·*ra*·kia baby squid

καλαμάρι ⑩ ka·la·*ma*·ri squid

— **γεμιστό** ye·mi·*sto* squid stuffed with rice & baked in a lemony broth

— **Λεβριανά** lev·ria·*na* squid stewed in dry red wine with green olives, tomatoes, onions & parsley

— **με ρύζι** me *ri*·zi fried squid with onions simmered with water, crushed tomatoes, rice & cinnamon

— **τηγανητό** ti·gha·ni·*to* squid cut in rings or strips, lightly battered & fried

καλιτσούνια ⑩ pl ka·lit·*su*·nia small cheese pies

καπαμάς ⑩ ka·pa·*mas* method of stewing meat with tomatoes, wine, cinnamon & sometimes red capsicum & cloves

κάππαρη ① *ka*·pa·ri capers, usually pickled & eaten as an appetiser

κάπρος ⑩ *ka*·pros wild boar

καραμέλα ① ka·ra·*me*·la candy • caramel

καραβίδα ① ka·ra·*vi*·tha crayfish

καρύδια ⑩ pl ka·*ri*·thia walnuts

— **γεμιστά** ye·mi·*sta* walnuts & roasted almonds preserved in syrup (Cyprus)

καρυδόπιτα ① ka·ri·*tho*·pi·ta rich moist walnut cake

κάσιου ⑩ *ka*·siu cashews

κατάϊφι ⑩ ka·ta·*i*·fi 'angel hair' pastry – syrupy nest-like nut-filled rolls

κατσικάκι ⑩ kat·si·*ka*·ki goat • kid

— **πατούδο** pa·*tu*·tho roast kid stuffed with liver, rice, bread-crumbs, feta & raisins or κεφαλοτύρι, bacon, rice & dill (Cyclades)

— **ψητό** psi·*to* roast kid, sometimes served with a spicy red wine sauce

καφές ⑩ ka·*fes* coffee

— **ελληνικός** e·li·ni·*kos* freshly brewed Greek coffee

— **γλυκός** ghli·*kos* sweet coffee

— **μέτριος** *me*·tri·os medium-strength coffee with a little sugar

— **πολλά βαρύς** po·*la* va·*ris* strong coffee

— **σκέτος** *ske*·tos sugarless coffee

— **βαρύγλυκος** va·*ri*·ghli·kos strong & sweet coffee

κεφαλάκι ⑩ ke·fa·*la*·ki head – usually refers specifically to lamb's head

κεφτεδάκια ⑩ pl kef·te·*tha*·kia
miniature meat rissoles served at parties
κεφαλοτύρι ⑩ ke·fa·lo·*ti*·ri *'head cheese'
– known as 'kefalotiri', a hard, pale
yellow cheese made from sheep and
goat's milk*
κεφτέδες ⑩ pl kef·*te*·thes
*small tasty rissoles, often made with
minced lamb, pork or veal*
   — **στη σχάρα** sti *skha*·ra
   chargrilled meat rissoles
κιχώρι ⑩ ki·*kho*·ri *chicory • green leaves*
κιμαδόπιτα ① ki·ma·*tho*·pi·ta
mincemeat pie
κιμάς ki·*mas* ⑩
*sauce made from mincemeat, onions &
tomatoes served with pasta or rice*
κληματόφυλλο ⑩ kli·ma·to·fi·lo *vine leaf*
κοφίσι ⑩ ko·*fi*·si *pie made from boiled &
shredded dried fish mixed with onion,
garlic, rice & tomatoes (Kefallonia)*
κόκκοι καφέ ⑩ pl *ko*·ki ka·*fe* *coffee beans*
κοκκινέλι ① ko·ki·*ne*·li *red resinated wine*
κόκκινη πιπεριά ① ko·*ki*·ni pi·pe·*ria*
red capsicum (pepper)
κοκκινιστό ⑩ ko·ki·ni·*sto*
*'reddened' – method of simmering meat,
chicken or rice with tomatoes*
κόκκινο φασόλι ⑩ *ko*·ki·no fa·*so*·li
red kidney bean
   — **λάχανο** *la*·kha·no *red cabbage*
κοκκινοπίπερο ⑩ ko·ki·no·*pi*·pe·ro
cayenne (spice)
κόκορας ⑩ *ko*·ko·ras *rooster*
   — **κρασάτος** kra·*sa*·tos
   *lightly floured rooster fried with onions &
   spices, then cooked in red wine sauce*
κοκορέτσι ⑩ ko·ko·*ret*·si
*chopped lamb offal wrapped in lamb's
intestines & grilled*
κοκορόζουμο ⑩ ko·ko·ro·zu·mo
*lemony rooster broth used as a post-
party pick-me-up (Cyclades)*
κολιός ⑩ ko·li·*os* *mackerel*
   — **λαδορίγανη** la·tho·*ri*·gha·ni
   *mackerel baked with oil, lemon, oregano,
   garlic & parsley*
   — **σε κληματόφυλλα** kli·ma·to·fi·la
   mackerel in vine leaves
κολιτσάνοι ⑩ pl ko·lit·*sa*·ni *a sea anemone*

κολοκέτα ① pl ko·lo·*ke*·ta
*pastries stuffed with red pumpkin,
raisins & cracked wheat (Cyprus)*
κολοκύθα ① ko·lo·*ki*·tha
marrow • pumpkin • squash
κολοκυθάκια ⑩ pl ko·lo·ki·*tha*·kia *zucchini*
   — **με αβγά** me av·*gha*
   zucchini & egg omelette
   — **τηγανητά** ti·gha·ni·*ta*
   *zucchini battered & deep-fried, served
   with lemon & σκορδαλιά*
   — **βραστά** vra·*sta* *boiled baby zucchini
   with oil & lemon dressing*
κολοκύθι ⑩ ko·lo·*ki*·thi
marrow • pumpkin • squash
κολοκυθόανθοι ⑩ pl ko·lo·ki·*tho*·an·thi
zucchini flowers
   — **τηγανητοί** ti·gha·ni·*ti*
   zucchini flowers & cheese fritters (Andros)
   — **γεμιστοί** ye·mi·*sti* *zucchini flower
   ντολμάδες stuffed with rice, tomato &
   parsley & simmered until tender*
κολοκυθοκεφτέδες
ko·lo·ki·tho·kef·*te*·thes *rissoles of puréed
zucchini, parsley, onion, mint & garlic*
κολοκυθόπιτα ①
ko·lo·ki·*tho*·pi·ta
zucchini pie
κόλυβα ⑩ pl ko·li·va *wheat mixed with
fruit, pomegranate seeds, sugar & nuts –
eaten after the death of a family member
& on the anniversary of their death*
κομπόστα ① ko·bo·sta
compote • stewed fruit
κονσερβολιά ① kon·ser·vo·*lia* *common
type of olive from the central mainland*
κοντοσούβλι ⑩ kon·do·*suv*·li
*spit-roast pieces of lamb or pork seasoned
with onions, oregano, salt & pepper*
κορωναίικη ① ko·ro·ne·*i*·ki *a smaller, oil-
bearing variety of the kalamata olive*
κοτόπιτα ① ko·to·pi·ta *chicken filo pastry*
κοτόπουλο ⑩ ko·to·pu·lo *chicken*
   — **χυλοπίτες** hi·lo·*pi*·tes *whole chicken &
   noodles simmered in tomato, onion &
   cinnamon broth until liquid is absorbed*
   — **λεμονάτο** le·mo·*na*·to *roast chicken
   basted with butter & lemon juice*
   — **με μπάμιες** me ba·mies *chicken &
   okra braised in tomato & onion gravy*

κοτόσουπα ⑪ ko·*to*·su·pa
soup made from boiled whole chicken

κρασί ⑪ kra·*si* wine
— **άσπρο** *a*·spro white wine
— **κόκκινο** *ko*·ki·no red wine
— **λευκό** lef·*ko* white wine
— **ροζέ** ro·*ze* rosé wine

κρέας ⑪ *kre*·as meat
— **ελαφιού** e·la·*fiu* venison
— **στη στάμνα** sti *stam*·na
meat cooked in a pot
— **στο φούρνο με πατάτες** sto *fur*·no
me pa·*ta*·tes roast meat with potatoes

κρεατικά ⑪ pl kre·a·ti·*ka*
meat dishes, mostly stewed or roasted

κρεατόπιτα ⑦ kre·a·*to*·pi·ta
lamb or veal pie, usually with cinnamon
— **Κεφαλλονίτικη** ke·fa·lo·*ni*·ti·ki
*meat pie cooked with onions, eggs, rice,
potatoes, tomatoes & spices (Kefallonia)*
— **της Κρήτης** tis *kri*·tis
*pie of alternating layers of cubed lamb
(or goat) & μυζήθρα covered in butter &
baked in shortcrust pastry (Crete)*

κρεατόσουπα ⑦ kre·a·to·su·pa *nourish-
ing broth made from boiled meat –
sometimes thickened with rice &
αβγολέμονο*

κρεμμυδόπιτα ⑦ kre·mi·*tho*·pi·ta
*pie with a filling of μυζήθρα, grated
onion, eggs & dill (Mykonos)*

Κρητική κρεατόπιτα ⑦
kri·ti·*ki* kre·a·*to*·pi·ta
see **κρεατόπιτα της Κρήτης**

κριθαράκι ⑪ kri·tha·*ra*·ki
*tiny spindle-shaped barley pasta used
for pasta dishes, soups & casseroles*
— **με βούτυρο και τυρί** me *vu*·ti·ro
ke ti·*ri* pasta baked with brown butter,
cheese, lemon juice & herbs*

κουκουβάγια ⑦ ku·ku·*va*·yia
see **παξιμάδια σαλάτα**

κουκιά ⑪ pl ku·*kia* broad beans
— **ξερά βραστά** kse·*ra* vra·*sta* broad
beans boiled in water & lemon juice &
served with oil, dill & onion rings*
— **με αγριαγκινάρες**
me a·ghri·ang·gi·*na*·res
broad beans with artichokes

κουλουκόφωμο ⑪ ku·lu·*kop*·so·mo
see **παξιμάδια με ντομάτες και φέτα**

κουλουράκια ⑪ pl ku·lu·*ra*·kia
cookies · biscuits · buns
— **με πετιμέζι** me pe·ti·*me*·zi
*sweet buns made with syrup, cinnamon
& spices*

κουλούρι ⑪ ku·*lu*·ri crisp sesame-coated
*bread rings sold on streets & outside
church after Sunday mass · generic
name for circular rolls, buns & biscuits*

κουλούρια αστυπαλίτικα ⑪ pl ku·*lu*·ri·a
a·sti·pa·*li*·ti·ka saffron biscuits (Astypalea)

κουμκουάτ ⑪ kum·ku·*at* cumquat
— **λικέρ** li·*ker* cumquat liqueur (Corfu)

Κουμμανταρία ⑦ ku·man·da·ri·a
*heavy dessert wine originally made
during the Crusades by the Knights of
the Order of St John (Cyprus)*

κουνέλι ⑪ ku·*ne*·li rabbit
— **κρασάτο** kra·*sa*·to rabbit casserole
with red wine, garlic & bay leaves*
— **με καρύδια** me ka·*ri*·thi marinated
rabbit, fried & simmered in white wine
infused with coarsely ground walnuts*
— **με γιαούρτι** me yia·*ur*·ti
*rabbit marinated in lemon juice & black
pepper, then baked with a creamy egg &
yogurt sauce*
— **στιφάδο** sti·*fa*·tho rabbit ragout
spiced with cloves, cinnamon & cumin

κουπέπια ⑪ pl ku·*pe*·pia **ντολμάδες**
*made with minced lamb & veal, served
hot with αβγολέμονο sauce (Cyprus)*

κούπες ⑦ pl *ku*·pes deep-fried pastries of
mincemeat, onion & spices (Cyprus)

κουραμπιέδες ⑪ pl ku·ra·*bie*·thes
buttery almond shortbread

κυδώνι ⑪ ki·*tho*·ni quince
— **μπελτές** bel·*tes* quince jelly
— **γλυκό** ghli·*ko* quince preserve
flavoured with rose geranium*
— **στο φούρνο** sto *fur*·no buttered
quince baked in a water & sugar solution
until liquid has caramelised*
— **γεμιστό** ye·mi·*sto*
*large quince stuffed with minced beef,
rice, onions, raisins, cloves & nutmeg*

υδωνόπαστο ⓝ ki·tho·no·pa·sto
dark-red quince paste dried until firm, cut
in small diamonds & dusted with sugar

Λ λ

αβράκι ⓝ lav·ra·ki sea bass
— **στο αλάτι** sto a·la·ti whole sea bass
buried in salt & baked – the salt-encrusted
skin is slit & the flesh is eaten from the
bone with an oil & lemon dressing
αγάνα ① la·gha·na bread sprinkled with
sesame seeds baked on the first day of Lent
αγός ⓜ la·ghos hare
— **στιφάδο** sti·fa·tho hare ragout
spiced with cumin & cloves, usually
marinated in vinegar prior to cooking
αγωτό ⓝ la·gho·to hare ragout (Kefallonia)
αδόξειδο ⓝ la·thok·si·tho vinaigrette of
oil, vinegar, parsley, salt & pepper
αδολέμονο ⓝ la·tho·le·mo·no
thick dressing of oil beaten with lemon
juice, salt & pepper
άχανα ⓝ la·kha·na seasonal wild greens
— **με λαρδί** me lar·thi casserole of seasonal greens & fatty bacon (Mykonos)
αχανικά ⓝ la·kha·ni·ka vegetables
— **της θάλασσας** tis tha·la·sas
sea vegetables
άχανο ⓝ la·kha·no cabbage
— **κοκκινιστό** ko·ki·ni·sto
cabbage stewed with tomatoes, onions,
parsley, dill & paprika (Corfu)
— **με κιμά** me ki·ma cabbage braised
with onions, mincemeat & tomatoes,
finished with fresh butter (Mykonos)
αχανοσαλάτα ① la·kha·no·sa·la·ta
shredded white cabbage sprinkled with
oil, lemon juice & salt
εμονάτος ⓜ le·mo·na·tos
method of cooking with oil & lemon juice
ιθρίνι ⓝ li·thri·ni sea bream
ουκάνικα ⓝ pl lu·ka·ni·ka pork sausages
seasoned with coriander & orange peel •
generic word for sausages & frankfurters
λουκανόπιτες ① pl lu·ka·no·pi·tes
filo-wrapped sausages
ουκουμάδες ⓜ pl lu·ku·ma·thes
rosette-shaped, light-as-air doughnuts
served hot with honey & cinnamon

λουκούμι ⓝ lu·ku·mi Turkish delight
λουκούμια ⓝ pl lu·ku·mia
wedding shortbread (Cyprus)
λούντζα ① lun·dza spicy ham made from
cured smoked pork fillet (Cyprus, Cyclades)
— **με χαλούμι** me kha·lu·mi grilled ham
topped with melted χαλούμι (Cyprus)
λουβιά ⓝ pl lu·via black-eyed peas
— **με λάχανα** me la·kha·na warm salad
of black-eyed peas & seasonal greens
with oil & lemon dressing (Cyprus)
λουζές ⓜ lu·zes salted fillet of pork stuffed
into thick pig's intestine & sun-dried
(Mykonos)
λιαστός ⓜ lia·stos sun-dried

Μ μ

μαγειρίτσα ① ma·yi·rit·sa lamb's offal
soup thickened with rice & **αβγολέμονο**,
eaten to celebrate the end of Lent
μακαρόνια ⓝ pl ma·ka·ro·nia
macaroni • spaghetti
— **με κιμά** me ki·ma pasta with a sauce of
mincemeat, tomatoes, onions & red wine
— **με σάλτσα** me sal·tsa pasta with
tomato, onion & oregano sauce
— **με βούτυρο και τυρί** me vu·ti·ro ke
ti·ri pasta with butter sauce & cheese
— **στο φούρνο** sto fur·no pasta baked
in cheese & butter sauce
μαντί ⓝ man·di small pasta pockets filled
with mincemeat, cooked in meat broth
seasoned with capsicum & served with a
yogurt & garlic sauce (Northern Greece)
μάραθο ⓝ ma·ra·tho fennel
— **με ούζο σούπα** me u·zo su·pa
ouzo & fennel soup
μαχαλεπί ⓝ ma·kha·le·pi creamy custard
pudding in rose-water syrup (Cyprus)
μαχλέπι ⓝ ma·khle·pi
pungent bitter-sweet black cherry pips
used for spicing breads & stuffings
μαρίδα πικάντικη ① ma·ri·tha
pi·kan·di·ki whitebait, tomato & mint
fritters (Rhodes)
μαρίδες ① pl ma·ri·thes whitebait
— **λιαστές** lia·stes whitebait seasoned
with oregano & strung out to dry then
chargrilled & served with oil & lemon juice

— **τηγανητές** ti-gha-ni-*tes* whitebait rolled in flour & deep fried until crisp, served with lemon wedges

μαστίχα ① ma-*sti*-kha mastic • crystallised resin from the mastic bush, eaten as chewing gum & used as a flavouring (Chios)

μαυρομάτικα φασόλια ⓝ pl mav-ro-*ma*-ti-ka fa-*so*-lia black-eyed peas

— **με χόρτα** me khor-ta black-eyed peas stewed with greens, onions, tomatoes, parsley, mint & garlic (Crete)

μεγαρίτικη ① me-gha-*ri*-ti-ki olives grown in Attica, near Athens, named after the city of Megara

μελανούρι ⓝ me-la-*nu*-ri sea bream

μεζές ⓜ me-*zes* snack

μεζεδάκι ⓝ me-ze-*tha*-ki tasty morsels served with ouzo – favourites include olives, salted cucumber slices, feta, salted anchovies, mackerel & mini-meat rissoles

μέλι ⓝ *me*-li honey

— **με ξηρούς καρπούς** me ksi-rus kar-*pus* honey poured over walnuts or almonds

μελιτζάνες ① pl me-li-*dza*-nes eggplant

— **στο φούρνο** sto *fur*-no sliced eggplant fried with potatoes, & baked with tomatoes, cumin, parsley & feta

— **τηγανητές** ti-gha-ni-*tes* see **κολοκυθάκια τηγανητά**

μελιτζανοσαλάτα ① me-li-dza-no-sa-*la*-ta smoky purée of grilled mashed eggplant, onion, garlic, oil & lemon

μελιτίνι ⓝ me-li-*ti*-ni golden pastry tarts filled with fresh cheese, eggs & sugar, traditionally eaten at Easter

μελόπιτα ① me-*lo*-pi-ta cheesecake made with μυζήθρα & clear honey

μηλοπιτάκια ⓝ pl mi-lo-pi-*ta*-kia crescent-shaped apple & walnut pies

μοσχάρι ⓝ mo-*sha*-ri veal

— **κατσαρόλας με αρακά** kat-sa-*ro*-las me a-ra-*ka* veal stewed with fresh peas in white wine & thyme

— **κοκκινιστό με μακαρόνια** ko-ki-ni-*sto* me ma-ka-*ro*-nia veal stewed with tomatoes, served with spaghetti

— **ψητό** psi-to rolled veal rubbed with lemon juice, pepper & salt, pot-roasted with onion, tomatoes & wine

— **στιφάδο** sti-*fa*-tho veal ragout with garlic, peppercorns & bay leaves

μουσακάς ⓜ mu-sa-*kas* thick-sliced eggplant & mincemeat arranged in layers, topped with béchamel & baked

— **με αγγινάρες** me ang-gi-*na*-res alternating layers of minced veal & artichoke hearts

μουσταλευριά ① mu-sta-lev-*ri*-a dark gelatinous pudding made from boiled grape must, thickened with flour & sprinkled with cinnamon, seeds & nuts

μούστος ⓜ *mu*-stos grape must collected from crushed wine grapes

— **κουλούρα** ku-*lu*-ra hard, turban-shaped grape must buns

μπακαλιάρος ⓜ ba-ka-*lia*-ros dried salt cod soaked for several hours prior to cooking

μπουρδέτο ⓝ bur-*the*-to salt cod stew

— **κροκετάκια** kro-ke-*ta*-kia deep-fried salt cod mashed with potato & nutmeg

— **πλακί** pla-*ki* salt cod simmered with onions, potatoes, celery, carrots & garlic in a tomato-based sauce

— **τηγανητός** ti-gha-ni-*tos* salt cod fried in crisp, golden batter, traditionally accompanied with **σκορδαλιά**

μπακλαβάς ⓜ pl ba-kla-*vas* nut-filled layers of filo bathed in honey syrup

μπάμιες ① pl *ba*-mies okra

— **λαδερές** la-*the*-res okra stewed in oil

— **γιαχνί** yia-*khni* okra braised with pulped tomatoes & onions

μπαρμπούνια ⓝ pl bar-*bu*-nia small, sweet-fleshed red mullet

— **ψητά στον άνιθο** psi-*ta* ston *a*-ni-tho red mullet on a bed of dill

— **στη σκάρα** sti *ska*-ra red mullet basted with oil & lemon & chargrilled

— **τηγανητά** ti-gha-ni-*ta* red mullet rolled in seasoned flour & fried

μπεκάτσα ⓝ be-*kat*-sa woodcock

— **κρασάτη** kra-*sa*-ti woodcock casserole with dry red wine, tomatoes & spices, served with bread

μπεκρή μεζέ ⓝ be-*kri* me-ze 'drunken μεζέ' – meat cooked in tomato & wine sauce

μπομπότα ⓕ bo·bo·ta
  sweet corn bread studded with raisins, walnuts, cloves & flavoured with cinnamon & orange juice (Zakynthos)
μπισκότα ⓕ pl bi·sko·ta biscuits • cookies
μπιζελόσουπα ⓕ bi·ze·lo·su·pa
  fragrant pea soup loaded with dill
μπόλια bo·li·a ⓕ
  lacy caul of fat encasing lamb's stomach
μπριάμι ⓝ bri·a·mi casserole of sliced potatoes, zucchini, capsicums, tomatoes & herbs · roast vegetables
μπριζόλες ⓕ pl bri·zo·les chops • steak
μπουγάτσα ⓕ bu·ghat·sa creamy semolina pudding wrapped in pastry & baked
μπουρδέτο ⓝ bur·the·to
  hot fish casserole spiked with paprika
μπουρεκάκια ⓝ pl bu·re·ka·kia little filo pies in cigar, cigarette & envelope shapes
μπουρέκια ⓝ pl bu·re·kia filo pies shaped into thin long rolls, batons & pinwheels
  — **με ανερί** me a·ne·ri deep-fried pastry pouches stuffed with cheese (Cyprus)
μυαλά ⓝ pl mia·la brains
  — **αρνίσια λαδολέμονο** ar·ni·si·a la·tho·le·mo·no poached lamb's brains
  — **τηγανητά** ti·gha·ni·ta fried brains
μύδια ⓝ pl mi·thia mussels
  — **κρασάτα** kra·sa·ta
  poached mussels in a white wine sauce
  — **τηγανητά** ti·gha·ni·ta mussels shucked, lightly battered, fried in hot oil & served with a garlic yogurt sauce
  — **γεμιστά** ye·mi·sta mussels stuffed with rice, onions & parsley, slow-simmered in fish stock, tomato purée & white wine
μυζήθρα ⓕ mi·zi·thra
  soft mild ricotta-like cheese made from sheep's or goat's milk (sweet or savoury)
μυζηθρόπιτες ⓕ pl mi·zi·thro·pi·tes delicate deep-fried pies with μυζήθρα (Crete)

N ν

νεγκόσκα ⓝ ne·go·ska variety of red grape
νεραντζάκι γλυκό ⓝ ne·ran·dza·ki ghli·ko preserved small bitter green oranges
νεράτη ⓕ ne·ra·ti
  variety of cheese pie (Crete)

νουμπουλό ⓝ num·bu·lo
  bacon-flavoured sausage (Corfu)
ντολμάδες dol·ma·thes ⓜ pl
  dolmades – parcels of rice-wrapped leaves (usually vine leaves) & cooked in water, oil & lemon juice
  — **φυλλιανές** fi·lia·nes Christmas & New Year dish of onion sleeves stuffed with minced veal, pork & rice (Lesvos)
  — **με αυγολέμονο** me av·gho·le·mo·no dolmades with rice, minced lamb, tomatoes, mint & cumin, served hot with αλευρολέμονο
  — **με κουκιά** me ku·kia
  dolmades with boiled & sliced broad beans & dried ox meat, cooked on a bed of beef bones (Northern Greece)
  — **με λαχανόφυλλα** me la·kha·no·fi·la stuffed cabbage leaves, served hot with αβγολέμονο
  — **γιαλαντζί** yia·lan·dzi
  'fraud' – stuffed meatless dolmades
  — **Σμυρναίικα** zmir·ne·i·ka
  dolmades stuffed with sautéed onions, rice, eggplant, oregano, dill, garlic & cooked in tomato broth
ντομάτες ⓕ pl do·ma·tes tomatoes
  — **λιαστές** lia·stes sun-dried tomatoes
  — **γεμιστές** ye·mi·stes
  large tomatoes stuffed with rice, tomato pulp, onion, garlic & herbs
ντοματοκεφτέδες ⓜ pl do·ma·to·kef·te·thes
  deep-fried tomato rissoles
ντοματομπελτές ⓜ do·ma·to·pel·tes
  tomato paste
ντοματόσουπα ⓕ do·ma·to·su·pa soup made with tomatoes & sometimes pasta
νυχάκι ⓝ ni·kha·ki kalamata table olive (Messenia & Laconia)

Ξ ξ

ξεροτήγανα ⓝ pl kse·ro·ti·gha·na see δίπλες
ξινόχοντρος ⓜ ksi·no·khon·dros ground wheat cooked in sour milk & dried
ξινομυζήθρα ⓕ ksi·no·mi·zi·thra
  savoury μυζήθρα

O o

οινοπνευματώδη ⓝ pl
i-nop-nev-ma-to-thi *alcoholic spirits*

οστρακοειδή ⓝ pl o-stra-ko-i-thi *shellfish*

ούζο ⓝ *u-zo clear spirit distilled from
grape seeds, stems & skins with a strong
aniseed flavour*

οφτή σαλάτα ⓕ of-ti sa-la-ta *grilled salad
of potatoes, onions & σταφιδολιές, foil-
wrapped & chargrilled (Crete)*

οφτό ⓝ of-to *sausage made from pig's
intestines, rice, walnuts, pistachios,
raisins, cinnamon & orange peel (Crete)*

ουρά βοδιού ⓕ u-ra vo-thiu *oxtail*

Π π

παϊδάκια ⓝ pl pa-i-tha-kia *chops • cutlets*

παξιμάδια ⓝ pl pak-si-ma-thia
*hard wheat or barley rusks eaten slightly
moistened with water at meal times
(both wheat & barley varieties are
common)*
— **με ντομάτες και φέτα** me do-ma-tes
ke fe-ta **παξιμάδια** *moistened with water
or tomato juice & topped with sliced
tomatoes, feta, oregano, oil, salt & pepper
– very popular snack or light lunch*
— **σαλάτα** sa-la-ta **παξιμάδια** *broken
into pieces, moistened with water &
sprinkled with diced tomatoes, crumbled
feta or oregano, oil, salt & pepper*

παλαμίδα ⓕ pa-la-mi-tha
bonito • tunny fish (a variety of tuna)
— **ψητή με χόρτα** psi-ti me khor-ta
marinated bonito steaks

παλικάρια ⓝ pl pa-li-ka-ri-a
*mix of legumes & grains boiled & tossed
with oil, onions & dill*

πανέ pa-ne *crumbed & fried*

παντρεμένοι ⓝ pl pan-dre-me-ni *beans
with other foods (rice, wheat, tomatoes)*

παντζάρι ⓝ pan-dza-ri *beetroot*
— **σαλάτα** sa-la-ta *boiled thickly sliced
beetroot dressed with vinaigrette &
served with σκορδαλιά*

παντσέττα ⓕ pan-tse-ta *pancetta*

— **γεμιστή στο φούρνο**
ye-mi-sti sto fur-no *pig's stomach stuffed
with parmesan, garlic, onions & oregano,
basted with oil, wine & lemon juice &
baked with potatoes (Zakynthos)*

πάπια ⓕ pa-pia *duck*
— **με σάλτσα ροδιού** me sal-tsa ro-thiu
*fried duck breast served with sauce made
from pomegranate seeds, lemon juice,
duck stock & walnuts (Northern Greece)*
— **σαλμί** sal-mi *whole duck seared in oil,
then jointed & cooked in its own juices,
wine, orange juice & onions*

πάπρικα ⓕ pa-pri-ka *paprika*

παπουτσάκι ⓝ pa-put-sa-ki *'little shoe' –
stuffed baby eggplant topped with
béchamel sauce & baked*

παρμεζάνα ⓕ par-me-za-na *parmesan*

πασατέμπος ⓝ pa-sa-te-bos
*'pass the time' – roasted pumpkin seeds
sold as a snack*

πάστα ⓕ pa-sta *gateau*

παστέλι ⓝ pa-ste-li
sweet honey & sesame seed wafers

παστιτσάδα ⓕ pa-stit-sa-tha *pot-roasted
veal with tomato, red wine, cloves,
cinnamon & paprika (Corfu)*

παστίτσιο ⓝ pa-stit-si-o *baked layers of
buttery macaroni & minced lamb topped
with white sauce & grated κεφαλοτύρι*

παστός pa-stos *salted & dried*

παστουρμάς ⓜ pa-stur-mas
spicy dried ox meat

πατάτες ⓕ pl pa-ta-tes *potatoes*
— **γιαχνί** yia-khni *potatoes stewed with
tomatoes, onions & oregano*
— **κεφτέδες** kef-te-thes
fried potato, feta & parsley rissoles
— **λεμονάτες** le-mo-na-tes
*potatoes roasted with oil, lemon juice,
oregano, salt & pepper*
— **πουρέ** pu-re *mashed potatoes*
— **στο φούρνο** sto fur-no *potatoes
baked or roasted with oil, salt & oregano*
— **τηγανητές** ti-gha-ni-tes
fried potato slices

πατατοσαλάτα ⓕ pa-ta-to-sa-la-ta
potato salad

πατατού pa-ta-tu
baked mashed potato pie (Cyclades)

πατσάς pat-*sas* ⓜ tripe • rich-textured & surprisingly delicate-flavoured soup made with the stomach of a young lamb & finished with **αβγολέμονο**

πατούδα ⓕ pa-*tu*-tha pastries filled with walnuts, almonds & cinnamon, baked, sprinkled with orange flower water & dredged in icing sugar (Crete)

πεϊνιρλί pe-i-nir-*li* savoury pastries with a variety of fillings such as mincemeat, feta, ham & egg, & dried ox meat

πέρδικες ⓕ pl *per*-thi-kes partridges
— **με ελιές και σέλινο** me e-*lies* ke *se*-li-no partridges browned in butter & simmered in their own juices with green olives, sliced olives & tomatoes

πέρκα ⓕ *per*-ka sea perch

πέστροφα ⓕ *pe*-stro-fa trout

πεταλίδες ⓕ pl pe-ta-*li*-thes limpets
— **με θαλασσινούς χοχλιούς** me tha-la-si-*nus* kho-khli-*us* limpets & sea snails stewed with ripe tomatoes, onions & black pepper (Lesvos)

πετιμέζι ⓝ pe-ti-*me*-zi syrup made from unfermented grape juice, used to flavour rolls, cakes & sweets – when mixed with cold water makes a refreshing drink

πιλάφι ⓝ pi-*la*-fi pilau – rice & stock cooked to a creamy consistency – served to complement boiled meat or chicken
— **με ντομάτες** me do-*ma*-tes pilau with the addition of tomatoes, meat stock, garlic, parsley, salt & pepper
— **με γαρίδες** me gha-*ri*-thes pilau with prawns, onions & oregano
— **με μύδια** me *mi*-thia pilau with fresh mussels, onions & white wine
— **με περδίκια** me per-*thi*-ki-a pilau with partridge, tomato & cloves (Kefallonia)

πιπέρι ⓝ pi-*pe*-ri black pepper

πιροσκί ⓝ pi-ro-*ski* deep-fried, dough-wrapped sausage roll

πίτα ⓕ *pi*-ta pie – filo is the most common pastry used • flat doughy circular bread seared on grill until golden, mainly used for wrapping **σουβλάκι** & **γύρος**

πιτσούνια ⓝ pl pit-*su*-nia squab • love-bird • any tiny bird used for cooking

— **κρασάτα** kra-*sa*-ta baby squabs doused in red wine, tomato pulp, cinnamon & cloves then braised
— **με κουκουνάρια** me ku-ku-*na*-ria squab ignited with brandy, splashed with retsina & dressed with a garlic cream sauce (Northern Greece)
— **με κουκιά** me ku-*kia* stewed squab & fresh broad beans cooked in chicken stock, white wine, dill, garlic & lots of black pepper

πλακί pla-*ki* method of baking or braising with tomatoes, onion, garlic & parsley

ποδαράκια ⓝ pl po-tha-*ra*-kia trotters
— **αρνίσια** a-*ni*-si-a boiled lamb's trotters browned in butter & garlic, roasted, then finished with egg & lemon sauce

πόρτο ⓝ *por*-to port

πορτοκάλι ⓝ por-to-*ka*-li orange
— **γλυκό** ghli-*ko* preserved orange

ποτό ⓝ po-*to* drinks • spirits (on menus)

πράσα ⓝ pl *pra*-sa leeks
— **αλευρολέμονο** a-lev-ro-*le*-mo-no braised leeks in lemony sauce
— **με δαμάσκηνα** me tha-*ma*-ski-na leeks & prunes sprinkled with cinnamon & nutmeg
— **με ρύζι** me *ri*-zi leeks & celery simmered with rice & crushed tomatoes

πρασάκια με πατάτες ⓝ pl pra-*sa*-ki-a me pa-*ta*-tes leeks & sliced potatoes cooked in butter, chicken stock, onions, oregano & parsley

πρασόπιτα ⓕ pra-*so*-pi-ta pie made with braised leeks, feta, **μυζήθρα** & skim milk (Western Greece)

P ρ

ραβιόλες ⓕ pl ra-vi-*o*-les pasta envelopes stuffed with a mixture of cheese & mint, served with melted butter & grated cheese (Cyprus)

ραδίκι ⓝ ra-*thi*-ki chicory • term used for common varieties of **χόρτα**
— **σαλάτα** sa-*la*-ta spring salad of young dandelion leaves splashed with oil & lemon

ρακί ⓝ ra-*ki* fiery village spirit made from grapes, like ouzo but without the aniseed taste, high in alcohol

ραφιόλια ⓝ pl ra-fi-o-li-a sweet half-moon filo pastries stuffed with cheese, eggs, cinnamon, orange rind & ouzo (Cyclades)

ρεβανί ⓝ re-va-*ni* very sweet semolina sponge, flavoured with vanilla & orange juice & smothered with honey syrup

ρεβίθια ⓝ pl re-*vi*-thia chickpeas
— **αλευρολεμονο** a-lev-ro-le-mo-no chickpeas simmered in a rich lemony broth
— **στο φούρνο** sto fur-no casserole of chickpeas, onions, garlic & bay leaves – favourite fasting food during Lent
— **σούπα** su-pa chickpea soup

ρεβιθοκεφτέδες ⓝ pl re-vi-tho-kef-*te*-thes rissoles of mashed chickpeas, potatoes, onion, parsley & black pepper

ρέγγα ⓕ reng-ga smoked herrings, eaten plain or grilled with oil & lemon

ρέσι ⓝ re-si pilau made with burghul & lamb (including the tail) & served at weddings (Cyprus)

ρετσίνα ⓕ ret-si-na retsina – pine-resinated wine, often served chilled

ριγανάτος ⓜ ri-gha-*na*-tos seasoned with oregano, salt & pepper

ρίγανη ⓕ *ri*-gha-ni pungent Greek oregano

ριζάδα ⓕ ri-*za*-tha thick soup made with rice & shellfish or tiny game birds (Corfu)

ριζόγαλο ⓝ ri-zo-gha-lo vanilla-flavoured rice pudding sprinkled with cinnamon

ρόδι ⓝ *ro*-thi pomegranate – used to flavour sweets, syrups, cakes & salads

ροδόνερο ⓝ ro-tho-ne-ro fragrant rose-water used to flavour cakes, pies & sweets

ροφός ⓜ ro-fos grouper • blackfish

ρολό από κιμά ⓝ ro-lo a-po ki-*ma* baked mincemeat roll with hard-boiled eggs cuddled in the middle

ρύζι ⓝ *ri*-zi rice

Σ σ

σαλάχι ⓝ sa-*la*-hi ray fish • skate
— **σαλάτα** sa-*la*-ta boiled ray fish salad dressed with λαδολεμονο

σαλιγκάρια ⓝ pl sa-ling-*ga*-ri-a snails – cooked in the shell & eaten with a fork

— **φρικασέ** fri-ka-se large snails sautéed in oil & stewed with zucchini, onions, fresh dill & finished with αβγολεμονο
— **με σάλτσα** me sal-tsa snails cooked with crushed tomatoes, tomato paste, onions & oregano
— **συμπεθεριό** sim-be-the-rio 'in-laws' – snails cooked with sliced eggplant, tomato pulp & ξινόχοντρος
— **στα κάρβουνα** sta kar-vu-na live snails chargrilled & doused with λαδολεμονο & bay leaves (Cyclades)
— **στιφάδο** sti-*fa*-tho snail ragout with bay leaves (Crete)

σαλμί ⓝ sal-*mi* method of casseroling game with red wine, vegetables & herbs

σάλτσα ⓕ *sal*-tsa sauce • generic term for tomato sauce
— **από ζωμό κρέατος** a-po zo-mo kre-a-tos gravy
— **άσπρη** *a*-spri béchamel sauce with egg
— **άσπρη ξινή** *a*-spri ksi-*ni* 'sharp white sauce' – made with butter, flour, meat stock, eggs & lemon
— **αυγολεμονο** av-gho-le-mo-no see αβγολεμονο
— **ντομάτα** do-*ma*-ta tomato sauce with bay leaves
— **ντομάτα με κιμά** do-*ma*-ta me ki-*ma* tomato & mincemeat sauce
— **μαρινάτα** ma-ri-*na*-ta marinade
— **μουστάρδα** mu-star-tha mustard & garlic beaten with lemon juice
— **ταρτάρ** tar-*tar* tartare sauce

Σάμος sa-mos rich golden dessert wine (Samos)

σαρακοστιανά ⓝ pl sa-ra-ko-sti-a-na see νηστησιμα

σαρδέλες ⓕ pl sar-*the*-les sardines
— **παστές** pa-stes salted sardines
— **στο φούρνο** sto fur-no sardines baked with oil, lemon, garlic & oregano

σαρμάς ⓜ sar-*mas* pie-like offal dish (Northern Greece)

σβίγγοι ⓜ pl zving-gi deep-fried fritters served with honey, cinnamon & cognac syrup

σελινόριζα ① se·li·no·ri·za *celeriac*
— **με αυγολέμονο** me av·gho·le·mo·no *creamy dish of celeriac in chicken stock & finished with egg & lemon sauce*
— **με πράσα** me pra·sa *braised celeriac wedges & leek strips thickened with* **αβγολέμονο**

σέσκουλο ① se·sku·lo *swiss chard, type of* **χόρτα**
— **με κιμά** me ki·ma *silverbeet sautéed with chopped onion in butter & cooked with minced lamb, rice, dill, lemon juice & salt*

σεσκουλόρυζο ① se·sku·lo·ri·zo *see* **σπανακόρυζο**

σεφταλιά ① sef·ta·lia *pork rissoles wrapped in sheep's caul & chargrilled (Cyprus)*

σκαλτσοτσέτα ① pl skal·tsot·se·ta *paper-thin slices of fillet steak skewered & simmered in oil, water & tomatoes*

σκορδαλιά ① skor·tha·lia *thick paste of walnuts, bread, potatoes, olive oil, lemon & garlic*

σκόρδο ① skor·tho *garlic*
— **στούμπι** stu·bi *vinegar bottled with a garlic bulb, used for dressing vegetable dishes & salads (Ionian Islands)*
— **τσιγαριστά** tsi·gha·ri·sta *fried whole garlic bulbs • peeled & sliced garlic cloves fried & simmered in white wine, tomato paste, salt & pepper (Ithaca)*

σκουμπρί ① sku·bri *mackerel*

σνακς ① pl snaks *snacks*

σοφρίτο ① so·fri·to *fried veal slices braised in a sauce of crushed garlic, wine vinegar, parsley, mint & brandy (Corfu)*

σοκολάτα ① so·ko·la·ta *chocolate*
— **γάλα** gha·la *hot chocolate*

σουσάμι ① su·sa·mi *sesame seed*

σούβλα ① suv·la *spit-roasted • skewers • method of chargrilling meat or fish*

σουβλάκι ① suv·la·ki *souvlaki – tender chunks of seasoned or marinated meat (or fish) skewered & chargrilled*
— **με πίτα** me pi·ta *souvlaki with* **πίτα**

σούγλι ① sugh·li *sun-dried baby bogue fish coated in batter & fried (Cyclades)*

σούπα ① su·pa *soup*
— **ειδάτη** ksi·tha·ti *sour soup of lentils, parsley & vinegar*

— **με τσουκνίδες** me tsuk·ni·thes *electric-green soup of stinging nettles & diced potatoes cooked in chicken stock & thickened with milk*

σουπιές ① pl su·pies *cuttlefish*
— **κρασάτες** kra·sa·tes *cuttlefish cooked in wine*
— **με σάλτσα μελάνης** me sal·tsa me·la·nis *cuttlefish cooked in a rich sauce made from its own black ink & wine (Crete)*
— **με σπανάκι** me spa·na·ki *cuttlefish cooked with spinach, onions, dill & mint*

σουτζουκάκια ① pl su·dzu·ka·kia *rissoles of minced lamb, veal or pork braised in a very spicy tomato gravy*

σουτζούκι ① su·dzu·ki *strings of almonds dipped in syrup & sun-dried*

σπάλα ① spa·la *shoulder of meat*
— **μοσχαρίσια** mos·kha·ri·si·a *silverside*

σπανακόπιτα ① spa·na·ko·pi·ta *spinach filo pie, often includes feta or* **κεφαλοτύρι**, *eggs & herbs*

σπανακόρυζο ① spa·na·ko·ri·zo *sautéed spinach, rice, spring onions & dill simmered in water until liquid is absorbed*

σπετζοφάι ① spe·dzo·fa·i *sliced pork sausages stewed with sweet green peppers, eggplant, tomatoes & oregano*

σπλήνα ① spli·na *spleen*
— **γεμιστή** ye·mi·sti *calf's spleen stuffed with chopped sautéed liver, onion, garlic & herbs, then roasted*

σπληνάντερο ① spli·nan·de·ro *spit-roast sausage made from intestine stuffed with sliced spleen & garlic*

σταφίδες ① pl sta·fi·thes *raisins • currants*

σταφιδολιές ① pl sta·fi·tho·lies *type of olive sun-dried until wrinkled, lightly salted & packed, or immersed in oil*

σταφιδωτά ① pl sta·fi·tho·ta *oval short-bread biscuits with chewy raisin centres*

σταφύλια ① pl sta·fi·li·a *grapes*

στάκα ① sta·ka *creamy butter made from fresh goat's or sheep's milk, used to flavour pies, stuffed vegetables & pilau*
— **με αβγά** me av·gha *omelette with* **στάκα** *(Crete)*

στάμνα ① stam-na method of cooking meat & potatoes in a pot sealed with wet clay & baked in charcoal embers

στιφάδο ⑩ sti-fa-tho
meat, game or seafood ragout

στραγάλια ① pl stra-gha-lia
roasted chickpeas for snacking

σύκο ⑩ si-ko fig
— **αποστολιάτικο** a-po-sto-lia-ti-ko young green fig
— **γλυκό** ghli-ko green fig preserve
— **στο φούρνο** sto fur-no figs baked in a syrup of honey, vanilla, orange juice & orange flower water

συκόπιτα ① si-ko-pi-ta fig cake (Corfu)

συκόψωμο ⑩ si-kop-so-mo heavy aromatic fig cake • dried green figs minced & mixed with ouzo shaped into balls, flattened, dried & wrapped in vine leaves

συκωταριά ① si-ko-ta-ria innards • offal

συκώτι ⑩ si-ko-ti liver
— **κρασάτα** kra-sa-ta chopped liver marinated in red wine
— **λαδορίγανη** la-tho-ri-gha-ni grilled liver with oil, lemon & oregano
— **μαρινάτα** ma-ri-na-ta thinly sliced livers fried & finished with vinegar, white wine & rosemary
— **με κρεμμυδάκια** me kre-mi-tha-kia livers fried with spring onions & cloves in a sauce of white wine & tomato juice

σφακιανόπιτες ① pl sfa-kia-no-pi-tes cheese pies consisting of balls of cheese wrapped in dough, then fried & served with a dollop of honey

σφουγγάτο ⑩ sfung-ga-to Spanish-style omelette made with more vegetables than eggs, fried or baked (Rhodes)

Τ τ

ταβάς ⑩ ta-vas casserole of seasoned beef or lamb, fried onions, diced tomatoes, oil, vinegar & cinnamon

ταλατούρι ⑩ ta-la-tu-ri τζατζίκι flavoured with mint (Cyprus)

ταραμάς ⑩ ta-ra-mas salted pressed roe of the grey mullet or cod

ταράξακο ⑩ ta-rak-sa-ko dandelion

ταχίνι ⑩ ta-hi-ni sesame seed paste

ταχινόσουπα ① ta-hi-no-su-pa creamy lemony soup made from sesame paste (popular during Lent)

τελεμές ⑩ te-le-mes heavily salted feta-style cheese

τηγανόψωμο ⑩ ti-gha-nop-so-mo fried tomato & spring onion bread (Santorini)

τίλιο ⑩ ti-li-o infusion of lime leaves

τζατζίκι ⑩ dza-dzi-ki refreshing purée of grated cucumber, yogurt & garlic

τσόχος ⑩ tso-khos milk thistle • mild sweet-tasting green used in warm salads, pies & stews • type of χόρτα

της ώρας tis o-ras dishes cooked to order, such as steaks or chops

τσουρέκι ⑩ tot-su-re-ki braided Easter bread spiced with lemon rind & cherry pips, sprinkled with almonds & crushed μαστίχα

τραχανόσουπα ① tra-kha-no-su-pa thick gruel of granulated pasta cooked in chicken broth with butter, lemon juice

τριαντάφυλλο γλυκό ⑩ tri-an-da-fi-lo ghli-ko delicate soft jam made from dark red rose petals

τσικουδιά ① tsi-ku-thia see ρακί

τσιπούρα ① tsi-pu-ra gilt head bream • snapper

τσίπουρο ⑩ tsi-pu-ro see ρακί

τσίρος ⑩ tsi-ros small dried mackerel

τσουκνίδες ① pl tsu-kni-thes stinging nettles used in salads & soups

τουρσί ⑩ tur-si pickles • pickled

τούρτα ① tur-ta cake • gateau • tart

τυρί ⑩ ti-ri cheese
— **μπλε** ble blue cheese
— **ημίσκληρο** i-mi-skli-ro semi-firm cheese
— **κατσίκισιο** kat-si-ki-si-o goat's cheese
— **κρεμώδες** kre-mo-thes cream cheese
— **μαλακή μυζήθρα** ma-la-ki mi-zi-thra cottage cheese
— **μαλακό** ma-la-ko soft cheese
— **σαγανάκι** sa-gha-na-ki sharp, hard cheese fried until crispy on the outside & soft in the centre, served with a squeeze of lemon juice
— **σκληρό** skli-ro hard cheese

τυρόπηγμα ⑩ ti-ro-pigh-ma curd

τυρόπιτα ⓝ ti·ro·pi·ta cheese pies, the classic mixture is feta & **κεφαλοτύρι** wrapped in flaky filo pastry & baked

τυροβολιά ⓕ ti·ro·vo·lia cheese variety

Φ φ

φάβα ⓕ fa·va yellow split pea purée served with raw onion rings
— **παντρεμένη** pan·dre·me·ni 'married' – leftover **φάβα** served as a hot dish with the addition of tomatoes & cumin

φαγρί ⓝ fa·ghri sea bream

φακές ⓕ pl fa·kes lentils
— **με μακαρόνια** me ma·ka·ro·nia lentils simmered in water & vinegar with mint, garlic & pearl pasta (Astypalea)
— **σούπα** su·pa lentil soup

Φανουρόπιτα ⓕ fa·nu·ro·pi·ta cake spiced with dried fruit, brandy & cinnamon – served on Saint Fanourios Day

φασκόμηλο ⓝ fa·sko·mi·lo sage

φασολάδα ⓕ fa·so·la·tha thick fragrant soup of beans, tomatoes, tomato paste, carrots, celery, garlic & parsley

φασολάκια ⓝ pl fa·so·la·kia green beans
— **λαδερά** la·the·ra green beans cooked in oil with tomatoes & onions
— **σαλάτα** sa·la·ta boiled fresh green beans with λαδολέμονο or λαδόξιδο

φασόλια ⓝ pl fa·so·li·a dried beans – usually refers to white haricot/lima beans
— **μάραθο** ma·ra·tho dried beans browned in oil & onions, simmered with tomato pulp & fennel leaves
— **σαλάτα** sa·la·ta bean salad

φέτα ⓕ fe·ta feta – white, crumbly, salty cheese
— **σχάρας** skha·ras grilled feta

φέτες ψαριού με ντομάτα και σταφίδες ⓕ pl fe·tes psa·riu me do·ma·ta ke sta·fi·thes fish with tomato & currants

φιλέτο ⓝ fi·le·to fillet • steak

φιρίκια ⓝ pl fi·ri·ki·a small crisp apples (Northern Greece)
— **με αμύγδαλα** me a·migh·tha·la baked **φιρίκια** stuffed with almonds
— **γεμιστά** ye·mi·sta **φιρίκια** stuffed with minced veal, coriander & cumin

φιστίκια ⓝ pl fi·sti·kia peanuts
— **Αιγίνης** e·yi·nis pistachios

φλαούνες ⓕ pl fla·u·nes baked savoury tarts (Cyprus)

φοινίκια ⓝ pl fi·ni·ki·a honey-dipped shortbread sprinkled with cinnamon & marked with a criss-cross design

φρικασέ ⓝ fri·ka·se meat or vegetable stew thickened & flavoured with **αβγολέμονο**

φρουταλιά ⓕ fru·ta·lia omelette-type dish consisting of eggs, potatoes, parsley & sliced smoked pork sausages (Andros)

φρυγαδέλια ⓝ pl fri·gha·the·lia liver parcels in lamb's caul, fried or skewered & chargrilled (Northern Greece, Thessaly)

φύλλο ⓝ fi·lo flaky tissue-thin pastry used for pies & sweet pastries

Χ χ

χαβιάρι ⓝ kha·via·ri caviar

χαλβάς ⓝ khal·vas rich creamy sweet made from sesame seeds & honey, flavoured with pistachio, chocolate or almonds
— **σιμιγδαλένιος** si·migh·tha·le·nios moist cake of semolina & honey, decorated with almonds & cinnamon
— **της Ρίνας** tis ri·nas baked semolina & almond cake served hot with sugar syrup

χαλορίνι ⓝ kha·lo·ri·ni pouch-shaped cheese filled with crushed coriander (Cyprus)

χαλούμι ⓝ kha·lu·mi firm, white, sheep's milk cheese with elastic texture & salty taste (Cyprus)

χαλουμπίτες ⓕ pl kha·lu·mo·pi·tes savoury cake made with **χαλούμι**, eggs, mint, sultanas & **μαστίχα** (Cyprus)

χαλουμόψωμο ⓝ kha·lu·mop·so·mo bread baked with chunks of **χαλούμι** (Cyprus)

χαμομήλι ⓝ kha·mo·mi·li chamomile

χαμψιά ⓕ kham·psia fresh anchovy

χαμψοπίλαφο ⓝ kham·pso·pi·la·fo onion & anchovy pilau seasoned with oregano

χείλη της χανούμισσας ⓝ pl kha·nu·mi·sas 'the Turkish lady's lips' – crunchy honey cakes (Rhodes)

χέλι ⓝ he·li eel
— **πλακί** pla·ki eel baked with tomatoes, onions, potatoes & herbs (Corfu)

χοιρινές ① pl hi-ri-nes pork chops
— **κρασάτες** kra-sa-tes pork chops simmered in red wine
— **στη σχάρα** sti skha-ra pork chops chargrilled with salt, pepper & lemon juice
— **τηγανητές** ti-gha-ni-tes fried pork chops

χοιρινό ① hi-ri-no pork
— **με κυδώνια** me ki-tho-nia pork & quinces simmered in red wine spiced with orange peel & cinnamon
— **με πράσα** me pra-sa pork & leek casserole
— **με σέλινο αυγολέμονο** me se-li-no av-gho-le-mo-no pork & celery in egg & lemon sauce
— **μπούτι ψητό** bu-ti psi-to crispy, roast leg of pork
— **παστό** pa-sto salted pork

χοιρομέρι ① hi-ro-me-ri cured leg of ham (Cyprus, Zakynthos)

χόντρος ⓜ khon-dros hand-milled wheat used in soups, dolmades, snail dishes & stews (see also **ξινόχοντρος**)

χόρτα ① pl khor-ta wild or cultivated greens used in salads, pie fillings, casseroles or boiled & served hot with an oil & lemon dressing
— **τσιγάρι** tsi-gha-ri lightly fried wild greens

χορτόπιτα ① khor-to-pi-ta pies made from seasonal greens

χορτοσαλάτα ① khor-to-sa-la-ta warm salad of greens dressed with salt, oil & lemon

χορτόσουπα ① khor-to-su-pa vegetable soup

χουρμάδες ⓜ pl khur-ma-thes dates

χοχλιοί ① pl kho-khli-i snails
— **μπουμπουριστοί** bu-bu-ri-sti 'upside-down' – live snails deep-fried & doused with vinegar & rosemary

χριστόψωμο ① khri-stop-so-mo sweet Christmas bread baked in the shape of a cross

χταπόδι ① khta-po-thi octopus
— **βραστό** vra-sto boiled octopus coated with oil & lemon sauce
— **κεφτέδες** kef-te-thes rissoles of minced octopus, onion, mint & cheese
— **κρασάτο** kra-sa-to octopus cooked in red wine sauce
— **λιαστό** lia-sto sun-dried, chargrilled octopus sprinkled with oil & lemon juice
— **με μακαρόνι κοφτό** me ma-ka-ro-ni kof-to casserole of octopus, tomatoes, macaroni & red wine
— **στα κάρβουνα** sta kar-vu-na grilled octopus
— **στιφάδο** sti-fa-tho octopus ragout
— **τουρσί** tur-si pickled octopus

χυλόφτα ① pl hi-lof-ta macaroni served with hot butter & grated cheese (Crete)

χωριάτικη σαλάτα ① kho-ria-ti-ki sa-la-ta 'village salad' – salad of tomatoes, cucumber, olives & feta (known outside Greece as 'Greek salad')

Ψ ψ

ψάρι ① psa-ri fish
— **μαρινάτο** ma-ri-na-to fish fried until golden, served with a piquant sauce of garlic, rosemary & vinegar (also called **ψάρι σαβόρι**)
— **πλακί** pla-ki whole fish basted with oil, lemon & parsley, baked on a bed of chopped tomatoes & onions
— **σαβόρι** sa-vo-ri see **ψάρι μαρινάτο**
— **Σπετσιώτο** spet-si-o-to fish baked with bread crumbs & white wine (Spetses)
— **στη σχάρα** sti skha-ra chargrilled fish
— **στο φούρνο λαδορίγανη** sto fur-no la-tho-ri-gha-ni sliced fish & potato wedges baked in a broth of oil, water & lemon juice
— **τηγανητό** ti-gha-ni-to battered fish
— **βραστό με λαχανικά** vra-sto me la-kha-ni-ka poached fish with vegetables – the broth is often strained, thickened with **αυγολέμονο**

ψαροκεφτέδες ⓜ pl psa-ro-kef-te-thes fried fish rissoles

ψαρονέφρι ① psa-ro-ne-fri pork fillet steak

ψαρόσουπα ① psa-ro-su-pa fish soup thickened with rice & **αυγολέμονο**

ψητός psi-tos an all-purpose term for grilling, baking & barbecueing

ψωμιά με ανάγλυφες διακοσμήσεις ① pl pso-mia me a-na-ghli-fes thia-koz-mi-sis decorated bread (usually made with doughs of different colours) eaten at festivals, baptisms & weddings

emergencies

έκτακτη ανάγκη

Help!	Βοήθεια!	vo·*i*·thia
Stop!	Σταμάτα!	sta·*ma*·ta
Go away!	Φύγε!	*fi*·ye
Thief!	Κλέφτης!	*klef*·tis
Fire!	Φωτιά!	fo·*tia*
Watch out!	Πρόσεχε!	*pro*·se·he

Call an ambulance!
Κάλεσε το ασθενοφόρο.　　　　*ka*·le·se to as·the·no·*fo*·ro

Call the doctor!
Κάλεσε ένα γιατρό.　　　　*ka*·le·se *e*·na yia·*tro*

Call the police!
Κάλεσε την αστυνομία.　　　　*ka*·le·se tin a·sti·no·*mi*·a

It's an emergency.
Είναι μια έκτακτη ανάγκη.　　　　*i*·ne mia *ek*·tak·ti a·*na*·gi

There's been an accident.
Έγινε ατύχημα.　　　　*e*·yi·ne a·*ti*·hi·ma

Could you please help?
Μπορείς να βοηθήσεις,　　　　bo·*ris* na vo·i·*thi*·sis
παρακαλώ;　　　　pa·ra·ka·*lo*

signs

Αστυνομία	a·sti·no·*mi*·a	Police
Αστυνομικός	a·sti·no·mi·*kos*	Police Station
Σταθμός	stath·*mos*	
Νοσοκομείο	no·so·ko·*mi*·o	Hospital
Σταθμός Πρώτων	stath·*mos pro*·ton	Emergency
Βοηθειών	vo·i·thi·*on*	Department

essentials

191

Is it safe ...?	Είναι ασφαλές ...;	i·ne as·fa·les ...
at night	τη νύχτα	ti nikh·ta
for gay people	για γκέι	yia ge·i
for travellers	για ταξιδιώτες	yia tak·si·thio·tes
for women	για γυναίκες	yia yi·ne·kes
on your own	χωρίς παρέα	kho·ris pa·re·a

I'm lost.

Έχω χαθεί. — e·kho kha·thi

Where are the toilets?

Πού είναι η τουαλέτα; — pu i·ne i tu·a·le·ta

Is that a UN zone?

Είναι αυτή η ζώνη του ΟΗΕ; — i·ne af·ti i zo·ni tu o·i·e

Where's the demarcation line?

Πού είναι η διαχωριστική γραμμή; — pu i·ne i thi·a·kho·ri·sti·ki ghra·mi

Are there military bases in this region?

Υπάρχουν στρατιωτικές βάσεις σ' αυτή την περιοχή; — i·par·khun stra·ti·o·ti·kes va·sis saf·ti tin pe·ri·o·hi

police

Where's the police station?

Πού είναι ο αστυνομικός σταθμός; — pu i·ne o a·sti·no·mi·kos stath·mos

Please telephone the Tourist Police.

Παρακαλώ τηλεφώνα την τουριστική αστυνομία. — pa·ra·ka·lo ti·le·fo·na tin tu·ri·sti·ki a·sti·no·mi·a

I want to report an offence.

Θέλω να αναφέρω μια παρανομία. — the·lo na a·na·fe·ro mia pa·ra·no·mi·a

It was him/her.

Ήταν αυτός/αυτή. — i·tan af·tos/af·ti

I have insurance.

Έχω ασφάλεια. — e·kho as·fa·li·a

I've been ...	Με έχουν ...	me *e*·khun ...
He/She has been ...	Τον/Την έχουν ...	ton/tin *e*·khun ...
assaulted	κακοποιήσει	ka·ko·pi·*i*·si
raped	βιάσει	vi·*a*·si
robbed	ληστέψει	li·*step*·si

---

the police may say ...

Κατηγορείσαι για ...	
ka·ti·gho·*ri*·se yia ...	**You're charged with ...**
Αυτός κατηγορείται για ...	
af·*ti* ka·ti·gho·*ri*·te yia ...	**He's charged with ...**
Αυτή κατηγορείται για ...	
af·*ti* ka·ti·gho·*ri*·te yia ...	**She's charged with ...**

διατάραξη	thi·a·*ta*·rak·si	disturbing the
ησυχίας	i·si·*hi*·as	peace
εξαγωγή	ek·sa·gho·*yi*	exporting
αρχαιοτήτων χωρίς	ar·he·o·*ti*·ton kho·*ris*	antiquities with-
άδεια	*a*·thi·a	out a permit
κακοποίηση	ka·ko·*pi*·i·si	assault
κλοπή από	klo·*pi* a·*po*	shoplifting
κατάστημα	ka·*ta*·sti·ma	
κλοπή	klo·*pi*	theft
μετακίνηση	me·ta·*ki*·ni·si	removing
αρχαιοτήτων	ar·he·o·*ti*·ton	antiquities
μη κατοχή	mi ka·to·*hi*	not having
βίζας	*vi*·zas	a visa
κατοχή	ka·to·*hi*	possession
(παράνομων	(pa·*ra*·no·mon	(of illegal
ουσιών)	u·si·*on*)	substances)
υπέρβαση της	i·*per*·va·si tis	overstaying
βίζας	*vi*·zas	a visa

Είναι πρόστιμο για ...	*i*·ne *pro*·sti·mo yia ...	It's a ... fine.
πάρκινγκ	*par*·king	parking
ταχύτητα	ta·*hi*·ti·ta	speeding

I've lost my ...	Έχασα ... μου.	e·kha·sa ... mu
My ... was/were stolen.	Έκλεψαν ... μου.	e·klep·san ... mu
bags	τις βαλίτσες	tis va·lit·se
money	τα χρήματά	ta khri·ma·ta
passport	το διαβατήριό	to thia·va·ti·rio

What am I accused of?

| Για τι πράγμα κατηγορούμαι; | yia ti pra·ghma ka·ti·gho·ru·me |

I didn't realise I was doing anything wrong.

| Δεν κατάλαβα ότι έκαμα κάτι λάθος. | then ka·ta·la·va o·ti e·ka·ma ka·ti la·thos |

I didn't do it.

| Δεν το έκαμα. | then to e·ka·ma |

I'm sorry.

| Συγνώμη. | sigh·no·mi |

Can I pay an on-the-spot fine?

| Μπορώ να πληρώσω ένα πρόστιμο επί τόπου; | bo·ro na pli·ro·so e·na pro·sti·mo e·pi to·pu |

I want to contact my embassy.

| Θέλω να έρθω σε επαφή με την πρεσβεία μου. | the·lo na er·tho se e·pa·fi me tin prez·vi·a mu |

Can I make a phone call?

| Μπορώ να κάμω ένα τηλεφώνημα; | bo·ro na ka·mo e·na ti·le·fo·ni·ma |

Can I have a lawyer (who speaks English)?

| Μπορώ να έχω ένα δικηγόρο (που να μιλάει αγγλικά); | bo·ro na e·kho e·na thi·ki·gho·ro (pu na mi·la·i ang·gli·ka) |

This drug is for personal use.

| Αυτό το φάρμακο είναι για προσωπική χρήση. | af·to to far·ma·ko i·ne yia pro·so·pi·ki hri·si |

I have a prescription for this drug.

| Έχω συνταγή για αυτό το φάρμακο. | e·kho si·da·yi yia af·to to far·ma·ko |

I (don't) understand.

| (Δεν) καταλαβαίνω. | (then) ka·ta·la·ve·no |

doctor

γιατρός

Where's the nearest …?	Πού είναι το πιο κοντινό…;	pu *i*·ne to pio ko·di·*no* …
emergency department	πρώτων βοηθειών	*pro*·ton vo·i·thi·*on*
hospital	νοσοκομείο	no·so·ko·*mi*·o
medical centre	ιατρικό κέντρο	i·a·tri·*ko* ke·dro
(night) pharmacy	(νυχτερινό) φαρμακείο	(nikh·te·ri·*no*) far·ma·*ki*·o

Where's the nearest …?	Πού είναι ο πιο κοντινός …;	pu *i*·ne o pio ko·di·*nos* …
dentist	οδοντίατρος	o·tho·di·a·*tros*
doctor	γιατρός	yia·*tros*
optometrist	οφθαλμίατρος	of·thal·*mi*·a·tros

I need a doctor (who speaks English).
Χρειάζομαι ένα γιατρό (που να μιλάει αγγλικά).
khri·*a*·zo·me *e*·na yia·*tro* (pu na mi·*la*·i ang·gli·*ka*)

Could I see a female doctor?
Μπορώ να δω μια γυναίκα γιατρό;
bo·*ro* na tho mia yi·*ne*·ka yia·*tro*

Could the doctor come here?
Μπορεί ο γιατρός να έρθει εδώ;
bo·*ri* o yia·*tros* na *er*·thi e·*tho*

Is there an after-hours emergency number?
Υπάρχει τηλεφωνικός αριθμός για επείγουσες ανάγκες τη νύχτα;
i·*par*·hi ti·le·fo·ni·*kos* a·rith·*mos* yia e·*pi*·ghu·ses a·*na*·ges ti *nikh*·ta

I've run out of my medication.
Μου έχουν τελειώσει τα φάρμακά μου.
mu *e*·khun te·li·*o*·si ta *far*·ma·*ka* mu

This is my usual medicine.

Αυτά είναι τα συνηθισμένα
μου φάρμακα.

af·*ta* i·ne ta si·ni·thiz·*me*·na
mu *far*·ma·ka

What's the correct dosage?

Ποια είναι η σωστή δόση;

pia *i*·ne i so·*sti* ţho·si

I don't want a blood transfusion.

Δεν θέλω μετάγγιση
αίματος.

ţhen *the*·lo me·*ta*·gi·si
e·ma·tos

Please use a new syringe.

Παρακαλώ χρησιμοποίησε
καινούργια σύριγγα.

pa·ra·ka·*lo* khri·si·mo·*pi*·i·se
ke·*nur*·yia si·ri·ga

I have my own syringe.

Έχω δική μου σύριγγα.

e·kho ţhi·*ki* mu si·ri·ga

I've been vaccinated against ...

Έχω κάμει εμβόλιο για ...

e·kho *ka*·mi em·*vo*·li·o yia

He/She has been vaccinated against ...	Αυτός/Αυτή έχει κάμει εμβόλιο για ...	af·*tos*/af·*ti* e·khi *ka*·mi em·*vo*·li·o yia ...
hepatitis	ηπατίτιδα	i·pa·*ti*·ti·ţha
A/B/C	A/B/C	*e*·i/bi/si
tetanus	τέτανο	*te*·ta·no
typhoid	τύφο	*ti*·fo

I need new ...	Χρειάζομα ...	khri·*a*·zo·me ...
contact lenses	καινούργιους φακούς επαφής	ke·*nur*·yius fa·*kus* e·pa·*fis*
glasses	καινούργια γιαλιά	ke·*nur*·yia yia·*lia*

My prescription is ...

Η συνταγή μου είναι ...

i si·da·*yi* mu *i*·ne ...

How much will it cost?

Πόσο θα κοστίσει;

po·so tha ko·*sti*·si

Can I have a receipt for my insurance?

Μπορώ να έχω μια
απόδειξη για την
ασφάλειά μου;

bo·*ro* na *e*·kho mia
a·*po*·ţhik·si yia tin
as·*fa*·li·a mu

the doctor may say ...

Ποιο είναι το πρόβλημα;
pio *i*-ne to *prov*-li-ma
What's the problem?

Πού πονάει;
pu po-*na*-i
Where does it hurt?

Έχετε πυρετό;
e-he-te pi-re-*to*
Do you have a temperature?

Πόσον καιρό είστε έτσι;
po-son ke-*ro i*-ste *et*-si
How long have you been like this?

Το είχατε αυτό πριν;
to *i*-kha-te af-*po* prin
Have you had this before?

Έχετε σεξουαλικές σχέσεις;
e-he-te sek-su-a-li-*kes she*-sis
Are you sexually active?

Μήπως είχατε σεξ χωρίς προφύλαξη;
mi-pos *i*-kha-te seks
kho-*ris* pro-*fi*-lak-si
Have you had unprotected sex?

Πίνετε;/Καπνίζετε;
pi-ne-te/ka-*pni*-ze-te
Do you drink/smoke?

Παίρνετε ναρκωτικά;
per-ne-te nar-ko-ti-*ka*
Do you take drugs?

Είστε αλλεργικός σε κάτι;
i-ste a-ler-yi-*kos* se *ka*-ti
Are you allergic to anything?

Παίρνετε φάρμακα;
per-ne-te *far*-ma-ka
Are you on medication?

Πόσον καιρό ταξιδεύετε;
po-son ke-*ro* tak-si-*the*-ve-te
How long are you travelling for?

Πρέπει να μπείτε στο νοσοκομείο.
pre-pi na *bi*-te sto no-so-ko-*mi*-o
You need to be admitted to hospital.

Πρέπει να το ελέγξετε όταν επιστρέψετε στη χώρα σας.
pre-pi na to e-*leng*-kse-te o-tan e-pi-*strep*-se-te sti *kho*-ra sas
You should have it checked when you go home.

symptoms & conditions

συμπτώματα και καταστάσεις

I'm sick.
Είμαι άρρωστος.   *i*·me a·ro·stos

My friend is (very) sick. (about a man)
Ο φίλος μου είναι   o *fi*·los mu *i*·ne
(πολύ) άρρωστος.   (po·*li*) a·ro·stos

My friend is (very) sick. (about a woman)
Η φίλη μου είναι   i *fi*·li mu *i*·ne
(πολύ) άρρωστη.   (po·*li*) a·ro·sti

My child is (very) sick.
Το παιδί μου   to pe·*thi* mu
είναι (πολύ) άρρωστο.   *i*·ne (po·*li*) a·ro·sto

He/She is having a/an ...	Αυτός/Αυτή έχει ...	af·*tos*/af·*ti* e·hi ...
allergic reaction	αλλεργική αντίδραση	a·ler·yi·*ki* a·*di*·thra·si
asthma attack	προσβολή από άσθμα	proz·vo·*li* a·*po* *as*·thma
epileptic fit	επιληπτική κρίση	e·pi·lip·ti·*ki* *kri*·si
heart attack	καρδιακή προσβολή	kar·thi·a·*ki* pros·vo·*li*

He/She has been ...	Αυτός/Αυτή ...	af·*tos*/af·*ti* ...
injured	έχει τραυματιστεί	*e*·hi trav·ma·ti·*sti*
vomiting	κάνει εμετό	*ka*·ni e·me·*to*

I've been …
injured	Έχω τραυματιστεί.	*e*·kho trav·ma·ti·*sti*
vomiting	Κάνω εμετό.	*ka*·no e·me·*to*

I've been bitten/
stung by a …
	Με έχει δαγκώσει/	me *e*·hi tha·*go*·si/
	τσιμπήσει …	tsi·*bi*·si …
bee	μέλισσα	*me*·li·sa
jellyfish	μέδουσα	*me*·thu·sa
sea urchin	αχινός	a·hi·*nos*
snake	φίδι	*fi*·thi
wasp	σφήκα	*sfi*·ka
weever fish	δράκαινα	*thra*·ke·na

I feel …
	Αισθάνομαι …	es·*tha*·no·me …
anxious	ανυπόμονος/η m/f	a·ni·*po*·mo·nos/i
better	καλύτερα m&f	ka·*li*·te·ra
depressed	θλιμμένος/η m/f	thli·*me*·nos/i
dizzy	ζαλάδα m&f	za·*la*·tha
hot and cold	ζέστη και κρύο m&f	ze·sti ke *kri*·o
nauseous	ναυτία m&f	naf·*ti*·a
shivery	ρίγος m&f	*ri*·ghos
strange	παράξενα m&f	pa·*rak*·se·na
weak	αδύνατος/η m/f	a·*thi*·na·tos/i
worse	χειρότερα m&f	hi·*ro*·te·ra

It hurts here.
Πονάει εδώ.   po·*na*·i e·*tho*

I can't sleep.
Δεν μπορώ να κοιμηθώ.   then bo·*ro* na ki·mi·*tho*

I think it's the medication I'm on.
Νομίζω είναι τα φάρμακα   no·*mi*·zo *i*·ne ta *far*·ma·ka
που παίρνω.   pu *per*·no

I'm on medication for …
Παίρνω φάρμακα για …   *per*·no *far*·ma·ka yia …

He/She is on medication for …
Αυτός/αυτή παίρνει   af·*tos*/af·*ti* per·ni
φάρμακα για …   *far*·ma·ka yia …

I have (a/an) …
Έχω …   *e·kho …*

He/She has (a/an) …
Αυτός/αυτή έχει …   *af·tos/af·ti e·hi …*

I've recently had (a/an) …
Είχα πρόσφατα …   *i·kha pros·fa·ta …*

He/She has recently had (a/an) …
Αυτός/αυτή είχε πρόσφατα … *af·tos/af·ti i·he pros·fa·ta …*

AIDS	Έηντς n	*e·idz*
asthma	άσθμα n	*as·thma*
burn	έγκαυμα n	*e·gav·ma*
cold	κρύωμα n	*kri·o·ma*
constipation	δυσκοιλιότητα f	*this·ki·li·o·ti·ta*
cough	βήχα m	*vi·kha*
dehydration	αφυδάτωση f	*a·fi·tha·to·si*
diabetes	διαβήτη m	*thia·vi·ti*
diarrhoea	διάρροια f	*thi·a·ri·a*
encephalitis	εγκεφαλίτιδα f	*e·ge·fa·li·ti·tha*
fever	πυρετό m	*pi·re·to*
headache	πονοκέφαλο m	*po·no·ke·fa·lo*
heatstroke	ηλιακή	*i·lia·ki*
	συμφόρηση f	*sim·fo·ri·si*
indigestion	δυσπεψία f	*this·pep·si·a*
(fungal)	(μυκητώδη)	*(mi·ki·to·thi)*
infection	μόλυνση f	*mo·lin·si*
insect bite	τσίμπημα από	*tsi·bi·ma a·po*
	έντομο n	*e·do·mo*
Lyme disease	νόσο του lyme f	*no·so tu la·im*
nausea	ναυτία f	*naf·ti·a*
pain	πόνο m	*po·no*
rabies	λύσσα f	*li·sa*
rash	εξάνθημα n	*ek·san·thi·ma*
sea sickness	ναυτία f	*naf·ti·a*
sore throat	πονόλαιμο m	*po·no·le·mo*
sprain	στραμπούλισμα n	*stra·bu·liz·ma*
stomachache	στομαχόπονο m	*sto·ma·kho·po·no*
sunburn	ηλιακό έγκαυμα n	*i·li·a·ko e·gav·ma*
tick typhus	τσιμπούρι τύφου n	*tsi·bu·ri ti·fu*

women's health

(I think) I'm pregnant.
(Νομίζω) Είμαι έγγυος.   (no·*mi*·zo) *i*·me e·*gi*·os

I'm on the pill.
Παίρνω το Χάπι.   *per*·no to *kha*·pi

I haven't had my period for (six) weeks.
Δεν έχω περίοδο για (έξι)   then e·kho pe·*ri*·o·tho yia (*ek*·si)
εβδομάδες.   ev·tho·*ma*·thes

I've noticed a lump here.
Παρατήρησα ένα   pa·ra·*ti*·ri·sa e·na
εξόγκωμα εδώ.   ek·*so*·go·ma e·*tho*

Do you have something for (period pain)?
Έχετε κάτι για (πόνο για   e·he·te *ka*·ti yia (*po*·no yia
την περίοδο);   tin pe·*ri*·o·tho)

I have a …	Έχω …	e·kho …
urinary tract	μόλυνση στον	*mo*·lin·si ston
infection	ουρικό σωλήνα	u·ri·*ko* so·*li*·na
yeast infection	μυκωτική	mi·ko·ti·*ki*
	μόλυνση	*mo*·lin·si

---

the doctor may say …

Χρησιμοποιείτε αντισυλληπτικά;
khri·si·mo·pi·*i*·te
a·di·si·lip·ti·*ka*   **Are you using contraception?**

Έχετε περίοδο;
e·he·te pe·*ri*·o·tho   **Are you menstruating?**

Είστε έγγυος;
i·ste e·*gi*·os   **Are you pregnant?**

Πότε είχατε περίοδο τελευταία;
po·te *i*·kha·te pe·*ri*·o·tho
te·lef·*te*·a   **When did you last have your period?**

Είστε έγγυος.
i·ste e·*gi*·os   **You're pregnant.**

I need (a/the) ...	Χρειάζομαι ...	khri·a·zo·me ...
contraception	αντισυλληπτικό	a·di·si·lip·ti·ko
morning-after pill	το χάπι του επόμενου πρωινού	to kha·pi tu e·po·me·nu pro·i·nu
pregnancy test	τεστ εγγυμοσύνης	test e·gi·mo·si·nis

allergies

I have a skin allergy.

Έχω αλλεργία στο δέρμα.   e·kho a·ler·yi·a sto ther·ma

I'm allergic to ...	Είμαι αλλεργικός/ αλλεργική ... m/f	i·me a·ler·yi·kos a·ler·yi·ki
He's allergic to ...	Αυτός είναι αλλεργικός ...	af·tos i·ne a·ler·yi·kos ...
She's allergic to ...	Αυτή είναι αλλεργική ...	af·ti i·ne a·ler·yi·ki ...
antibiotics	στα αντιβιωτικά	sta a·di·vi·o·ti·ka
anti- inflammatories	στα αντιφλεγμονώδη	sta a·di·flegh·mo·no·thi
aspirin	στην ασπιρίνη	stin as·pi·ri·ni
bees	στις μέλισσες	stis me·li·ses
codeine	στην κωδεΐνη	stin ko·the·i·ni
penicillin	στην πενικιλλίνη	stin pe·ni·ki·li·ni
pollen	στη γύρη	sti yi·ri
sulphur-based drugs	στα φάρμακα με θείο	sta far·ma·ka me thi·o
wasps	στις σφήκες	stis sfi·kes

inhaler	αναπνευστήρας m	a·nap·nef·sti·ras
injection	ένεση f	e·ne·si
antihistamines	αντισταμίνες f	a·di·i·sta·mi·nes

For food-related allergies, see **vegetarian & special meals**, page 173.

parts of the body

My ... hurts.
Πονάει ...   po·*na*·i ...

I can't move my ...
Δεν μπορώ να κουνήσω ...   țhen bo·*ro* na ku·*ni*·so ...

I have a cramp in my ...
Έχω κράμπα ...   e·kho *kra*·ba ...

My ... is swollen.
Είναι πρησμένο ...   *i*·ne priz·*me*·no ...

It hurts when you touch it.
Πονάει όταν το αγγίζεις.   po·*ne* o·tan to a·*gi*·zis

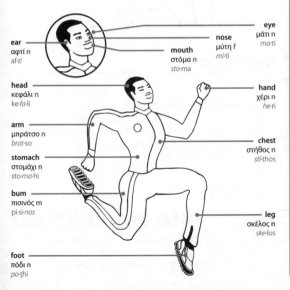

ear
αφτί n
af·*ti*

nose
μύτη f
mi·ti

eye
μάτι n
ma·ti

mouth
στόμα n
sto·ma

head
κεφάλι n
ke·*fa*·li

hand
χέρι n
he·ri

arm
μπράτσο n
brat·so

chest
στήθος n
sti·thos

stomach
στομάχι n
sto·*ma*·hi

bum
πισινός m
pi·si·*nos*

leg
σκέλος n
ske·los

foot
πόδι n
po·țhi

health

203

alternative treatments

I don't use (Western medicine).
Δεν χρησιμοποιώ   ţhen khri·si·mo·pi·o
(συμβατική ιατρική).   (sim·va·ti·ki i·a·tri·ki)

I prefer …	Προτιμώ …	pro·ti·mo …
Can I see someone	Μπορώ να δω	bo·ro na ţho
who practises …?	κάποιον που	ka·pion pu
	ασκεί …;	a·ski …
acupuncture	βελονισμό	ve·lo·niz·mo
naturopathy	φυσική θεραπεία	fi·si·ki the·ra·pi·a
reflexology	αντανακλαστική	a·da·na·kla·sti·ki

pharmacist

I need something for (a headache).
Χρειάζομαι   khri·a·zo·me
κάτι για (πονοκέφαλο).   ka·ti yia (po·no·ke·fa·lo)

Do I need a prescription for (antihistamines)?
Χρειάζομαι συνταγή για   khri·a·zo·me si·da·yi yia
(αντιισταμίνες);   (a·di·i·sta·mi·nes)

I have a prescription.
Έχω συνταγή.   e·kho si·da·yi

---

come again?

If you need something repeated in a consultation or conversation, say Ορίστε; o·ris·te (Sorry?). Use Συγνώμη sigh·no·mi (Sorry) when you need to apologise.

How many times a day?
    Πόσες φορές την ημέρα;   *po·*ses fo·*res* tin i·*me·*ra

Will it make me drowsy?
    Θα με κάμει να νυστάζω;   tha me *ka·*mi na ni·*sta·*zo

antiseptic	αντισηπτικό n	a·di·sip·ti·*ko*
condoms	προφυλακτικά n pl	pro·fi·lakh·ti·*ka*
contraceptives	αντισυλληπτικά n pl	a·di·si·lip·ti·*ka*
insect repellent	εντομοαπωθητικό n	e·do·mo·a·po·thi·ti·*ko*
laxative	καθαρτικό n	ka·thar·ti·*ko*
painkillers	παυσίπονα	paf·*si·*po·na
(for infants)	(για μωρά) n pl	(yia mo·*ra*)
rehydration	ενυδρωτικά	en·i·thro·ti·*ka*
salts	άλατα n pl	*a·*la·ta
spray for insect	σπρέι για	*spre·*i yia
bites	τσιμπήματα	tsi·*bi·*ma·ta
	κουνουπιών n	ku·nu·*pion*
sunburn lotion	λοσιόν για ηλιακό	lo·*sion* yia i·li·a·*ko*
	έγκαυμα n	*e·*gav·ma
sunscreen	αντιηλιακό n	a·di·i·li·a·*ko*
talcum powder	ταλκ n	talk
thermometer	θερμόμετρο n	ther·*mo·*me·tro
zinc cream	ψευδαργυρούχος	psev·thar·yi·*ru·*khos
	αλοιφή f	a·li·*fi*

---

dentist

I have a ...	Έχω ...	e·ho ...
broken tooth	ένα σπασμένο δόντι	e·na spaz·me·no tho·di
cavity	ένα κούφιο δόντι	e·na ku·fio tho·di
toothache	πονόδοντο	po·no·tho·do

I've lost a filling.
Έχασα ένα σφράγισμα.　　　　e·kha·sa e·na sfra·yiz·ma

My dentures are broken.
Οι μασέλες μου έσπασαν.　　　i ma·se·les mu e·spa·san

My gums hurt.
Πονούν τα ούλα μου.　　　　　po·nun ta u·la mu

I need an anaesthetic/a filling.
Χρειάζομαι αναισθητικό/　　　khri·a·zo·me a·nes·thi·ti·ko/
σφράγισμα.　　　　　　　　　sfra·yiz·ma

I don't want it extracted.
Δεν θέλω να το βγάλω.　　　　then the·lo na to vgha·lo

Ouch!
Όου!　　　　　　　　　　　　o·u

---

the dentist may say ...

Ανοίξτε το στόμα πολύ a·nik·ste to sto·ma po·li.	**Open wide.**
Δεν θα πονέσει καθόλου. then tha po·ne·si ka·tho·lu	**This won't hurt a bit.**
Δαγκώστε αυτό. tha·go·ste af·to	**Bite down on this.**
Μην κινείστε. min ki·ni·ste	**Don't move.**
Ξεβγάλτε! ksev·ghal·te	**Rinse!**
Γυρίστε πίσω, δεν τελείωσα. yi·ri·ste pi·so then te·li·o·sa	**Come back, I haven't finished.**

DICTIONARY > english–greek

Greek nouns in the **dictionary** have their gender indicated by ⓜ masculine, ⓕ feminine or ⓝ neuter. If it's a plural noun you'll also see pl. When a word that could be either a noun or a verb has no gender indicated, it's a verb. Adjectives are given in the masculine form only – see **adjectives & adverbs** in the **phrasebuilder** for more on how to form feminine and neuter adjectives. Both nouns and adjectives are provided in the nominative case only – refer to the **phrasebuilder** for more information on **case**. Note that we've also added the abbreviations a adjective and v verb for added clarity where required.

A

aboard (επάνω στο) κατάστρωμα ⓝ
(e·*pa*·no sto) ka·*tas*·tro·ma

abortion έκτρωση ⓕ *ek*·tro·si

about περίπου pe·*ri*·pu

above από πάνω a·*po pa*·no

abroad στο εξωτερικό sto ek·so·te·ri·*ko*

accident ατύχημα ⓝ a·*ti*·hi·ma

accommodation κατάλυμα ⓝ ka·*ta*·li·ma

account λογαριασμός ⓜ lo·gha·riaz·*mos*

across απέναντι a·*pe*·na·di

activist ακτιβιστής/ακτιβίστρια ⓜ/ⓕ
a·kti·vi·*stis*/a·kti·*vi*·stri·a

actor ηθοποιός ⓜ&ⓕ i·tho·pi·*os*

acupuncture βελονισμός ⓜ ve·lo·niz·*mos*

adaptor μετασχηματιστής ⓜ
me·ta·shi·ma·ti·*stis*

addiction εθισμός ⓜ e·thiz·*mos*

address διεύθυνση ⓕ thi·*ef*·thin·si

administration διοίκηση ⓕ thi·*i*·ki·si

admission (price) τιμή εισόδου ⓕ
ti·*mi* i·*so*·thu

admit δέχομαι *the*·kho·me

adult ενήλικος/ενήλικη ⓜ/ⓕ
e·*ni*·li·kos/e·*ni*·li·ki

advertisement διαφήμιση ⓕ thi·a·*fi*·mi·si

advice συμβουλή ⓕ sim·vu·*li*

Aegean Αιγαίο ⓝ e·*ye*·o

aerobics αερόμπικς ⓝ pl a·e·ro·biks

aeroplane αεροπλάνο ⓝ a·e·ro·*pla*·no

Africa Αφρική ⓕ a·fri·*ki*

after μετά me·*ta*

(this) afternoon (αυτό το) απόγευμα ⓝ
(af·*to* to) a·*po*·yev·ma

aftershave κολόνια ξυρίσματος ⓕ
ko·*lo*·ni·a ksi·*riz*·ma·tos

again πάλι *pa*·li

age ηλικία ⓕ i·li·*ki*·a

(three days) ago (τρεις μέρες) πριν
(tris *me*·res) prin

agree συμφωνώ sim·fo·*no*

agriculture γεωργία ⓕ ye·or·*yi*·a

ahead εμπρός e·*bros*

AIDS Έηντς ⓝ *e*·idz

air αέρας ⓜ a·*e*·ras

air-conditioned με ερκοντίσιον
me er·kon·*di*·si·on

air conditioning έρκοντίσιον ⓝ
er kon·*di*·si·on

airline αερογραμμή ⓕ a·e·ro·ghra·*mi*

airmail αεροπορικό ταχυδρομείο ⓝ
a·e·ro·po·ri·*ko* ta·hi·*thro*·mi·o

airplane αεροπλάνο ⓝ a·e·ro·*pla*·no

airport αεροδρόμιο ⓝ a·e·ro·*thro*·mi·o

airport tax δασμός αεροδρομίου ⓜ
thaz·*mos* a·e·ro·*thro*·mi·u

aisle (on plane) διάδρομος (αεροπλάνου)
ⓜ thi·*a*·thro·mos (a·e·ro·*pla*·nu)

alarm clock ξυπνητήρι ⓝ ksi·pni·*ti*·ri

Albania Αλβανία ⓕ al·va·*ni*·a

alcohol αλκοόλ ⓝ al·ko·*ol*

all όλοι ⓜ *o*·li

allergy αλλεργία ⓕ a·ler·*yi*·a

almond αμύγδαλο ⓝ a·*migh*·tha·lo

almost σχεδόν she·*thon*

alone μόνος *mo*·nos

already ήδη *i*·thi

also επίσης e·*pi*·sis

altar βωμός ⑩ vo-*mos*
altitude ύψος ⑩ *ip*-sos
always πάντα pa-da
ambassador πρέσβης/πρέσβειρα ⑩/①
  prez-vis/*prez*-vi-ra
ambulance νοσοκομειακό ⑩
  no-so-ko-mi-a-*ko*
America Αμερική ① a-me-ri-*ki*
American football
  Αμερικανικό ποδόσφαιρο ⑩
  a-me-ri-ka-ni-ko po-*thos*-fe-ro
amphitheatre αμφιθέατρο ⑩
  am-fi-*the*-a-tro
anaemia αναιμία ① a-ne-*mi*-a
anarchist αναρχικός/αναρχική ⑩/①
  a-nar-hi-*kos*/a-nar-hi-*ki*
ancient a αρχαίος ar-*he*-os
and και ke
angry θυμωμένος thi-mo-*me*-nos
animal ζώο ⑩ zo-o
ankle αστράγαλος ⑩ a-*stra*-gha-los
another ένας άλλος e-nas a-los
answer απάντηση ① a-*pa*-di-si
ant μυρμήγκι ⑩ mir-*mi*-gi
antibiotics αντιβιοτικά ⑩ pl a-di-vi-o-ti-*ka*
antinuclear αντιπυρηνικό ⑩
  a-di-pi-ri-ni-*ko*
antique αντίκα ① an-*ti*-ka
antiseptic αντισηπτικό ⑩ a-di-si-lip-*ti*-ko
any καθόλου ka-*tho*-lu
anxious ανυπόμονος/ανυπόμονη ⑩/①
  a-ni-*po*-mo-nos/a-ni-*po*-mo-ni
apartment διαμέρισμα ⑩ ἱhi-a-*me*-riz-ma
appendix (body) σκωληκοειδίτης ⑩
  sko-li-ko-i-*thi*-tis
apple μήλο ⑩ *mi*-lo
appointment ραντεβού ra-de-*vu*
apricot βερύκοκο ⑩ ve-*ri*-ko-ko
April Απρίλιος ⑩ a-*pri*-li-os
archaic αρχαϊκός ar-kha-i-*kos*
archaeological αρχαιολογικός
  ar-he-o-lo-yi-*kos*
architect αρχιτέκτονας ⑩&①
  ar-hi-*tek*-to-nas
architecture αρχιτεκτονική ①
  ar-hi-tek-to-ni-*ki*
argue συζητώ si-zi-*to*
arm χέρι ⑩ *he*-ri
aromatherapy αρωμαθεραπεία ①
  a-ro-mo-the-ra-*pi*-a

arrest v συλλαμβάνω si-lam-*va*-no
arrivals αφίξεις ① pl a-*fik*-sis
arrive φτάνω *fta*-no
art τέχνη ① *tekh*-ni
art gallery πινακοθήκη ① pi-na-ko-*thi*-ki
artist καλλιτέχνης/καλλιτέχνιδα ⑩/①
  ka-li-*tekh*-nis/ka-li-*tekh*-ni-ṭha
ashtray σταχτοθήκη ① stakh-to-*thi*-ki
Asia Ασία ① a-*si*-a
ask (a question) ρωτάω ro-*ta*-o
ask (for something) ζητάω zi-*ta*-o
asparagus σπαράγγι ⑩ spa-*ra*-gi
aspirin ασπιρίνη ① a-spi-*ri*-ni
asthma άσθμα ① *asth*-ma
astrology αστρολογία ① a-stro-lo-*yi*-a
at σε se
athletics αθλητικά ⑩ pl a-thli-ti-*ka*
atmosphere ατμόσφαιρα ① at-*mos*-fe-ra
aubergine μελιτζάνα ⑩ me-li-*dza*-na
August Αύγουστος ⑩ *av*-ghu-stos
aunt θεία ① *thi*-a
Australia Αυστραλία ① af-stra-*li*-a
Australian Rules Football
  Αυστραλέζικο ποδόσφαιρο ⑩
  af-stra-*le*-zi-ko po-*thos*-fe-ro
automated teller machine (ATM)
  αυτόματη μηχανή χρημάτων ①
  af-*to*-ma-ti mi-kha-*ni* khri-*ma*-ton
autumn φθινόπωρο ⑩ fthi-*no*-po-ro
avenue λεωφόρος ① le-o-*fo*-ros
avocado αβοκάντο ⑩ a-vo-ka-do
awful απαίσιος a-*pe*-si-os

B

B&W (film) μαυρόασπρο (φιλμ) ⑩
  mav-ro-a-spro (film)
baby μωρό ⑩ mo-ro
baby food φαγητό για μωρά ⑩
  fa-yi-*to* yia mo-*ra*
baby powder ταλκ ⑩ talk
babysitter μπέιμπι σίτερ ① be-i-bi *si*-ter
back (body) πλάτη ① *pla*-ti
back (position) πίσω pi-so
backgammon τάβλι ⑩ *tav*-li
backpack σακίδιο ⑩ sa-*ki*-ṭhi-o
bacon μπέικον ⑩ *be*-i-kon
bad κακός ka-*kos*
bag σάκος ⑩ *sa*-kos

baggage αποσκευές ① pl a-po-ske-*ves*

baggage allowance
επιτρεπόμενες αποσκευές ① pl
e-pi-tre-*po*-me-nes a-po-ske-*ves*

baggage claim παραλαβή αποσκευών
① pa-ra-la-*vi* a-po-ske-*von*

bakery φούρνος ⑩ *fur*-nos

balance (account) υπόλοιπο
(λογαριασμού) ⑩
i-*po*-li-po (lo-gha-riaz-*mu*)

Balcans Βαλκάνια ⑩ pl val-*ka*-ni-a

balcony μπαλκόνι ⑪ bal-*ko*-ni

bail (sport) μπάλα ① *ba*-la

ballet μπαλέτο ⑪ ba-*le*-to

banana μπανάνα ① ba-*na*-na

band (music) μπάντα ① *ba*-da

bandage επίδεσμος ⑩ e-*pi*-thez-mos

Band-Aid τσιρότο ⑩ tsi-*ro*-to

bank τράπεζα ① *tra*-pe-za

bank account τραπεζικός λογαριασμός
⑩ tra-pe-zi-kos lo-gha-riaz-*mos*

banknote χαρτονόμισμα ①
khar-to-*no*-miz-ma

baptism βάπτιση ① *vap*-ti-si

bar μπαρ ⑩ bar

barber κουρέας ⑩ ku-*re*-as

bar work δουλειά σε μπαρ ① thu-*lia* se bar

baseball μπέιζμπολ ⑩ *be*-iz-bol

basket καλάθι ① ka-*la*-thi

basketball μπάσκετ ⑪ *ba*-sket

bath μπάνιο ⑩ *ba*-nio

bathing suit μαγιό ① ma-*yio*

bathroom μπάνιο ⑪ *ba*-nio

battery μπαταρία ① ba-ta-*ri*-a

be είμαι *i*-me

beach παραλία ① pa-ra-*li*-a

beach volleyball βόλεϊ παραλίας ⑩
vo-le-i pa-ra-*li*-as

bean φασόλι ⑪ fa-*so*-li

beansprouts φύτρα φασολιών ⑪
fit-ra fa-so-*lion*

beautiful όμορφος o-*mor*-fos

beauty salon ινστιτούτο αισθητικής ⑪
in-sti-*tu*-to es-thi-ti-*kis*

because διότι thi-o-ti

bed κρεβάτι ⑪ kre-*va*-ti

bedding σκεπάσματα ⑪ pl ske-*paz*-ma-ta

bed linen σεντόνια ① pl se-*do*-nia

bedroom υπνοδωμάτιο ⑪
ip-no-tho-*ma*-ti-o

bee μέλισσα ① *me*-li-sa

beef βοδινό ⑪ vo-thi-*no*

beer μπύρα ① *bi*-ra

beetroot παντζάρι ① pat-*za*-ri

before πριν prin

beggar ζητιάνος/ζητιάνα ⑩/①
zi-*tia*-nos/zi-*tia*-na

behind πίσω *pi*-so

Belgium Βέλγιο ⑩ *vel*-yi-o

below κάτω *ka*-to

beside δίπλα *thi*-pla

best a ο καλύτερος o ka-*li*-te-ros

bet στοίχημα ① *sti*-hi-ma

better καλύτερος/καλύτερη ⑩/①
ka-*li*-te-ros/ka-*li*-te-ri

between ανάμεσα a-*na*-me-sa

bible Βίβλος ① *viv*-los

bicycle ποδήλατο ⑩ po-*thi*-la-to

big μεγάλος me-*gha*-los

bigger μεγαλύτερος me-gha-*li*-te-ros

biggest ο μεγαλύτερος o me-gha-*li*-te-ros

bike ποδήλατο ⑪ po-*thi*-la-to

bike chain αλυσίδα ποδηλάτου ①
a-li-*si*-tha po-thi-*la*-tu

bike lock κλειδαριά ποδηλάτου ①
kli-tha-*ria* po-thi-*la*-tu

bike path δρόμος ποδηλάτου ①
thro-mos po-thi-*la*-tu

bike shop κατάστημα ποδηλάτου ⑩
ka-*ta*-sti-ma po-thi-*la*-tu

bill (restaurant etc) λογαριασμός ⑩
lo-gha-riaz-*mos*

billiards μπιλιάρδο ① bi-*liar*-tho

binoculars κιάλια ⑩ pl *kia*-lia

bird πουλί ⑪ pu-*li*

birthday γενέθλια ① pl ye-*ne*-thli-a

birth certificate πιστοποιητικό
γεννήσεως ⑪ pi-sto-pi-i-ti-ko ye-*ni*-se-os

biscuit μπισκότο ⑪ bi-*sko*-to

bite (dog) δαγκωματιά ① tha-go-ma-*tia*

bite (insect) τσίμπημα ⑪ *tsi*-bi-ma

bitter πικρός pi-*kros*

black a μαύρος *mav*-ros

bladder κύστη ① *ki*-sti

blanket κουβέρτα ① ku-*ver*-ta

blind a τυφλός ti-*flos*

blister φουσκάλα ① fu-*ska*-la

blocked μπλοκαρισμένος blo-ka-riz-*me*-nos

blood αίμα ⑪ *e*-ma

blood group ομάδα αίματος ①
o-*ma*-tha *e*-ma-tos

blood pressure πίεση αίματος ⓕ
pi·e·si e·ma·tos

blood test εξέταση αίματος ⓕ
ek·se·ta·si e·ma·tos

blue a μπλε ble

board (transport) v ανεβαίνω a·ne·ve·no

boarding house πανσιόν ⓕ pan·sion

boarding pass κάρτα επιβίβασης ⓕ
kar·ta e·pi·vi·va·sis

boat βάρκα ⓕ var·ka

body σώμα ⓝ so·ma

boiled βρασμένος vraz·me·nos

bone κόκαλο ⓝ ko·ka·lo

book βιβλίο ⓝ viv·li·o

book (reserve) v κλείνω θέση kli·no the·si

booked out πλήρες pli·res

bookshop βιβλιοπωλείο ⓝ viv·li·o·po·li·o

boot (footwear) μπότα ⓕ bo·ta

boots (footwear) μπότες ⓕ pl bo·tes

border σύνορο ⓝ si·no·ro

bored βαριεστημένος va·ri·e·sti·me·nos

boring ανιαρός a·ni·a·ros

borrow δανείζομαι tha·ni·zo·me

botanical garden βοτανικός κήπος ⓜ
vo·ta·ni·kos ki·pos

both και οι δύο ke i thi·o

bottle μπουκάλι ⓝ bu·ka·li

bottle opener ανοιχτήρι ⓝ a·nikh·ti·ri

bottle shop κάβα ⓕ ka·va

bottom (body) πισινός ⓜ pi·si·nos

bottom (position) κάτω ka·to

bouzouki (traditional music)
μπουζούκι ⓝ bu·zu·ki

bouzouki place μπουζουκτσίδικο ⓝ
bu·zuk·tsi·thi·ko

bowl μπωλ ⓝ bol

box κουτί ⓝ ku·ti

boxer shorts σλιπάκι ⓝ sli·pa·ki

boxing μποξ ⓝ boks

boy αγόρι ⓝ a·gho·ri

boyfriend φίλος ⓜ fi·los

bra σουτιέν ⓝ su·ti·en

brakes φρένα ⓝ pl fre·na

brandy κονιάκ ⓝ ko·niak

brave γενναίος ye·ne·os

bread ψωμί ⓝ pso·mi

bread rolls ψωμάκια ⓝ pl pso·ma·kia

break v σπάω spa·o

break down χαλάω ha·la·o

breakfast πρόγευμα ⓝ pro·yev·ma

breast (body) στήθος ⓝ sti·thos

breathe αναπνέω a·nap·ne·o

bribe v δωροδοκώ tho·ro·tho·ko

bridge γεφύρι ⓝ ye·fi·ri

briefcase ⓜ χαρτοφύλακας khar·to·fi·la·kas

brilliant λαμπρός la·bros

bring φέρνω fer·no

broccoli μπρόκολο ⓝ bro·ko·lo

brochure μπροσούρα ⓕ bro·su·ra

broken σπασμένος spaz·me·nos

broken down χαλασμένος
kha·laz·me·nos

bronchitis βρογχίτιδα ⓕ vro·hi·ti·tha

bronze μπρούτζος ⓜ bru·dzos

brother αδερφός ⓜ a·ther·fos

brown καφέ ka·fe

bruise σημάδι από χτύπημα ⓝ
si·ma·thi a·po khti·pi·ma

brush βούρτσα ⓕ vur·tsa

bucket κουβάς ⓜ ku·vas

Buddhist Βουδιστής/Βουδίστρια
vu·thi·stis/vu·thi·stri·a ⓜ/ⓕ

budget προϋπολογισμός ⓜ
pro·i·po·lo·yiz·mos

buffet μπουφές ⓜ bu·fes

bug κοριός ⓜ ko·rios

build v χτίζω khti·zo

builder χτίστης ⓜ khti·stis

building κτήριο ⓝ kti·ri·o

Bulgaria Βουλγαρία ⓕ vul·gha·ri·a

bumbag πορτοφόλι μέσης ⓝ
por·to·fo·li me·sis

burn έγκαυμα ⓝ e·gav·ma

burnt καμένος ka·me·nos

bus (city) αστικό λεωφορείο ⓝ
a·sti·ko le·o·fo·ri·o

bus (intercity) υπεραστικό λεωφορείο ⓝ
i·per·as·ti·ko le·o·fo·ri·o

bus station σταθμός λεωφορείου ⓜ
stath·mos le·o·fo·ri·u

bus stop στάση λεωφορείου ⓕ
sta·si le·o·fo·ri·u

business επιχείρηση ⓕ e·pi·hi·ri·si

business class μπίζνες κλασ biz·nes klas

businessperson επιχειρηματίας ⓜ&ⓕ
e·pi·hi·ri·ma·ti·as

business trip ταξίδι εργασίας ⓝ
tak·si·thi er·gha·si·as

busker περιοδεύων τραγουδιστής ⓜ
pe·ri·o·the·von tra·ghu·thi·stis
περιοδεύουσα τραγουδίστρια ⓕ
pe·ri·o·the·vu·sa tra·ghu·thi·stri·a

busy απασχολημένος a·pa·skho·li·me·nos
but αλλά a·la
butcher χασάπης ⓜ kha·sa·pis
butcher's shop κρεοπωλείο ⓝ kre·o·po·li·o
butter βούτυρο ⓝ vu·ti·ro
butterfly πεταλούδα ⓕ pe·ta·lu·tha
button κουμπί ⓝ ku·bi
buy v αγοράζω a·gho·ra·zo
Byzantine Βυζαντινός vi·za·di·nos

C

cabin καμπίνα ⓕ ka·bi·na
cabbage μάπα ⓕ ma·pa
cable car τελεφερίκ ⓝ te·le·fe·rik
café καφεστιατόριο ⓝ ka·fe·sti·a·to·ri·o
cafeteria καφετηρία ⓕ ka·fe·ti·ri·a
cake γλυκό ⓝ ghli·ko
cake shop ζαχαροπλαστείο ⓝ
za·kha·ro·pla·sti·o
calculator αριθμομηχανή ⓕ
a·rith·mo·mi·kha·ni
calendar ημερολόγιο ⓝ i·me·ro·lo·yi·o
call v καλώ ka·lo
camera φωτογραφική μηχανή ⓕ
fo·to·ghra·fi·ki mi·kha·ni
camera shop κατάστημα φωτογραφικών
ειδών ⓝ ka·ta·sti·ma fo·to·ghra·fi·kon
i·thon
camp v κατασκηνώνω ka·ta·ski·no·no
camping ground χώρος για κάμπινγκ ⓜ
kho·ros yia kam·ping
camping store
κατάστημα ειδών κατασκήνωσης
ka·ta·sti·ma i·thon ka·ta·ski·no·sis
campsite χώρος για κάμπινγκ ⓜ
kho·ros yia kam·ping
can (be able) v μπορώ bo·ro
can (tin) κουτί ⓝ ku·ti
can opener ανοιχτήρι ⓝ a·nikh·ti·ri
Canada Καναδάς ⓜ ka·na·thas
cancel ακυρώνω a·ki·ro·no
cancer καρκίνος ⓜ kar·ki·nos
candle κερί ⓝ ke·ri
candy καραμέλα ⓕ ka·ra·me·la
cantaloupe πεπόνι ⓝ pe·po·ni
capsicum πιπεριά ⓕ pi·pe·ria
car αυτοκίνητο ⓝ af·to·ki·ni·to
caravan τροχόσπιτο ⓝ tro·kho·spi·to
cardiac arrest καρδιακή προσβολή ⓕ
kar·thi·a·ki proz·vo·li

cards (playing) χαρτιά ⓝ pl khar·tia
care (for someone) φροντίζω fro·di·zo
car hire ενοικίαση αυτοκινήτου ⓕ
e·ni·ki·a·si af·to·ki·ni·tu
carob χαρούπι ⓝ kha·ru·pi
car owner's title
τίτλος κατόχου αυτοκινήτου ⓜ
tit·los ka·to·khu af·to·ki·ni·tu
car park χώρος στάθμευσης αυτικινήτων
ⓜ kho·ros stath·mef·sis af·to·ki·ni·tu
carpenter μαραγκός ⓜ ma·ra·gos
car registration
άδεια κυκλοφορίας αυτοκινήτου ⓕ
a·thia ki·klo·fo·ri·as af·to·ki·ni·tu
carrot καρότο ⓝ ka·ro·to
carry μεταφέρω me·ta·fe·ro
carton χαρτοκιβώτιο ⓝ khar·to·ki·vo·ti·o
cash μετρητά ⓝ pl me·tri·ta
cash (a cheque) v εξαργυρώνω
ek·sar·yi·ro·no
cash register ταμείο ⓝ ta·mi·o
cashew κάσιου ⓝ ka·si·u
cashier ταμίας ⓜ&ⓕ ta·mi·as
casino καζίνο ⓝ ka·zi·no
cassette κασέτα ⓕ ka·se·ta
castle κάστρο ⓝ ka·stro
casual work ημερομίσθια εργασία ⓕ
i·me·ro·mi·sthi·a er·gha·si·a
cat γάτα ⓕ gha·ta
catamaran καταμαράν ka·ta·ma·ran
cathedral μητρόπολη ⓕ mi·tro·po·li
Catholic Καθολικός/Καθολική ⓜ/ⓕ
ka·tho·li·kos/ka·tho·li·ki
cauliflower κουνουπίδι ⓝ ku·nu·pi·thi
cave σπηλιά ⓕ spi·lia
CD σι ντι ⓝ si di
celebration γιορτή ⓕ yior·ti
cellphone κινητό ⓝ ki·ni·to
cemetery κοιμητήριο ⓝ ki·mi·ti·ri·o
cent σεντ ⓝ sent
centimetre εκατοστόμετρο ⓝ
e·ka·to·sto·me·tro
centre κέντρο ⓝ ke·dro
ceramics κεραμικά ⓝ pl ke·ra·mi·ka
cereal δημητριακά ⓝ pl ţhi·mi·tri·a·ka
certificate πιστοποιητικό ⓝ pi·sto·pi·i·ti·ko
chain αλυσίδα ⓕ a·li·si·ţha
chair καρέκλα ⓕ ka·re·kla
chairlift (skiing) τελεφερίκ ⓝ te·le·fe·rik
champagne σαμπάνια ⓕ sam·pa·nia

championships αγώνες πρωταθλήματος ⓜ pl *a·gho·*nes pro·ta·*thli·*ma·tos

chance πιθανότητα ① pi·tha·*no·*ti·ta

change αλλαγή ① a·la·*yi*

change (coins) ψιλά ⓝ pl psi·*la*

change (from sale) ρέστα ⓝ pl *re·*sta

change (money) v αλλάζω a·*la·*zo

changing room (in shop) δοκιμαστήριο ρούχων ⓝ tho·ki·ma·*sti·*ri·o *ru·*khon

charming χαριτωμένος kha·ri·to·*me·*nos

charter flight πτήση τσάρτερ ①
*pti·*si *tsar·*ter

chat up (somebody) v ψήνω *psi·*no

cheap φτηνός fti·*nos*

cheat απατεώνας/απατεώνισσα ⓜ/①
a·pa·te·*o·*nas/a·pa·te·*o·*ni·sa

check v ελέγχω e·*leng·*kho

check (banking) προσωπική επιταγή ①
pro·so·pi·*ki* e·pi·ta·*yi*

check (bill) λογαριασμός ⓜ
lo·gha·riaz·*mos*

check-in (desk) ρεσεψιόν ① *re·*sep·*sion*

checkpoint σημείο ελέγχου ⓝ
si·*mi·*o e·*leng·*khu

cheese τυρί ⓝ ti·*ri*

cheese shop τυροπωλείο ⓝ ti·ro·po·*li·*o

chef ⓜ σεφ sef

chemist (shop) φαρμακείο ⓝ far·ma·*ki·*o

chemist (pharmacist) φαρμακοποιός
ⓜ&① far·ma·ko·pi·*os*

cheque προσωπική επιταγή ①
pro·so·pi·*ki* e·pi·ta·*yi*

cherry κεράσι ⓝ ke·*ra·*si

chess σκάκι ⓝ *ska·*ki

chessboard σκακιέρα ① ska·*kie·*ra

chest (body) στήθος ⓝ *sti·*thos

chestnut κάστανο ⓝ *ka·*sta·no

chewing gum μαστίχα ① ma·*sti·*kha

chicken κοτόπουλο ⓝ ko·*to·*pu·lo

chicken pox ανεμοβλογιά ①
a·ne·mov·lo·*yia*

chickpea στραγάλι ⓝ stra·*gha·*li

child παιδί ⓝ pe·*thi*

childminding επιτήρηση παιδιών ①
e·pi·*ti·*ri·si pe·*thion*

children παιδιά ⓝ pl pe·*thia*

child seat παιδικό κάθισμα ⓝ
pe·*thi·*ko *ka·*thiz·ma

chilli πιπεριά ① pi·pe·*ria*

chilli sauce σάλτσα πιπεριάς ①
*sal·*tsa pi·pe·*rias*

chipura τσίπουρο ⓝ *tsi·*pu·ro

chiropractor χειροπράκτωρ ⓜ&①
hi·ro·*prak·*stor

chocolate σοκολάτα ① so·ko·*la·*ta

chopping board σανίδα κοπής ①
sa·*ni·*tha ko·*pis*

chopsticks τσοπ στικς ⓝ pl tsop stiks

Christian Χριστιανός/Χριστιανή ⓜ/①
khri·sti·a·*nos*/khri·sti·a·*ni*

Christian name μικρό όνομα ⓝ
mi·*kro* o·no·ma

Christmas Χριστούγεννα ⓝ pl
khri·*stu·*ye·na

Christmas Day ημέρα Χριστουγέννων ①
i·*me·*ra khri·stu·*ye·*non

Christmas Eve παραμονή Χριστουγέννων
① pa·ra·mo·*ni* khri·stu·*ye·*non

church εκκλησία ① e·kli·*si·*a

cider κρασί από μήλο ⓝ kra·*si* a·po *mi·*lo

cigar πούρο ⓝ *pu·*ro

cigarette τσιγάρο ⓝ tsi·*gha·*ro

cigarette lighter αναπτήρας ⓜ a·nap·*ti·*ras

cinema σινεμά ⓝ si·ne·*ma*

circus τσίρκο ⓝ *tsir·*ko

citizenship ιθαγένεια ① i·tha·*ye·*ni·a

city πόλη ① *po·*li

city centre κέντρο της πόλης ⓝ
*ke·*dro tis *po·*lis

civil rights πολιτικά δικαιώματα ⓝ pl
po·li·ti·*ka* thi·ke·*o·*ma·ta

civil servant δημόσιος υπάλληλος ⓜ&①
thi·*mo·*si·os i·*pa·*li·los

class (category) τάξη ① *tak·*si

classical κλασικός kla·si·*kos*

class system ταξικό σύστημα ⓝ
tak·si·*ko* *si·*sti·ma

clean a καθαρός ka·tha·*ros*

clean v καθαρίζω ka·tha·*ri·*zo

cleaning καθάρισμα ⓝ ka·*tha·*riz·ma

client πελάτης/πελάτισσα ⓜ/①
pe·*la·*tis/pe·*la·*ti·sa

cliff γκρεμός ⓜ gre·*mos*

climb v αναρριχούμαι a·na·ri·*khu·*me

cloakroom ιματιοφυλάκιο ⓝ
i·ma·ti·o·fi·*la·*ki·o

clock ρολόι ⓝ ro·*lo·*i

close a κοντινός ko·di·*nos*

close v κλείνω *kli·*no

closed κλεισμένος kliz·*me·*nos

clothesline μύλος (για ρούχα) ⓜ
mi-los (yia *ru*-kha)

clothing ρούχα ⓝ pl *ru*-kha

clothing store κατάστημα ρούχων ⓝ
ka·*ta*·sti·ma *ru*·khon

cloud σύννεφο ⓝ *si*-ne-fo

cloudy συννεφιασμένος si-ne-fiaz-me-nos

clutch (car) συμπλέκτης ⓜ si-*ble*-ktis

coach (sport) προπονητής/προπονήτρια
ⓜ/ⓕ pro-po-ni-*tis*/pro-po-*ni*-tri-a

coalition συνασπισμός ⓜ sin-as-piz-*mos*

coast ακτή ⓕ ak-*ti*

coat παλτό ⓝ pal-*to*

cocaine κοκαΐνη ⓕ ko-ka-*i*-ni

cockroach κοριός ⓜ ko-*rios*

cocktail κοκτέιλ ⓝ kok-*te*-il

cocoa κακάο ⓝ ka-*ka*-o

coconut ινδική καρύδα ⓕ in-*thi*-ki ka-*ri*-tha

coffee καφές ⓜ ka-*fes*

coffee shop καφενείο ⓝ ka-fe-*ni*-o

coins κέρματα ⓝ pl *ker*-ma-ta

cold κρύο ⓝ *kri*-o

cold a κρυωμένος kri-o-*me*-nos

colleague συνάδελφος/συναδέλφισσα
ⓜ/ⓕ si-*na*-thel-fos/si-na-*thel*-fi-sa

collect call
κλήση με αντιστροφή της επιβάρυνσης
ⓕ *kli*-si me a-dis-tro-*fi* tis e-pi-*va*-rin-sis

college κολλέγιο ⓝ ko-*le*-yi-o

colour χρώμα ⓝ *khro*-ma

column κολώνα ⓕ ko-*lo*-na

comb χτένα ⓕ *khte*-na

come έρχομαι *er*-kho-me

comedy κωμωδία ⓕ ko-mo-*thi*-a

comfortable άνετος *a*-ne-tos

commission προμήθεια ⓕ pro-*mi*-thi-a

communications (profession)
επικοινωνίες ⓕ pl e-pi-ki-no-*ni*-es

communion κοινωνία ⓕ ki-no-*ni*-a

communist κομμουνιστής/κομμουνίστρια
ⓜ/ⓕ ko-mu-ni-*stis*/ko-mu-*ni*-stri-a

companion σύντροφος/συντρόφισσα
ⓜ/ⓕ *si*-dro-fos/si-dro-fi-sa

company (firm) εταιρεία ⓕ e-te-*ri*-a

company (friends) συντροφιά ⓕ si-dro-*fia*

compass πυξίδα ⓕ pik-*si*-tha

complain παραπονούμαι pa-ra-po-*nu*-me

complaint παράπονο ⓝ pa-*ra*-po-no

complimentary (free) δωρεάν tho-re-*an*

computer κομπιούτερ ⓝ kom-*piu*-ter

computer game παιχνίδι στο κομπιούτερ
ⓝ pegh-*ni*-thi sto kom-*piu*-ter

concert κονσέρτο ⓝ kon-*ser*-to

concussion κλονισμός ⓜ klo-niz-*mos*

conditioner (hair) κοντίσιονερ ⓝ
kon-di-si-o-ner

condom προφυλακτικό ⓝ pro-fi-lak-ti-*ko*

conference (big) συνέδριο ⓝ si-ne-*thri*-o

conference (small) σεμινάριο ⓝ
se-mi-*na*-ri-o

confession εξομολόγηση ⓕ
ek-so-mo-*lo*-ghi-si

confirm (a booking) επικυρώνω
e-pi-ki-*ro*-no

conjunctivitis επιπεφυκίτις ⓜ
e-pi-pe-fi-*ki*-tis

connection σύνδεσμος ⓜ *sin*-thez-mos

conservative a συντηρητικός si-di-ri-ti-*kos*

constipation δυσκοιλία ⓕ *this*-ki-li-a

consulate προξενείο ⓝ prok-se-*ni*-o

contact lenses φακοί επαφής ⓜ pl
fa-*ki* e-pa-*fis*

contact lens solution υγρό φακών
επαφής ⓝ i-*ghro* fa-*kon* e-pa-*fis*

contraceptives αντισυλληπτικά ⓝ pl
a-di-si-lip-ti-*ka*

contract συμβόλαιο ⓝ sim-*vo*-le-o

convenience store σούπερ μάρκετ ⓝ
su-per *mar*-ket

convent μοναστήρι γυναικών ⓝ
mo-na-*sti*-ri yi-ne-*kon*

cook μάγειρας/μαγείρισσα ⓜ/ⓕ
ma-yi-ras/ma-*yi*-ri-sa

cook v μαγειρεύω ma-yi-*re*-vo

cookie μπισκότο ⓝ bis-*ko*-to

cooking μαγείρεμα ⓝ ma-*yi*-re-ma

cool (temperature) δροσερό thro-se-*ro*

copper χαλκός ⓜ khal-*kos*

copy αντίγραφο ⓝ a-*di*-ghra-fo

Corinthian Κορινθιακός ko-rin-thi-a-*kos*

corkscrew ανοιχτήρι ⓝ a-nikh-*ti*-ri

corn καλαμπόκι ⓝ ka-la-*bo*-ki

corner γωνία ⓕ gho-*ni*-a

cornflakes κορν φλέικς ⓝ pl korn *fle*-iks

corrupt διεφθαρμένος thi-ef-thar-*me*-nos

cost v κοστίζω ko-*sti*-zo

cotton βαμβάκι ⓝ va-*ba*-ki

cotton balls μπαλάκια από βαμβάκι ⓝ pl
ba-*la*-kia a-po va-*ba*-ki

cotton buds ξιλάκι με βαμβάκι ⓝ
ksi-*la*-ki me va-*ba*-ki

cough v βήχω *vi*·kho
cough medicine φάρμακο για το βήχα ⓝ *far*·ma·ko yia to *vi*·kha
count v μετράω me·*tra*·o
counter (at bar) πάγκος ⓜ *pa*·gos
country χώρα ⓕ *kho*·ra
countryside εξοχή ⓕ ek·so·*hi*
coupon κουπόνι ⓝ ku·*po*·ni
courgette κολοκυθάκι ⓝ ko·lo·ki·*tha*·ki
court (legal) δικαστήριο ⓝ ᵭhi·ka·*sti*·ri·o
court (tennis) γήπεδο ⓝ *yi*·pe·ᵭho
couscous κουσκούς ⓝ kus·*kus*
cover charge προσαύξηση τιμής ⓕ pro·*saf*·ksi·si ti·*mis*
cow γελάδα ⓕ ye·*la*·ᵭha
cracker (biscuit) γαλέτα ⓕ gha·*le*·ta
craft τέχνη ⓕ *tekh*·ni
crash v κρότος *kro*·tos
crazy τρελλός tre·*los*
cream κρέμα ⓕ *kre*·ma
crèche παιδικός σταθμός ⓜ pe·ᵭhi·*kos* stath·*mos*
credit πίστωση ⓕ *pi*·sto·si
credit card πιστωτική κάρτα ⓕ pi·sto·ti·*ki kar*·ta
cricket (sport) κρίκετ ⓝ *kri*·ket
crop σοδειά ⓕ so·*ᵭhia*
cross (religious) σταυρός ⓜ stav·*ros*
crowded γεμάτο (κόσμο) ye·*ma*·to (*koz*·mo)
cruise κρουαζέρα ⓕ kru·a·*ze*·ra
cucumber αγγούρι ⓝ a·*gu*·ri
cup φλυτζάνι ⓝ fli·*dza*·ni
cupboard ντουλάπι ⓝ du·*la*·pi
currency exchange τιμή συναλλάγματος ⓕ ti·*mi* si·na·*lagh*·ma·tos
current (electricity) ρεύμα ⓝ *rev*·ma
current affairs επίκαιρα θέματα ⓝ pl e·*pi*·ke·ra *the*·ma·ta
curry κάρι ⓝ *ka*·ri
cushion cover μαξιλαροθήκη ⓕ mak·si·la·ro·*thi*·ki
custom έθιμο ⓝ *e*·thi·mo
customs τελωνείο ⓝ te·lo·*ni*·o
cut v κόβω *ko*·vo
cutlery μαχαιροπήρουνα ⓝ pl ma·he·ro·*pi*·ru·na
CV βιογραφικό σημείωμα ⓝ vi·o·ghra·fi·*ko* si·*mi*·o·ma
Cycladic Κυκλαδικός ki·kla·ᵭhi·*kos*

cycle v κάνω ποδήλατο *ka*·no po·*ᵭhi*·la·to
cycling ποδηλασία ⓕ po·ᵭhi·la·*si*·a
cyclist ποδηλάτης/ποδηλάτισσα ⓜ/ⓕ po·ᵭhi·*la*·tis/po·ᵭhi·*la*·ti·sa
Cypriot (person) Κύπριος/Κύπρια ⓜ/ⓕ *ki*·pri·os/*ki*·pri·a
Cypriot (wine etc) κυπριακός/κυπριακή ⓜ/ⓕ ki·pri·a·*kos*/ki·pri·a·*ki*
Cyprus Κύπρος ⓕ *ki*·pros
cystitis κύστη ⓕ *ki*·sti

D

dad μπαμπάς ⓜ ba·*bas*
daily καθημερινός ka·thi·me·ri·*nos*
dairy shop γαλακτοπωλείο ⓝ gha·lak·to·po·*li*·o
dance v χορεύω kho·*re*·vo
dancing χορός kho·*ros*
dangerous επικίνδυνος e·pi·*kin*·ᵭhi·nos
dark (night) a σκοτεινός sko·ti·*nos*
dark (colour) a σκούρος *sku*·ros
date (a person) v βγαίνω (με κάποιον) *vye*·no (me *ka*·pion)
date (appointment) ραντεβού ⓝ ra·de·*vu*
date (day) ημερομηνία ⓕ i·me·ro·mi·*ni*·a
date (fruit) χουρμάς ⓜ khur·*mas*
date of birth ημερομηνία γεννήσεως ⓕ i·me·ro·mi·*ni*·a ye·*ni*·se·os
daughter κόρη ⓕ *ko*·ri
dawn αυγή ⓕ av·*yi*
day ημέρα ⓕ i·*me*·ra
day after tomorrow μεθαύριο me·*thav*·ri·o
day before yesterday προχθές prokh·*tes*
dead a νεκρός ne·*kros*
deaf a κουφός ku·*fos*
deal (cards) μοιράζω (χαρτιά) mi·*ra*·zo (khar·*tia*)
December Δεκέμβριος ⓜ de·*kem*·vri·os
decide αποφασίζω a·po·fa·*si*·zo
deck κατάστρωμα ⓝ ka·*ta*·stro·ma
deep βαθύς va·*this*
deforestation αποδάσωση ⓕ a·po·*tha*·so·si
degrees (temperature) βαθμοί ⓜ pl vath·*mi*

dehydration αφυδάτωση ⓕ a·fi·*tha*·to·si

delay καθυστέρηση ⓕ ka·thi·*ste*·ri·si

delicatessen ντελικατέσεν ⓕ de·li·ka·*te*·sen

delineation line διαχωριστική γραμμή ⓕ thi·a·kho·ri·sti·*ki* ghra·*mi*

deliver παραδίνω pa·ra·*thi*·no

democracy δημοκρατία ⓕ thi·mo·kra·*ti*·a

demonstration διαδήλωση ⓕ thi·a·*thi*·lo·si

Denmark Δανία ⓕ tha·*ni*·a

dental floss οδοντιατρική κλωστή ⓕ o·tho·di·a·tri·*ki* klo·*sti*

dentist οδοντίατρος ⓜ&ⓕ o·tho·*di*·a·tros

deodorant αποσμητικό ⓝ a·poz·mi·ti·*ko*

depart (leave) αναχωρώ a·na·kho·*ro*

department store κατάστημα ⓝ ka·*ta*·sti·ma

departure αναχώρηση ⓕ a·na·*kho*·ri·si

departure gate θύρα αναχώρησης ⓕ *thi*·ra a·na·*kho*·ri·sis

deposit (bank) κατάθεση ⓕ ka·*ta*·the·si

deposit (on house etc) προκαταβολή ⓕ pro·ka·ta·vo·*li*

depressed θλιμμένος/θλιμμένη ⓜ/ⓕ thli·*me*·nos/thli·*me*·ni

derailleur εκτροχιασμός ⓜ ek·tro·hi·az·*mos*

descendent απόγονος ⓜ a·*po*·gho·nos

desert έρημος ⓕ *e*·ri·mos

design σχέδιο ⓝ *skhe*·thi·o

dessert επιδόρπιο ⓝ e·pi·*thor*·pi·o

destination προορισμός ⓜ pro·o·riz·*mos*

details λεπτομέρειες ⓕ pl lep·to·*me*·ri·es

diabetes διαβήτης ⓜ thi·a·*vi*·tis

dial tone ήχος κλήσης ⓜ *i*·khos *kli*·sis

diaper πάνα ⓕ *pa*·na

diaphragm διάφραγμα ⓝ thi·a·ghra·ma

diarrhoea διάρροια ⓕ thi·a·ri·a

diary ημερολόγιο ⓝ i·me·ro·*lo*·yi·o

diaspora διασπορά ⓕ thi·a·spo·*ra*

dice ζάρια ⓝ pl *za*·ria

dictionary λεξικό ⓝ lek·si·*ko*

die v πεθαίνω pe·*the*·no

diet δίαιτα ⓕ *thi*·e·ta

different διαφορετικός thia·fo·re·ti·*kos*

difficult δύσκολος *thi*·sko·los

digital a ψηφιακός psi·fi·a·*kos*

dining car βαγόνι φαγητού ⓝ va·*gho*·ni fa·yi·*tu*

dinner δείπνο ⓝ *thip*·no

direct a άμεσος *a*·me·sos

direct-dial κατ' ευθείαν γραμμή ⓕ ka·tef·*thi*·an gra·*mi*

direction κατεύθυνση ⓕ ka·*tef*·thin·si

director διευθυντής/διευθύντρια ⓜ/ⓕ thi·ef·thi·*dis*/thi·ef·*thi*·dri·a

dirty a βρώμικος *vro*·mi·kos

disabled a ανάπηρος a·*na*·pi·ros

disco ντισκοτέκ ⓕ di·sko·*tek*

discount έκπτωση ⓕ *ek*·pto·si

discrimination διάκριση ⓕ thi·a·kri·si

disease ασθένεια ⓕ a·*sthe*·ni·a

dish πιάτο ⓝ *pia*·to

disk (CD-ROM) σι ντι ρομ ⓝ si di rom

disk (floppy) δισκέτα ⓕ thi·*ske*·ta

diving βουτιά ⓕ vu·*tia*

diving equipment εξαρτήματα βουτηχτή ⓝ pl ek·sar·*ti*·ma·ta vu·tikh·*ti*

divorced a διαζευγμένος/διαζευγμένη ⓜ/ⓕ thi·a·zev·*ghme*·nos/thi·a·zev·*ghme*·ni

dizzy ζαλισμένος/ζαλισμένη ⓜ/ⓕ za·liz·*me*·nos/za·liz·*me*·ni

do v κάνω *ka*·no

doctor γιατρός ⓜ&ⓕ yia·*tros*

documentary ντοκυμαντέρ ⓝ do·ki·man·*ter*

dog σκυλί ⓝ ski·*li*

dole επίδομα ανεργίας ⓝ e·*pi*·tho·ma an·er·*yi*·as

doll κούκλα ⓕ *ku*·kla

dollar δολλάριο ⓝ tho·*la*·ri·o

dolphin δελφίνι ⓝ thel·*fi*·ni

dhomatia (room for rent) δωμάτια (για νοίκιασμα) ⓝ pl tho·*ma*·ti·a (yia *ni*·kiaz·ma)

dominoes ντόμινο ⓝ *do*·mi·no

door πόρτα ⓕ *por*·ta

dope (drugs) ναρκωτικά ⓝ pl nar·ko·ti·*ka*

Doric Δωρικός tho·ri·*kos*

double a διπλός thi·*plos*

double bed διπλό κρεβάτι ⓝ thi·*plo* kre·*va*·ti

double room διπλό δωμάτιο ⓝ thi·*plo* tho·*ma*·ti·o

down κάτω *ka*·to

downhill κατηφορικά ka·ti·fo·ri·*ka*

dozen ντουζίνα ⓕ du·*zi*·na

drama δράμα ⓝ *thra*·ma

dream όνειρο ⓝ o·ni·ro

dress ⓝ φόρεμα ⓝ *fo*·re·ma

dried ξηρός ksi·ros

dried fruit ξηρά φρούτα ⓝ pl ksi·*ra* fru·ta

drink ποτό ⓝ po·*to*

drink v πίνω *pi*·no

drink (alcoholic) ποτό (αλκοολικό) ⓝ po·*to* (al·ko·o·li·ko)

drive v οδηγώ o·*thi*·gho

drivers licence άδεια οδήγησης ⓕ *a*·thi·a o·*thi*·yi·sis

drizzle ψιχάλα ⓕ psi·*kha*·la

drug (illegal) ναρκωτικό ⓝ nar·ko·ti·*ko*

drug addiction εθισμός στα ναρκωτικά ⓜ e·*thiz*·mos sta nar·ko·ti·*ka*

drug dealer έμπορος ναρκωτικών ⓜ *e*·bo·ros nar·ko·ti·*kon*

drug trafficking κυκλοφορία ναρκωτικών ⓕ ki·klo·fo·ri·*a* nar·ko·ti·*kon*

drug user ναρκομανής ⓜ&ⓕ nar·ko·ma·*nis*

drugs (illicit) ναρκωτικά ⓝ pl nar·ko·ti·*ka*

drum τύμπανο ⓝ *ti*·ba·no

drunk μεθυσμένος me·thiz·*me*·nos

dry a στεγνός stegh·*nos*

dry v στεγνώνω stegh·*no*·no

duck πάπια ⓕ *pa*·pia

dummy (pacifier) πιπίλα ⓕ pi·*pi*·la

DVD Ντι-Βι-Ντί ⓝ di·vi·*di*

E

each καθένας ka·*the*·nas

ear αυτί ⓝ af·*ti*

early νωρίς no·*ris*

earn κερδίζω ker·*thi*·zo

earplugs ωτοασπίδες ⓕ pl o·to·a·*spi*·thes

earrings σκουλαρίκια ⓝ pl sku·la·*ri*·kia

Earth Γη ⓕ yi

earthquake σεισμός ⓜ *siz*·mos

east ανατολή ⓕ a·na·to·*li*

Easter Πάσχα ⓝ *pas*·kha

easy εύκολο ef·ko·lo

eat τρώγω *tro*·gho

economy class τουριστική θέση ⓕ tu·ri·sti·*ki* the·si

ecstasy (drug) έκσταση ⓕ *ek*·sta·si

eczema έκζεμα ⓝ *ek*·ze·ma

education εκπαίδευση ⓕ ek·*pe*·thef·si

egg αβγό ⓝ av·*gho*

eggplant μελιτζάνα ⓕ me·li·*dza*·na

election εκλογή ⓕ ek·lo·*yi*

electrical store κατάστημα ηλεκτρικών ειδών ⓝ ka·*ta*·sti·ma i·lek·tri·*kon* i·*thon*

electricity ηλεκτρισμός ⓜ i·lek·triz·*mos*

elevator ασανσέρ ⓝ a·san·*ser*

email ημέιλ ⓝ *i·me*·il

embarrassed αμήχανος a·*mi*·kha·nos

embassy πρεσβεία ⓕ pre·zvi·a

embroidery κέντημα ⓝ *ke*·di·ma

emergency έκτακτη ανάγκη ⓕ *ek*·tak·ti a·*na*·gi

emotional συναισθηματικός si·ne·sthi·ma·ti·kos

employee υπάλληλος ⓜ&ⓕ i·*pa*·li·los

employer εργοδότης/εργοδότρια ⓜ/ⓕ er·gho·*tho*·tis/er·gho·*tho*·tri·a

empty a άδειο *a*·thi·o

end τέλος ⓝ *te*·los

endangered species είδη υπό εξαφάνιση ⓝ pl *i*·thi i·*po* ek·sa·fa·*ni*·si

engaged (to marry) αρραβωνιασμένος/αρραβωνιασμένη ⓜ/ⓕ a·ra·vo·niaz·*me*·nos/ a·ra·vo·niaz·*me*·ni

engagement (undertaking) υποχρέωση ⓕ i·po·*khre*·o·si

engine μηχανή ⓕ mi·kha·*ni*

engineer μηχανικός ⓜ&ⓕ mi·kha·ni·*kos*

engineering μηχανική ⓕ mi·kha·ni·*ki*

England Αγγλία ⓕ ang·*gli*·a

English (language) Αγγλικά ⓝ pl ang·gli·*ka*

enjoy oneself απολαμβάνω a·po·lam·*va*·no

enough αρκετά ar·ke·*ta*

enter μπαίνω be·no

entertainment guide οδηγός διασκέδασης ⓜ o·*thi*·ghos thia·*ske*·tha·sis

entry είσοδος ⓕ *i*·so·thos

envelope φάκελος ⓜ *fa*·ke·los

environment περιβάλλον ⓝ pe·ri·va·lon

epilepsy επιληψία ⓕ e·pi·lip·*si*·a

erosion διάβρωση ⓕ thi·*av*·ro·si

equal opportunity ίσες ευκαιρίες ⓕ pl *i*·ses ef·ke·ri·es

equality ισότητα ⓕ i·*so*·ti·ta

equipment εξοπλισμός ⓜ ek·so·pliz·*mos*

escalator κυλιόμενες σκάλες ⓕ pl ki·li·o·me·nes *ska*·les

estate agency κτηματομεσιτικό γραφείο ⓝ kti·ma·to·me·si·ti·ko ghra·fi·o

euro ευρώ ⓝ ev·ro

Europe Ευρώπη ⓕ ev·ro·pi
European Union Ευρωπαϊκή Ένωση ⓕ ev·ro·pa·i·ki e·no·si
euthanasia ευθανασία ⓕ ef·tha·na·si·a
evening βράδι ⓝ vra·thi
every κάθε ka·the
everyone καθένας ⓜ ka·the·nas
everything καθετί ⓝ ka·the·ti
exactly ακριβώς a·kri·vos
example παράδειγμα ⓝ pa·ra·thigh·ma
excavation ανασκαφή ⓕ a·na·ska·fi
excellent εξαιρετικός ek·se·re·ti·kos
excess (baggage) υπέρβαρο (φορτίο) ⓝ i·per·va·ro (for·ti·o)
exchange συνάλλαγμα ⓝ si·na·lagh·ma
exchange v ανταλλάσσω a·da·la·so
exchange rate τιμή συναλλάγματος ⓕ ti·mi si·na·lagh·ma·tos
excluded εξαιρούμενος ek·se·ru·me·nos
exhaust (car) εξάτμιση ⓕ ek·sat·mi·si
exhibition έκθεση ⓕ ek·the·si
exhibit έκθεμα ⓝ ek·the·ma
exit έξοδος ⓕ ek·so·thos
expensive ακριβός a·kri·vos
experience εμπειρία ⓕ e·bi·ri·a
exploitation εκμετάλλευση ⓕ ek·me·ta·lef·si
export permit άδεια εξαγωγής ⓕ a·thi·a ek·sa·gho·yis
(by) express mail επείγον (ταχυδρομείο) ⓝ e·pi·ghon (ta·hi·thro·mi·o)
extension (visa) παράταση ⓕ pa·ra·ta·si
eye μάτι ⓝ ma·ti
eye drops σταγόνες ματιών ⓕ pl sta·gho·nes ma·ti·on
eyes μάτια ⓝ pl ma·tia

F

fabric ύφασμα ⓝ i·faz·ma
face πρόσωπο ⓝ pro·so·po
face cloth πετσέτα προσώπου ⓕ pet·se·ta pro·so·pu
factory εργοστάσιο ⓝ er·gho·sta·si·o
factory worker εργάτης εργοστασίου ⓜ er·gha·tis er·gho·sta·si·u
    εργάτρια εργοστασίου ⓕ er·gha·tri·a er·gho·sta·si·u
falcon γεράκι ⓝ ye·ra·ki

fall (autumn) φθινόπωρο ⓝ fthi·no·po·ro
fall (down) πτώση ⓕ pto·si
family οικογένεια ⓕ i·ko·ye·ni·a
family name επώνυμο ⓝ e·po·ni·mo
famous a φημισμένος fi·miz·me·nos
fan (machine) ανεμιστήρας ⓜ a·ne·mi·sti·ras
fan (of sport) οπαδός ⓜ o·pa·thos
fanbelt λουρί ⓝ lu·ri
far μακριά ma·kri·a
fare εισιτήριο ⓝ i·si·ti·ri·o
farm φάρμα ⓕ far·ma
farmer γεωργός ⓜ&ⓕ ye·or·ghos
fashion μόδα ⓕ mo·tha
fast a γρήγορος ghri·gho·ros
fat a παχύς pa·his
father πατέρας ⓜ pa·te·ras
father-in-law πεθερός ⓜ pe·the·ros
faucet βρύση ⓕ vri·si
fault (someone's) λάθος ⓝ la·thos
faulty ελαττωματικός e·la·to·ma·ti·kos
fax machine μηχανή φαξ ⓕ mi·kha·ni faks
February Φεβρουάριος ⓜ fev·ru·a·ri·os
feed v ταΐζω ta·i·zo
feel (touch) v αγγίζω a·gi·zo
feeling (physical) αφή ⓕ a·fi
feelings αισθήματα ⓝ pl es·thi·ma·ta
female a θηλυκός thi·li·kos
fence φράχτης ⓜ frakh·tis
fencing (sport) ξιφομαχία ⓕ ksi·fo·ma·hi·a
ferry φέρυ ⓝ fe·ri
festival φεστιβάλ ⓝ fe·sti·val
fever πυρετός ⓜ pi·re·tos
few λίγοι li·yi
fiancé αρραβωνιαστικός ⓜ a·ra·vo·nia·sti·kos
fiancée αρραβωνιαστικιά ⓕ a·ra·vo·nia·sti·kia
fiction μυθοπλασία ⓕ mi·tho·pla·si·a
fig σύκο ⓝ si·ko
fight πάλη ⓕ pa·li
filigree (jewellery) φιλιγκράν ⓝ fi·li·gran
fill γεμίζω ye·mi·zo
fillet φιλέτο ⓝ fi·le·to
film (camera/cinema) φιλμ ⓝ film
film speed ταχύτητα φιλμ ⓕ ta·hi·ti·ta film
filtered φιλτραρισμένος fil·tra·riz·me·nos
find βρίσκω vri·sko
fine (penalty) πρόστιμο ⓝ pros·ti·mo
fine (weather) a ωραίος o·re·os

finger δάκτυλο ⓝ *thak*·ti·lo
finish τελείωμα ⓝ te·*li*·o·ma
finish v τελειώνω te·li·*o*·no
Finland Φιλανδία ⓕ fi·lan·*thi*·a
fire φωτιά ⓕ fo·*tia*
firewood καυσόξυλα ⓝ pl kaf·*sok*·si·la
first a πρώτος *pro*·tos
first class πρώτη τάξη ⓕ *pro*·ti tak·si
first-aid kit κυτίο πρώτων βοηθειών ⓝ ki·*ti*·o *pro*·ton vo·i·thi·on
first name μικρό όνομα ⓝ mi·*kro* o·no·ma
fish ψάρι ⓝ *psa*·ri
fishing ψάρεμα ⓝ *psa*·re·ma
fish monger ιχθυοπώλης/ιχθυοπώλισσα ⓜ/ⓕ ikh·thi·o·*po*·lis/ikh·thi·o·*po*·li·sa
fish shop ιχθυοπωλείο ⓝ ikh·thi·o·po·*li*·o
flag σημαία ⓕ si·*me*·a
flannel φανέλλα (ύφασμα) ⓕ fa·*ne*·la (*i*·faz·ma)
flashlight φλας ⓝ flas
flat a επίπεδος e·*pi*·pe·thos
flat (apartment) διαμέρισμα ⓝ thi·a·*me*·riz·ma
flea market παζάρι ⓝ pa·*za*·ri
flight πτήση ⓕ *pti*·si
flood πλημμύρα ⓕ pli·*mi*·ra
floor πάτωμα ⓝ *pa*·to·ma
floor (storey) όροφος ⓝ o·ro·fos
florist ανθοπώλης/ανθοπώλισσα ⓜ/ⓕ an·tho·*po*·lis/an·tho·po·li·sa
flour αλεύρι ⓝ a·*lev*·ri
flower λουλούδι ⓝ lu·*lu*·thi
flu γρίππη ⓕ *ghri*·pi
fly v πετάω v pe·*ta*·o
foggy ομιχλώδης o·mi·*khlo*·this
folk (art) a λαϊκός la·i·*kos*
follow ακολουθώ a·ko·lu·*tho*
food φαγητό ⓝ fa·yi·*to*
food supplies προμήθειες φαγητού ⓝ pl pro·*mi*·thi·es fa·yi·*tu*
foot πόδι ⓝ *po*·thi
football (soccer) ποδόσφαιρο ⓝ po·*thos*·fe·ro
footpath πεζοδρόμιο ⓝ pe·zo·*thro*·mi·o
foreign ξένος *kse*·nos
forest δάσος ⓝ *tha*·sos
forever πάντα *pa*·da
forget ξεχνώ ksekh·*no*
forgive συγχωρώ sing·kho·*ro*
fork πιρούνι ⓝ pi·*ru*·ni

fortnight δεκαπενθήμερο ⓝ da·ka·pen·*thi*·me·ro
fortune teller μάντης/μάντισσα ⓜ/ⓕ *ma*·dis/*ma*·di·sa
foul φάουλ ⓝ *fa*·ul
foyer φουαγέ ⓝ fu·a·*ye*
fragile εύθραυστος ef·*thraf*·stos
France Γαλλία ⓕ gha·*li*·a
free (available) διαθέσιμος thi·a·*the*·si·mos
free (gratis) δωρεάν tho·re·*an*
free (not bound) ελεύθερος e·*lef*·the·ros
freeze παγώνω pa·*gho*·no
fresco φρέσκο ⓝ *fre*·sko
fresh φρέσκος *fre*·skos
Friday Παρασκευή ⓕ pa·ra·ske·*vi*
fridge ψυγείο ⓝ psi·*yi*·o
fried τηγανισμένος ti·gha·niz·*me*·nos
friend φίλος/φίλη ⓜ/ⓕ *fi*·los/*fi*·li
from από a·*po*
frost παγωνιά ⓕ pa·gho·*nia*
frozen παγωμένος pa·gho·*me*·nos
fruit φρούτα ⓝ pl *fru*·ta
fruit picking μάζεμα φρούτων ⓝ *ma*·ze·ma *fru*·ton
fry v τηγανίζω ti·gha·*ni*·zo
frying pan τηγάνι ⓝ ti·*gha*·ni
full γεμάτο ye·*ma*·to
full-time πλήρους απασχόλησης *pli*·rus a·pa·*skho*·li·sis
fun a διασκεδαστικό thia·ske·tha·sti·*ko*
funeral κηδεία ⓕ ki·*thi*·a
funny αστείος a·*sti*·os
furniture έπιπλα ⓝ pl e·pi·pla
future μέλλον ⓝ *me*·lon

G

game (football) ματς ⓝ mats
game (sport) παιγνίδι ⓝ pegh·*ni*·thi
garage γκαράζ ⓝ ga·*raz*
garbage σκουπίδια ⓝ pl sku·*pi*·thia
garbage can σκουπιδοτενεκές ⓝ sku·pi·tho·te·ne·*kes*
garden κήπος ⓜ *ki*·pos
gardener κηπουρός ⓜ&ⓕ ki·pu·*ros*
gardening κηπουρική ⓕ ki·pu·ri·*ki*
garlic σκόρδο ⓝ *skor*·tho
gas (for cooking) πετρογκάζ ⓝ pe·tro·*gaz*
gas (petrol) βενζίνα ⓕ ven·*zi*·na

gas cartridge μπουκάλα γκαζιού ①
bu·*ka*·la ga·zi·*u*

gastroenteritis γαστροεντερίτιδα ①
gha·stro·e·de·*ri*·ti·tha

gate (airport etc) θύρα ① *thi*·ra

gauze αραχνοΰφαντος ⑩
a·rakh·no·*i*·fa·dos

gay γκέι *ge*·i

gelatine ζελατίνη ① ze·la·*ti*·ni

Germany Γερμανία ① yer·ma·*ni*·a

get παίρνω *per*·no

get off (transport) κατεβαίνω ka·te·*ve*·no

gift δώρο ⑩ *tho*·ro

gig παράσταση ① pa·ra·sta·si

gin τζιν ⑩ dzin

girl κορίτσι ⑩ ko·*rit*·si

girlfriend φιλενάδα ① fi·le·*na*·tha

give δίνω *thi*·no

given name μικρό όνομα ⑩
mi·kro o·no·ma

glandular fever αδενώδης πυρετός ⑩
a·the·no·*this* pi·re·*tos*

glass (drinking) ποτήρι ⑩ po·*ti*·ri

glasses (spectacles) γιαλιά ⑩ pl yia·*lia*

glove γάντι ⑩ *ghan*·ti

gloves γάντια ⑩ pl *ghan*·tia

glue κόλα ① *ko*·la

go πηγαίνω pi·*ye*·no

go out βγαίνω *vye*·no

go out with (a male) βγαίνω με κάποιον
vye·no me *ka*·pi·on

go out with (a female) βγαίνω με κάποια
vye·no me *ka*·pia

go shopping πάω για ψώνια
pa·o yia *pso*·nia

goal (score/point) γκολ ⑩ gol

goalkeeper τερματοφύλακας ⑩&①
ter·ma·to·*fi*·la·kas

goat κατσίκα ① kat·*si*·ka

god (general) θεός ⑩ the·*os*

goddess θεά ① the·*a*

goggles προστατευτικά γιαλιά ⑩ pl
pro·sta·tef·ti·*ka* yia·*lia*

goggles (swimming)
προστατευτικά γιαλιά για κολύμπι
⑩ pl pro·sta·tef·ti·*ka* yia·*lia* yia ko·*li*·bi

gold χρυσάφι ⑩ khri·*sa*·fi

golf ball μπαλάκι του γκολφ ⑩
ba·*la*·ki tu golf

golf course γήπεδο του γκολφ ⑩
yi·pe·tho tu golf

good καλός ka·*los*

government κυβέρνηση ① ki·*ver*·ni·si

gram γραμμάριο ⑩ ghra·*ma*·ri·o

granddaughter εγγονή ① e·go·*ni*

grandfather παππούς ⑩ pa·*pus*

grandmother γιαγιά ① yia·*yia*

grandson εγγονός ⑩ e·go·*nos*

grapefruit γκρέιπ φρουτ ⑩ *gre*·ip frut

grapes σταφύλια ⑩ pl sta·*fi*·lia

grass γρασίδι ⑩ ghra·*si*·thi

grateful ευγνώμων ev·*ghno*·mon

grave τάφος ⑩ *ta*·fos

gray γκρίζος *gri*·zos

great (fantastic) απίθανος a·*pi*·tha·nos

Greece Ελλάδα ① e·*la*·tha

Greek (language) Ελληνικά ⑩ pl
e·li·ni·*ka*

Greek (people) Έλληνες ⑩ pl *e*·li·nes

green πράσινος *pra*·si·nos

greengrocer
οπωροπώλης/οπωροπώλισσα ⑩/①
o·po·ro·*po*·lis/o·po·ro·*po*·li·sa

grey γκρίζος *gri*·zos

grilled ψημένο στη σχάρα
psi·*me*·no sti *skha*·ra

grocery οπωροπωλείο ⑩ o·po·ro·po·*li*·o

groundnut φυστίκι ⑩ fi·*sti*·ki

grow μεγαλώνω me·ga·*lo*·no

guaranteed εγγυημένος e·ghi·i·*me*·nos

guess v μαντεύω ma·*de*·vo

guesthouse ξενώνας ⑩ *kse*·no·nas

guide (audio) μαγνητοφωνημένες
οδηγίες ① pl magh·ni·to·fo·ni·*me*·nes
o·dhi·*yi*·es

guide (person) οδηγός ⑩&① o·thi·*ghos*

guidebook τουριστικός οδηγός ⑩
tu·ri·sti·*kos* o·thi·*ghos*

guide dog σκυλί οδηγός ⑩ ski·*li* o·thi·*ghos*

guided tour περιήγηση με οδηγό ①
pe·ri·*i*·yi·si me o·thi·*gho*

guilty a ένοχος *e*·no·khos

guitar κιθάρα ① ki·*tha*·ra

gum μαστίχα ① ma·*sti*·kha

gun όπλο ⑩ o·plo

gym (fitness) γυμναστήριο ⑩
yim·na·*sti*·ri·o

gymnastics γυμναστική ① yim·na·sti·*ki*

gynaecologist γυναικολόγος ⑩&①
yi·ne·ko·*lo*·ghos

gyros γύρος ⑩ *yi*·ros

H

hair μαλλιά ⓝ pl ma-*lia*
hairbrush βούρτσα μαλλιών ⓕ
   vur-tsa ma-*lion*
haircut κούρεμα ⓝ *ku*-re-ma
hairdresser κομμωτής/κομμώτρια ⓜ/ⓕ
   ko-mo-*tis*/ko-mo-tri-a
halal χαλάλ kha-*lal*
half μισό mi-so
hallucination παραίσθηση ⓕ pa-*res*-thi-si
ham ζαμπόν ⓝ za-*bon*
hammer σφυρί ⓝ sfi-*ri*
hammock αιώρα ⓕ e-o-ra
hand χέρι ⓝ he-ri
handbag τσάντα ⓕ *tsa*-da
handball χάντμπολ ⓝ *khand*-bol
handicrafts εργόχειρα ⓝ pl er-*gho*-hi-ra
handkerchief μαντήλι ⓝ ma-*di*-li
handlebars χειρολαβή ⓕ hi-ro-la-*vi*
handmade a χειροποίητο hi-ro-*pi*-i-to
handsome όμορφος *o*-mor-fos
happy ευτυχισμένος ef-ti-hiz-*me*-nos
harassment παρενόχληση ⓕ
   pa-re-*no*-khli-si
harbour λιμάνι ⓝ li-*ma*-ni
hard (not soft) σκληρός skli-*ros*
hard-boiled σφιχτός sfikh-*tos*
hardware store κατάστημα σιδερικών ⓝ
   ka-ta-sti-ma si-the-ri-*kon*
hash τουρλού ⓝ tur-*lu*
hat καπέλο ⓝ ka-*pe*-lo
have έχω e-kho
have a cold έχω κρύωμα e-kho kri-o-ma
have fun διασκεδάζω thia-ske-*tha*-zo
hay fever ρινική αλλεργία ⓕ
   ri-ni-*ki* a-ler-*yi*-a
hazelnut φουντούκι ⓝ fu-*du*-ki
he αυτός ⓝ af-*tos*
head κεφάλι ⓝ ke-*fa*-li
headache πονοκέφαλος ⓜ po-no-ke-fa-los
headlights μεγάλα φώτα αυτοκινήτου
   ⓝ pl me-*gha*-la fo-ta af-to-ki-*ni*-tu
health υγεία ⓕ i-*yi*-a
hear ακούω a-*ku*-o
hearing aid ακουστικά ⓝ pl a-ku-sti-*ka*
heart καρδιά ⓕ kar-*thia*
heart attack καρδιακή προσβολή ⓕ
   kar-thi-a-*ki* proz-vo-*li*

heart condition καρδιακή κατάσταση ⓕ
   kar-thi-a-*ki* ka-*ta*-sta-si
heat ζέστη ⓕ ze-sti
heated ζεσταμένος ze-sta-*me*-nos
heater σόμπα ⓕ so-ba
heating θέρμανση ⓕ *ther*-man-si
heatstroke θερμοπληξία ⓕ
   ther-mo-plik-*si*-a
heatwave καύσωνας ⓜ *kaf*-so-nas
heavy βαρύς va-*ris*
Hellenistic Ελληνιστικός e-li-ni-sti-*kos*
helmet περικεφαλαία ⓕ pe-ri-ke-fa-*le*-a
help βοήθεια ⓝ vo-*i*-thi-a
help v βοηθώ vo-i-*tho*
hepatitis ηπατίτιδα ⓕ i-pa-*ti*-ti-tha
her (ownership/direct object) της tis
herb βότανο ⓝ *vo*-ta-no
herbalist βοτανολόγος ⓜ&ⓕ
   vo-ta-no-*lo*-ghos
here εδώ e-*tho*
heroin ηρωίνη ⓕ i-ro-*i*-ni
herring ρέγκα ⓕ *re*-ga
high ψηλός psi-*los*
highchair καρέκλα για μωρά
   ka-*re*-kla yia mo-*ro*
high school γυμνάσιο ⓝ yim-*na*-si-o
highway δημόσιος δρόμος ⓜ
   thi-*mo*-si-os *thro*-mos
hike v πεζοπορώ pe-zo-po-*ro*
hiking πεζοπορία ⓕ pe-zo-po-*ri*-a
hiking boots μπότες πεζοπορίας ⓕ pl
   bo-tes pe-zo-po-*ri*-as
hiking route δρόμος πεζοπορίας ⓜ
   thro-mos pe-zo-po-*ri*-as
hill λόφος ⓜ *lo*-fos
Hindu Ινδουιστής/Ινδουίστρια ⓜ/ⓕ
   in-thu-i-*stis*/in-thu-i-stri-a
hire v ενοικιάζω e-ni-ki-*a*-zo
his (ownership/direct object) του tu
historical ιστορικός i-sto-ri-*kos*
history ιστορία ⓕ i-sto-*ri*-a
hitchhike v ταξιδεύω με ωτοστόπ
   tak-si-*the*-vo me o-to-*stop*
HIV έιτς άι βι ⓝ e-idz a-i vi
hockey χόκι ⓝ *kho*-ki
holiday αργεία ⓕ ar-*yi*-a
holidays διακοπές ⓕ pl thi-a-ko-*pes*
home σπίτι ⓝ *spi*-ti
homeless άστεγος a-ste-ghos
homemaker νοικοκύρης/νοικοκυρά
   ⓜ/ⓕ ni-ko-*ki*-ris/ni-ko-ki-*ra*

homeopathy ομοιοπαθητική ① o-mi-o-pa-thi-ti-*ki*

homosexual ομοφυλόφιλος ⑩ o-mo-fi-*lo*-fi-los

honey μέλι ⑩ *me*-li

honeymoon ταξίδι του μέλιτος ⑩ tak-*si*-thi tu *me*-li-tos

horoscope ωροσκόπιο ⑩ o-ro-*sko*-pi-o

horse άλογο ⑩ *a*-lo-gho

horse riding ιππασία ① i-pa-*si*-a

hospital νοσοκομείο ⑩ no-so-ko-*mi*-o

hospitality φιλοξενία ① fi-lok-se-*ni*-a

hot ζεστός ze-*stos*

hotel ξενοδοχείο ⑩ kse-no-tho-*hi*-o

hot water ζεστό νερό ⑩ ze-*sto* ne-*ro*

hour ώρα ① *o*-ra

house σπίτι ⑩ *spi*-ti

housework νοικοκυριό ⑩ ni-ko-ki-*rio*

how πώς pos

how much πόσο *po*-so

hug v αγκαλιάζω a-ga-*lia*-zo

huge πελώριος pe-*lo*-ri-os

humanities ανθρωπιστικές σπουδές ① pl an-thro-pi-sti-*kes* spu-*thes*

human resources ανθρώπινο δυναμικό ⑩ an-*thro*-pi-no thi-na-mi-*ko*

human rights ανθρώπινα δικαιώματα ⑩ pl an-*thro*-pi-na thi-ke-o-ma-ta

hundred εκατό e-ka-*to*

hungry (be) v πεινάώ pi-*no*

hunting κυνήγι ⑩ ki-*ni*-yi

hurt v πληγώνω pli-*gho*-no

husband σύζυγος ⑩ *si*-zi-ghos

hydrofoil ιπτάμενο φελγίνι ⑩ ip-*ta*-me-no thel-*fi*-ni

I

I εγώ e-*gho*

ice πάγος ⑩ *pa*-ghos

ice cream παγωτό ⑩ pa-gho-*to*

ice-cream parlour παγωτατζίδικο ⑩ pagho-ta-*dzi*-thi-ko

ice hockey άις χόκεϊ ① *a*-is kho-ke-i

icon εικόνα ① i-*ko*-na

identification (ID) ταυτότητα ① taf-*to*-ti-ta

idiot βλάκας ⑩ *vla*-kas

if αν an

ill άρρωστος *a*-ro-stos

immigration μετανάστευση ① ma-ta-*na*-stef-si

important σπουδαίος spu-*the*-os

impossible αδύνατος a-*thi*-na-tos

in μέσα *me*-sa

in a hurry βιαστικός via-sti-*kos*

in front of μπροστά bro-*sta*

included συμπεριλαμβανομένου si-be-ri-lam-va-no-*me*-nu

income tax φόρος εισοδήματος ⑩ *fo*-ros i-so-*thi*-ma-tos

India Ινδίες ① pl in-*thi*-es

indicator δείχτης ⑩ *thikh*-tis

indigestion δυσπεψία ① this-pep-*si*-a

indoor εσωτερικός ⑩ e-so-te-ri-*kos*

industry βιομηχανία ① vi-o-mi-kha-*ni*-a

infection μόλυνση ① *mo*-lin-si

inflammation φλεγμονή ① flegh-mo-*ni*

inflation πληθωρισμός ⑩ pli-tho-riz-*mos*

influenza γρίπη ① *ghri*-pi

information πληροφορία ① pli-ro-fo-*ri*-a

ingredient συστατικό ⑩ si-sta-ti-*ko*

inject v κάνω ένεση *ka*-no *e*-ne-si

injection ένεση ① *e*-ne-si

injured πληγωμένος pli-gho-*me*-nos

injury πληγή ① pli-*yi*

inner tube (bicycle) εσωτερική σαμπρέλλα ① e-so-te-ri-*ki* sa-*bre*-la

innocent a αθώος a-*tho*-os

insect έντομο ⑩ *e*-do-mo

inside μέσα *me*-sa

instructor δάσκαλος/δασκάλα ⑩/① *tha*-ska-los/*tha*-ska-la

insurance ασφάλεια ① as-*fa*-li-a

interest (hobby) ενδιαφέρον ⑩ en-*thia*-fe-ron

interesting ενδιαφέρων en-*thia*-fe-ron

intermission διάλειμμα ⑩ *thia*-li-ma

international διεθνής thi-eth-*nis*

Internet διαδίκτυο ⑩ thi-a-*thik*-ti-o

Internet café καφενείο διαδικτύου ⑩ ka-fe-*ni*-o thi-a-*thik*-ti-u

interpreter διερμηνέας ⑩&① thi-er-mi-*ne*-as

interview συνέντευξη ① si-*ne*-def-ksi

invite v προσκαλώ pros-ka-*lo*

Ioanian Ιωνικός i-o-ni-*kos*

Ireland Ιρλανδία ① ir-lan-*thi*-a

iron (for clothes) σίδερο ⑩ *si*-the-ro

iris (eye) ίρις ① *i*-ris

island νησί ⑩ ni-*si*

Israel Ισραήλ ⑩ iz-ra-*il*
it αυτό af-*to*
IT πληροφορική ① pli-ro-fo-ri-*ki*
Italy Ιταλία ① i-ta-*li*-a
itch φαγούρα ① fa-*ghu*-ra
itemised αναλυτικός a-na-li-ti-*kos*
itinerary κατάλογος ⑩ ka-*ta*-lo-ghos
IUD (contraceptive)
ενδομήτριο αντισυλληπτικό ⑩
en-tho-*mi*-tri-o a-di-si-lip-ti-*ko*

J

jacket ζακέτα ① za-*ke*-ta
jail φυλακή ① fi-la-*ki*
jam μαρμελάδα ① mar-me-*la*-tha
January Ιανουάριος ⑩ i-a-nu-*a*-ri-os
Japan Ιαπωνία ① i-a-po-*ni*-a
jar βάζο ⑩ *va*-zo
jaw σαγόνι ⑩ sa-*gho*-ni
jealous ζηλιάρης zi-*lia*-ris
jeans τζιν ⑩ dzin
jeep τζιπ ⑩ dzip
jellyfish μέδουσα ① *me*-thu-sa
jet lag τζετ λαγκ ⑩ dzet lag
jewellery κοσμήματα ⑩ pl koz-*mi*-ma-ta
Jewish Ιουδαϊκός/Ιουδαϊκή ⑩/①
i-u-tha-i-*kos*/i-u-tha-i-*ki*
job δουλειά ① du-*lia*
jogging τρέξιμο ⑩ *trek*-si-mo
joke αστείο ⑩ a-*sti*-o
journalist δημοσιογράφος ⑩&①
thi-mo-si-o-*ghra*-fos
journey ταξίδι ⑩ tak-si-*thi*
judge δικαστής ⑩&① thi-ka-*stis*
jug κανάτα ① ka-*na*-ta
juice χυμός ⑩ hi-*mos*
July Ιούλιος ⑩ i-*u*-li-os
junta χούντα ① *khu*-da
jump v πηδώ pi-*tho*
jumper (sweater) πουλόβερ ⑩ pu-*lo*-ver
jumper leads καλώδια μπαταρίας ⑩ pl
ka-*lo*-thi-a ba-ta-*ri*-as
June Ιούνιος ⑩ i-*u*-ni-os

K

kebab shop σουβλατζίδικο ⑩
suv-la-*tzi*-thi-ko
ketchup σάλτσα ① *salt*-sa

key κλειδί ⑩ kli-*thi*
keyboard πληκτρολόγιο ⑩ plik-tro-*lo*-yi-o
kick v κλωτσάω klot-*sa*-o
kidney νεφρό ⑩ ne-*fro*
kilo κιλό ⑩ ki-*lo*
kilogram χιλιόγραμμο ⑩ hi-*lio*-gra-mo
kilometre χιλιόμετρο ⑩ hi-*lio*-me-tro
kind (nice) καλός ka-*los*
kindergarten νηπιαγωγείο ⑩
ni-pi-a-gho-*yi*-o
king βασιλιάς ⑩ va-si-*lias*
kiosk περίπτερο ⑩ pe-*rip*-te-ro
kiss φιλί ⑩ fi-*li*
kiss v φιλώ fi-*lo*
kitchen κουζίνα ① ku-*zi*-na
kiwifruit ακτινίδιο ⑩ ak-ti-*ni*-thi-o
knee γόνατο ⑩ *gho*-na-to
knife μαχαίρι ⑩ ma-*he*-ri
know v ξέρω *kse*-ro
kosher a κόσια *ko*-si-a

L

labourer εργάτης/εργάτρια ⑩/①
er-*gha*-tis/er-*gha*-tri-a
labyrinth λαβύρινθος ⑩ la-*vi*-rin-thos
lace δαντέλα ① tha-*de*-la
lake λίμνη ① *li*-mni
lamb αρνί ⑩ ar-*ni*
land ξηρά ① ksi-*ra*
landlady νοικοκυρά ① ni-ko-ki-*ra*
landlord ιδιοκτήτης ⑩ i-thi-ok-*ti*-tis
language γλώσσα ① *ghlo*-sa
laptop λάπτοπ ① *lap*-top
large μεγάλος me-*gha*-los
last (previous) προηγούμενος
pro-i-*ghu*-me-nos
last week περασμένη εβδομάδα
pe-raz-*me*-ni ev-tho-*ma*-tha
late καθυστερημένος ka-thi-ste-ri-*me*-nos
later αργότερα ar-*gho*-te-ra
laugh v γελάω ye-*la*-o
launderette πλυντήριο ⑩ pli-*di*-ri-o
laundry (place) πλυντήριο ⑩ pli-*di*-ri-o
law νόμος ⑩ *no*-mos
law (study, profession) νομικά ⑩ no-mi-*ka*
lawyer δικηγόρος ⑩&① thi-ki-gho-ros
laxative καθαρτικό ⑩ ka-thar-ti-*ko*
lazy τεμπέλης te-*be*-lis

leader αρχηγός ⑩&① ar-hi-*ghos*
leaf φύλλο ⑪ *fi*-lo
learn μαθαίνω ma-*the*-no
leather δέρμα ⑪ *ther*-ma
lecturer λέκτορας ⑩&① *lek*-to-ras
ledge ξέρες ① pl *kse*-res
leek πράσο ⑩ *pra*-so
left (direction) αριστερός ⑩ a-ri-ste-*ros*
left-luggage (office)
(γραφείο) φύλαξη αποσκευών
(gra-*fi*-o) *fi*-lak-si a-po-ske-*von*
left-wing αριστερά ① a-ri-ste-*ra*
leg πόδι ⑪ *po*-thi
legal νόμιμος *no*-mi-mos
legislation νομοθεσία ① no-mo-the-*si*-a
legume όσπρια ⑪ pl os-pri-a
lemon λεμόνι ⑪ le-*mo*-ni
lemonade λεμονάδα ① le-mo-*na*-tha
lens φακός ⑩ fa-*kos*
Lent Σαρακοστή ① sa-ra-ko-*sti*
lentil φακές ① pl fa-*kes*
lesbian λεσβία ① les-*vi*-a
less λιγότερο li-*gho*-te-ro
letter (mail) γράμμα ⑪ *ghra*-ma
lettuce μαρούλι ⑩ ma-*ru*-li
liar ψεύτης/ψεύτρα ⑩/① *psef*-tis/*psef*-tra
library βιβλιοθήκη ① viv-li-o-*thi*-ki
licence άδεια ① *a*-thi-a
license plate number αριθμός
κυκλοφορίας ⑩ a-rith-*mos* ki-klo-fo-*ri*-as
lie (not stand) κείτομαι *ki*-to-me
life ζωή ① zo-*i*
life jacket σωσίβιο ⑪ so-*si*-vi-o
lift (elevator) ασανσέρ ⑩ a-san-*ser*
light φως ⑪ fos
light (colour) a ανοιχτός a-nikh-*tos*
light (weight) a ελαφρύς e-la-*fris*
light bulb λάμπα ① *lam*-pa
light meter μετρητής ρεύματος ⑩
me-tri-*tis* *rev*-ma-tos
lighter αναπτήρας ⑩ a-nap-*ti*-ras
like ν μου αρέσει mu a-re-si
lime (fruit) κιτρολέμονο ⑪ ki-tro-*le*-mo-no
linen (material) λινό ⑪ li-*no*
linen (sheets) σεντόνια ⑩ pl se-*do*-nia
lip balm αλοιφή για τα χείλη
a-li-*fi* yia ta *hi*-li
lips χείλη ⑪ pl *hi*-li
lipstick κραγιόν ⑪ kra-*yion*
liquor store κάβα ① *ka*-va

listen (to) ακούω a-*ku*-o
little (quantity) λίγο *li*-gho
little (size) μικρός mi-*kros*
live (somewhere) ν μένω *me*-no
liver συκώτι ⑪ si-*ko*-ti
lizard σαύρα ① *sav*-ra
local a τοπικός to-pi-*kos*
lock κλειδαριά ① kli-tha-*ria*
lock ν κλειδώνω kli-*tho*-no
locked κλειδωμένος kli-tho-*me*-nos
lollies καραμέλες ① pl ka-ra-*me*-les
long a μακρύς ma-*kris*
look ν κοιτάζω ki-*ta*-zo
look after προσέχω pro-*se*-kho
look for ψάχνω *psakh*-no
lookout παρατηρητήριο ⑩ pa-ra-ti-ri-*ti*-ri-o
loose a χαλαρός kha-la-*ros*
loose change ψιλά ⑪ pl psi-*la*
lose χάνω *kha*-no
lost a χαμένος kha-*me*-nos
lost property office γραφείο
απωλεσθέντων αντικειμένων ⑩ gra-*fi*-o
a-po-les-*the*-don a-di-ki-*me*-non
(a) lot πολύ po-*li*
lotion λοσιόν ① lo-*sion*
loud δυνατός thi-na-*tos*
love αγάπη ① a-*gha*-pi
love ν αγαπώ a-gha-*po*
lover εραστής/ερωμένη ⑩/①
e-ra-*stis*/e-ro-*me*-ni
low a χαμηλός kha-mi-*los*
lubricant λιπαντικό ⑪ li-pa-di-*ko*
luck τύχη ① *ti*-hi
lucky a τυχερός ti-he-*ros*
luggage αποσκευές ① pl a-po-ske-*ves*
luggage lockers φύλαξη αποσκευών ①
fi-lak-si a-po-ske-*von*
luggage tag ταμπέλα αποσκευών ①
ta-*be*-la a-po-ske-*von*
lump εξόγκωμα ⑪ ek-so-gho-ma
lunch μεσημεριανό φαγητό ⑪
me-si-me-ria-no fa-yi-*to*
lung πνευμόνι ⑪ pnev-*mo*-ni
luxury πολυτέλεια ① po-li-*te*-li-a

M

Macedonia Μακεδονία ① ma-ke-*tho*-*ni*-a
machine μηχανή ① mi-kha-*ni*
magazine περιοδικό ⑩ pe-ri-o-*thi*-ko

mail (letters) αλληλογραφία ⓕ
a·li·lo·ghra·**fi**·a

mail (postal system) ταχυδρομείο ⓝ
ta·hi·**thro**·mi·o

mailbox ταχυδρομικό κουτί ⓝ
ta·hi·**thro**·mi·ko ku·**ti**

main κύριος **ki**·ri·os

main road κύριος δρόμος ⓜ
ki·ri·os **thro**·mos

make v κάνω **ka**·no

make-up καλλυντικά ⓝ pl ka·li·di·**ka**

mammogram μαμμογράφημα ⓝ
ma·mo·**ghra**·fi·ma

man (male) άντρας ⓜ **a**·dras

manager διευθυντής/διευθύντρια ⓜ/ⓕ
thi·ef·thi·**dis**/thi·ef·**thi**·dri·a

mandarin μανταρίνι ⓝ ma·da·**ri**·ni

mango μάνγκο ⓜ **man**·go

manual work χειρωνακτική εργασία ⓕ
hi·ro·nak·ti·**ki** er·gha·**si**·a

many πολλοί po·**li**

map χάρτης ⓜ **khar**·tis

March Μάρτιος ⓜ **mar**·ti·os

margarine μαργαρίνη ⓕ mar·gha·**ri**·ni

marijuana μαριχουάνα ⓕ ma·ri·khu·**a**·na

marine reserve θαλάσσια αποθέματα
ⓝ pl tha·**la**·si·a a·po·**the**·ma·ta

marital status γαμήλια κατάσταση ⓕ
gha·**mi**·li·a ka·**ta**·sta·si

market αγορά ⓕ a·gho·**ra**

marmalade μαρμελάδα ⓕ mar·me·**la**·tha

marriage γάμος ⓜ **gha**·mos

married a παντρεμένος/παντρεμένη
ⓜ/ⓕ pa·dre·**me**·nos/pa·dre·**me**·ni

marry παντρεύομαι pa·**dre**·vo·me

martial arts πολεμική τέχνη ⓕ
po·le·mi·**ki tekh**·ni

mass (Catholic) λειτουργία ⓕ li·tur·**yi**·a

massage μασάζ ⓝ ma·**saz**

masseur μασέρ ⓜ ma·**ser**

masseuse μασέζ ⓕ ma·**sez**

mat χαλί ⓝ kha·**li**

match (sports) ματς ⓝ mats

matches (for lighting) σπίρτα ⓝ pl **spir**·ta

mattress στρώμα ⓝ **stro**·ma

May Μάιος ⓜ **ma**·i·os

maybe ίσως **i**·sos

mayonnaise μαγιονέζα ⓕ ma·yi·o·**ne**·za

mayor δήμαρχος ⓜ&ⓕ **thi**·mar·khos

me εγώ e·**gho**

meal γεύμα ⓝ **yev**·ma

measles ιλαρά ⓕ i·la·**ra**

meat κρέας ⓝ **kre**·as

mechanic μηχανικός ⓜ mi·kha·ni·**kos**

media μέσα ενημέρωσης ⓝ pl
me·sa e·ni·**me**·ro·sis

medicine (medication) φάρμακο ⓝ
far·ma·ko

medicine (study, profession) ιατρική ⓕ
i·a·tri·**ki**

meditation αυτοσυγκέντρωση ⓕ
af·to·si·**ge**·dro·si

Mediterranean Μεσογειακός ⓜ
me·so·yi·a·**kos**

meet v συναντώ si·na·**do**

melon πεπόνι ⓝ pe·**po**·ni

member μέλος ⓝ **me**·los

menstruation περίοδος ⓕ pe·**ri**·o·thos

menu μενού ⓝ me·**nu**

message μήνυμα ⓝ **mi**·ni·ma

metal μέταλλο ⓝ **me**·ta·lo

metre μέτρο ⓝ **me**·tro

metro (train) μετρό ⓝ me·**tro**

metro station σταθμός μετρό ⓜ
stath·**mos** me·**tro**

microwave (oven)
φούρνος μικροκυμάτων ⓜ
fur·nos mi·kro·ki·**ma**·ton

midday (noon) μεσημέρι ⓝ me·si·**me**·ri

midnight μεσάνυχτα ⓝ pl me·**sa**·nikh·ta

migraine ημικρανία ⓕ i·mi·kra·**ni**·a

mild μαλακός ma·la·**kos**

military a στρατιωτικός stra·ti·o·ti·**kos**

military base στρατιωτική βάση ⓕ
stra·ti·o·ti·**ki va**·si

military service στρατιωτική θητεία ⓕ
stra·ti·o·ti·**ki** thi·**ti**·a

milk γάλα ⓝ **gha**·la

millimetre χιλιοστόμετρο ⓝ
hi·li·o·**sto**·me·tro

million εκατομμύριο ⓝ e·ka·to·**mi**·ri·o

mince κιμάς ⓜ ki·**mas**

mineral water μεταλλικό νερό ⓝ
me·ta·li·ko ne·**ro**

Minoan Μινωικός mi·no·i·**kos**

minute λεπτό ⓝ lep·**to**

mirror καθρέφτης ⓜ ka·**thref**·tis

miscarriage αποβολή ⓕ a·po·vo·**li**

Miss Δις ⓕ the·spi·**nis**

miss (feel absence of) μου λείπει mu **li**·pi

mistake λάθος ⓝ *la*·thos
mix v ανακατώνω a·na·ka·to·no
mixed plate ποικιλία ⓕ pi·ki·*li*·a
mobile phone κινητό ⓝ ki·ni·*to*
modem μόντεμ ⓝ *mo*·dem
modern μοντέρνος mo·*der*·nos
moisturiser υγραντική κρέμα ⓕ
i·ghra·di·*ki* *kre*·ma
monarchy μοναρχία ⓕ mo·nar·*hi*·a
monastery μοναστήρι ⓝ mo·na·*sti*·ri
Monday Δευτέρα ⓕ def·*te*·ra
money χρήματα ⓝ pl *khri*·ma·ta
monk καλόγερος ⓜ ka·*lo*·ye·ros
monk seal φώκια ⓕ *fo*·ki·a
month μήνας ⓜ *mi*·nas
monument μνημείο ⓝ mni·*mi*·o
moon φεγγάρι ⓝ fe·*ga*·ri
more περισσότερος pe·ri·*so*·te·ros
morning πρωί ⓝ pro·*i*
morning sickness πρωινή αδιαθεσία ⓕ
pro·i·*ni* a·thi·a·the·*si*·a
mosaic μωσαϊκό ⓝ mo·sa·i·*ko*
mosque τζαμί ⓝ dza·*mi*
mosquito κουνούπι ⓝ ku·*nu*·pi
mosquito coil φιδάκι για κουνούπια ⓝ
fi·*dha*·ki yia ku·*nu*·pia
mosquito net κουνουπιέρα ⓕ ku·nu·pi·*e*·ra
motel μοτέλ ⓝ mo·*tel*
mother μητέρα ⓕ mi·*te*·ra
mother-in-law πεθερά ⓕ pe·the·*ra*
motorbike μηχανάκι ⓝ mi·kha·*na*·ki
motorboat βενζινάκατος ⓕ
ven·zi·*na*·ka·tos
motorcycle μοτοσυκλέτα ⓕ mo·to·si·*kle*·ta
motorway (tollway) αυτοκινητόδρομος
ⓜ af·to·ki·ni·*to*·thro·mos
mountain βουνό ⓝ vu·*no*
mountain bike ποδήλατο για βουνό ⓝ
po·*thi*·la·to yia vu·*no*
mountain path μονοπάτι ⓝ mo·no·*pa*·ti
mountain range οροσειρά ⓕ o·ro·si·*ra*
mountaineering ορειβασία ⓕ o·ri·va·*si*·a
mouse ποντικός ⓜ po·di·*kos*
mouth στόμα ⓝ *sto*·ma
movie φιλμ ⓝ film
Mr Κος ⓜ *khi*·ri·os
Mrs Κα ⓕ khi·*ri*·a
Ms Δις the·spi·*ni*s
mud λάσπη ⓕ *la*·spi
muesli δημητριακά ⓝ pl thi·mi·tri·a·*ka*

mum μαμά ⓕ ma·*ma*
mumps μαγουλάδες ⓜ pl ma·ghu·*la*·thes
murder δολοφονία ⓕ tho·lo·fo·*ni*·a
murder v δολοφονώ tho·lo·fo·*no*
muscle μυς ⓜ mis
museum μουσείο ⓝ mu·*si*·o
mushroom μανιτάρι ⓝ ma·ni·*ta*·ri
music μουσική ⓕ mu·si·*ki*
music shop κατάστημα μουσικών ειδών
ⓝ ka·*ta*·sti·ma mu·si·*kon* i·*thon*
musician μουσικός ⓜ&ⓕ mu·si·*kos*
Muslim Μουσουλμάνος/Μουσουλμάνα
ⓜ/ⓕ mu·sul·*ma*·nos/mu·sul·*ma*·na
mussel μύδι ⓝ *mi*·thi
mustard μουστάρδα ⓕ mus·*tar*·tha
mute a βουβός vu·*vos*
my μου mu
Mycenean Μυκηναϊκός mi·ki·na·i·*kos*
mythological μυθολογικός
mi·tho·lo·yi·*kos*

N

nail clippers νυχοκόπτης ⓜ ni·kho·*kop*·tis
name όνομα ⓝ o·no·ma
napkin πετσετάκι ⓝ pet·se·*ta*·ki
nappy πάνα ⓕ *pa*·na
nappy rash ερεθισμός από πάνα ⓜ
e·re·thiz·*mos* a·po *pa*·na
national park εθνικό πάρκο ⓝ
eth·ni·*ko* *par*·ko
nationality εθνικότητα ⓕ eth·ni·*ko*·ti·ta
NATO ΝΑΤΟ ⓝ *na*·to
nature φύση ⓕ *fi*·si
naturopathy φυσιοθεραπευτική ⓕ
fi·si·o·the·ra·pef·ti·*ki*
nausea ναυτία ⓕ naf·*ti*·a
near(by) κοντά ko·*da*
nearest το πιο κοντινό to pio ko·di·*no*
necessary αναγκαίο a·na·ge·o
neck λαιμός ⓜ le·*mos*
necklace κολιέ ⓝ ko·li·*e*
nectarine νεκταρίνι ⓝ nek·ta·*ri*·ni
need v χρειάζομαι khri·*a*·zo·me
needle (sewing) βελόνα ⓕ ve·*lo*·na
needle (syringe) σύριγκα ⓕ *si*·ri·ga
negative a αρνητικός ar·ni·ti·kos
neither κανένα από τα δύο
ka·*ne*·na a·po ta *thi*·o
net δίκτι ⓝ *thik*·ti
Netherlands Ολλανδία ⓕ o·lan·*thi*·a

never ποτέ po-*te*

new νέος *ne*-os

New Year's Day Πρωτοχρονιά ⓕ pro-to-khro-*nia*

New Year's Eve Παραμονή Πρωτοχρονιάς ⓕ pa-ra-mo-*ni* pro-to-khro-*nias*

New Zealand Νέα Ζηλανδία ⓕ *ne*-a zi-lan-*thi*-a

news νέα ⓝ pl *ne*-a

newsagency πρακτορείο εφημερίδων ⓝ prak-to-*ri*-o e-fi-me-*ri*-thon

newspaper εφημερίδα ⓕ e-fi-me-*ri*-tha

newsstand περίπτερο ⓝ pe-*rip*-te-ro

next a επόμενος e-*po*-me-nos

next to δίπλα *thi*-pla

nice ωραίος o-*re*-os

nickname παρατσούκλι ⓝ pa-rat-*su*-kli

night νύχτα ⓕ *nikh*-ta

night out ξενύχτι ⓝ kse-*nikh*-ti

nightclub νάιτ κλαμπ ⓝ *na*-it klab

no όχι o-*hi*

noisy θορυβώδης tho-ri-*vo*-this

none κανένας ka-*ne*-nas

nonsmoking μη καπνίζοντες mi kap-*ni*-zo-des

noodles λαζάνια ⓝ pl la-*za*-nia

noon μεσημέρι ⓝ me-si-*me*-ri

north βοράς ⓜ vo-*ras*

Norway Νορβηγία ⓕ nor-vi-*yi*-a

nose μύτη ⓕ *mi*-ti

not όχι o-*hi*

notebook σημειωματάριο ⓝ si-mi-o-ma-*ta*-ri-o

nothing τίποτε *ti*-po-te

November Νοέμβριος ⓜ no-*em*-vri-os

now τώρα *to*-ra

nuclear energy πυρηνική ενέργεια ⓕ pi-ri-ni-*ki* e-*ner*-yi-a

nuclear testing πυρηνικές δοκιμές ⓕ pl pi-ri-ni-*kes* tho-ki-*mes*

nuclear waste πυρηνικά απόβλητα ⓝ pl pi-ri-ni-*ka* a-*pov*-li-ta

number αριθμός ⓜ a-rith-*mos*

numberplate αριθμός κυκλοφορίας ⓜ a-rith-*mos* ki-klo-fo-*ri*-as

nun καλόγρια ⓕ ka-*lo*-ghri-a

nurse νοσοκόμος/νοσοκόμα ⓜ/ⓕ no-so-*ko*-mos/no-so-*ko*-ma

nut καρύδι ⓝ ka-*ri*-thi

O

oats βρώμη ⓕ *vro*-mi

ocean ωκεανός ⓜ o-ke-a-*nos*

October Οκτώβριος ⓜ ok-*tov*-ri-os

off (food) μπαγιάτικος ba-*yia*-ti-kos

office γραφείο ⓝ ghra-*fi*-o

often συχνά sikh-*na*

oil (cooking) λάδι ⓝ *la*-thi

oil (car) λάδι αυτοκινήτου ⓝ *la*-thi af-to-ki-*ni*-tu

old παλιός pa-*lios*

olive ελιά ⓕ e-*lia*

olive oil λάδι ελιάς ⓝ *la*-thi e-*lias*

Olympic Games Ολυμπιακοί Αγώνες ⓜ o-li-bi-a-*ki* a-*gho*-nes

omelette ομελέττα ⓕ o-me-*le*-ta

on πάνω *pa*-no

on time στην ώρα stin *o*-ra

once μια φορά mia fo-*ra*

one ένα *e*-na

one-way (ticket) απλό εισιτήριο ⓝ a-*plo* i-si-*ti*-ri-o

onion κρεμμύδι ⓝ kre-*mi*-thi

only μόνο *mo*-no

open a ανοιχτός a-nikh-*tos*

open v ανοίγω a-*ni*-gho

opening hours ώρες λειτουργίας ⓕ pl *o*-res li-tur-*yi*-as

opera (house) όπερα ⓕ *o*-pe-ra

operation (medical) εγχείρηση ⓕ eng-*hi*-ri-si

operator χειριστής/χειρίστρια ⓜ/ⓕ hi-ri-*stis*/hi-ri-stri-a

opinion γνώμη ⓕ *ghno*-mi

opposite απέναντι a-*pe*-na-di

optometrist οφθαλμίατρος ⓜ&ⓕ of-thal-*mi*-a-tros

or ή i

oracle χρησμός ⓜ khriz-*mos*

orange (fruit) πορτοκάλι ⓝ por-to-*ka*-li

orange (colour) a πορτοκαλής por-to-ka-*lis*

orange juice χυμός πορτοκάλι ⓜ hi-*mos* por-to-*ka*-li

orchestra ορχήστρα ⓕ or-*hi*-stra

orchid ορχιδέα ⓕ or-hi-*the*-a

order σειρά ⓕ si-*ra*

order v διατάζω thia-*ta*-zo

ordinary συνηθισμένος si·ni·thiz·*me*·nos

orgasm οργασμός ⓜ or·ghaz·*mos*

original αρχικός ar·hi·*kos*

Orthodox Ορθόδοξος/Ορθόδοξη ⓜ/ⓕ or·tho·*thok*·sos/or·tho·*thok*·si

other άλλος *a*·los

Ottoman a Οθωμανικός o·tho·ma·ni·*kos*

our μας mas

outside έξω *ek*·so

ouzo ούζο ⓝ *u*·zo

ouzeria ουζερί ⓝ u·ze·*ri*

ovarian cyst ωοθηκική κύστη ⓕ o·o·thi·ki·*ki ki*·sti

ovary ωοθήκη ⓕ o·o·*thi*·ki

oven φούρνος ⓜ *fur*·nos

overcoat πανωφόρι ⓝ pa·no·*fo*·ri

overdose υπερβολική δόση ⓕ i·per·vo·li·*ki tho*·si

overnight ολονυχτίς o·lo·nikh·*tis*

overseas εξωτερικό ek·so·te·ri·*ko*

owe οφείλω o·*fi*·lo

owner κάτοχος ⓜ *ka*·to·khos

oxygen οξυγόνο ⓝ ok·si·*gho*·no

oyster στρείδι ⓝ *stri*·thi

ozone layer στρώμα όζοντος ⓝ *stro*·ma o·zo·dos

P

pacemaker βηματοδότης ⓜ vi·ma·to·*tho*·tis

pacifier (dummy) πιπίλα ⓕ pi·*pi*·la

package πακέτο ⓝ pa·*ke*·to

packet πακέτο ⓝ pa·*ke*·to

padlock κλειδαριά ⓕ kli·tha·*ria*

page σελίδα ⓕ se·*li*·tha

pain πόνος ⓜ *po*·nos

painful οδυνηρός o·thi·ni·*ros*

painkiller παυσίπονο ⓝ paf·*si*·po·no

painter ζωγράφος ⓜ&ⓕ zo·*ghra*·fos

painting (a work) πίνακας ⓜ *pi*·na·kas

painting (the art) ζωγραφική ⓕ zo·ghra·fi·*ki*

pair (couple) ζευγάρι ⓝ zev·*gha*·ri

palace παλάτι ⓝ pa·*la*·ti

pan κατσαρόλα ⓕ kat·sa·*ro*·la

pants (trousers) παντελόνι ⓝ pa·de·*lo*·ni

panty liners πετσετάκι υγείας ⓝ pet·se·ta·ki i·*yi*·as

pantyhose καλτσόν ⓝ kal·*tson*

paper χαρτί ⓝ khar·*ti*

papers (documents) πιστοποιητικά ⓝ pl pi·sto·pi·i·ti·*ka*

paperwork προετοιμασία ⓕ εγγράφων pro·e·ti·ma·*si*·a e·*gra*·fon

paprika πάπρικα ⓕ *pa*·pri·ka

pap smear τεστ παπ ⓝ test pap

paraplegic παραπληγικός ⓜ pa·ra·pli·yi·*kos*

parcel δέμα ⓝ *the*·ma

parents γονείς ⓜ pl gho·*nis*

park πάρκο ⓝ *par*·ko

park (a car) παρκάρω par·*ka*·ro

parliament Βουλή ⓕ vu·*li*

part (component) εξάρτημα ⓝ ek·*sar*·ti·ma

part-time μερική απασχόληση me·ri·*ki* a·pas·*kho*·li·si

party (night out) πάρτυ ⓝ *par*·ti

party (politics) κόμμα ⓝ *ko*·ma

pass v περνάω per·*na*·o

passenger επιβάτης/επιβάτισσα ⓜ/ⓕ e·pi·*va*·tis/e·pi·*va*·ti·sa

passionfruit πάσιον φρουτ ⓝ *pa*·si·on frut

passport διαβατήριο ⓝ thia·va·*ti*·ri·o

passport number αριθμός διαβατηρίου ⓝ a·rith·*mos* thia·va·ti·*ri*·u

past παρελθόν ⓝ pa·rel·*thon*

pasta ζυμαρικά ⓝ pl zi·ma·ri·*ka*

pastry φύλλο ⓝ *fi*·lo

path μονοπάτι ⓝ mo·no·*pa*·ti

patisserie ζαχαροπλαστείο ⓝ za·kha·ro·pla·*sti*·o

pay v πληρώνω pli·*ro*·no

payment πληρωμή ⓕ pli·ro·*mi*

pea αρακάς ⓜ a·ra·*kas*

peace ειρήνη ⓕ i·*ri*·ni

peach ροδάκινο ⓝ ro·*tha*·ki·no

peak (mountain) κορυφή ⓕ ko·ri·*fi*

peanut φυστίκι ⓝ fi·*sti*·ki

pear αχλάδι ⓝ a·*khla*·thi

pedal πετάλι ⓝ pe·*ta*·li

pedestrian πεζός ⓜ pe·*zos*

pelican πελεκάνος ⓜ pe·le·*ka*·nos

pen (ballpoint) στυλό ⓝ sti·*lo*

pencil μολύβι ⓝ mo·*li*·vi

penis πέος ⓝ *pe*·os

penknife σουγιάς ⓜ su·*yias*

pension σύνταξη ⓕ *si*·dak·si

pensioner συνταξιούχος/συνταξιούχα ⑩/① si-dak-si-*u*-khos/si-dak-si-*u*-kha

people κόσμος ⑩ *koz*-mos

pepper πιπέρι ⑪ pi-*pe*-ri

pepper (bell) πιπεριέρα ① pi-pe-rie-ra

per κάθε *ka*-the

per cent τοις εκατό tis e-ka-*to*

perfect a τέλειος *te*-li-os

performance απόδοση ① a-*po*-tho-si

perfume άρωμα ⑪ *a*-ro-ma

period pain πόνος περιόδου ⑩ *po*-nos pe-ri-*o*-thu

permission άδεια ① *a*-thi-a

permit άδεια ① *a*-thi-a

person πρόσωπο ⑪ *pro*-so-po

petition συλλογή υπογραφών ① si-lo-*yi* i-po-ghra-*fon*

petrol πετρέλαιο ⑪ pe-*tre*-le-o

petrol station πρατήριο βενζίνας ⑪ pra-*ti*-ri-o ven-*zi*-nas

pharmacist φαρμακοποιός ⑩&① far-ma-ko-pi-os

pharmacy φαρμακείο ⑪ far-ma-*ki*-o

phone book τηλεφωνικός κατάλογος ⑩ ti-le-fo-ni-*kos* ka-*ta*-lo-ghos

phone box δημόσιο τηλέφωνο ⑪ thi-*mo*-si-o ti-*le*-fo-no

phonecard τηλεκάρτα ① ti-le-*kar*-ta

photo φωτογραφία ① fo-to-gra-*fi*-a

photographer φωτογράφος ⑩&① fo-to-*ghra*-fos

photography φωτογραφική ① fo-to-ghra-fi-*ki*

phrasebook βιβλίο φράσεων ① viv-*li*-o fra-se-on

pickaxe τσεκούρι ⑪ tse-*ku*-ri

pickles τουρσί ⑪ tur-*si*

picnic πίκνικ ⑪ pik-*nik*

pie πίτα ① *pi*-ta

piece κομμάτι ⑪ ko-*ma*-ti

pig γουρούνι ⑪ ghu-*ru*-ni

pill χάπι ⑪ *kha*-pi

the pill το Χάπι ⑪ to *kha*-pi

pillow μαξιλάρι ⑪ mak-si-*la*-ri

pillowcase μαξιλαροθήκη ① mak-si-la-ro-*thi*-ki

pine πεύκο ⑪ *pef*-ko

pineapple ανανάς ⑩ a-na-*nas*

pink ροζ roz

pistachio φυστίκι ⑪ fi-*sti*-ki

place θέση ① *the*-si

place of birth τόπος γεννήσεως ⑩ *to*-pos ye-*ni*-se-os

plane αεροπλάνο ⑪ a-e-ro-*pla*-no

planet πλανήτης ⑩ pla-*ni*-tis

plant φυτό ⑪ fi-*to*

plastic a πλαστικός pla-sti-*kos*

plate πιάτο ⑪ *pia*-to

plateau πλατό ⑪ pla-*to*

platform πλατφόρμα ① plat-*for*-ma

play (theatre) θεατρικό έργο ⑪ the-a-tri-ko *er*-gho

play cards v παίζω χαρτιά pe-zo khar-*tia*

play guitar v παίζω κιθάρα pe-zo ki-*tha*-ra

plug (bath) βούλωμα ⑪ vu-lo-ma

plug (electricity) βύσμα ⑪ *viz*-ma

plum δαμάσκηνο ⑪ tha-*ma*-ski-no

poached ποσέ po-se

pocket τσέπη ① tse-pi

pocket knife σουγιάς ⑩ su-*yias*

poetry ποίηση ① pi-*i*-si

point σημείο ⑪ si-*mi*-o

point v δείχνω *thi*-khno

poisonous δηλητηριώδης thi-li-ti-ri-o-*this*

police αστυνομία ① a-sti-no-*mi*-a

police officer (in city) αστυφύλακας/αστυφυλακίνα ⑩/① a-sti-fi-la-kas/a-sti-fi-la-ki-na

police officer (in country) χωροφύλακας/χωροφυλακίνα ⑩/① kho-ro-fi-la-kas/kho-ro-fi-la-*ki*-na

police station αστυνομικός σταθμός ⑩ a-sti-no-mi-*kos* stath-*mos*

policy πολιτική ① po-li-ti-*ki*

politician πολιτικός ⑩&① po-li-ti-*kos*

politics πολιτικά ⑪ pl po-li-ti-*ka*

pollen γύρη ① *yi*-ri

pollution ρύπανση ① *ri*-pan-si

pool (game) μπιλιάρδο ⑪ bi-*liar*-tho

pool (swimming) πισίνα ① pi-*si*-na

poor a φτωχός fto-*khos*

popular δημοφιλής thi-mo-fi-*lis*

pork χοιρινό ⑪ hi-ri-no

pork sausage χοιρινό λουκάνικο ⑪ hi-ri-no lu-ka-ni-ko

port (sea) λιμάνι ⑪ li-*ma*-ni

positive a θετικός the-ti-kos

possible δυνατός thi-na-*tos*

post v ταχυδρομώ ta-hi-thro-*mo*

postage ταχυδρομικά τέλη ⑪ pl ta-hi-thro-mi-*ka* te-li

postcard κάρτα ① *kar*-ta
postcode ταχυδρομικός τομέας ⓜ
ta-hi-ᶿ͟hro-mi-*kos* to-*me*-as
post office ταχυδρομείο ⓝ
ta-hi-ᶿ͟hro-*mi*-o
poster πόστερ ⓝ *po*-ster
pot (ceramics) κεραμικό ⓝ ke-ra-mi-*ko*
pot (dope) μαριχουάνα ① ma-ri-khu-*a*-na
potato πατάτα ① pa-*ta*-ta
pottery αγγειοπλαστική ① a-gi-o-pla-sti-*ki*
pound (money) λίρα ① *li*-ra
pound (weight) λίτρα ① *li*-tra
poverty φτώχεια ① *fto*-hia
powder πούδρα ① *pu*-ᶿ͟hra
power δύναμη ① *ᶿ͟hi*-na-mi
prawn γαρίδα ① gha-*ri*-ᶿ͟ha
prayer προσευχή ① pro-sef-*hi*
prayer book βιβλίο προσευχών ⓝ
viv-*li*-o pro-sef-*khon*
prefer προτιμώ pro-ti-*mo*
pregnancy test kit τεστ εγκυμοσύνης ⓝ
test e-gi-mo-*si*-nis
pregnant a έγκυος *e*-gi-os
prehistoric προϊστορικός pro-i-sto-ri-*kos*
premenstrual tension ένταση πριν την
περίοδο ① *e*-da-si pri tin pe-*ri*-o-ᶿ͟ho
prepare προετοιμάζω pro-e-ti-*ma*-zo
prescription συνταγή ① si-da-*yi*
present (gift) δώρο ⓝ *ᶿ͟ho*-ro
present (time) παρόν ⓝ pa-*ron*
president πρόεδρος ⓜ&① *pro*-e-ᶿ͟hros
pressure πίεση ① *pi*-e-si
pretty όμορφος o-*mor*-fos
price τιμή ① ti-*mi*
priest παπάς ⓜ pa-*pas*
prime minister πρωθυπουργός ⓜ&①
pro-ᶿ͟hi-pur-*ghos*
printer (computer) εκτυπωτής ⓜ
ek-ti-po-*tis*
prison φυλακή ① fi-la-*ki*
prisoner φυλακισμένος ⓜ fi-la-kiz-*me*-nos
private a ιδιωτικός i-ᶿ͟hi-o-ti-*kos*
problem πρόβλημα ⓝ *pro*-vli-ma
produce v παράγω pa-*ra*-gho
profit κέρδος ⓝ *ker*-ᶿ͟hos
program πρόγραμμα ⓝ *pro*-gra-ma
projector προβολέας ⓜ pro-vo-*le*-as
promise v υπόσχομαι i-*pos*-kho-me
prostitute πόρνη ① *por*-ni
protect προστατεύω pro-sta-*te*-vo

protected (species) προστατευόμενα
(είδη) ⓝ pl pro-sta-te-*vo*-me-na (*i*-ᶿ͟hi)
protest διαμαρτυρία ① ᶿ͟hi-a-mar-ti-*ri*-a
protest v διαμαρτύρομαι
ᶿ͟hi-a-mar-*ti*-ro-me
provisions προμήθειες ① pl pro-*mi*-ᶿ͟hi-es
prune (dried fruit) ξηρό δαμάσκηνο ⓝ
ksi-*ro* ᶿ͟ha-*ma*-ski-no
pub (bar) μπυραρία ① bi-ra-*ri*-a
public gardens εθνικός κήπος ⓜ
eth-ni-*kos* *ki*-pos
public relations δημόσιες σχέσεις ① pl
ᶿ͟hi-*mo*-si-es *she*-sis
public telephone δημόσιο τηλέφωνο ⓝ
ᶿ͟hi-*mo*-si-o ti-*le*-fo-no
public toilet δημόσια αποχωρητήρια ⓝ pl
ᶿ͟hi-*mo*-si-a a-po-kho-ri-*ti*-ria
pulse σφυγμός ⓜ sfigh-*mos*
pull v τραβάω tra-*va*-o
pump τρόμπα ① *tro*-ba
pumpkin κολοκύθι ⓝ ko-lo-*ki*-thi
puncture τρύπα ρόδας ① *tri*-pa *ro*-ᶿ͟has
punch (ticket) v ακυρώνω a-ki-*ro*-no
pure a καθαρός ka-tha-*ros*
purple μαβής ma-*vis*
purse πορτοφόλι ⓝ por-to-*fo*-li
push v σπρώχνω *sprokh*-no
put βάζω *va*-zo

Q

quadriplegic παραπληγικός ⓜ
pa-ra-pli-yi-*kos*
qualifications προσόντα ⓝ pl pro-*so*-da
quality ποιότητα ① pi-o-ti-ta
quarantine καραντίνα ① ka-ra-*di*-na
quarter τέταρτο ⓝ *te*-tar-to
queen βασίλισσα ① va-*si*-li-sa
question ερώτηση ① e-ro-ti-si
queue ουρά ① u-*ra*
quick a γρήγορος *ghri*-gho-ros
quiet a ήσυχος *i*-si-khos
quit v παραιτούμαι pa-re-*tu*-me

R

rabies λύσσα ① *li*-sa
rabbit κουνέλι ⓝ ku-*ne*-li
race (sport) ιπποδρομία ① i-po-ᶿ͟hro-*mi*-a

racetrack ιππόδρομος ⑩ i·po·thro·mos

racing bike ποδήλατο κούρσας ⑩ po·thi·la·to kur·sas

racism ρατσισμός ⑩ rat·sis·mos

racquet ρακέτα ① ra·ke·ta

radiator ψυγείο αυτοκινήτου ⑩ psi·yi·o af·to·ki·ni·tu

radio ράδιο ⑩ ra·thi·o

radish ραπάνι ① ra·pa·ni

railway station σιδηροδρομικός σταθμός ⑩ si·thi·ro·thro·mi·kos stath·mos

rain ① βροχή vro·hi

raincoat αδιάβροχο ⑩ a·thi·av·ro·ho

raisin σταφίδα ① sta·fi·tha

rally ράλι ⑩ ra·li

rape βιασμός ⑩ vi·az·mos

rape v βιάζω vi·a·zo

rare (uncommon) σπάνιος spa·ni·os

rare (food) μισοψημένο a mi·so·psi·me·no

rash εξάνθημα ⑩ ek·san·thi·ma

raspberry βατόμουρο ⑩ va·to·mu·ro

rat ποντίκι ⑩ po·di·ki

raw ωμός o·mos

razor ξυριστική μηχανή ① ksi·ri·sti·ki mi·kha·ni

razor blade ξυράφι ⑩ ksi·ra·fi

read διαβάζω thia·va·zo

reading διάβασμα ⑩ thia·vaz·ma

ready έτοιμος e·ti·mos

real estate agent κτηματομεσίτρια/κτηματομεσίτρια ⑩/① kti·ma·to·me·si·tis/kti·ma·to·me·si·tri·a

realistic ρεαλιστικός re·a·li·sti·kos

rear (seat etc) οπίσθιος o·pi·sthi·os

reason αιτία ① e·ti·a

receipt απόδειξη ① a·po·thik·si

recently πρόσφατα pros·fa·ta

recommend συνιστώ si·ni·sto

record v καταγράφω ka·ta·ghra·fo

recording καταγραφή ① ka·ta·ghra·fi

recyclable ανακυκλώσιμο a·na·ki·klo·si·mo

recycle ανακυκλώνω a·na·ki·klo·no

red κόκκινο ko·ki·no

referee διαιτητής/διαιτήτρια ⑩/① thi·e·ti·tis/thi·e·ti·tri·a

reference (letter) συστατική επιστολή ① si·sta·ti·ki e·pi·sto·li

reflexology αντανακλαστική ① a·da·na·kla·sti·ki

refrigerator ψυγείο ⑩ psi·yi·o

refugee πρόσφυγας ⑩&① pros·fi·ghas

refund ① επιστροφή χρημάτων e·pi·stro·fi khri·ma·ton

refuse v αρνούμαι ar·nu·me

regional τοπικός to·pi·kos

(by) registered mail συστημένο sis·ti·me·no

rehydration salts υδρωτικά άλατα ⑩ pl i·thro·ti·ka a·la·ta

relationship σχέση ① she·si

relax v χαλαρώνω kha·la·ro·no

relic κειμήλιο ⑩ ki·mi·li·o

religion θρησκεία ① thri·ski·a

religious a θρήσκος thri·skos

remote a απόμακρος a·po·mak·ros

remote control τηλεκατεύθυνση ① ti·le·ka·tef·thin·si

rent v ενοικιάζω e·ni·ki·a·zo

repair v επισκευάζω e·pi·ske·va·zo

republic δημοκρατία ① thi·mo·kra·ti·a

reservation (booking) κράτηση ① kra·ti·si

residency permit άδεια παραμονής ① a·thi·a pa·ra·mo·nis

rest v ξεκουράζομαι kse·ku·ra·zo·me

restaurant εστιατόριο ⑩ e·sti·a·to·ri·o

restriction περιορισμός ⑩ pe·ri·o·riz·mos

résumé (CV) βιογραφικό σημείωμα ⑩ vi·o·ghra·fi·ko si·mi·o·ma

retired συνταξιούχος si·dak·si·u·khos

retsina (drink) ρετσίνα ① ret·si·na

return (come back) v επιστρέφω e·pi·stre·fo

return (ticket) εισιτήριο μετ' επιστροφής ⑩ i·si·ti·ri·o me·te·pis·tro·fis

review αναθεώρηση ① a·na·the·o·ri·si

rhythm ρυθμός ⑩ rith·mos

rib πλευρό ⑩ plev·ro

rice ρύζι ⑩ ri·zi

rich (wealthy) πλούσιος plu·si·os

ride (horse) ιππασία ① i·pa·si·a

ride (horse) v ιππεύω i·pe·vo

right (correct) a σωστός so·stos

right (direction) δεξιός thek·si·os

right-wing δεξιά ① thek·si·a

ring (jewellery) δαχτυλίδι ⑩ thakh·ti·li·thi

ring (phone) v τηλεφωνάω ti·le·fo·na·o

rip-off γδάρσιμο ⑩ gthar·si·mo

risk ρίσκο ⑩ ri·sko

river ποτάμι ⑩ po·ta·mi

road δρόμος ⑩ thro·mos

road map οδικός χάρτης ⓜ
o·thi·kos khar·tis
roasted ψημένος psi·me·nos
rob ληστεύω li·ste·vo
rock βράχος ⓜ vra·khos
rock climbing αναρρίχηση ⓕ a·na·ri·hi·si
rock music μουσική ροκ ⓕ mu·si·ki rok
rockfalls κατολίσθηση ⓕ ka·to·lis·thi·si
rock group μπάντα ροκ ⓕ ba·da rok
rockmelon πεπόνι ⓝ pe·po·ni
roll (bread) ψωμάκι ⓝ pso·ma·ki
rollerblading τροχοπέδιλο ⓝ
tro·kho·pe·thi·lo
Roman Ρωμαϊκός ro·ma·i·kos
romantic ρομαντικός ro·ma·di·kos
room δωμάτιο ⓝ tho·ma·ti·o
room number αριθμός δωματίου ⓜ
a·rith·mos tho·ma·ti·u
rope σκοινί ⓝ ski·ni
round a στρογγυλός stro·gi·los
roundabout κυκλική διασταύρωση ⓕ
ki·kli·ki thi·a·stav·ro·si
route δρόμος ⓜ thro·mos
rowing κωπηλασία ⓕ ko·pi·la·si·a
rubbish σκουπίδια ⓝ pl sku·pi·thia
rubella ερυθρά ⓕ e·ri·thra
rug χαλί ⓝ kha·li
rugby ράγκμπυ ⓝ rag·bi
ruins ερρίπια ⓝ pl e·ri·pi·a
rule ⓝ κανόνας ka·no·nas
rum ρούμι ⓝ ru·mi
run v τρέχω tre·kho
running τρέξιμο ⓝ trek·si·mo
runny nose τρέξιμο μύτης ⓝ
trek·si·mo mi·tis

S

sad λυπημένος li·pi·me·nos
saddle σέλλα ⓕ se·la
safe ασφάλεια ⓕ as·fa·li·a
safe a ασφαλής as·fa·lis
safe sex ασφαλές σεξ ⓝ as·fa·les seks
saint άγιος/αγία ⓜ/ⓕ a·yi·os/a·yi·a
sailing ιστίο ⓝ i·sti·o
salad σαλάτα ⓕ sa·la·ta
salami σαλάμι ⓝ sa·la·mi
salary μισθός ⓜ mis·thos
sale πώληση ⓕ po·li·si

sales tax φόρος πώλησης ⓜ fo·ros po·li·sis
salmon σολομός ⓜ so·lo·mos
salt αλάτι ⓝ a·la·ti
same ίδιος i·thi·os
sand άμμος ⓜ a·mos
sandal σανδάλι ⓝ sa·da·li
sanitary napkin πετσετάκι υγείας ⓝ
pet·se·ta·ki i·yi·as
sardine σαρδέλα ⓕ sar·the·la
Saturday Σάββατο ⓝ sa·va·to
sauce σάλτσα ⓕ sal·tsa
saucepan κατσαρόλα ⓕ kat·sa·ro·la
sauna σάουνα ⓕ sa·u·na
sausage λουκάνικο ⓝ lu·ka·ni·ko
savoury πικάντικος pi·ka·di·kos
say v λέγω le·gho
scalp κρανίο ⓝ kra·ni·o
scarf κασκόλ ⓝ ka·skol
school σχολείο ⓝ skho·li·o
science επιστήμη ⓕ e·pi·sti·mi
scientist επιστήμονας ⓜ&ⓕ
e·pi·sti·mo·nas
scissors ψαλίδι ⓝ psa·li·thi
score v σκοράρω sko·ra·ro
scoreboard πίνακας σκορ ⓜ pi·na·kas skor
Scotland Σκωτία ⓕ sko·ti·a
scrambled χτυπητά (αβγά)
khti·pi·ta (av·gha)
sculpture γλυπτική ⓕ ghlip·ti·ki
sea θάλασσα ⓕ tha·la·sa
seafood θαλασσινά ⓝ pl tha·la·si·na
(be) seasick πάσχει από ναυτία
pa·shi a·po naf·ti·a
seasickness ναυτία ⓕ naf·ti·a
seaside παραλία ⓕ pa·ra·li·a
season εποχή ⓕ e·po·hi
seat (place) θέση ⓕ the·si
seatbelt ζώνη καθίσματος ⓕ
zo·ni ka·thiz·ma·tos
sea turtle θαλάσσια χελώνα ⓕ
tha·la·si·a he·lo·na
sea urchin αχινός ⓜ a·hi·nos
second δευτερόλεπτο ⓝ thef·te·ro·lep·to
second a δεύτερος thef·te·ros
second class δεύτερη τάξη ⓕ
thef·te·ri tak·si
second-hand a μεταχειρισμένος
me·ta·hi·riz·me·nos
second-hand shop παλαιοπωλείο ⓝ
pa·le·o·po·li·o

secretary γραμματέας ⑩&① ghra·ma·*te*·as

see βλέπω *vle*·po

self-employed a ιδιωτικός υπάλληλος i·thi·o·ti·*kos* i·*pa*·li·los

selfish ατομιστής a·to·mi·*stis*

self-service ⑩ σελφ σέρβις self *ser*·vis

sell v πουλάω pu·*la*·o

seminar σεμινάριο ⑩ se·mi·*na*·ri·o

send στέλνω *stel*·no

sensible συνετός si·ne·*tos*

sensual αισθησιακός e·sthi·si·a·*kos*

separate a χωριστός kho·ri·*stos*

September Σεπτέμβριος ⑩ sep·*tem*·vri·os

serious σοβαρός so·va·*ros*

service υπηρεσία ① i·pi·re·*si*·a

service charge τιμή εξυπηρέτησης ① ti·*mi* ek·si·pi·*re*·ti·sis

service station βενζινάδικο ⑩ ven·zi·*na*·thi·ko

serviette πετσέτα φαγητού ① pet·*se*·ta fa·yi·*tu*

several μερικοί me·ri·*ki*

sew v ράβω *ra*·vo

sex (intercourse) σεξ ⑩ seks

sexism σεξισμός ⑩ sek·siz·*mos*

sexy σέξυ *sek*·si

shade σκιά ① ski·*a*

shadow σκιά ① ski·*a*

shampoo σαμπουάν v sam·pu·*an*

shape σχήμα ⑩ *shi*·ma

share (with) μοιράζομαι mi·*ra*·zo·me

shave v ξυρίζω ksi·*ri*·zo

shaving cream κρέμα ξυρίσματος ① *kre*·ma ksi·*riz*·ma·tos

she αυτή af·*ti*

sheep πρόβατο ⑩ *pro*·va·to

sheet (bed) σεντόνι ① se·*do*·ni

shelf ράφι ⑩ *ra*·fi

shiatsu σιάτσου ⑩ si·*at*·su

shield ασπίδα ① as·*pi*·tha

shingles (illness) έρπης ⑩ *er*·pis

ship πλοίο ⑩ *pli*·o

shirt πουκάμισο ⑩ pu·*ka*·mi·so

shoe παπούτσι ⑩ pa·*put*·si

shoes παπούτσια ⑩ pl pa·*put*·si·a

shoe shop υποδηματοποιείο ⑩ i·po·thi·ma·to·pi·*i*·o

shoot v πυροβολώ pi·ro·vo·*lo*

shop μαγαζί ⑩ ma·gha·*zi*

shop v ψωνίζω pso·*ni*·zo

shopping ψώνια ⑩ pl *pso*·nia

shopping centre αγορά ① a·gho·*ra*

short (height) κοντός ko·*dos*

shortage έλλειψη ① e·lip·si

shorts σορτς ⑩ sorts

shoulder ώμος ⑩ o·mos

shout v φωνάζω fo·*na*·zo

show επίδειξη ① e·*pi*·thik·si

show v δείχνω *thikh*·no

shower ντουζ ⑩ duz

shrine βωμός ⑩ vo·*mos*

shut a κλειστός kli·*stos*

shy a ντροπαλός dro·pa·*los*

sick a άρρωστος a·ro·stos

side πλευρά ① plev·*ra*

siesta μεσημεριανή ανάπαυση ① me·si·me·ria·ni a·na·paf·si

sign πινακίδα ① pi·na·*ki*·tha

signature υπογραφή ① i·po·ghra·*fi*

silk μετάξι ⑩ me·*tak*·si

silver ασήμι ⑩ a·*si*·mi

similar παρόμοιος pa·*ro*·mi·os

simple απλός a·plos

since (May) από (το Μάη) a·po (to *ma*·i)

sing v τραγουδώ tra·ghu·*tho*

Singapore Σιγγαπούρη ① sing·ga·*pu*·ri

singer τραγουδιστής/τραγουδίστρια ⑩/① tra·ghu·*thi*·stis/tra·ghu·*thi*·stri·a

single (person) a εργένης/εργένισσα ⑩/① er·*ye*·nis/er·*ye*·ni·sa

single room μονό δωμάτιο ⑩ mo·no tho·*ma*·tio

singlet φανελλάκι ① fa·ne·*la*·ki

sister αδερφή ① a·ther·*fi*

sit κάθομαι *ka*·tho·me

size μέγεθος ① *me*·ye·thos

skate v παγοδρομώ pa·gho·thro·*mo*

skateboarding πατίνι ⑩ pa·*ti*·ni

ski v κάνω σκι *ka*·no ski

skiing σκι ⑩ ski

skim milk άπαχο γάλα ⑩ *a*·pa·kho *gha*·la

skin δέρμα ⑩ *ther*·ma

skirt φούστα ① *fu*·sta

skull κρανίο ⑩ kra·*ni*·o

sky ουρανός ⑩ u·ra·*nos*

sleep v κοιμάμαι ki·*ma*·me

sleeping bag σλίπινγκ μπαγκ ⑩ *sli*·ping bag

sleeping berth κρεββατάκι ⑩ kre·va·*ta*·ki

sleeping car βαγκόν λι ⓝ va·gon li
sleeping pills υπνωτικά χάπια ⓝ pl ip·no·ti·ka hha·pia
sleepy νυσταγμένος nis·tagh·me·nos
slice φέτα ⓕ fe·ta
slide (film) σλάιντ ⓝ sla·id
slow a αργός ar·ghos
slowly αργά ar·gha
small μικρός mi·kros
smaller μικρότερος mi·kro·te·ros
smallest ο μικρότερος o mi·kro·te·ros
smell μυρουδιά ⓕ mi·ru·thia
smile v χαμογελώ hha·mo·ye·lo
smog νέφος ⓝ ne·fos
smoke v καπνίζω kap·ni·zo
snack μικρό γεύμα ⓝ mi·kro ghev·ma
snail σαλιγκάρι ⓝ sa·li·ga·ri
snake φίδι ⓝ fi·dhi
snorkelling υπόγεια κατάδυση ⓕ i·po·yi·a ka·ta·thi·si
snow χιόνι ⓝ hio·ni
snowboarding σκι με χιονοσανίδα ⓝ ski me hio·no·sa·ni·tha
snow pea αρακάς ⓜ a·ra·kas
soap σαπούνι ⓝ sa·pu·ni
soap opera αισθηματικό σίριαλ ⓝ es·thi·ma·ti·ko si·ri·al
soccer ποδόσφαιρο ⓝ po·thos·fe·ro
social welfare κοινωνική πρόνοια ⓕ ki·no·ni·ki pro·ni·a
socialist σοσιαλιστής/σοσιαλίστρια ⓜ/ⓕ so·si·a·li·stis/so·si·a·li·stri·a
sock κάλτσα ⓕ kal·tsa
socks κάλτσες ⓕ pl kal·tses
soft drink αναψυκτικό ⓝ a·nap·sik·ti·ko
soft-boiled μελάτο ⓝ me·la·to
soldier στρατιώτης ⓜ stra·ti·o·tis
some μερικοί me·ri·ki
someone κάποιος ka·pi·os
something κάτι ka·ti
sometimes μερικές φορές me·ri·kes fo·res
son γιος ⓜ yios
song τραγούδι ⓝ tra·ghu·thi
soon σύντομα si·do·ma
sore a πονεμένος po·ne·me·nos
soup σούπα ⓕ su·pa
sour cream ξινή κρέμα ⓕ ksi·ni kre·ma
south νότος ⓜ no·tos
souvenir σουβενίρ ⓝ su·ve·nir
souvenir shop κατάστημα για σουβενίρ ⓝ ka·ta·sti·ma yia su·ve·nir

souvlaki σουβλάκι ⓝ suv·la·ki
soy milk γάλα σόγια ⓝ gha·la so·yi·a
soy sauce σάλτσα σόγια ⓕ sόγια sal·tsa so·yi·a
space διάστημα ⓝ thi·a·sti·ma
Spain Ισπανία ⓕ i·spa·ni·a
sparkling wine σαμπάνια ⓕ sam·pa·ni·a
speak μιλάω mi·la·o
special a ειδικός i·thi·kos
specialist σπεσιαλίστας/σπεσιαλίστρια ⓜ/ⓕ spe·si·a·li·stas/spe·si·a·li·stri·a
speed (velocity) ταχύτητα ⓕ ta·hi·ti·ta
speed limit όριο ταχύτητας ⓝ o·ri·o ta·hi·ti·tas
speedometer ταχύμετρο ⓝ ta·hi·me·tro
spider αράχνη ⓕ a·rakh·ni
spinach σπανάκι ⓝ spa·na·ki
spoiled (food) χαλασμένος kha·laz·me·nos
spoke ακτίνα τροχού ⓕ ak·ti·na tro·khu
spoon κουτάλι ⓝ ku·ta·li
sport σπορ ⓝ spor
sportsman σπόρτσμαν ⓜ sports·man
sportswoman σπορτσγούμαν ⓕ sports·ghu·man
sports store κατάστημα των σπορ ⓝ ka·ta·sti·ma ton spor
sprain στραμπούλισμα ⓝ stra·bu·liz·ma
spring (coil) ελατήριο ⓝ e·la·ti·ri·o
spring (season) άνοιξη ⓕ a·nik·si
square (town) πλατεία ⓕ pla·ti·a
spray σπρέι ⓝ spre·i
stadium στάδιο ⓝ sta·thi·o
stairway σκάλα ⓕ ska·la
stale μπαγιάτικος ba·yia·ti·kos
stamp γραμματόσημο ⓝ ghra·ma·to·si·mo
stand-by ticket εισιτήριο σταντ μπάι ⓝ i·si·ti·ri·o stand ba·i
star (sky) αστέρι ⓝ a·ste·ri
start αρχή ⓕ ar·hi
start v αρχίζω ar·hi·zo
station σταθμός ⓜ stath·mos
stationer's χαρτοπωλείο ⓝ khar·to·po·li·o
statue άγαλμα ⓝ a·ghal·ma
stay μένω me·no
steak (beef) μπριζόλα ⓕ bri·zo·la
steal κλέβω kle·vo
steep απόκρημνος a·po·krim·nos
step βήμα ⓝ vi·ma
stereo στέρεο ⓝ ste·re·o
still water νερό χωρίς ανθρακικό ⓝ ne·ro kho·ris an·thra·ki·ko

sting v τσιμπάω tsi-*ba*-o
stock (food) ζουμί @ zu-*mi*
stockings καλτσόν ① kal-*tson*
stolen κλεμμένο kle-*me*-no
stomach στομάχι ① sto-*ma*-hi
stomachache στομαχόπονος @
  sto-ma-*kho*-po-nos
stone πέτρα ① *pe*-tra
stoned (drugged) μαστουρωμένος
  ma-stu-ro-*me*-nos
stop (bus etc) στάση ① *sta*-si
stop (cease) v σταματάω sta-ma-*ta*-o
stop (prevent) v εμποδίζω e-bo-*thi*-zo
storm καταιγίδα ① ka-te-*yi*-tha
story ιστορία ① i-sto-*ri*-a
stove ηλεκτρική κουζίνα ①
  i-lek-tri-*ki* ku-*zi*-na
straight ίσιος *i*-si-os
strange παράξενος pa-*rak*-se-nos
stranger (person) ξένος/ξένη @/①
  kse-nos/*kse*-ni
strawberry φράουλα ① *fra*-u-la
stream ατμός @ at-*mos*
street οδός ① o-*thos*
street market λαϊκή ① la-i-*ki*
strike απεργία ① a-per-*yi*-a
string κλωστή ① klo-*sti*
stroke (health) εγκεφαλικό @ e-ge-fa-li-*ko*
stroller καροτσάκι @ ka-rot-*sa*-ki
strong δυνατός thi-na-*tos*
stubborn ισχυρογνώμων is-hi-rog-*no*-mon
student σπουδαστής/σπουδάστρια
  @/① spu-tha-*stis*/spu-*tha*-stri-a
studio στούντιο @ *stu*-di-o
stupid χαζός kha-*zos*
style στυλ @ stil
subtitles υπότιτλοι @ pl i-*po*-ti-tli
suburb προάστειο ① pro-*a*-sti-o
subway a υπόγειος i-*po*-yi-os
subway (train) υπόγειος σιδηρόδρομος
  @ i-po-yi-os si-*thi*-ro-*thro*-mos
sugar ζάχαρη ① *za*-kha-ri
suitcase βαλίτσα ① va-*lit*-sa
sultana σταφίδα ① sta-*fi*-tha
summer καλοκαίρι @ ka-lo-*ke*-ri
sun ήλιος @ *i*-li-os
sunblock αντιηλιακό @ a-di-i-li-a-*ko*
sunburn ηλιακό έγκαυμα @
  i-li-a-*ko* e-*gav*-ma
Sunday Κυριακή ① ki-ria-*ki*

sunglasses γιαλιά ηλίου @ pl yia-*lia* i-*li*-u
sunny ηλιόλουστος i-li-o-lu-stos
sunrise ανατολή ① a-na-to-*li*
sunset δύση ① *thi*-si
sunstroke ηλιοπληξία ① i-li-o-plik-*si*-a
supermarket σουπερμάρκετ @
  su-per-*mar*-ket
superstition πρόληψη ① *pro*-lip-si
supporter (politics, sport) οπαδός
  @&① o-pa-*thos*
surf σερφ @ serf
surface mail (land) δια ξηράς thi-a ksi-*ras*
surface mail (sea) ατμοπλοϊκώς
  at-mo-plo-i-kos
surfboard σέρφμπορντ @ *serf*-bord
surfing σέρφινγκ @ *ser*-fing
surname επώνυμο ① e-*po*-ni-mo
surprise έκπληξη ① *ek*-plik-si
sweater ζακέτα ① za-*ke*-ta
Sweden Σουηδία ① su-i-*thi*-a
sweet a γλυκός ghli-*kos*
sweets γλυκά @ pl ghli-*ka*
swelling πρήξιμο @ *prik*-si-mo
swim v κολυμπώ ko-li-*bo*
swimming (sport) κολύμπι @ ko-*li*-bi
swimming pool πισίνα ① pi-*si*-na
swimsuit μαγιό @ ma-*yio*
Switzerland Ελβετία ① el-ve-*ti*-a
sword σπαθί @ spa-*thi*
synagogue συναγωγή ① si-na-gho-*yi*
synthetic a συνθετικός sin-the-ti-*kos*
syringe σύριγκα ① *si*-ri-ga

T

table τραπέζι ① tra-*pe*-zi
tablecloth τραπεζομάντηλο @
  tra-pe-zo-*ma*-di-lo
table tennis πινγκ πονγκ @ ping pong
tail ουρά ① u-*ra*
tailor ράφτης/ράφτρα @/① *raf*-tis/*raf*-tra
take παίρνω *per*-no
take a photo βγάζω φωτογραφία
  vga-zo fo-to-gra-*fi*-a
talk v μιλάω mi-*la*-o
tall ψηλός psi-*los*
tampon ταμπόν @ ta-*bon*
tanning lotion λοσιόν για μαύρισμα @
  lo-*sion* yia *mav*-riz-ma

tap βρύση ⓕ *vri*·si
tap water νερό βρύσης ⓝ *ne*·ro vri·sis
tasty νόστιμος *no*·sti·mos
taverna ταβέρνα ⓕ ta·*ver*·na
tax φόρος ⓜ *fo*·ros
taxi ταξί tak·si
taxi stand στάση ταξί ⓕ *sta*·si tak·*si*
tea τσάι ⓝ *tsa*·i
teacher δάσκαλος/δασκάλα ⓜ/ⓕ
tha·ska·los/tha·*ska*·la
team ομάδα ⓕ o·*ma*·tha
teaspoon κουτάλι τσαγιού ⓝ
ku·*ta*·li tsa·*yiu*
technique τεχνική ⓕ tekh·ni·*ki*
teeth δόντια ⓝ *tho*·dia
telegram τηλεγράφημα ⓝ ti·le·*ghra*·fi·ma
telephone τηλέφωνο ⓝ ti·*le*·fo·no
telephone ν τηλεφωνώ ti·le·fo·*no*
telephone box δημόσιο τηλέφωνο ⓝ
thi·mo·si·o ti·*le*·fo·no
telephone centre τηλεφωνικό κέντρο ⓝ
ti·le·fo·ni·*ko ke*·dro
telescope τηλεσκόπιο ⓝ ti·le·*sko*·pi·o
television τηλεόραση ⓕ ti·le·*o*·ra·si
tell λέγω *le*·gho
temperature (fever) πυρετός ⓜ pi·re·*tos*
temperature (weather) θερμοκρασία ⓕ
ther·mo·kra·*si*·a
temple (church) ναός ⓜ na·*os*
tennis τένις ⓝ *te*·nis
tennis court γήπεδο του τένις ⓝ
yi·pe·tho tu *te*·nis
tent τέντα ⓕ *te*·da
tent peg πάσαλος τέντας ⓜ
pa·sa·los *te*·das
terracotta pot αγγείο τερακότα ⓝ
a·*gi*·o te·ra·*ko*·ta
terrible τρομερός tro·me·*ros*
test τεστ ⓝ test
thank ευχαριστώ ef·kha·ri·*sto*
that (one) εκείνο e·*ki*·no
theatre θέατρο ⓝ *the*·a·tro
their τους tus
there εκεί e·*ki*
they αυτοί af·*ti*
thick πυκνός pik·*nos*
thief κλέφτης ⓜ *klef*·tis
thin λεπτός lep·*tos*
think νομίζω no·*mi*·zo
third τρίτος *tri*·tos

thirsty διψασμένος thip·saz·*me*·nos
this (one) αυτός ⓜ af·*tos*
thread κλωστή ⓕ klo·*sti*
throat λαιμός ⓜ le·*mos*
thrush (health) μυκητώδης στοματίτις ⓜ
mi·ki·to·this sto·ma·*ti*·tis
thunderstorm καταιγίδα ⓕ ka·te·*yi*·tha
Thursday Πέμπτη ⓕ *pem*·ti
tick τσιμπούρι ⓝ tsi·*bu*·ri
ticket εισιτήριο ⓝ i·si·*ti*·ri·o
ticket collector εισπράκτορας ⓜ&ⓕ
is·*prak*·to·ras
ticket machine μηχανή εισιτηρίων ⓕ
mi·kha·*ni* i·si·ti·*ri*·on
ticket office γραφείο εισιτηρίων ⓝ
ghra·*fi*·o i·si·ti·*ri*·on
tide παλίρροια ⓕ pa·*li*·ri·a
tight σφιχτός sfikh·*tos*
time ώρα ⓕ *o*·ra
time difference διαφορά ώρας ⓕ
thia·fo·*ra o*·ras
timetable πρόγραμμα ⓝ *pro*·ghra·ma
tin (can) κουτί ⓝ ku·*ti*
tin opener ανοιχτήρι ⓝ a·nikh·*ti*·ri
tiny μικροσκοπικός mi·kro·sko·pi·*kos*
tip (gratuity) φιλοδώρημα ⓝ
fi·lo·*tho*·ri·ma
tire λάστιχο ⓝ *la*·sti·kho
tired κουρασμένος ku·raz·*me*·nos
tissues χαρτομάντηλα ⓝ pl
khar·to·*ma*·di·la
to σε se
toast τοστ ⓝ tost
toaster τοστιέρα ⓕ to·sti·*e*·ra
tobacco καπνός ⓜ kap·*nos*
tobacconist
καπνοπώλης/καπνοπώλισσα ⓜ/ⓕ
ka·pno·*po*·lis/ka·pno·po·*li*·sa
today σήμερα *si*·me·ra
toe δάχτυλο ποδιού ⓝ *thakh*·ti·lo po·*thiu*
tofu τόφου ⓝ *to*·fu
together μαζί ma·*zi*
toilet τουαλέτα ⓕ tu·a·*le*·ta
toilet paper χαρτί υγείας ⓝ khar·*ti* i·*yi*·as
tomato ντομάτα ⓕ do·*ma*·ta
tomato sauce σάλτσα ⓕ *sal*·tsa
tomb μνήμα ⓝ *mni*·ma
tomorrow αύριο *av*·ri·o
tomorrow afternoon αύριο το απόγευμα
av·ri·o to a·*po*·yev·ma

tomorrow evening αύριο το βράδι
*av·ri·*o to *vra·*thi

tomorrow morning αύριο το πρωί
*av·ri·*o to *pro·i*

tonight απόψε *a·pop·*se

too (excess) πάρα πολύ *pa·ra* po·*li*

tooth δόντι ⓝ *tho·*di

toothache πονόδοντος ⓜ po·*no·*tho·dos

toothbrush οδοντόβουρτσα ⓕ
o·tho·*do·*vur·tsa

toothpaste οδοντόπαστα ⓕ
o·tho·*do·*pa·sta

toothpick οδοντογλυφίδα ⓕ
o·tho·do·ghli·*fi·*tha

torch (flashlight) φακός ⓜ fa·*kos*

touch v αγγίζω a·*gi·*zo

tour περιήγηση ⓕ pe·ri·*i·*yi·si

tourist τουρίστας/τουρίστρια ⓜ/ⓕ
tu·*ri·*stas/tu·*ri·*stri·a

tourist office τουριστικό γραφείο ⓝ
tu·ri·sti·*ko* ghra·*fi·*o

towards προς pros

towel πετσέτα ⓕ pet·*se·*ta

tower πύργος ⓜ *pir·*ghos

toxic waste τοξικά απόβλητα ⓝ pl
tok·si·*ka* a·*pov·*li·ta

toy shop κατάστημα παιγνιδιών ⓝ
ka·*ta·*sti·ma pegh·ni·*thion*

track (path) μονοπάτι ⓝ mo·no·*pa·*ti

track (sport) στίβος ⓜ *sti·*vos

trade εμπόριο ⓝ e·*bo·*ri·o

tradesperson έμπορος ⓜ&ⓕ e·bo·ros

traffic κυκλοφορία ⓕ ki·klo·fo·*ri·*a

traffic light φανάρι ⓝ fa·*na·*ri

trail μονοπάτι ⓝ mo·no·*pa·*ti

train τρένο ⓝ *tre·*no

train station σταθμός τρένου ⓜ
stath·*mos* tre·nu

tram τραμ ⓝ tram

transit lounge αίθουσα τράνζιτ ⓕ
*e·*thu·sa *tran·*zit

translate μεταφράζω me·ta·*fra·*zo

transport μεταφορά ⓕ me·ta·fo·*ra*

travel v ταξιδεύω tak·si·*the·*vo

travel agency ταξιδιωτικό γραφείο ⓝ
tak·si·thi·o·ti·*ko* ghra·*fi·*o

travel sickness ναυτία ⓕ naf·*ti·*a

travellers cheque ταξιδιωτική επιταγή ⓕ
tak·si·thi·o·ti·*ki* e·pi·ta·*yi*

tree δέντρο ⓝ *the·*dro

trip (journey) ταξίδι ⓝ tak·*si·*thi

trolley καροτσάκι ⓝ ka·rot·*sa·*ki

trolley bus τρόλεϋ ⓝ *tro·*le·i

trousers παντελόνι ⓝ pa·de·*lo·*ni

truck φορτηγό ⓝ for·ti·*gho*

trust v εμπιστεύομαι e·bi·*ste·*vo·me

try (attempt) προσπαθώ pros·pa·*tho*

T-shirt μπλουζάκι ⓝ blu·*za·*ki

tube (tyre) σαμπρέλα ⓕ sa·*bre·*la

Tuesday Τρίτη ⓕ *tri·*ti

tumour όγκος ⓜ *o·*gos

tuna τόνος ⓜ *to·*nos

tune σκοπός ⓜ sko·*pos*

tunic χιτώνας ⓜ hi·*to·*nas

Turkey Τουρκία ⓕ tur·*ki·*a

turkey γαλοπούλα ⓕ gha·lo·*pu·*la

Turkish (language) Τουρκικά tur·ki·*ka*

Turkish (people) Τούρκοι ⓜ pl *tur·*ki

turn v γυρίζω yi·*ri·*zo

TV τηλεόραση ⓕ ti·le·o·*ra·*si

tweezers τσιμπιδάκι ⓝ tsi·bi·*tha·*ki

twice δυο φορές thio fo·*res*

twin beds δίκλινο δωμάτιο ⓝ
*thi·*kli·no tho·*ma·*ti·o

twins δίδυμα ⓝ pl *thi·*thi·ma

two δύο *thi·*o

type τύπος ⓜ *ti·*pos

typhus τύφος ⓜ *ti·*fos

typical τυπικός ti·pi·*kos*

tyre λάστιχο ⓝ *la·*sti·kho

U

ultrasound υπερηχητικό κύμα ⓝ
i·pe·ri·hi·ti·*ko ki·*ma

umbrella ομπρέλα ⓕ o·*bre·*la

uncomfortable άβολος a·vo·los

understand καταλαβαίνω ka·ta·la·*ve·*no

underwear εσώρουχα ⓝ pl e·*so·*ru·kha

unemployed a άνεργος/άνεργη ⓜ/ⓕ
*a·*ner·ghos/*a·*ner·yi

unfair άδικος a·thi·kos

uniform στολή ⓕ sto·*li*

universe σύμπαν ⓝ *si·*ba

university πανεπιστήμιο ⓝ
pa·ne·pi·*sti·*mi·o

unleaded (petrol) αμόλυβδος ⓕ
a·*mo·*liv·thos

unsafe ανασφαλής a·nas·fa·*lis*

until μέχρι *me·*khri

unusual ασυνήθιστος a·si·*ni·*thi·stos

UN zone ζώνη των Ηνωμένων Εθνών ⓕ *zo·*ni ton i·no·*me·*non *e·*thnon

up πάνω *pa·*no

uphill ανηφορικά a·ni·fo·ri·*ka*

urgent επείγον e·*pi·*ghon

urinary infection ουρική μόλυνση ⓕ u·ri·*ki* mo·lin·si

USA ΗΠΑ ⓕ *i·*pa

useful χρήσιμος khri·si·mos

V

vacancy κενή θέση ⓕ ke·*ni* the·si

vacant ελεύθερος e·*lef·*the·ros

vacation διακοπές ⓕ pl thia·ko·*pes*

vaccination εμβόλιο ⓝ em·*vo·*li·o

vagina κόλπος γυναίκας ⓜ *kol·*pos yi·*ne·*kas

validate επικυρώνω e·pi·ki·*ro·*no

valley κοιλάδα ⓕ ki·*la·*tha

valuable πολύτιμος po·*li·*ti·mos

value (price) αξία ⓕ ak·*si·*a

van φορτηγάκι ⓝ for·ti·*gha·*ki

VAT (Value Added Tax) Φ.Π.Α. ⓕ fpa

veal μοσχάρι ⓝ mos·*kha·*ri

vegan βέγκαν ⓜ&ⓕ *ve·*gan

vegetable λαχανικά ⓝ pl la·kha·ni·*ka*

vegetarian a χορτοφάγος ⓜ&ⓕ khor·to·*fa·*ghos

vein φλέβα ⓕ *fle·*va

venereal disease αφροδισιακό νόσημα ⓝ a·fro·thi·si·a·*ko* no·si·ma

venue χώρος ⓜ *kho·*ros

very πολύς po·*lis*

vessel σκάφος ⓝ *ska·*fos

video recorder βίντεο ρεκόρντερ ⓝ *vi·*de·o re·*kor·*der

video tape βιντεοταινία ⓕ *vi·*de·o·te·*ni·*a

view θέα ⓕ *the·*a

village χωριό ⓝ kho·*rio*

vine κλήμα ⓝ *kli·*ma

vinegar ξύδι ⓝ *ksi·*thi

vineyard αμπέλι ⓝ a·*be·*li

virus ιός ⓜ i·*os*

visa βίζα ⓕ *vi·*za

visit επίσκεψη ⓕ e·*pi·*skep·si

visit v επισκέπτομαι e·pi·*ske·*pto·me

vitamins βιταμίνες ⓕ pl vi·ta·*mi·*nes

vodka βότκα ⓕ *vot·*ka

voice φωνή ⓕ fo·*ni*

volleyball ⓝ βόλεϊ *vo·*le·i

vote v ψηφίζω psi·*fi·*zo

W

wage μισθός ⓜ mis·*thos*

wait (for) περιμένω pe·ri·*me·*no

waiter γκαρσόν ⓝ gar·*son*

waiting room αίθουσα αναμονής ⓕ *e·*thu·sa a·na·mo·*nis*

waitress σερβιτόρα ⓕ ser·vi·*to·*ra

wake (someone) up ξυπνάω ksip·*na·*o

walk v περπατάω per·pa·*ta·*o

wall (outer) τείχος ⓝ *ti·*khos

wallet πορτοφόλι ⓝ por·to·*fo·*li

want θέλω *the·*lo

war πόλεμος ⓜ *po·*le·mos

wardrobe ντουλάπα ⓕ du·*la·*pa

warm a ζεστός ze·*stos*

warn ζεσταίνω ze·*ste·*no

wash (oneself) v πλένομαι *ple·*no·me

wash (something) v πλένω *ple·*no

wash cloth (flannel) σφουγγάρι ⓝ sfu·*ga·*ri

washing machine πλυντήριο ⓝ pli·*di·*ri·o

wasp σφήκα ⓕ *sfi·*ka

watch v κοιτάζω ki·*ta·*zo

watch ρολόι ⓝ ro·*lo·*i

water νερό ⓝ ne·*ro*

water bottle μπουκάλι νερού ⓝ bu·*ka·*li ne·*ru*

water bottle (hot) θερμοφόρα ⓕ ther·mo·*fo·*ra

waterfall καταράχτης ⓜ ka·ta·*rakh·*tis

watermelon καρπούζι ⓝ kar·*pu·*zi

waterproof a αδιάβροχος a·*thi·*av·ro·khos

waterskiing θαλάσσιο σκι ⓝ tha·*la·*si·o ski

wave κύμα ⓝ *ki·*ma

way δρόμος ⓜ *thro·*mos

we εμείς e·*mis*

weak a αδύνατος a·*thi·*na·tos

wealthy πλούσιος ⓜ *plu·*si·os

wear v φοράω fo·*ra·*o

weather καιρός ⓜ ke·*ros*

weaving υφαντό ⓝ i·fa·*do*

wedding γάμος ⓜ *gha·*mos

wedding cake γαμήλια τούρτα ⓕ
gha·*mi*·li·a *tur*·ta
wedding present γαμήλιο δώρο ⓝ
gha·*mi*·li·o *tho*·ro
Wednesday Τετάρτη ⓕ te·*tar*·ti
week εβδομάδα ⓕ ev·tho·*ma*·tha
weekend Σαββατοκύριακο ⓝ
sa·va·to·*ki*·ria·ko
weigh ζυγίζω zi·*yi*·zo
weight βάρος ⓝ *va*·ros
weights βάρη ⓝ pl *va*·ri
welcome v καλωσορίζω ka·lo·so·*ri*·zo
welfare πρόνοια ⓕ *pro*·ni·a
well (health) καλά ka·*la*
west δύση ⓕ *thi*·si
wet a βρεγμένος vregh·*me*·nos
what τι ti
wheel τροχός ⓜ tro·*khos*
wheelchair αναπηρική καρέκλα ⓕ
a·na·pi·ri·*ki* ka·*re*·kla
when όταν o·tan
where πού pu
which ποιος pios
whisky ουίσκυ ⓝ u·*i*·ski
white άσπρος as·pros
who ποιος pios
wholemeal bread ψωμί ολικής αλέσεως
ⓝ pso·*mi* o·li·*kis* a·*le*·se·os
why γιατί yia·*ti*
wide πλατύς pla·*tis*
wife σύζυγος ⓕ *si*·zi·ghos
wildflowers αγριολούλουδα ⓝ pl
a·ghri·o·*lu*·lu·tha
win v κερδίζω ker·*thi*·zo
wind άνεμος ⓜ *a*·ne·mos
window παράθυρο ⓝ pa·*ra*·thi·ro
windscreen παμπρίζ ⓝ pa·*briz*
windsurfing γουιντσέρφινγκ ⓝ
ghu·id·*ser*·fing
wine κρασί ⓝ kra·*si*
wings φτερούγες ⓕ pl fte·ru·ghes
winner νικητής ⓜ ni·ki·*tis*
winter χειμώνας ⓜ hi·*mo*·nas
wire καλώδιο ⓝ ka·*lo*·thi·o
wish v εύχομαι ef·kho·me
with με me
within (an hour) εντός e·*dos*
without χωρίς kho·*ris*
wok γουόκ ⓝ ghu·*ok*

woman γυναίκα ⓕ yi·*ne*·ka
wonderful θαυμάσιος thav·*ma*·si·os
wood δάσος ⓝ *tha*·sos
wool μαλλί ⓝ ma·*li*
word λέξη ⓕ *lek*·si
work δουλειά ⓕ thu·*lia*
work v δουλεύω thu·*le*·vo
work experience πείρα εργασίας ⓕ
pi·ra er·gha·*si*·as
workout εξάσκηση ⓕ ek·*sa*·ski·si
work permit άδεια εργασίας ⓕ
a·thi·a er·gha·*si*·as
workshop εργαστήρι ⓝ er·gha·*sti*·ri
world κόσμος ⓜ *koz*·mos
World Cup Παγκόσμιο Κύπελο ⓝ
pa·*goz*·mi·o *ki*·pe·lo
worm σκουλίκι ⓝ sku·*li*·ki
worried ανήσυχος a·*ni*·si·khos
worship v λατρεύω la·*tre*·vo
wrist καρπός ⓜ kar·pos
write γράφω *ghra*·fo
writer συγγραφέας ⓜ&ⓕ si·gra·*fe*·as
wrong a λανθασμένος lan·thaz·*me*·nos

year χρόνος ⓜ *khro*·nos
(this) year (αυτό το) χρόνο
(af·to to) *khro*·no
yellow a κίτρινος *ki*·tri·nos
yes ναι ne
yesterday χτες khtes
(not) yet (όχι) ακόμη (o·hi) a·*ko*·mi
yoga γιόγκα ⓕ *yiog*·ka
yogurt γιαούρτι ⓝ yia·*ur*·ti
you sg inf εσύ e·*si*
you sg pol & pl inf&pol εσείς e·*sis*
young νέος *ne*·os
your sg pol & pl inf&pol σας sas
your sg inf σου su
youth hostel γιουθ χόστελ ⓝ yuth kho·stel

zip/zipper φερμουάρ ⓝ fer·mu·*ar*
zodiac ζωδιακός ⓜ zo·thi·a·*kos*
zoo ζωολογικός κήπος ⓜ
zo·o·lo·yi·*kos* *ki*·pos
zucchini κολοκυθάκι ⓝ ko·lo·ki·*tha*·ki

Greek nouns in the **dictionary** have their gender indicated by ⑩ masculine, ⑥ feminine or ⑩ neuter. If it's a plural noun you'll also see pl. When a word that could be either a noun or a verb has no gender indicated, it's a verb. In the masculine form only – see **adjectives & adverbs** in the **phrasebuilder** for more on how to form feminine and neuter adjectives. Both nouns and adjectives are provided in the nominative case only – refer to the **phrasebuilder** for more information on **case**. You'll also find the English words marked as a adjective and v verb, sg singular, pl plural, inf informal, or pol polite where necessary.

The **greek–english dictionary** has been ordered according to the Greek alphabet:

Α α	Β β	Γ γ	Δ δ	Ε ε	Ζ ζ	Η η	Θ θ	Ι ι	Κ κ	Λ λ	Μ μ
Ν ν	Ξ ξ	Ο ο	Π π	Ρ ρ	Σ σ/ς	Τ τ	Υ υ	Φ φ	Χ χ	Ψ ψ	Ω ω

Α α

άβολος a·vo·los uncomfortable
αγάπη a·gha·pi ① love
αγαπώ a·gha·po love ⓥ
Αγγλία ① ang·gli·a England
Αγγλικά ⑩ pl ang·gli·ka English (language)
αγορά ① a·gho·ra market • shopping centre
αγοράζω a·gho·ra·zo buy ⓥ
αγόρι ⑩ a·gho·ri boy
άδειο a·thi·o empty a
αδερφή ① a·ther·fi sister
αδερφός ⑩ a·ther·fos brother
αδιάβροχο ⑩ a·thi·av·ro·ho raincoat
αδύνατος a·thi·na·tos impossible a
αερογραμμή ① a·e·ro·ghra·mi airline
αεροδρόμιο a·e·ro·thro·mi·o ⑩ airport
αεροπλάνο a·e·ro·pla·no ⑩ airplane
αίθουσα αναμονής
 e·thu·sa a·na·mo·nis ① waiting room
αίθουσα τράνζιτ ① e·thu·sa tran·zit
 transit lounge
αίμα e·ma ⑩ blood
ακριβός a·kri·vos expensive
ακριβώς a·kri·vos exactly
ακυρώνω a·ki·ro·no cancel
αλλαγή a·la·yi ① change
αλλεργία a·ler·yi·a ① allergy
αλληλογραφία a·li·lo·ghra·fi·a ① mail
άλλος a·los other
άμεσος a·me·sos direct a
αναπηρική καρέκλα
 a·na·pi·ri·ki ka·re·kla ① wheelchair

ανάπηρος a·na·pi·ros disabled a
αναπτήρας ⑩ a·nap·ti·ras cigarette lighter
ανατολή ① a·na·to·li east • sunrise
αναχώρηση ① a·na·kho·ri·si departure
αναχωρώ a·na·kho·ro depart ⓥ • leave ⓥ
ανεβαίνω a·ne·ve·no board (transport) ⓥ
ανεμιστήρας a·ne·mi·sti·ras
 fan (machine)
άνετος a·ne·tos comfortable
ανθοπώλης ⑩ an·tho·po·lis florist
ανθοπώλισσα ① an·tho·po·li·sa florist
ανιαρός a·ni·a·ros boring
άνοιξη ① a·nik·si spring (season)
ανοιχτήρι ① a·nikh·ti·ri bottle opener •
 can opener • corkscrew
ανοιχτός a·nikh·tos light (colour) • open a
ανταλλάσσω a·da·la·so exchange ⓥ
αντιβιοτικά ⑩ pl a·di·vi·o·ti·ka antibiotics
αντίγραφο ⑩ a·di·ghra·fo copy
αντηλιακό ⑩ a·di·li·a·ko sunblock
αντισηπτικό ⑩ a·di·si·lip·ti·ko antiseptic
άντρας ⑩ a·dras man
απαίσιος a·pe·si·os awful
απασχολημένος a·pa·skho·li·me·nos busy
απεργία ① a·per·yi·a strike
απίθανος a·pi·tha·nos fantastic • great
απλό εισιτήριο ⑩ a·plo i·si·ti·ri·o
 one-way (ticket)
απόγευμα ⑩ a·po·yev·ma afternoon
απόδειξη ① a·po·thik·si receipt
αποσκευές ⑥ pl a·po·ske·ves baggage
αποσμητικό ⑩ a·poz·mi·ti·ko deodorant
απόψε a·pop·se tonight

αργά ar·gha *slowly*

αργότερα ar·gho·te·ra *later*

αριθμομηχανή ① a·rith·mo·mi·kha·ni *calculator*

αριθμός a·rith·mos *number*

αριθμός διαβατηρίου ⑩ a·rith·mos thia·va·ti·ri·u *passport number*

αριθμός δωματίου ⑩ a·rith·mos tho·ma·ti·u *room number*

αριθμός κυκλοφορίας αυτοκινήτου ① a·rith·mos ki·klo·fo·ri·as af·to·ki·ni·tu *car registration*

αριθμός οδήγησης ① a·rith·mos o·thi·yi·sis *drivers licence*

αριστερός a·ri·ste·ros *left (direction)* a

αρκετά ar·ke·ta *enough*

αρραβωνιασμένη ① a·ra·vo·niaz·me·ni *engaged (to marry)*

αρραβωνιασμένος ⑩ a·ra·vo·niaz·me·nos *engaged (to marry)*

αρραβωνιαστικιά ① a·ra·vo·nia·sti·kia *fiancée*

αρραβωνιαστικός ⑩ a·ra·vo·nia·sti·kos *fiancé*

άρρωστος a·ro·stos *ill • sick*

αρχιτέκτονας ⑩&① ar·hi·tek·to·nas *architect*

αρχιτεκτονική ① ar·hi·tek·to·ni·ki *architecture*

άρωμα ⑩ a·ro·ma *perfume*

ασανσέρ a·san·ser *elevator • lift*

ασήμι ⑩ a·si·mi *silver*

άσπρος as·pros *white*

αστείος a·sti·os *funny*

αστικό λεωφορείο ⑩ a·sti·ko le·o·fo·ri·o *bus*

αστράγαλος ⑩ a·stra·gha·los *ankle*

αστυνομία ① a·sti·no·mi·a *police*

αστυνομικός σταθμός ⑩ a·sti·no·mi·kos stath·mos *police station*

αστυφύλακας ⑩ a·sti·fi·la·kas *police officer*

αστυφυλακίνα ① a·sti·fi·la·ki·na *police officer*

ασφάλεια ① as·fa·li·a *insurance*

ασφαλές σεξ ⑩ as·fa·les seks *safe sex*

ατύχημα ⑩ a·ti·hi·ma *accident*

αυγή ① av·yi *dawn*

αύριο av·ri·o *tomorrow*

αυτοκίνητο ⑩ af·to·ki·ni·to *car*

αυτοκινητόδρομος ⑩ af·to·ki·ni·to·thro·mos *motorway • tollway*

αυτόματη μηχανή χρημάτων ① af·to·ma·ti mi·kha·ni khri·ma·ton *ATM*

αυτός ⑩ af·tos *he • this (one)*

αφή ① a·fi *feeling (physical)*

αφίξεις ① pl a·fik·sis *arrivals*

αφτί ⑩ af·ti *ear*

Β β

βαγκόν λι ⑩ va·gon li *sleeping car*

βαγόνι φαγητού ⑩ va·gho·ni fa·yi·tu *dining car*

βαλίτσα ① va·lit·sa *suitcase*

βαμπάκι ⑩ va·ba·ki *cotton*

βάρκα ① var·ka *boat*

βαρύς va·ris *heavy*

βγάζω φωτογραφία vga·zo fo·to·gra·fi·a *take a photo*

βγαίνω vye·no *go out*

βελόνα ① ve·lo·na *needle (sewing)*

βενζίνα ① ven·zi·na *gas • petrol*

βενζινάδικο ⑩ ven·zi·na·thi·ko *service station*

βήχω vi·kho *cough* ⓥ

βιαστικός via·sti·kos *in a hurry*

βιβλίο ⑩ viv·li·o *book*

βιβλιοθήκη ① viv·li·o·thi·ki *library*

βιβλιοπωλείο ⑩ viv·li·o·po·li·o *bookshop*

βιβλίο φράσεων ① viv·li·o fra·se·on *phrasebook*

βίζα ① vi·za *visa*

βιντεοταινία ① vi·de·o·te·ni·a *video tape*

βοήθεια ① vo·i·thi·a *help*

βοηθώ vo·i·tho *help* ⓥ

βοράς ⑩ vo·ras *north*

βούλωμα ⑩ vu·lo·ma *plug (bath)*

βουνό ⑩ vu·no *mountain*

βούρτσα ① vur·tsa *brush*

βράδι ⑩ vra·thi *evening*

βροχή ① vro·hi *rain*

βρύση ① vri·si *faucet • tap*

βρώμικος a vro·mi·kos *dirty*

βύσμα ⑩ viz·ma *plug (electricity)*

Γ γ

γάλα ⑩ gha·la *milk*

γαστροεντερίτιδα ① gha·stro·e·de·ri·ti·tha *gastroenteritis*

γεμάτο ye·ma·to *full*

γενέθλια ⑩ pl ye·ne·thli·a *birthday*

Γερμανία ① ye·rma·ni·a *Germany*

γεύμα ⑩ yev·ma *meal*

γεφύρι ⑩ ye·fi·ri *bridge*

Γη ① yi *Earth*

γήπεδο ⑩ *yi*-pe-tho *court (tennis)*
— **του γκολφ** ⑩ tu golf *golf course*
— **του τένις** ⑩ tu *te*-nis *tennis court*

γιαγιά ① yia-*yia grandmother*

γιαλιά ⑩ pl yia-*lia glasses • spectacles*

γιαλιά ηλίου ⑩ pl yia-*lia* i-*li*-u *sunglasses*

γιατί yia-*ti why*

γιατρός ⑩&① yia-*tros doctor*

γιος ⑩ yios *son*

γιουθ χόστελ ⑩ yuth *kho*-stel *youth hostel*

γκαρσόν ⑩ gar-*son waiter*

γκέι ge-i *gay* a

γκρίζος *gri*-zos *gray • grey* a

γλυκός ghli-*kos sweet* a

γλυπτική ① ghlip-ti-*ki sculpture*

γλώσσα ① *ghlo*-sa *language*

γόνατο ⑩ *gho*-na-to *knee*

γονείς ⑩ pl gho-*nis parents*

γράμμα ⑩ *ghra*-ma *letter (mail)*

γραμμάριο ⑩ ghra-*ma*-ri-o *gram*

γραμματόσημο ⑩ ghra-ma-*to*-si-mo *stamp*

γραφείο απολεσθέντων αντικειμένων ⑩ gra-*fi*-o a-po-le-*sthe*-don a-di-ki-*me*-non *left-luggage office*

γραφείο εισιτηρίων ghra-*fi*-o i-si-ti-*ri*-on ⑩ *ticket office*

γράφω *ghra*-fo *write*

γρήγορος a *ghri*-gho-ros *fast*

γρίπη ① *ghri*-pi *influenza • flu*

γυμναστήριο ⑩ yi-mna-*sti*-ri-o *gym (place)*

γυναίκα ① yi-*ne*-ka *woman*

Δ δ

δάκτυλο ⑩ *thak*-ti-lo *finger*

δασμός αεροδρομίου ⑩ thaz-*mos* a-e-ro-thro-*mi*-u *airport tax*

δάσος ⑩ *tha*-sos *forest • wood*

δαχτυλίδι ⑩ thakh-ti-*li*-thi *ring (on finger)*

δείπνο ⑩ *thip*-no *dinner*

δείχνω *thi*-khno *point • show* ⓥ

δεκαπενθήμερο ⑩ tha-ka-pen-*thi*-me-ro *fortnight*

δέμα ⑩ *the*-ma *parcel*

δεξιός *thek*-si-os *right (direction)* a

δέρμα ⑩ *ther*-ma *leather • skin*

δεύτερη τάξη ① *thef*-te-ri *tak*-si *second class*

δημόσια αποχωρητήρια ⑩ pl thi-*mo*-si-a a-po-kho-ri-*ti*-ria *public toilet*

δημόσιο τηλέφωνο ⑩ thi-*mo*-si-o ti-*le*-fo-no *phone box • public telephone*

δημοσιογράφος ⑩&① thi-mo-si-o-*ghra*-fos *journalist*

δημόσιος δρόμος ⑩ thi-*mo*-si-os *thro*-mos *highway*

δια ξηράς thi-a ksi-*ras surface mail*

διαβατήριο ⑩ thia-va-*ti*-ri-o *passport*

διαδίκτυο ⑩ thi-a-*thik*-ti-o *Internet*

διάδρομος ⑩ thi-*a*-thro-mos *aisle*

διαζευγμένη ① thi-a-zev-*ghme*-ni *divorced* a

διαζευγμένος ⑩ thi-a-zev-*ghme*-nos *divorced* a

διαθέσιμος thi-a-*the*-si-mos *free (available)*

διακοπές ① pl thia-ko-*pes vacation*

διάλειμμα ⑩ *thia*-li-ma *intermission*

διαμέρισμα ⑩ thia-*me*-riz-ma *apartment*

διάρροια ① thi-*a*-ri-a *diarrhoea*

διαφορά ώρας ① thia-fo-*ra* o-ras *time difference*

διαφορετικός thia-fo-re-ti-*kos different*

διαχωριστική γραμμή ① thi-a-kho-ri-sti-*ki* ghra-*mi delineation line*

διερμηνέας ⑩&① thi-er-mi-*ne*-as *interpreter*

διεύθυνση ① thi-*ef*-thin-si *address*

δικηγόρος ⑩&① thi-ki-*gho*-ros *lawyer*

δίκλινο δωμάτιο ⑩ *thi*-kli-no tho-*ma*-ti-o *twin beds*

δίπλα *thi*-pla *beside • next to*

διπλό δωμάτιο ⑩ thi-*plo* tho-*ma*-ti-o *double room*

διπλό κρεβάτι ⑩ thi-*plo* kre-*va*-ti *double bed*

Δις ① the-spi-*nis Ms • Miss*

δισκέτα ① thi-*ske*-ta *disk (floppy)*

διψασμένος thip-saz-*me*-nos *thirsty*

δοκιμάζω tho-ki-*ma*-zo *try* ⓥ

δοκιμαστήριο ρούχων ⑩ tho-ki-ma-*sti*-ri-o *ru*-khon *changing room (in shop)*

δολλάριο ⑩ tho-*la*-ri-o *dollar*

δουλειά ① thu-*lia job • work*

δρόμος ⑩ *thro*-mos *road • route • way*

δροσερό thro-se-*ro cool (temperature)*

δυνατός thi-na-*tos loud • strong • possible*

δύο *thi*-o *two*

δύση ① *thi*-si *sunset • west*

δυσπεψία ① thi-spep-*si*-a *indigestion*

δωμάτιο ⑩ tho-*ma*-ti-o *room*

δωρεάν tho-re-*an complimentary • free*

δώρο ⑩ *tho*-ro *gift • present*

Ε ε

εβδομάδα ① ev·tho·ma·tha week
εγγονή ① e·go·ni granddaughter
εγγονός ⑩ e·go·nos grandson
εγγυημένος e·ghi·i·me·nos guaranteed
έγκαυμα ⑪ e·gav·ma burn
έγκυος e·gi·os pregnant
εγώ e·gho me
εδώ e·tho here
έθιμο ⑪ e·thi·mo custom
εισιτήριο ⑪ i·si·ti·ri·o fare • ticket
   — **μετ' επιστροφής** ① me·te·pi·stro·fis return ticket
   — **σταντ μπάι** ⑩ stand ba·i stand-by ticket
είσοδος ① i·so·thos entry
εκατοστόμετρο ⑪ e·ka·to·sto·me·tro centimetre
εκεί e·ki there
εκείνα e·ki·no that (one)
έκθεμα ⑪ ek·the·ma exhibit
έκθεση ① ek·the·si exhibition
εκκλησία ① e·kli·si·a church
έκπτωση ① ek·pto·si discount
έκτακτη ανάγκη ① ek·tak·ti a·na·gi emergency
εκτυπωτής ⑩ ek·ti·po·tis printer (computer)
ελαττωματικός e·la·to·ma·ti·kos faulty
ελαφρύ γεύμα ① e·laf·ri ghev·ma snack
ελαφρύς e·la·fris light (weight)
ελεύθερος e·lef·the·ros vacant
Ελλάδα ① e·la·tha Greece
Έλληνες ⑩ pl e·li·nes Greek (people)
Ελληνικά ⑪ pl e·li·ni·ka Greek (language)
εμβόλιο ⑪ em·vo·li·o vaccination
ένα e·na one
ένας άλλος e·nas a·los another
ένεση ① e·ne·si injection
ενοικιάζω ⑲ e·ni·ki·a·zo hire ⑲ • rent ⑲
ενοικίαση αυτοκινήτου ①
   e·ni·ki·a·si af·to·ki·ni·tu car hire
εξαργυρώνω ⑲ ek·sar·yi·ro·no cash a cheque
έξοδος ① ek·so·thos exit
εξοχή ① ek·so·hi countryside
εξπρές eks·pres express mail a
έξω ek·so outside
εξωτερικό ⑪ ek·so·te·ri·ko overseas
επάνω e·pa·no aboard
επείγον e·pi·ghon urgent
   — **ταχυδρομείο** ⑩ ta·hi·thro·mi·o by express mail

επιβάτης ⑩ e·pi·va·tis passenger
επιβάτισσα ① e·pi·va·ti·sa passenger
επίδειξη ① e·pi·thik·si show
επίδεσμος ⑩ e·pi·thez·mos bandage
επιδόρπιο ⑪ e·pi·thor·pi·o dessert
επικίνδυνος e·pi·kin·thi·nos dangerous
επικυρώνω e·pi·ki·ro·no confirm (booking) • validate
έπιπλα ⑪ pl e·pi·pla furniture
επισκευάζω e·pi·ske·va·zo repair ⑲
επιστήμη ① e·pi·sti·mi science
επιστήμονας ⑩&① e·pi·sti·mo·nas scientist
επιστρέφω e·pi·stre·fo come back • return ⑲
επιστροφή χρημάτων ①
   e·pi·stro·fi khri·ma·ton refund
επίτηρηση παιδιών ①
   e·pi·ti·ri·si pe·thion childminding
επιτρεπόμενες αποσκευές ① pl
   e·pi·tre·po·me·nes a·po·ske·ves baggage allowance
επιχείρηση ① e·pi·hi·ri·si business
επόμενος e·po·me·nos next a
εποχή ① e·po·hi season
επώνυμο ⑪ e·po·ni·mo surname
εργόχειρα ⑪ pl er·gho·hi·ra handicrafts
ερείπια ⑪ pl e·ri·pi·a ruins
εσείς e·sis you sg pol & pl
εστιατόριο ⑪ e·stia·to·ri·o restaurant
εσύ e·si you sg inf
εσώρουχα ⑪ pl e·so·ru·kha underwear
εταιρεία ① e·te·ri·a company (firm)
ευγνώμων ev·ghno·mon grateful
εύθραυστος ef·thraf·stos fragile
ευτυχισμένος ef·ti·hiz·me·nos happy
εφημερίδα ① e·fi·me·ri·tha newspaper
έχω e·kho have

Ζ ζ

ζακέτα ① za·ke·ta jacket • sweater
ζαχαροπλαστείο ⑪ za·kha·ro·pla·sti·o cake shop
ζεστός ze·stos hot • warm a
ζωγραφική ① zo·ghra·fi·ki painting (the art)
ζωγράφος ⑩&① zo·ghra·fos painter
ζώνη καθίσματος ① zo·ni ka·thiz·ma·tos seatbelt
ζωολογικός κήπος ⑩
   zo·o·lo·yi·kos ki·pos zoo

H η

ηθοποιός ⓜ&ⓕ i·tho·pi·os *actor*
ηλεκτρισμός ⓜ i·lek·triz·mos *electricity*
ηλιακό έγκαυμα ⓝ i·li·a·ko e·gav·ma
sunburn
ήλιος ⓜ i·li·os *sun*
ημέρα ⓕ i·me·ra *day*
ημερολόγιο ⓝ i·me·ro·lo·yi·o *diary*
ημερομηνία ⓕ i·me·ro·mi·ni·a *date (day)*
— **γεννήσεως** ⓕ ye·ni·se·os *date of birth*
ΗΠΑ ⓕ i·pa *USA*
ήσυχος i·si·khos *quiet* a
ήχος κλήσης ⓜ i·khos kli·sis *dial tone*

Θ θ

θάλασσα ⓕ tha·la·sa *sea*
θέα ⓕ the·a *view*
θεά ⓕ the·a *goddess*
θεατρικό έργο ⓝ the·a·tri·ko er·gho
play (theatre)
θέατρο ⓝ the·a·tro *theatre*
θεία ⓕ thi·a *aunt*
θερμοκρασία ⓕ ther·mo·kra·si·a
temperature (weather)
θερμοπληξία ⓕ ther·mo·plik·si·a
heatstroke
θερμοφόρα ⓕ ther·mo·fo·ra
(hot) water bottle
θηλυκός a thi·li·kos *female*
θορυβώδης tho·ri·vo·this *noisy*
Φ.Π.Α. ⓜ fpa *VAT (Value Added Tax)*

I ι

ιατρική ⓕ i·a·tri·ki *medicine (job, study)*
ιδιωτικός i·thi·o·ti·kos *private* a
ιματιοφυλάκιο ⓝ i·ma·ti·o·fi·la·ki·o
cloakroom
ινστιτούτο αισθητικής ⓝ
in·sti·tu·to es·thi·ti·kis *beauty salon*
ιππασία ⓕ i·pa·si·a *horse riding • ride*
ιχθυοπωλείο ⓝ ikh·thi·o·po·li·o *fish shop*

K κ

Κα ⓕ khi·ri·a *Mrs*
καθαρίζω ka·tha·ri·zo *clean* ⓥ
καθάρισμα ⓝ ka·tha·riz·ma *cleaning*

καθαρός ka·tha·ros *clean* a
καθαρτικό ⓝ ka·thar·ti·ko *laxative*
κάθε ka·the *every • per*
καθένας ka·the·nas *each • everyone*
καθετί ⓝ ka·the·ti *everything*
καθημερινός ka·thi·me·ri·nos *daily*
καθρέφτης ⓜ ka·thref·tis *mirror*
καθυστερημένος ka·thi·ste·ri·me·nos *late*
καθυστέρηση ka·thi·ste·ri·si *delay* ⓥ
και ke *and*
και οι δύο ke i thi·o *both*
κακός ka·kos *bad*
καλλιτέχνης ⓜ ka·li·tekh·nis *artist*
καλλιτέχνιδα ⓕ ka·li·tekh·ni·tha *artist*
καλλυντικά ⓝ pl ka·li·di·ka *make-up*
καλοκαίρι ⓝ ka·lo·ke·ri *summer*
καλός ka·los *good* a • *kind* a
κάλτσες ⓕ kal·tses *socks*
καλύτερος ka·li·te·ros *better*
καλώ ka·lo *call* ⓥ
Καναδάς ⓜ ka·na·thas *Canada*
καπέλο ⓝ ka·pe·lo *hat*
καπνίζω kap·ni·zo *smoke* ⓥ
καρδιά ⓕ kar·thia *heart*
καρδιακή κατάσταση ⓕ kar·dhi·a·ki
ka·ta·sta·si *heart condition*
καρέκλα ⓕ ka·re·kla *chair*
καροτσάκι ⓝ ka·rot·sa·ki *stroller • trolley*
κάρτα ⓕ kar·ta *postcard*
— **επιβίβασης** ⓕ e·pi·vi·va·sis
boarding pass
— **τηλεφώνου** ⓕ ti·le·fo·nu *phonecard*
κασέτα ⓕ ka·se·ta *cassette*
κασκόλ ⓝ ka·skol *scarf*
κάστρο ⓝ ka·stro *castle*
κατ' ευθείαν γραμμή ⓕ
ka·tef·thi·an gra·mi *direct-dial*
κατάθεση ⓕ ka·ta·the·si *deposit (bank)*
κατάλογος ⓜ ka·ta·lo·ghos *itinerary*
κατάλυμα ⓝ ka·ta·li·ma *accommodation*
κατάστημα ⓝ ka·ta·sti·ma
department store
— **για σουβενίρ** ⓝ yia su·ve·nir
souvenir shop
— **ηλεκτρικών ειδών** ⓝ
i·lek·tri·kon i·thon *electrical store*
— **μουσικών ειδών** ⓝ
mu·si·kon i·thon *music shop*
— **ρούχων** ⓝ ruk·hon *clothing store*
— **των σπορ** ⓝ ton spor *sports shop*
κατεβαίνω ka·te·ve·no *get off (train, etc)*
κατεύθυνση ⓕ ka·tef·thin·si *direction*

καύσωνας ⓜ kaf·so·nas *heatwave*
καφέ ka·*fe* *brown* a
καφενείο ⓝ ka·fe·*ni*·o *coffee shop*
— **διαδικτύου** ⓝ thi·a·*thik*·ti·u
Internet café
καφές ka·*fes* *coffee*
καφεστιατόριο ⓝ ka·fe·sti·a·*to*·ri·o *café*
κενή θέση ⓕ ke·*ni the*·si *vacancy*
κέντημα ⓝ ke·di·ma *embroidery*
κέντρο ⓝ ke·dro *centre*
κέντρο της πόλης ⓝ ke·dro tis *po*·lis
city centre
κέρματα ⓝ pl ker·ma·ta *coins*
κεφάλι ⓝ ke·*fa*·li *head*
κήπος ⓜ *ki*·pos *garden*
κινητό ⓝ ki·ni·*to* *mobile phone*
κίτρινος *ki*·tri·nos *yellow* a
κλειδί ⓝ kli·*thi* *key*
κλειδωμένος kli·tho·me·nos *locked*
κλειδώνω kli·*tho*·no *lock* ⓥ
κλείνω *kli*·no *close* ⓥ
— **θέση** *the*·si *book* ⓥ
κλεισμένος kliz·me·nos *closed*
κλειστός kli·*stos* *shut*
κλεμμένο kle·me·no *stolen*
κλήση με αντιστροφή της επιβάρυνσης
ⓕ *kli*·si me a·dis·tro·*fi* tis e·pi·*va*·rin·sis
collect call
κλονισμός ⓜ klo·niz·*mos* *concussion*
κόβω *ko*·vo *cut* ⓥ
κοιμάμαι ki·*ma*·me *sleep* ⓥ
κοιμητήριο ⓝ ki·mi·*ti*·ri·o *cemetery*
κόκκινο *ko*·ki·no *red*
κολιέ ⓝ ko·li·*e* *necklace*
κολυμπώ ko·li·*bo* *swim* ⓥ
κολώνα ⓕ ko·*lo*·na *column*
κολόνια ξυρίσματος ⓕ
ko·*lo*·ni·a ksi·*riz*·ma·tos *aftershave*
κομμωτής ⓜ ko·mo·*tis* *hairdresser*
κομμώτρια ⓕ ko·*mo*·tri·a *hairdresser*
κοντά ko·*da* *near • nearby*
κοντινός ko·di·*nos* *close* a
κοντός ko·*dos* *short (height)*
κόρη ⓕ *ko*·ri *daughter*
κορίτσι ⓝ ko·*rit*·si *girl*
Κος ⓜ *khi*·ri·os *Mr*
κοσμήματα ⓝ pl koz·*mi*·ma·ta *jewellery*
κοστίζω ko·*sti*·zo *cost* ⓥ
κοτόπουλο ⓝ ko·*to*·pu·lo *chicken*
κουβέρτα ⓕ ku·*ver*·ta *blanket*
κουζίνα ⓕ ku·*zi*·na *kitchen*
κουμπί ⓝ ku·*bi* *button*
κουρασμένος ⓜ ku·raz·*me*·nos *tired*

κούρεμα ⓝ ku·re·ma *haircut*
κουτάλι ⓝ ku·*ta*·li *spoon*
— **τσαγιού** ⓝ tsa·yiu *teaspoon*
κουτί ⓝ ku·*ti* *box • can • tin*
κραγιόν ⓝ pl kra·yion *lipstick*
κρασί ⓝ kra·*si* *wine*
κράτηση ⓕ *kra*·ti·si *booking • reservation*
κρέας ⓝ *kre*·as *meat*
κρεβάτι ⓝ kre·*va*·ti *bed*
κρέμα ⓕ *kre*·ma *cream*
— **ξυρίσματος** ⓕ ksi·*riz*·ma·tos
shaving cream
κρεοπωλείο ⓝ kre·o·po·*li*·o *butcher's shop*
κρυωμένος kri·o·me·nos *cold* a
κτηματομεσιτικό γραφείο ⓝ
kti·ma·to·me·si·ti·ko ghra·*fi*·o
estate agency
κτήριο ⓝ *kti*·ri·o *building*
κυλιόμενες σκάλες ⓕ pl ki·li·o·me·nes
ska·les *escalator*
κυτίο πρώτων βοηθειών ⓝ
ki·ti·o *pro*·ton vo·i·*thi*·on *first-aid kit*

Λ λ

λάδι ⓝ *la*·thi *oil*
— **αυτοκινήτου** ⓝ af·to·ki·*ni*·tu *oil (car)*
λαϊκή ⓕ la·i·*ki* *street market*
λαιμός ⓜ le·*mos* *throat*
λάστιχο ⓝ *la*·sti·kho *tire • tyre*
λαχανικά ⓝ pl la·kha·ni·*ka* *vegetable*
λαιμός ⓜ le·*mos* *neck*
λεξικό ⓝ lek·si·*ko* *dictionary*
λεπτό ⓝ lep·*to* *minute*
λεσβία ⓕ lez·*vi*·a *lesbian*
λιγότερο li·*gho*·te·ro *less*
λίμνη ⓕ *lim*·ni *lake*
λινό ⓝ li·*no* *linen (material)*
λιπαντικό ⓝ li·pa·di·*ko* *lubricant*
λίρα ⓕ *li*·ra *pound (money)*
λίτρα ⓕ *lit*·ra *pound (weight)*
λογαριασμός ⓜ lo·gha·riaz·*mos*
account • bill • check
λοσιόν ⓝ lo·*sion* *lotion*
— **για μαύρισμα** ⓝ yia mav·*riz*·ma
tanning lotion

Μ μ

μαβής ma·*vis* *purple*
μαγαζί ⓝ ma·gha·*zi* *shop*
μάγειρας ⓜ *ma*·yi·ras *cook*

μαγείρισσα ⓕ ma·*yi*·ri·sa *cook*
μαγειρεύω ma·yi·*re*·vo *cook* ⓥ
μαγιό ⓝ ma·*yio* *swimsuit*
μαζί ma·*zi* *together*
μαθαίνω ma·*the*·no *learn*
μακριά ma·kri·*a* *far*
μακρύς ma·*kris* *long* a
μαντήλι ⓝ ma·*di*·li *handkerchief*
μαξιλάρι ⓝ mak·si·*la*·ri *pillow*
μαξιλαροθήκη ⓕ mak·si·la·ro·*thi*·ki
   pillowcase
μας mas *our*
μάτι ⓝ *ma*·ti *eye*
μάτια ⓝ pl *ma*·tia *eyes*
ματς ⓝ mats *game* • *match*
μαυρόασπρο (φιλμ) ⓝ mav·ro·a·spro
   (film) *B&W (film)*
μαύρος *mav*·ros *black*
μαχαίρι ⓝ ma·*he*·ri *knife*
μαχαιροπήρουνα ⓝ pl ma·he·ro·*pi*·ru·na
   cutlery
με ερκοντίσιον me er·kon·*di*·si·on
   air-conditioned
μεγάλα φώτα αυτοκινήτου
   ⓝ pl me·*gha*·la *fo*·ta af·to·ki·*ni*·tu
   headlights
μεγάλος me·*gha*·los *big* • *large*
μεγαλύτερος me·gha·*li*·te·ros *bigger*
μέγεθος ⓝ *me*·ye·thos *size (general)*
μεθαύριο me·*thav*·ri·o *day after tomorrow*
μεθυσμένος me·thiz·*me*·nos *drunk*
μενού ⓝ me·*nu* *menu*
μέσα *me*·sa in • *inside*
μεσάνυχτα ⓝ pl me·*sa*·nikh·ta *midnight*
μεσημέρι ⓝ me·si·*me*·ri *midday* • *noon*
μεσημεριανό φαγητό ⓝ
   me·si·me·ria·*no* fa·yi·*to* *lunch*
μετά me·*ta* *after*
μεταλλικό νερό ⓝ me·ta·li·*ko* ne·*ro*
   mineral water
μετάξι ⓝ me·*tak*·si *silk*
μετασχηματιστής ⓜ
   me·ta·shi·ma·ti·*stis* *adaptor*
μεταφράζω me·ta·*fra*·zo *translate*
μετρητά ⓝ pl me·tri·*ta* *cash*
μέχρι *me*·khri *until*
μη καπνίζοντες mi kap·*ni*·zo·des
   nonsmoking
μήνας ⓜ *mi*·nas *month*
μήνυμα ⓝ *mi*·ni·ma *message*
μητέρα ⓕ mi·*te*·ra *mother*
μητρόπολη ⓕ mi·*tro*·po·li *cathedral*

μηχανή ⓕ mi·kha·*ni* *engine* • *machine*
   — εισιτηρίων ⓕ i·si·ti·*ri*·on
   ticket machine
   — φαξ faks *fax machine*
μηχανική ⓕ mi·kha·ni·*ki* *engineering*
μηχανικός ⓜ&ⓕ mi·kha·ni·*kos*
   engineer • *mechanic*
μικρό όνομα ⓝ mi·*kro* *o*·no·ma *first name*
μικρότερος mi·*kro*·te·ros *smaller*
μιλάω mi·*la*·o *speak* • *talk* ⓥ
μισό mi·*so* *half*
μόδα ⓕ *mo*·tha *fashion*
μοιράζομαι mi·*ra*·zo·me *share with*
μολύβι ⓝ mo·*li*·vi *pencil*
μόλυνση ⓕ mo·lin·si *infection*
μονό δωμάτιο ⓝ mo·*no* tho·*ma*·tio
   single room
μονοπάτι ⓝ mo·no·*pa*·ti *path* • *track* • *trail*
μόνος *mo*·nos *alone*
μου mu *my* • *to me*
μου αρέσει mu a·*re*·si *like* ⓥ
μπαγιάτικος ba·*yia*·ti·kos *off (spoiled)* • *stale*
μπαίνω be·no *enter*
μπαλάκια από βαμπάκι ⓝ pl
   ba·*la*·kia a·po va·*ba*·ki *cotton balls*
μπάνιο ⓝ *ba*·nio *bath* • *bathroom*
μπάντα ⓕ *ba*·da *band (music)*
μπαρ ⓝ bar *bar*
μπαταρία ⓕ ba·ta·*ri*·a *battery*
μπέμπι σίτερ ⓕ *be*·i·bi *si*·ter *babysitter*
μπίζνες κλας *biz*·nes klas *business class*
μπλε ble *blue* a
μπλοκαρισμένος blo·ka·riz·*me*·nos
   blocked
μπλουζάκι ⓝ blu·*za*·ki *T-shirt*
μπότα ⓕ *bo*·ta *boot (footwear)*
μπουκάλι ⓝ bu·*ka*·li *bottle*
μπουφές ⓜ bu·*fes* *buffet*
μπροσούρα ⓕ bro·su·*ra* *brochure*
μπύρα ⓕ *bi*·ra *beer*
μπυραρία ⓕ bi·ra·*ri*·a *bar* • *pub*
μπωλ ⓝ bol *bowl*
μυρουδιά ⓕ mi·ru·*thia* *smell*
μύτη ⓕ *mi*·ti *nose*
μωρό ⓝ mo·*ro* *baby*

N ν

ναι ne *yes*
ναρκωτικά ⓝ pl nar·ko·ti·*ka* *illegal drugs*
ναυτία ⓕ naf·*ti*·a
   nausea • *seasickness* • *travel sickness*

νέα ⑩ pl *ne*·a **news**
Νέα Ζηλανδία ① *ne*·a zi·lan·*thi*·a **New Zealand**
νέος *ne*·os **new • young**
νερό ⑩ ne·*ro* **water**
νοικοκυρά ① ni·ko·ki·*ra* **housewife**
νοικοκύρης ⑩ ni·ko·*ki*·ris **head of the house**
νησί ⑩ ni·*si* **island**
νομικά ⑩ no·mi·*ka* **law (study, profession)**
νοσοκόμος ⑩ no·so·*ko*·mos **nurse**
νοσοκόμα ① no·so·*ko*·ma **nurse**
νοσοκομειακό ⑩ no·so·ko·mi·a·*ko* **ambulance**
νοσοκομείο ⑩ no·so·ko·*mi*·o **hospital**
νόστιμος *no*·sti·mos **tasty**
νότος *no*·tos **south**
ντελικατεσέν ⑩ de·li·ka·*te*·sen **delicatessen**
ντουζ ⑩ duz **shower**
νύχτα ① *nikh*·ta **night**
νωρίς no·*ris* **early**

Ξ ξ

ξενοδοχείο ⑩ kse·no·tho·*hi*·o **hotel**
ξένη ① *kse*·ni **foreign a • stranger** ①
ξένος ⑩ *kse*·nos **foreign a • stranger** ⑩
ξενώνας ⑩ kse·*no*·nas **guesthouse**
ξυπνάω ksip·na·*o* **wake • wake (someone) up**
ξυπνητήρι ⑩ ksip·ni·*ti*·ri **alarm clock**
ξυράφι ⑩ ksi·*ra*·fi **razor blade**
ξυρίζω ksi·*ri*·zo **shave** ⓥ
ξυριστική μηχανή ① ksi·ri·sti·*ki* mi·kha·*ni* **razor**

Ο ο

ο καλύτερος o ka·*li*·te·ros **best** a
ο μεγαλύτερος o me·gha·*li*·te·ros **biggest**
ο μικρότερος o mi·*kro*·te·ros **smallest**
οδηγός ⑩&① o·*thi*·ghos **driver • guide (person)**
  — διασκέδασης ⑩ thia·*ske*·tha·sis **entertainment guide**
οδηγώ o·*thi*·gho **drive** ⓥ
οδοντιατρική κλωστή ① o·tho·di·a·tri·*ki* klo·*sti* **dental floss**
οδοντίατρος ⑩&① o·tho·*di*·a·tros **dentist**
οδοντόβουρτσα ① o·tho·*do*·vur·tsa **toothbrush**
οδοντόπαστα ① o·tho·*do*·pa·sta **toothpaste**
οδός ① o·*thos* **street**

οδυνηρός o·thi·ni·*ros* **painful**
Οθωμανικός o·tho·ma·ni·*kos* **Ottoman** a
οικογένεια ① i·ko·*ye*·ni·a **family**
Ολλανδία ① o·lan·*thi*·a **Netherlands**
όλοι *o*·li **all**
ολονυχτίς o·lo·nikh·*tis* **overnight**
ομάδα αίματος ① o·*ma*·tha e·ma·tos **blood group**
όμορφος o·*mor*·fos **beautiful • handsome**
ομοφυλόφιλος o·mo·*fi*·lo·fi·los **homosexual**
όνομα ⑩ *o*·no·ma **name**
οπίσθιος o·*pi*·sthi·os **rear (seat etc)**
οπωροπωλείο ⑩ o·po·ro·po·*li*·o **grocery**
όριο ταχύτητας ⑩ o·ri·o ta·*hi*·ti·tas **speed limit**
όροφος ⑩ o·ro·fos **floor (storey)**
όταν o·*tan* **when**
όχι o·hi **no • not**

Π π

πάγος ⑩ *pa*·ghos **ice**
παγωμένος pa·gho·*me*·nos **frozen**
παγωτό ⑩ pa·gho·*to* **ice cream**
παζάρι ⑩ pa·*za*·ri **fleamarket**
παιδί ⑩ pe·*thi* **child**
παιδιά ⑩ pl pe·*thia* **children**
παιδικό κάθισμα ⑩ pe·thi·*ko* *ka*·thiz·ma **child seat**
παιδικός σταθμός ⑩ pe·thi·*kos* stath·*mos* **crèche**
παλάτι ⑩ pa·*la*·ti **palace**
πάλι *pa*·li **again**
παλιός pa·*lios* **old** a
παλτό ⑩ pal·*to* **coat**
πάνα ① *pa*·na **diaper • nappy**
πανεπιστήμιο ⑩ pa·ne·pi·*sti*·mi·o **university**
παντελόνι ⑩ pa·de·*lo*·ni **pants • trousers**
παντρεμένη ① pa·dre·*me*·ni **married**
παντρεμένος ⑩ pa·dre·*me*·nos **married**
πάνω pa·no **on • up**
παπούς ⑩ pa·*pus* **grandfather**
παπούτσι ⑩ pa·*put*·si **shoe**
πάρα πολύ *pa*·ra po·*li* **too (expensive etc)**
παράθυρο ⑩ pa·*ra*·thi·ro **window**
παραλαβή αποσκευών ① pa·ra·la·*vi* a·po·ske·*von* **baggage claim**
παραλία ① pa·ra·*li*·a **beach • seaside**
Παραμονή Πρωτοχρονιάς ① pa·ra·mo·*ni* pro·to·khro·*nias* **New Year's Eve**

παράπονο ⓝ pa·ra·po·no *complaint*
παράσταση ⓕ pa·ra·sta·si *gig*
παρκάρω par·ka·ro *park a car*
Πάσχα ⓝ pas·kha *Easter*
πατέρας ⓜ pa·te·ras *father*
παυσίπονο ⓝ paf·si·po·no *painkiller*
παχύς ⓜ pa·his *fat*
πάω για ψώνια pa·o yia pso·nia
 go shopping
πεζοδρόμιο ⓝ pe·zo·thro·mi·o *footpath*
πεζοπορία ⓕ pe·zo·po·ri·a *hiking*
πεζοπορώ pe·zo·po·ro *hike*
πεθερά ⓕ pe·the·ra *mother-in-law*
πεθερός ⓜ pe·the·ros *father-in-law*
πεινάω pi·na·o *(be) hungry* ⓥ
πελάτης ⓜ pe·la·tis *client*
πελάτισσα ⓕ pe·la·ti·sa *client*
πέος ⓝ pe·os *penis*
περιήγηση ⓕ pe·ri·i·yi·si *tour*
 — με οδηγό ⓜ me o·thi·gho *guided tour*
περιμένω pe·ri·me·no *wait* ⓥ
περίπτερο ⓝ pe·rip·te·ro *kiosk*
περισσότερος pe·ri·so·te·ros *more*
περπατάω per·pa·ta·o *walk* ⓥ
πετάω pe·ta·o *fly* ⓥ
πετρέλαιο ⓝ pe·tre·le·o *petrol*
πετρογκάζ ⓝ pe·tro·gaz *gas (for cooking)*
πετσέτα ⓕ pet·se·ta *towel*
πετσετάκι ⓝ pet·se·ta·ki *napkin*
 — υγείας i·yi·as ⓝ
 panty liners · sanitary napkins
πηγαίνω pi·ye·no *go*
πιάτο ⓝ pia·to *dish · plate*
πικρός pi·kros *bitter* ⓐ
πίνακας ⓜ pi·na·kas *painting (a work)*
πινακοθήκη ⓕ pi·na·ko·thi·ki *art gallery*
πίνω pi·no *drink* ⓥ
πιπίλα ⓕ pi·pi·la *dummy · pacifier*
πιρούνι ⓝ pi·ru·ni *fork*
πισίνα ⓕ pi·si·na *swimming pool*
πίστωση ⓕ pi·sto·si *credit*
πιστωτική κάρτα ⓕ pi·sto·ti·ki kar·ta
 credit card
πλατεία ⓕ pla·ti·a *square (town)*
πλάτη ⓕ pla·ti *back (body)*
πλατφόρμα ⓕ plat·for·ma *platform*
πλένω ple·no *wash* ⓥ
πληγή ⓕ pli·yi *injury*
πληγωμένος pli·gho·me·nos *injured* ⓐ
πληροφορία ⓕ pli·ro·fo·ri·a *information*
πληροφορική ⓕ pli·ro·fo·ri·ki *IT*
πληρωμή ⓕ pli·ro·mi *payment*
πλυντήριο ⓝ pli·di·ri·o *launderette ·
 laundry · washing machine*

ποδήλατο ⓝ po·thi·la·to *bicycle · bike*
πόδι ⓝ po·thi *foot · leg*
ποδόσφαιρο ⓝ po·thos·fe·ro *football*
ποιος pios *which · who*
πόλη ⓕ po·li *city*
πολυτέλεια ⓕ po·li·te·li·a *luxury*
πολύτιμος po·li·ti·mos *valuable*
πονόδοντος ⓜ po·no·tho·dos *toothache*
πονοκέφαλος ⓜ po·no·ke·fa·los *headache*
πόνος ⓜ po·nos *pain*
πόρνη ⓕ por·ni *prostitute*
πορτοκαλής por·to·ka·lis *orange (colour)*
πορτοφόλι ⓝ por·to·fo·li *purse*
ποτάμι ⓝ po·ta·mi *river*
ποτήρι ⓝ po·ti·ri *drinking glass*
ποτό ⓝ po·to *drink*
πού pu *where*
πουκάμισο ⓝ pu·ka·mi·so *shirt*
πουλόβερ ⓝ pu·lo·ver *jumper · sweater*
πούρο ⓝ pu·ro *cigar*
πρακτορείο εφημερίδων ⓝ
 prak·to·ri·o e·fi·me·ri·thon *newsagency*
πράσινος pra·si·nos *green*
πρατήριο βενζίνας ⓝ pra·ti·ri·o ven·zi·nas
 petrol station
πρεσβεία ⓕ prez·vi·a *embassy*
πριν prin *before*
πρόγευμα ⓝ pro·yev·ma *breakfast*
πρόγραμμα ⓝ pro·ghra·ma *timetable*
προετοιμασία εγγράφων ⓕ
 pro·e·ti·ma·si·a e·gra·fon *paperwork*
προηγούμενος pro·i·ghu·me·nos
 last · previous
προκαταβολή ⓕ pro·ka·ta·vo·li
 deposit (on house etc)
προμήθεια ⓕ pro·mi·thi·a *commission*
προμήθειες φαγητού ⓕ pl
 pro·mi·thi·es fa·yi·tu *food supplies*
προξενείο ⓝ prok·se·ni·o *consulate*
προορισμός ⓜ pro·o·riz·mos *destination*
προσαύξηση τιμής ⓕ pro·saf·ksi·si
 ti·mis *cover charge*
πρόστιμο ⓝ pros·ti·mo *fine (penalty)*
προσωπική επιταγή ⓕ pro·so·pi·ki
 e·pi·ta·yi *check (banking) · cheque*
πρόσωπο ⓝ pro·so·po *face · person*
προϋπολογισμός ⓜ pro·i·po·lo·yiz·mos
 budget
προφυλακτικό ⓝ pro·fi·lak·ti·ko *condom*
προχθές prokh·tes *day before yesterday*
πρωί ⓝ pro·i *morning*
πρώτη τάξη ⓕ pro·ti tak·si *first class*
Πρωτοχρονιά ⓕ pro·to·khro·nia
 New Year's Day

πτήση ① *pti*-si *flight*
πυρετός ⑩ *pi*-re-*tos fever*

P ρ

ράδιο ⑩ *ra*-thi-o *radio*
ραντεβού ⑩ ra-de-*vu appointment • date*
ράφτης ⑩ *raf*-tis *tailor*
ράφτρα ① *raf*-tra *tailor*
ρεσεψιόν ① re-sep-*sion check-in (desk)*
ρέστα ⑪ pl *re*-sta *change (money)*
ρεύμα ⑩ *rev*-ma *current (electricity)*
ρινική αλλεργία ① ri-ni-*ki* a-ler-*yi*-a *hay fever*
ροζ *roz pink*
ρούχα ⑩ pl *ru*-kha *clothing*

Σ σ

Σαββατοκύριακο ⑩ sa-va-to-*ki*-ria-ko *weekend*
σακίδιο ⑩ sa-*ki*-thi-o *backpack*
σάκος ⑩ *sa*-kos *bag*
σαμπάνια ① sam-*pa*-nia *champagne*
σαπούνι ⑩ sa-*pu*-ni *soap*
σε se *at • to*
σεισμός ⑩ siz-*mos earthquake*
σελφ σέρβις ⑩ self *ser*-vis *self-service*
σεμινάριο ⑩ se-mi-*na*-ri-o *conference (small) • seminar*
σεντόνι ⑩ se-*do*-ni *sheet (bed)*
σεντόνια ⑪ pl se-*do*-nia *bed linen*
σερβιτόρα ① ser-vi-*to*-ra *waitress*
σεξ ⑩ seks *sex*
σεφ ⑩ sef *chef • cook*
σημειωματάριο ⑩ si-mi-o-ma-*ta*-ri-o *notebook*
σήμερα *si*-me-ra *today*
σι ντι ① si di *CD*
σι ντι ρομ ① si di rom *disk (CD-ROM)*
σίδερο ⑩ *si*-the-ro *iron (for clothes)*
σιδηροδρομικός σταθμός ⑩
si-thi-ro-thro-mi-*kos* stath-*mos railway station*
σκάλα ① *ska*-la *stairway*
σκιά ① ski-*a shade*
σκληρός skli-*ros hard (not soft)*
σκοτεινός sko-ti-*nos dark* a
σκουλαρίκια ⑩ pl sku-la-*ri*-kia *earrings*
σκουπιδοτενεκές ⑩ sku-pi-*tho*-te-ne-*kes garbage can*
σκούρος *sku*-ros *dark (colour)* a

σκυλί ⑩ ski-*li dog*
Σκωτία ① sko-*ti*-a *Scotland*
σλάιντ ⑩ *sla*-id *slide (film)*
σοκολάτα ① so-ko-*la*-ta *chocolate*
σορτς ⑩ sorts *shorts*
σουβενίρ ⑩ su-ve-*nir souvenir*
σουγιάς ⑩ su-*yias penknife*
σουτιέν ① su-ti-en *bra*
σπασμένος spaz-*me*-nos *broken*
σπίρτα ⑪ pl *spir*-ta *matches (for lighting)*
σπίτι ⑩ *spi*-ti *home*
σπουδαίος spu-*the*-os *important*
σπουδαστής ⑩ spu-tha-*stis student*
σπουδάστρια ① spu-*tha*-stri-a *student*
σπρέι ⑩ *spre*-i *spray*
σταθμός ⑩ stath-*mos station*
σταθμός λεωφορείου ⑩ stath-*mos* le-o-fo-*ri*-u *bus station*
σταθμός μετρό ⑩ stath-*mos* me-*tro metro station*
σταθμός τρένου ⑩ stath-*mos* *tre*-nu *train station*
στάση ① *sta*-si *stop (bus, tram, etc)*
 — λεωφορείου ⑩ le-o-fo-*ri*-u *bus stop*
 — ταξί ① tak-*si taxi stand*
σταχτοθήκη ① stakh-to-*thi*-ki *ashtray*
στεγνός stegh-*nos* dry a
στήθος ⑩ *sti*-thos *chest (body)*
στην ώρα stin o-ra *on time*
στόμα ⑩ *sto*-ma *mouth*
στομάχι ⑩ sto-*ma*-hi *stomach*
στομαχόπονος ⑩ sto-ma-*kho*-po-nos *stomachache*
στραμπούλισμα ① stra-*bu*-liz-ma *sprain*
στρώμα ⑩ *stro*-ma *mattress*
στυλό ⑩ sti-*lo pen (ballpoint)*
σύζυγος ⑩&① *si*-zi-ghos *husband • wife*
συμπεριλαμβανομένου si-be-ri-lam-va-no-*me*-nu *included*
συνάδελφος ⑩ si-*na*-thel-fos *colleague*
συναδέλφισσα ① si-na-*thel*-fi-sa *colleague*
συνάλλαγμα ⑩ si-*na*-lagh-ma *exchange*
σύνδεσμος ⑩ *sin*-thez-mos *connection*
συνέδριο ① si-*ne*-thri-o *conference (big)*
συνεισφέρω si-nis-*fe*-ro *contribute*
συνιστώ si-ni-*sto recommend*
σύνορο ⑩ *si*-no-ro *border*
συνταγή ① si-da-*yi prescription*
σύνταξη ① *si*-dak-si *pension*
συνταξιούχα ① si-dak-si-*u*-kha *pensioner*
συνταξιούχος ⑩ si-dak-si-*u*-khos *pensioner*
σύντομα *si*-do-ma *soon*
συντροφιά ① si-dro-*fia company (friends)*

σύντροφος ⓜ *si·dro·fos companion*
συντρόφισσα ⓕ *si·dro·fi·sa companion*
συστημένο *sis·ti·me·no by registered mail*
σωσίβιο ⓝ *so·si·vi·o life jacket*

Τ τ

ταμείο ⓝ *ta·mi·o cash register*
ταμίας ⓜ&ⓕ *ta·mi·as cashier*
ταμπόν ⓝ *ta·bon tampon*
ταξίδι ⓝ *tak·si·thi journey · trip*
 — εργασίας ⓝ *er·gha·si·as business trip*
 — του μέλιτος ⓝ *tu me·li·tos honeymoon*
ταξίδι με ωτοστόπ *tak·si·thi me o·to·stop hitchhike* Ⓥ
ταξιδιωτική επιταγή ⓕ *tak·si·thi·o·ti·ki e·pi·ta·yi travellers cheque*
ταξιδιωτικό γραφείο ⓝ *tak·si·thi·o·ti·ko ghra·fi·o travel agency*
ταυτότητα ⓕ *taf·to·ti·ta identification · identification card*
ταχυδρομείο ⓝ *ta·hi·thro·mi·o mail · post office*
ταχυδρομικό κουτί ⓝ *ta·hi·thro·mi·ko ku·ti mailbox*
ταχυδρομικός τομέας ⓜ *ta·hi·thro·mi·kos to·me·as postcode*
ταχυδρομώ *ta·hi·thro·mo post* Ⓥ
ταχύτητα φιλμ ⓕ *ta·hi·ti·ta film film speed*
τελεφερίκ ⓝ *te·le·fe·rik chairlift (skiing)*
τέλος ⓝ *te·los end*
τελωνείο ⓝ *te·lo·ni·o customs*
τένις ⓝ *te·nis tennis*
τέχνη ⓕ *tekh·ni craft · art*
τηγάνι ⓝ *ti·gha·ni frying pan*
τηγανίζω *ti·gha·ni·zo fry* Ⓥ
τηλεγράφημα ⓝ *ti·le·ghra·fi·ma telegram*
τηλεκατεύθυνση ⓕ *ti·le·ka·tef·thin·si remote control*
τηλεόραση ⓕ *ti·le·o·ra·si television · TV*
τηλεφωνικός κατάλογος ⓜ *ti·le·fo·ni·kos ka·ta·lo·ghos phone book*
τηλέφωνο ⓝ *ti·le·fo·no telephone*
τηλεφωνώ *ti·le·fo·no telephone* Ⓥ
της *tis her (ownership/direct object)*
τιμή ⓕ *ti·mi price*
 — εισόδου ⓕ *i·so·thu admission (price)*
 — εξυπηρέτησης ⓕ *ek·si·pi·re·ti·sis service charge*
 — συναλλάγματος ⓕ *sina·lagh·ma·tos currency exchange · exchange rate*

τίποτε *ti·po·te nothing*
τίτλος κατόχου αυτοκινήτου ⓜ *tit·los ka·to·khu af·to·ki·ni·tu car owner's title*
το πιο κοντινό *to pio ko·di·no nearest*
τοπικός *to·pi·kos local* a
τοστ ⓝ *tost toast*
τοστιέρα ⓕ *to·stie·ra toaster*
του *tu his (ownership/direct object)*
τουαλέτα ⓕ *tu·a·le·ta toilet*
τουριστική θέση ⓕ *tu·ri·sti·ki the·si economy class*
τουριστικό γραφείο ⓝ *tu·ri·sti·ko ghra·fi·o tourist office*
τουριστικός οδηγός ⓜ *tu·ri·sti·kos o·thi·ghos guidebook*
τράπεζα ⓕ *tra·pe·za bank*
τραπεζικός λογαριασμός ⓜ *tra·pe·zi·kos lo·gha·riaz·mos bank account*
τρένο ⓝ *tre·no train*
τρόλεϋ ⓝ *tro·le·i trolley bus*
τρώγω *tro·gho eat* Ⓥ
τσάντα ⓕ *tsa·da handbag*
τσιγάρο ⓝ *tsi·gha·ro cigarette*
τσιμπιδάκι ⓝ *tsi·bi·tha·ki tweezers*
τσίρκο ⓝ *tsir·ko circus*
τσιρότο ⓝ *tsi·ro·to Band-Aid*
τυρί ⓝ *ti·ri cheese*
τώρα *to·ra now*

Υ υ

υπεραστικό λεωφορείο ⓝ *i·pe·ra·sti·ko le·o·fo·ri·o intercity bus*
υπέρβαρο φορτίο ⓝ *i·per·va·ro for·ti·o excess baggage*
υπηρεσία ⓕ *i·pi·re·si·a service*
υπνοδωμάτιο ⓝ *ip·no·tho·ma·ti·o bedroom*
υπόγειος *i·po·yi·os subway* a
 — σιδηρόδρομος ⓜ *si·thi·ro·thro·mos subway train*
υποδηματοποιείο ⓝ *i·po·thi·ma·to·pi·i·o shoe shop*
υπότιτλοι ⓜ pl *i·po·ti·tli subtitles*
υποχρέωση ⓕ *i·po·khre·o·si engagement · obligation*

Φ φ

φαγητό ⓝ *fa·yi·to food*
 — για μωρά ⓝ *yia mo·ra baby food*
φαγούρα ⓕ *fa·ghu·ra itch*

φάκελος ⓜ *fa*-ke-los envelope
φακοί επαφής ⓜ pl fa-*ki* e-pa-fis contact lenses
φακός ⓜ fa-kos lens • flashlight • torch
φαρμακείο ⓝ far-ma-*ki*-o pharmacy
φάρμακο ⓝ *far*-ma-ko medicine
— **για το βήχα** ⓝ yia to *vi*-kha cough medicine
φαρμακοποιός ⓜ&ⓕ far-ma-ko-pi-os pharmacist
φερμουάρ ⓝ fer-mu-*ar* zip • zipper
φέρυ ⓝ *fe*-ri ferry
φέτα ⓕ *fe*-ta slice
φθινόπωρο ⓝ fthi-*no*-po-ro autumn • fall
φιλενάδα ⓕ fi-le-*na*-ţha girlfriend
φίλη ⓕ *fi*-li friend
φιλμ ⓝ *fi*-lm film • movie
φιλοδώρημα ⓝ fi-lo-*ţho*-ri-ma gratuity • tip
φίλος ⓜ *fi*-los boyfriend • friend
φλας ⓝ flas flashlight
φλυτζάνι ⓝ fli-*dza*-ni cup
φόρεμα ⓝ fo-*re*-ma dress
φούρνος ⓜ *fur*-nos bakery • oven
— **μικροκυμάτων** ⓝ mi-kro-ki-*ma*-ton microwave oven
φουσκάλα ⓕ fu-*ska*-la blister
φούστα ⓕ *fu*-sta skirt
φρένα ⓝ pl *fre*-na brakes
φρέσκος *fre*-skos fresh
φρούτα ⓝ pl *fru*-ta fruit
φτηνός fti-*nos* cheap a
φύλαξη αποσκευών ⓕ *fi*-lak-si a-po-ske-*von* luggage lockers
φως ⓝ fos light
φωτογραφία ⓕ fo-to-gra-*fi*-a photo
φωτογραφική ⓕ fo-to-ghra-fi-*ki* photography
φωτογραφική μηχανή ⓕ fo-to-ghra-fi-*ki* mi-kha-*ni* camera
φωτογράφος ⓜ&ⓕ fo-to-*ghra*-fos photographer

χαλασμένος kha-laz-*me*-nos broken down • out of order • spoiled (food)
χαλκός ⓜ khal-*kos* copper
χαμένος kha-me-nos lost a
χάπι ⓝ *kha*-pi pill
χάρτης ⓜ *khar*-tis map (of country/town)
χαρτί ⓝ khar-*ti* paper
— **υγείας** ⓝ i-*yi*-as toilet paper

χαρτομάντηλα ⓝ pl khar-to-*ma*-di-la tissues
χαρτονόμισμα ⓝ khar-to-*no*-miz-ma banknote
χαρτοπωλείο ⓝ khar-to-po-*li*-o stationer's shop
χαρτοφύλακας ⓜ khar-to-*fi*-la-kas briefcase
χειμώνας ⓜ hi-*mo*-nas winter
χειροποίητο hi-ro-*pi*-i-to handmade a
χέρι ⓝ *he*-ri arm • hand
χιλιόγραμμο ⓝ hi-*lio*-gra-mo kilogram
χιλιόμετρο ⓝ hi-*lio*-me-tro kilometre
χιόνι ⓝ *hio*-ni snow
χορεύω kho-*re*-vo dance ⓥ
χορός ⓜ kho-*ros* dancing
χορτοφάγος ⓜ&ⓕ khor-to-*fa*-ghos vegetarian a
χρήματα ⓝ pl *khri*-ma-ta money
Χριστούγεννα ⓝ pl khri-*stu*-ye-na Christmas
χρόνος ⓜ *khro*-nos year
χρυσάφι ⓝ khri-*sa*-fi gold
χρώμα ⓝ *khro*-ma colour
χτένα ⓕ *khte*-na comb
χτες khtes yesterday
χωρίς kho-*ris* without
χώρος ⓜ *kho*-ros venue • place
— **για κάμπινγκ** ⓝ yia *kam*-ping camping ground • campsite
χωροφύλακας ⓜ kho-ro-*fi*-la-kas police officer
χωροφυλακίνα ⓕ kho-ro-fi-la-*ki*-na police officer

ψαλίδι ⓝ psa-*li*-ţhi scissors
ψάρεμα ⓝ *psa*-re-ma fishing
ψηφιακός psi-fi-a-*kos* digital a
ψηλός psi-los high • tall
ψιλά ⓝ pl psi-*la* change (money)
ψιχάλα ⓕ psi-*kha*-la drizzle
ψυγείο ⓝ psi-yi-o fridge • refrigerator
ψωμί ⓝ pso-*mi* bread
ψωνίζω pso-*ni*-zo shop ⓥ

ώμος ⓜ *o*-mos shoulder
ώρα ⓕ *o*-ra hour • time
ώρες λειτουργίας ⓕ pl *o*-res li-tur-*yi*-as opening hours

A

B

C

KEY PATTERNS

When's (the next bus)?	Πότε είναι (το επόμενο λεωφορείο);	*po·te i·*ne (to e·*po·*me·no le·o·fo·*ri·*o)
Where's (the station)?	Πού είναι (ο σταθμός);	pu *i·*ne (o stath·*mos*)
How much is it (per night)?	Πόσο είναι (για κάθε νύχτα);	*po·*so *i·*ne (yia *ka·*the *nikh·*ta)
I'm looking for (Ampfilohos).	Ψάχνω για (το Αμφίλοχος).	*psakh·*no yia (to am·*fi·*lo·khos)
Do you have (a local map)?	Έχετε οδικό (τοπικό χάρτη);	e·he·te o·thi·*ko* (to·pi·*ko* khar·ti)
Is there a (lift)?	Υπάρχει (ασανσέρ);	i·*par·*hi (a·san·*ser*)
Can I (try it on)?	Μπορώ να (το προβάρω);	bo·*ro* na (to pro·*va·*ro)
Do I need (to book)?	Χρειάζεται (να κλείσω θέση);	khri·*a·*ze·te (na *kli·*so *the·*si)
I have (a reservation).	Έχω (κλείσει δωμάτιο).	e·kho (*kli·*si tho·*ma·*ti·o)
I need (assistance).	Χρειάζομαι (βοήθεια).	khri·*a·*zo·me (vo·*i·*thi·a)
I'd like (to hire a car).	Θα ήθελα (να ενοικιάσω ένα αυτοκίνητο).	tha *i·*the·la (na e·ni·ki·*a·*so e·na af·to·*ki·*ni·to)
Could you (please help)?	Μπορείς να (βοηθήσεις, παρακαλώ);	bo·*ris* na (vo·*i·thi·*sis pa·ra·ka·*lo*)